PELICAN BOOKS

A 389

THE MUSIC MASTERS

VOLUME TWO

The Music Masters

VOLUME ONE

FROM THE SIXTEENTH CENTURY
TO THE TIME OF BEETHOVEN

VOLUME TWO

AFTER BEETHOVEN TO WAGNER

VOLUME THREE

THE ROMANTIC AGE

VOLUME FOUR

THE TWENTIETH CENTURY

*

EDITED BY

A. L. BACHARACH

EDITOR OF

The Musical Companion
British Music of Our Time
ETC.

PENGUIN BOOKS

The Music Masters

VOLUME TWO

AFTER BEETHOVEN TO WAGNER

BY

GERALD ABRAHAM
W. R. ANDERSON
STANLEY BAYLISS
F. BONAVIA
MARTIN COOPER
A. E. F. DICKINSON
ROBERT ELKIN
EDWIN EVANS
WILLIAM GLOCK
RALPH HILL
HERBERT HUGHES
DYNELEY HUSSEY
COLIN MASON
LESLIE ORREY
MAX PIRANI
FRANCIS TOYE
NILS L. WALLIN
JOHN S. WEISSMANN
RALPH WOOD

PENGUIN BOOKS

Penguin Books Ltd, Harmondsworth, Middlesex

U.S.A.: Penguin Books Inc., 3300 Clipper Mill Road, Baltimore 11, Md

AUSTRALIA: Penguin Books Pty Ltd, 762 Whitehorse Road,
Mitcham, Victoria

—

First published by Cassell 1950
Published in Pelican Books 1958

Made and printed in Great Britain
by The Whitefriars Press Ltd
London and Tonbridge

CONTENTS

PREFACE TO VOLUME TWO

The thirty-eight composers whose lives are described in this second volume of *The Music Masters* may well seem to have been selected on a basis so arbitrary as to be meaningless. But for the historical facts that Auber and Paganini were born in 1782, Brahms in 1833, and all the others in between, they would not have found themselves a-jostle in one book. At the other chronological end, Borodin has just got pushed into Volume III, for no esoteric reason whatever, but merely to balance the lengths of the two books.

Errors and omissions excepted, therefore, our biographies are grouped into their four volumes in order of the composers' birth years: which dates begin and end the volumes is determined by considerations of space. The year of death would also have served – though it is no less arbitrary and is fortunately not applicable to all the composers included in Volume IV. Anyhow, the secret is out; the volume division of *The Music Masters* is based on nothing more recondite than birthdays and numbers of words! And yet – is there not something more than date of birth common to the composers whose lives thus fall into Volume II?

Is this volume not concerned with the great period when music became both romantic and, for the first time since Elizabethan days in this this country, democratic? Have not Berlioz, Brahms, Chopin, Liszt, Mendelssohn, Rossini, Schubert, Schumann, Verdi, Wagner, and Weber – the 'Great Composers' assembled here – something in common, not only with one another, but also with Bruckner, Donizetti, Gounod, Meyerbeer, Offenbach, Smetana, the Strauss's – to mention but a few of those who join them in this book? Certain it is that, whatever the justification for putting all their lives between the same covers, their compositions, written from the turn of the eighteenth century right up to late Victorian days, show almost unbelievable changes in the methods and even the aims of their art – from Bellini and Auber to Verdi and Wagner, from Hummel to Liszt and Berlioz, even from Glinka to Lalo. This upheaval should in itself confer a special interest on the biographies of its mediators, apart from any inherent fascination of the epoch during which most of them lived, worked, and triumphed.

A. L. BACHARACH

London NW3
June 1950

DANIEL FRANÇOIS ESPRIT AUBER

1782–1871

RALPH W. WOOD

Early Years

The wife of Louis XVI's '*officier des chasses royales*' was far from her Parisian home, she was on a journey in Normandy (the region, as a matter of fact, from which old Daniel Auber, her father-in-law, had departed to the capital when very young to seek his fortune), she was at Caen, it has been suggested that she was in the very travelling coach, when she was overtaken by the necessity of ending her husband's speculations whether it would be a boy or a girl. Not the best of lying-in places, especially at that season – the date was 29 January.

It was a boy, upon whom in due course and form were bestowed the names Daniel François Esprit. And upon him began, in due course and form, to be bestowed the type of upbringing he had a right to expect in a family so rich, indeed so nearly aristocratic, as his.

'Began' is the word because, the year of his birth being 1782, he was hardly beyond infancy when the Revolution interrupted all things. At one point it was only by going into hiding that the ex-'officier des chasses royales' escaped having his very existence interrupted, then and there, for good. But with the coming of the Directoire the atmosphere lightened: the boy was then 13. In the Rue Saint-Lazare M. Auber had opened an establishment where he published and sold prints. By the time the Consulat had arrived he was again in a very prosperous way of business. Also he – this enthusiast in 1784 had entered the Société académique des Enfants d'Apollon both as a painter and as '*amateur de chant et de violon*' and had in the last-named capacity tutored his son – was again the centre of a coterie of the cultured, his salon the resort of artists of all kinds and the scene of constant music-makings. And Auber fils had been able, after all, to receive the benefits of a brilliant education.

At 16 the youngster played several instruments, sang, knew Italian. To that year belongs his first definitely dated composition. In fact, however, we are told that from the age of 11 he had been producing ballads and 'romances', some of which were sung by the *nymphes décolletées du Directoire*; one at least, *Le Bonjour*, was quite a popular success.

Auber the Man

Those, then, were the beginnings of the composer of *Masaniello, Fra Diavolo*, and *Le Cheval de Bronze*. Almost as vivid and quite as enigmatic as a character in Proust, Auber is for us a person of whom, despite a certain wealth of material that could serve to make him live again for us, we are left with a feeling that much has remained hidden. One kind of mysteriousness, perhaps present in all composers of his type, is the musical one that is covered by Rossini's famous mot about Auber's *petite musique d'un grand musicien*. But there is also his life outside music – a life that, for all his methodical and pervasive diligence as a composer, did clearly exist.

Auber died in his ninetieth year. He was the familiar of royalties, entitled to cover the breast of his dress-suit with decorations from all over the globe, Director of the Conservatoire (for more than a quarter of a century since), imperial *Maître de chapelle* (for a not much shorter period), a member – of forty-two years' standing – of the Académie . . . and an extremely alert and vivacious old gentleman of proverbial wit and no less proverbial *galanterie pour le beau sexe*. He was living quietly, among domestics of forty years' devoted service, and of course horses – to answer an enthusiasm carried over, almost equally with that for music, from his father – in his house, Rue Saint-Georges, where he was still in the habit of rising daily at 6.0 a.m. and working like one a quarter of his age. His chronicler in *Grove's* has it that: 'His habits were gentle and benevolent, slightly tinged with epicureanism.'

To that picture must be added the plain record that over a period of some sixty-four years he had composed forty-four stage-pieces, not to speak of ceremonial trifles such as a song to celebrate the victory of Magenta, a march for the opening of an exhibition in London and even an '*air national mexique*' – for the new emperor of Mexico.

His poise on social occasions, a poise from which were harvested the many bon-mots attributed to him, was matched – exactly, indeed, as his long practice and great success as a composer would lead us to expect – by a professional savoir faire, not to say aplomb, an adequacy to every occasion, expressed in a blend of the mercurial and the masterly and operating with a speed scarcely outdone by even the most celebrated Mozartian or Rossinian exploits.

What turns this sufficiently pleasant figure into a striking one, and at the same time perhaps in a way reconciles us – if we are still idealistic enough to be feeling resentful – to the contrast between his position in the world and the really quite 'petite' character of the fruits with which his musicianship, however intrinsically 'grand', acquired it, is the fact that Auber throughout his life was possessed by, in one shape or another, a very formidable degree of shyness and diffidence. This indeed is arresting. Whether or not a symptom of something more profound, whether or not we find its source possibly in his disturbed childhood, it makes of him a personality wanting only a few colourful splashes of hysteria (or is it only a few non-discreet correspondents and biographers that are lacking?) to be comparable to a Tchaikovsky.

Away from Music

Out of the childhood period, in which we are mostly so different from each other, Auber passed – a brilliant youth – through adolescence into the salad late teens and early twenties when we tend to be mostly so much alike. That critical point was chosen to be signalized by him with a manifestation that places him in startling, and rather comic, contrast to all other composers whatever – good, bad, or indifferent. In the face not only of his own propensities but of his father's encouragement and, indeed, pressure, he actually demurred at an artistic career and asked instead to be put in the way of becoming a bank-clerk and man of business! It is true that only a short spell in an office was needed to give him a strong distaste for such employment. Whereupon, no doubt in some embarrassment, he made a desire to improve his knowledge of affairs and to learn English the pretext for a mission to London. Once there, he discarded all his commercial *lettres d'introduction* and troubled to pass through only such doors as his musical talents opened for him. They were the doors of fashionable drawing-rooms, where soon, with his 'romances' and his quartets for harp, violin, bass, and piano, he became an established success. Of all things, the breaking of the Treaty of Amiens put a term to this interlude, and he was forced to go back to France sixteen months after he had left it.

It seems to have got settled between him and his father at this juncture that he was not, after all, to be tied to a career of commerce, though he still refused to be tied to one of music. At the request of an eminent cellist but indifferent composer, Lamarre, he wrote four cello concertos to be passed off as being from Lamarre's own pen. At the request of Mazas, when quite speedily the Lamarre fraud had been exploded by force of internal evidence, he wrote a violin concerto, which in its proper composer's name was performed with great success. Then in 1805 at the request of his father (it was as far as he could be got to go for the time being) he wrote a one-act comic-opera, *L'Erreur d'un Moment*. It was written, characteristically in a week, for a company of amateurs. One sequel was Auber's friendship with Ingres, who was one of the six performers (the master-to-be of pencil and brush happened also to dabble at violin-playing) that constituted the amateurs' entire orchestra. It was sixty-two years after this event, and the two were still friends then, that Mirecourt published his sketch of Auber, in the very year of Ingres' death (at the age of 87) and four years before Auber's. A more important result of the production of *L'Erreur d'un Moment*, which in fact turned out to be just the opposite of the error of Auber's whole career, was that Cherubini, who was in the audience, was favourably impressed and accepted him as a pupil.

Cherubini's Tutelage

It is interesting to note that Auber, during the period of Cherubini's guidance, through that stretch from twenty-three to thirty-one certainly quite unproductive financially and not, one gathers, really very productive at all, was in the position of being able to spend five to six months every year at the Belgian home of the Comte de Caramen (subsequently Prince de Chimay), a refuge of many artists, abode of a permanent literary circle, scene of poetry-readings and dramatic performances. For the Chimay private chapel Auber wrote a Mass, a portion of which eventually became famous in the guise of the *a cappella* prayer in *Masaniello*. For the Chimay private theatre Auber in 1812 wrote, to the libretto of another guest, an opera called *Couvin*. It was much applauded.

Only at that point could the timid composer be induced to face the test of a professional stage. This whole era, in the light of its antecedents, not to speak of the brilliant success that constituted most of the long remainder of Auber's life, seems rather fantastic. Indeed his first two professional attempts (in 1813 and 1819) were failures. Planard, the librettist of both, had to be pushed hard and long to produce the second. Cherubini's persuasion it was that eventually got it out of him, and Cherubini it was who, when that was a failure, obtained from him yet a third, demanding something really good and promising success for it. In 1820 the outcome, *La Bergère Châtelaine*, resoundingly, gigantically, fulfilled Cherubini's promise; and in 1821 *Emma* did equally well. Not long after that, the famous Scribe with laudable astuteness made approaches to Auber. In 1823 they met, and two successful operas resulted that same year. Thus began a prolific alliance that only ceased with Scribe's death in 1861.

Operas and Libretti

It can hardly be without importance that during the long wait for Planard's second libretto Auber *père* had, through speculation, lost his fortune. Three months after the production of *La Bergère Châtelaine* he died. Perhaps necessity must be judged to have had something to do with the termination of that phase of his son's diffidence.

There can be little doubt that the unsuccess of Auber's first two collaborations with Planard was largely due to the composer's method of work. It was, in fact, his custom already, and it always remained so, to conceive his music independently, and very often in advance, of the words it was to accompany. As Loménie puts it, 'It is said that M. Auber in general draws little inspiration from his subjects. His ideas most of the time come to him unpremeditatedly, while he is riding in the woods. He notes them down on bits of paper, and all find a place one day in some score.' Scribe before long became thoroughly broken-in to the kind of libretto-writing that this implied, where it was a question, quite literally, of fitting words to music instead of vice versa.

But neither the uninterrupted success that Auber's works henceforward enjoyed, nor the miraculous ease and speed with which he continued to create them, nor the honours that came his way, nor the assurance with which he seemed to move alike in his profession and in society – none of these did more than throw into relief the shyness into which his irresolution had turned. When he accused himself, as he liked to do, of laziness ('*Je n'aime que les femmes, les chevaux, les boulevards et le Bois de Boulogne*'), it was only a comic pretence: but when he said '*Si j'assistais à un de mes ouvrages, je n'écrivais de ma vie une note de musique*' he was telling what he believed to be the truth. He not only never conducted, he was never even present at, a performance of one of his own compositions. . . .

Dauriac, a critic who found in Auber much affinity with Haydn, reports that Auber was said to have copied out Haydn's quartets with his own hand.

VINCENZO BELLINI

1801–35

F. BONAVIA

Lyrical Music

It is a singular phenomenon that while the present generation of English music lovers has seen a revival of interest in both Rossini and Donizetti, it has been allowed to remain in complete ignorance as to the works of their contemporary and rival, Bellini. Wagner, whose opinion influenced European tastes for many years, disliked Donizetti, while at least in his early years showing a distinct partiality for Bellini. Even that stern judge of contemporaries, Hector Berlioz, had praise for the finale of the second act of Bellini's *I Capuletti e i Montecchi*. That some technical obstacles prevent a Bellini revival cannot be denied; the modern singer trained to meet the demands of the romantics must find Bellini uncongenial. But the even more difficult style of Rossini has not stood in the way of respectable performances of operas as exacting as *Cenerentola* and *L'Italiana in Algeri*. Bellini had some influence on another great composer, Chopin; Rossini and Donizetti had no direct influence on their immediate successors.

A more probable cause of neglect is the present distrust of music that is essentially lyrical. The movements and schools that have sprung up in the last fifty years have given us, besides original work of great value, music inspired by the fashions of other times. We have had neo-classics and neo-romantics; there has been no attempt to return to the pure lyric – much to the delight of a small group of conservatives who still maintain that any man of talent can give a very passable imitation of a technical masterpiece, but only genius can produce a work of lyrical beauty. Bellini is first and foremost a lyrical artist.

Early Years and Successes

He was born in Catania on 1 November 1801. The father, an organist, did not love his profession well enough to encourage the son to follow in his footsteps. It was only with difficulty and under pressure from friends that he allowed the boy to enter the Naples *conservatorio* (then known as the Collegio di San Sebastiano) directed by Nicolo Antonio Zingarelli, a prolific composer whose reputation rose high enough to warrant an invitation from Birmingham to contribute a new oratorio for the festival of 1829. A future director of the *conservatorio*, Saverio Mercadante, was Bellini's fellow-student. Progress at that institution appears to have been satisfactory. His school-leaving essay, an opera entitled *Adelson e Salvina*, impressed the examiners so favourably that they decided to give it a public performance. Among those who heard it was a certain Dojenico Barbaja, an impresario who controlled the two most important theatres in Italy – the San Carlo at Naples and La Scala at Milan. Barbaja did not accept *Adelson*, but liked it well enough to ask the composer to write another opera, which he promised to produce in Naples. The outcome was *Bianca e Fernando* (the title was changed to *Bianca e Gernando* because Fernando happened to be the name of the king of Naples, a very distrustful and suspicious monarch) and the Neapolitan public gave it so warm a reception that Barbaja commissioned another opera to be produced in Milan. *Il Pirata*, performed in 1827, was successful at La Scala. Performances in Rome and other European capitals followed and marked a turning point in the composer's career. With *Il Pirata* Bellini won international fame.

The opera is not comparable with the best in the Bellinian repertory. But it has the essential qualities of his style. It has arias in which the melody flows easily; it has a tenderness that captivates. The writing shows understanding of what the human voice can do to express pathetic emotion. It is uneven, some pages bearing signs of haste or carelessness, while elsewhere, and notably in the quintet that concludes the first act, there is abundant evidence of technical skill. Counterpoint is there so neatly contrived that a modern Italian critic points to it as a significant example of what Bellini could have done had he believed counterpoint necessary or useful. His conclusion is that the avoidance of complexity and the slight character of the accompanying parts in Bellini's scores was deliberate and consistent with the belief in the power of melody to affect the listener without the aid of 'science'. It is certain that while the technical elements are generally somewhat mechanical and casual the melody has been treated with utmost care. Bellini rewrote the best known of his cavatinas – 'Casta Diva' in *Norma* – eight times.

Set-backs and Triumphs

The next opera, *La Straniera*, given in Milan in 1829, was less successful, in spite of an excellent performance by some of the most famous singers of the day. Less successful still was *Zaira*, first heard at Parma in the same year. *I Capuletti e i Montecchi* (an arrangement of *Romeo and Juliet*) was given in Venice the following year and met with general approval. But it was with *La Sonnambula* that Bellini added to his reputation. The idyllic subject suited his gentle temperament and a good libretto by Felice Romani gave him the impulse he needed to do his best. Performed for the first time at Milan (Teatro Carcano) in March 1831, by a cast that included Maria Malibran, it had an enthusiastic reception and soon established itself in the repertory of every important opera house.

Norma, produced at La Scala in December of the same year, is generally considered to touch the high water mark of Bellini's achievement. The subject is tragic and deals with a Druid priestess who, having broken her vows of chastity, discovers that her Roman lover is unfaithful; in despair she makes public avowal of her guilt. In spite of the transparent simplicity of harmonic invention, Bellini uses the medium so aptly that he conveys an impression of dramatic tension as well as of great pathos. The title role was a favourite part of Pasta and the other great singers of the time, including Grisi and Tietjens. It was last sung at Covent Garden by Lili Lehmann in 1899. *Norma* has a vigour that is not found in the other operas of the composer.*

Rossini

Two more operas, *Il Fù e il Sarà*, which was performed in private, and *Beatrice di Tenda*, performed in Venice in 1833, were practically failures and Bellini, after staying for some time in London, went to Paris (1833) where Rossini was dictator of the Théâtre Italien. At first relations between the two composers were not very friendly. Shortly after his arrival in Paris Bellini wrote that Rossini had persuaded the Théâtre Italien to accept a work of Donizetti instead of one of his own and suspected the Pesarese of plotting against his interest. But in time relations improved. 'Rossini,' wrote Bellini in 1834, 'speaks well of me and my work. And I know that this time his praise is sincere.' At

* For a detailed study of *Norma*, see Ildebrande Pizzetti, *Le opere di Vincenzo Bellini*.

any rate it was Rossini who persuaded the Théâtre Italien to produce *I Puritani*, Bellini's last opera. Performed for the first time on 25 January 1835, *I Puritani* was an immediate success, and a few days later Rossini himself presented his colleague with the insignia of the Legion of Honour conferred on him by Louis Philippe. The original cast consisted of Grisi, Rubini, Tamburini, and Lablache.

Shortly after the first performance Bellini was taken ill while on a visit to some English friends at Puteaux and died there on 23 September. He was buried in Paris, the funeral service being arranged by Rossini and Cherubini. The night before the funeral the Théâtre Italien had opened for a new season with *I Puritani*, and the artists who took part in its performance sang the choral parts of the service. Forty years later his remains were exhumed and taken to his birthplace, Catania.

Evaluation

In London *I Puritani* was more successful than any other opera of Bellini. Grisi, the 'honeyed elegance' of Rubini, not less than the music and especially 'Son Vergin vezzosa', the Polacca, 'entranced the town'. London, wrote Henry Chorley, is steeped in the music of *Puritani*. 'Organs ground it, amateurs dare it and the singers themselves sang it to such satiety as to lose all consciousness of what they were engaged in.' Yet Chorley, a conservative who wanted the singer and not the orchestra to predominate in opera, was no out-and-out admirer of Bellini. In point of science he thought Bellini little more than an amateur. His treatment of the orchestra he considered 'either violently noisy or uselessly feeble', his modulations 'awkward and hampered'. It is significant that he concludes his criticism with the statement that he had found 'crudities cruder than Bellini's' in the work of young German composers who 'set them forth as the discoveries belonging to an era of emancipation'. By a curious irony Bellini is cold-shouldered now because of the alleged lack of initiative and of his over-sweet melodies.

Rossini, Chorley, and most biographers lament Bellini's early death and express the opinion that had he lived longer he would have written much greater things. It seems idle to speculate what Bellini or Pergolesi and Mozart might have done if they had reached three score years and ten. Some composers, like Puccini, follow attentively and are affected by the progress of music. Others, like Mascagni, are utterly impervious to reform. The artist gives us his own vision, his own conception of beauty. The critic can only consider the evidence before him and nothing supports the view that Bellini would have changed his style if he had lived as long as Methuselah or could have appreciated the orchestral genius of a Berlioz or the symphonic mastery of a Wagner. Bellini was no reformer; neither was he a reactionary. He was perfectly sincere in his belief that thematic elaboration, polyphonic combinations and complexity generally tend to rhetoric and are a liability, not an asset to the dramatic writer. In all probability his training did not encourage daring or experiment. But we know that he was aware of abuses in the opera house of his time and that he sought to improve conditions to the best of his ability. He used a toy pistol where what was wanted was an atomic bomb. But that was part of his gentle nature – an honest, simple soul, believing in the power of simple things, yet scrupulous in artistic matters. While others boasted of the rapidity with which they turned out new scores (Rossini wrote four operas in 1812 and four more in 1813) he was determined not to write more than one in twelve months 'so as to put into it all I have to give.' Methodical in his approach to a new subject, he began by studying closely each character, turning to composition only when 'I can become as they are, speak as they speak.' He paced the room declaiming loudly the lines, noting the rise and fall of the voice quickened by the sentiment appropriate to the situation, seeking in the voice the rhythm that, later, harmony was to translate into music – not a bad plan for a dramatic composer. He sought beauty and dramatic truth according to his lights and, according to his lights, he found them.

The music of Bellini, said Rossini, is a perfect reflection of his friendly, sweet countenance. That it is not free from weakness must be admitted. His partiality for melodic progressions in thirds and sixths does pall after a time. He undoubtedly failed to appreciate the importance of 'science', of careful and sound craftsmanship, while he overestimated the worth of fluent, singable melody. To modern ears his harmonic devices seem well worn, and there are to-day but few singers who can do full justice to his arias. But given the right interpreters, the art of Bellini can still cast a spell.

LOUIS HECTOR BERLIOZ

1803–69

EDWIN EVANS

Origins and Early Years

If one draws a straight line on the map from Vienne, on the Rhône below Lyons, to Grènoble, the old capital of the Dauphiné, there will be found on it, towards the centre but slightly nearer to the former city, a small country town called La Côte-Saint-André. It lies on the slope of the Banchet hills, with splendid views across country. There dwelt, for about four centuries before the composer was born, the family of Berlioz, whose name may perhaps indicate that it originally hailed from Savoy. Its members had attained to some distinction in official and professional life. The composer's father, Louis Joseph Berlioz (1776–1848), had studied medicine at Montpelier, established himself as a physician and been appointed medical officer of health. His mother came from Meylan, a village three miles beyond Grenoble in the direction of Savoy and bore before her marriage the name of Marmion, in which Berlioz took increased pride after he had become acquainted with Walter Scott's poem. The first child of the marriage, he was born at La Côte, and baptized when five days old with the names of Louis Hector. He had five brothers and sisters, two of whom died in childhood. Of the others, Nancy (1806–50) married a magistrate of Grenoble and Adèle (1814–60) a lawyer of Vienne. Prosper, the youngest, was born seventeen years after the composer. His death in Paris at the age of nineteen was a sad blow to the eldest son.

The boy's father was an enlightened liberal-minded man whose wide culture embraced an amateur's knowledge of music. His mother had strict religious views, which included a narrow prejudice against music, probably because of its association with the stage, more conspicuous in France and Italy than in Germany or England. Heredity can thus have played but a small part in forming young Hector's predisposition. This asserted itself at his First Communion when, as he related in his Memoirs, 'a new world of love and feeling was revealed' to him in the fresh young voices raised in the eucharistic hymn. In after years he was to discover that the melody which had so affected him had been adapted from D'Alayrac's opera *Nina*, but he was then happily unaware of its secular origin. Not long afterwards he discovered in the house an old flageolet from which he strove to coax the tune of *Malbrouk* with such effect that, in self-defence, his father taught him the rudiments of music. At the age of ten he was sent to a local school, but did not stay there long, his father taking charge of his general education. This included the reading of the classics and laid the foundation of that deep love of Virgil which was, many years afterwards, to bear fruit in *Les Troyens*. In the library at home he also discovered Florian's *Estelle et Némorin*, which he devoured in secret, and which became one of his favourite books. With it is associated a strange love of his boyhood, wherein is revealed that remarkable capacity for intense emotion that was to remain through life a salient characteristic. The children were accustomed to pay a yearly visit to their maternal relations at Meylan. Not far away was a villa at which a certain Madame Gautier spent the summer with her two nieces, of whom the elder, aged eighteen, was named Estelle. For her the twelve-year-old boy developed an extraordinary infatuation, which threatened to make him the laughing stock of the country-side, especially as he suffered all the pangs of an intense jealousy concerning her. To him it was so far from being a laughing matter that when he saw her again, many years after, a married woman with a family, his heart was still stirred and to the end, though he had forgotten the colour of her hair, he still remembered her eyes.

About the same time his father attempted to begin his instruction in anatomy, with a view to his following his own profession, but from the first the boy held the subject in aversion. His love of music had meanwhile increased, and his father tried to turn it to account by promising him as a reward for his anatomical studies a new flute, an instrument on which he had already acquired some prowess, but his efforts were fated to be in vain. On the other hand, Berlioz *père*, having taught his son what he knew of music, suggested to his neighbours that they should combine with him to bring a music teacher from Lyons. This led to the engagement of a violinist named Imbert, who was provided with twelve pupils. Under his guidance the young musician, then fourteen, made rapid progress with the aid of an old copy he had discovered of Rameau's *Harmony* in the simplified edition of d'Alembert, and subsequently of the more practical treatise of Catel. Imbert was succeeded by an Alsatian named Dorant, whose accomplishments included the guitar. Berlioz was thus able to record himself in his Memoirs, 'master of three potent and incomparable instruments, the flagelot, flute and guitar'. Before that he had begun to compose: a *Potpourri Concertant* for flute, horn, and strings, two quintets for flute and strings, and a number of songs, mostly settings of verses from Florian's idyll, very sad and in a minor key. He even aspired to appear in print, for in the spring of 1819 he wrote to two Paris publishers offering them his *Potpourri*. All these works were destroyed before he left for Paris, but memories of two of them survive. The melody in B minor introduced by the violins soon after the beginning of the Allegro in the overture of *Les Francs Juges* hails from the second of the quintets, and the air for the violins at the opening of the Largo of the *Symphonie Fantastique* was originally a setting of some lines of La Fontaine which expressed his anguish at leaving the places hallowed by the footsteps of his Estelle.

Medicine or Music?

In October 1821, Hector Berlioz and his cousin Alphonse Robert arrived in Paris, where they were to study medicine. The latter remained faithful to his task and became a well-known Paris doctor. Berlioz was at first animated by a sense of duty to his father. Although his first experience of the dissecting-room produced such horror that he jumped from the window and ran home, he strove to overcome this disgust and assiduously attended lectures. But music proved too strong for him. He began to frequent the opera. First he heard Salieri's *Les Danaïdes*, with the dance-music added by Spontini. The following week he heard Méhul's *Stratonice* followed by Persuis' ballet of *Nina* in which he recognized, played on the cor anglais, the tune borrowed from D'Alayrac's opera of the same name that had so impressed him in childhood. He also discovered that the library of the Conservatoire was open to the public and spent many hours immersed in the scores of Gluck when he should have been studying medical treatises. It was a performance of that composer's *Iphigénie en Tauride* that decided him. He wrote to his father that music must henceforth be his profession. At the library he had become acquainted with a Conservatoire student named Gerono, a pupil of Lesueur, who offered to present him to his teacher. Berlioz agreed and took with him a cantata for bass and orchestra, *Le Cheval Arabe*, and a three-part canon which Lesueur pronounced to be full of vitality – and of faults. He arranged for Gerono to 'coach' his friend until he was ready for more advanced teaching. Early in 1823 Lesueur pronounced him ripe and accepted him as a personal pupil.

Meanwhile Hector's correspondence with his father upon the subject had been slow in coming to a head because, the École de Médecine having twice been closed for political causes, Berlioz could give good reasons for non-attendance, and his allowance of one hundred and twenty francs per month had not been stopped. Perhaps also the father may have had illusions concerning the rapidity of possible advancement in the musical profession and expected some result from his son's enthusiasm. No sooner had young Berlioz been accepted by Lesueur than he must needs write an opera on the subject of Florian's *Estelle*, adapted by his friend Gerono. He afterwards declared himself fortunate in that nobody ever heard a note of it. This was followed by a scene for bass with orchestra from Saurin's drama *Beverley, ou le Joueur*, known in England as *The Gamester*. Then Masson, conductor at the Church of St Roch, invited him to write a Mass for Holy Innocents' Day, the choirboys' feast-day, 28 December 1823. He did so. Inadequately performed, it was a complete failure. He presented himself as a candidate at the Conservatoire and failed to pass. Although Lesueur wrote personally to his father, the latter stopped the allowance and recalled his son to La Côte, where he had a hard struggle to overcome the parental opposition. He was, however, to have another chance. The allowance was restored and he was permitted to attend the Conservatoire. Returning to Paris he wrote an oratorio, *Le Passage de la Mer Rouge*. But the failure of his Mass still troubled him. Augustin de Pons, an amateur whose acquaintance he had made at the Opéra, advanced him twelve hundred francs to defray the cost of a worthy performance which took place on 10 July 1825. It aroused much enthusiasm among his friends . . . and left him owing twelve hundred francs. He went to live in a garret, made his meals of dry bread with prunes or dates, and gave lessons until he had reduced the debt by one half. Then unfortunately de Pons, distressed at such privations or possibly in need of the balance, wrote to his father, with the result that he was paid, and the allowance was once more suspended. But Berlioz recruited pupils, to whom he taught singing, the flute, and the guitar, and presently he secured an engagement as chorister at the Théâtre des

Nouveautés that was sufficient to enable one of such frugal tastes as his to keep the wolf from the door. He shared rooms with a compatriot, Antoine Charbonnel, whose father had succeeded Berlioz senior as mayor of La Côte, and somehow contrived to purchase a piano for one hundred and ten francs.

The Prix de Rome

Meanwhile his studies at the Conservatoire were progressing under Lesueur and Reicha, to whom Cherubini had assigned him for counterpoint. He was also busily engaged in composition. To this period belong the 'heroic scena' called *La Révolution Grecque* and the monologue and bacchanale *La Mort d'Orphée* with which he competed unsuccessfully for the Prix de Rome in 1827. His friend Humbert Ferrand having provided him with a libretto, he began the composition of an opera, *Les Francs Juges*, the overture of which he considered to be his first important orchestral work. It was followed soon afterwards by the *Waverley Overture*. In 1828 he competed again and won the second prize with the lyrical scena *Herminie et Tancrède*. At the same time he was already engaged upon the eight scenes from Goethe's *Faust* that, completed in 1829, were subsequently to form the nucleus of *La Damnation de Faust*. The same year he competed again for the Prix de Rome with *La Mort de Cléopâtre*, in which he excelled himself, but the most striking original passage in the whole work proved too much for the judges, who decided not to award any first prize that year. In 1830 he again competed, with *Sardanapale*, but by now he had learned his lesson. He sent the work in without the final conflagration, and this time, at last, he was awarded the long-coveted premier prix. He had now lost all illusions concerning the artistic aspect of the competition, but had persisted in his candidature, in view of the importance attached to a Prix de Rome, not only by the French musical world, but more especially by his father.

There had now, moreover, been two performances of note. On St Cecilia's Day, 22 November 1827, his Mass was performed at St Eustache, on which occasion he made his first appearance as conductor. On 26 May 1828, he gave a concert of his works at the Conservatoire. The programme consisted of the overtures to *Waverley* and *Les Francs Juges*, an aria and a trio with chorus from the latter work, *La Révolution Grecque*, and the *Resurrexit* from the Mass. Apart from the trio, in which the chorus missed its cue, the concert went well, and brought the composer fame as 'the Byron of music'. The two overtures and the *Resurrexit* were heard again at the Conservatoire on 1 November 1829, as well as a vocal sextet, *Concert des Sylphes*, from the *Faust* music. This was rather poorly executed by Conservatoire students and missed fire, but the other works were more successful than ever. This concert actually showed a profit of 150 francs. The Prix de Rome was then not yet won, but Berlioz had 'arrived'.

Shakespeare, Harriet, and 'Camille'

Two years earlier, however, events had taken place that were to have a profound effect both on Berlioz's life and on his music. The romantic movement was at its height and Shakespeare, previously known only to the curious, was beginning to be widely read on the Continent. French students knew him through the adaptations of Ducis. Thereupon, in the autumn of 1827, Charles Kemble brought to the Odéon an English company, which included Harriet Smithson. She was then twenty-seven years old, having been born at Ennis, Ireland, on 18 March 1800. All literary Paris flocked to the theatre. Shakespeare became 'the rage'. Berlioz relates that he was struck as by lightning, not only by Shakespeare, but by Miss Smithson as Ophelia and Juliet. He raved. He was exalted. There are fantastic stories, probably exaggerated but not without foundation, concerning his behaviour at that time. He did not speak her language, could not even pronounce her name, but he was madly in love. His letters remaining unanswered, he poured out his passion in settings of Moore's *Irish Melodies*. It was mainly to attract her attention that he gave that concert in May 1828, and she did not even hear of it. Not until the eve of her departure for Holland did she learn of the musician's infatuation and then she declared that it was hopeless, but he was elated because at least she was aware of his existence. It was in this love-fever that he began the composition of the *Symphonie Fantastique; Episode in the Life of an Artist*, in which the *idée fixe* represents his obsession. He heard some scandal concerning his idol – its nature has not been recorded – and the horror he felt is included in the 'programme' of his symphony, which became in turns a tribute and an indictment according to the state of his feelings. He sought what he calls in his Memoirs a 'violent distraction'. Her name was Marie-Félicité-Denise Moke, but she was commonly known as 'Camille' Moke and afterwards she became a famous pianist as Mme Camille Pleyel. Ferdinand Hiller, who was in love with her, asked Berlioz to be his intermediary, with the result that he was supplanted. Berlioz called her his 'Ariel' and after some rebuffs succeeded in obtaining her mother's consent to their engagement.

Italian Days

In October 1830, the time arrived for the official performance of *Sardanapale*, to which the composer had meanwhile added the all-important final conflagration, but although it had been duly rehearsed the horns missed a vital cue, the percussion, relying upon them, were afraid to 'come in', and the whole effect was a failure. The composer was so mortified that he flung the score at the orchestra and created a scandal. To retrieve the catastrophe he gave another concert at the Conservatoire on 5 December, the programme of which comprised, among other works, both *Sardanapale* and the *Symphonie Fantastique*. It was to pillory Miss Smithson's turpitude, but of this she remained blissfully unaware. Meanwhile, on 7 November, at a benefit concert, there had been performed a *fantaisie dramatique* with chorus, on Shakespeare's *The Tempest*, a work that subsequently became the final section of *Lélio*. At the end of the year he left for La Côte to spend a few weeks with his parents, during which he was much troubled by the silence of his fiancée, and in February he set out from Lyons for the obligatory sojourn in Rome.

It may be expedient to review his position as a composer at this date. Too often has it been said that he arrived at Paris in a state of raw ignorance. As a matter of fact he had studied with good effect and knew theoretically far more than has commonly been credited to him. What he lacked was mainly experience. He had heard next to nothing. This, however, he quickly remedied on his arrival, even before his meeting with Lesueur, by attending performances at the opera and elsewhere and by assiduously studying scores at the Conservatoire library, which he knew so thoroughly that his ejaculations over inaccuracies at public performances became notorious. To refer to him as ill-equipped for his tasks is to fly in the face of facts. Heterodox his knowledge may have been, but it was extensive and thorough. By the time he left for Rome he had written an immense quantity of music, much of which he destroyed, retaining what he considered to be of value for incorporation in later works. The surviving compositions included the original version of *Faust*, the two overtures, *Waverley* and *Les Francs Juges*, *La Mort de Cléopatre*, the *Irish Melodies*, and the *Symphonie Fantastique* – quite enough to make of him the outstanding figure in French music of his day.

The route chosen by Berlioz for his journey to Italy was an unusual one. Having no desire to attempt the crossing of the Alps in winter, he travelled first to Marseilles, where he spent a few days waiting for a ship. Eventually he fell in with some young fellows who had arranged to cross to Leghorn on a Sardinian brig. They had to provide their own food and were not unwilling that he should 'mess' with them. They encountered terrible weather. The journey which should have taken five days took eleven, three of which were spent in sight of Nice where a head wind made progress impossible. Happily Berlioz was a good sailor and enjoyed the experience. Among his fellow passengers was a Venetian who claimed to have commanded Byron's corvette during the poet's adventures in the Adriatic and the Greek islands. The composer confesses that he was much too pleased to find himself in the company of a man who had possibly shared Childe Harold's Pilgrimage to question his veracity. It was this experience that gave him the original idea of his overture *The Corsair*, of which he wrote the first version the following year in Rome. He duly arrived at the Villa Medici, then under the direction of the painter Horace Vernet, where they had almost ceased to expect him, and was received with great hilarity by the students. The following day he made the acquaintance of Mendelssohn, his relations with whom appear somewhat strange in the light of their correspondence. Berlioz wrote to his Paris friends that he thought Mendelssohn to be one of the greatest musical intellects of the day, a fine fellow, and 'one of those frank beings whom one so rarely meets'. Mendelssohn wrote to his mother that Berlioz was a caricature without a shadow of talent, groping in the darkness but with boundless conceit. Another famous musician whom he met in Rome was Glinka, the father of modern Russian music. He, at all events, was a kindred soul.

Berlioz had still no news of his fiancée, Mlle Moke, but indirectly he heard rumours impugning her fidelity. Quite suddenly he decided to return home and learn the truth. He was detained at Florence by a sore throat and, on collecting his letters, found among them one from his prospective mother-in-law overwhelming him with vague reproaches and announcing her daughter's marriage to Camille Pleyel. In a jealous rage he resolved to hasten to Paris to 'kill two guilty women and an innocent man', but as news of his approach might reach them he first procured as a disguise the attire of a lady's maid. But in changing coaches at Pietra Santa he lost his disguise and had to wait at Genoa while another was being made. This gave time for reflection, with the result that he proceeded no further than Nice, whence, after a few pleasant weeks, during which he composed the overture to *King Lear*, he retraced his steps. On the way back to Rome he composed *Lélio*, incorporating in it fragments of earlier works, with the Fantasy on Shakespeare's *The Tempest* as concluding movement. In Rome he composed *The Corsair* and *Rob Roy* overtures and one or two minor works. He left on 1 May 1832, and arrived at Grenoble on 31 May on his way to La Côte. His sojourn in Italy had brought him little but boredom. He had no liking for the music he heard and spent his time rambling over the countryside, gathering impressions that were to fructify later in *Harold in Italy*. He became sufficiently interested in Horace Vernet's daughter to refuse the heiress his father had meanwhile found him, but soon forgot her afterwards. He spent some time in the Dauphiné revising various works and did not reach Paris until 6 November, when he found accommodation in an apartment that happened to have been previously occupied by Miss Smithson. Possibly this association rekindled his flame for her, which blazed up anew.

Married Life

On 9 December Berlioz gave a concert of his works at the Conservatoire. The programme included the overture of *Les Francs Juges*, the *Symphonie Fantastique*, of which the literary basis had been so modified as to become once more a tribute to the actress, and its sequel, *Lélio*, or *The Return to Life*. Bocage, a famous actor, declaimed the monologues of the latter and the concert was such a success that it was repeated within the month. By the intermediary of Schlesinger, the original publisher of his *Faust*, Berlioz had sent an invitation to Harriet Smithson, who attended the concert and was so touched at finding herself the heroine of a great dramatic work that at last she consented to meet him. The actress had begun a season on 21 November with her own company, first at the Théâtre Italien where four performances were given and then at other theatres. But the novelty of the English players had worn off, and the venture was a ruinous failure. By 30 March, when the season petered out completely, Miss

Smithson was in dire straits. She was entirely without means and owed 14,000 francs. As an additional misfortune, during the preparations of a concert for her benefit she broke her leg whilst alighting from a carriage. At this time Berlioz was constantly proving his devotion and alternating between extremes of hope and despair during which he even threatened suicide in her presence. It is small wonder that, probably against her better judgement, Harriet eventually yielded. They were married on 3 October 1833, at the British Embassy, in the face of violent objections from both families.

Whatever chances there may have been of the marriage proving a success were probably ruined by the material position of the couple. Harriet was not merely a waning star. Her stage career was practically at an end. Despite two benefit performances she was not clear of debt, and her attempts to recover her popularity were in vain. Berlioz on his wedding day possessed 300 francs. He had long been a musical journalist, and he now wrote more copiously than ever, besides giving concerts, but, although he came to be recognized as one of the most brilliant of critics, his earnings continued precarious. Meanwhile Harriet was gradually becoming embittered at her own failure as a contributor to the family fortunes. Her temper grew shrewish and undermined Berlioz's affection, whilst at the same time hers, which had at first been rather cool, developed into a jealous passion. She also became self-indulgent and began to lose her good looks. Scenes were frequent and her stage experience helped her to make them effective. Berlioz appears to have held out for some time, but towards the end of 1841 he became acquainted with Marie Martin, professionally known as Marie Recio, and in September 1842, when he left for his first foreign tour, it was in her company.

Paganini

During those nine years the composer's fame had spread through Europe, enhanced by important new works. The first of these was the symphony, *Harold in Italy*. After one of his concerts, given on 22 December 1833, at which the *Symphonie Fantastique* had been performed, he was stopped in the corridor by 'a man with long hair, piercing eyes, a strange and haggard face, a genius, a Titan among the giants'. This was Paganini, whom he had not previously met, and who pressed his hand, overwhelming him with praise of the work. He had recently acquired a Stradivarius viola, which he was anxious to play in public. With that purpose in view he called on Berlioz and requested him to write a work for viola and orchestra. Berlioz warned him that such a work as he would write was not likely to be what a virtuoso required, but Paganini insisted, and he wrote the first movement of a then nameless symphony, with a viola solo, using for the purpose a theme from the *Rob Roy* overture, which he intended discarding. As he expected, Paganini was dissatisfied. There were too many rests for the soloist. He must be playing the whole time. A few days later Paganini left for Nice and the two did not meet for three years, but Berlioz did not abandon his symphony. Drawing upon his Italian memories he made of the viola a kind of melancholy dreamer, after the manner of Byron's *Childe Harold*, and called the symphony *Harold in Italy*. It was first performed at the Conservatoire on 23 November 1834, but Paganini did not hear it until 16 December 1838. Two days later he wrote Berlioz an enthusiastic letter, enclosing a draft upon Messrs Rothschild for the sum of twenty thousand francs. This munificent and unexpected gift was the means of relieving the composer of his immediate necessities and thereby providing him with the requisite leisure for the composition of his *Romeo and Juliet* symphony, so that we are indebted to Paganini for the incentive to two of Berlioz's greatest compositions.

The Siege of the 'Opéra'

Berlioz did not share the views of his countrymen, who held at that time, and long afterwards, that a composer could not be deemed great until he had triumphed in opera. He declared that 'music has huge wings which she can never unfold to their fullest extent within the walls of a theatre'. Nevertheless he was far from desiring to exclude opera from the scope of his ambitions. In 1834 he accepted a libretto written for him by Léon de Wailly and Auguste Barbier on the subject of Benvenuto Cellini, and the three of them submitted it to the Opéra Comique, but it was rejected. Then began a siege of the Opéra, conducted in the Press and behind the scenes, which lasted until the beginning of 1837. The management agreed at last, after the production of two works that it had in prospect, to perform Berlioz's opera, upon which he had begun to work during the previous year. He had been since 1835 the musical critic of the *Journal des Débats*, and in this capacity he praised an opera *Esmeralda*, by Louise Angélique Bertin, whose father owned the newspaper. He was even accused of having helped her in the composition of the work, a charge that he vigorously denied, but it can be readily imagined to what use the insinuation was put in the Press campaign which raged round the name of Berlioz. He had, however, completed his opera by April 1837, except the overture, which was added when production appeared imminent.

Meanwhile he had succeeded in obtaining from the Ministry of the Interior a commission to compose a Requiem Mass for the second anniversary of the funeral of victims of 28 July 1835, when Fieschi's attempt on the life of King Louis-Philippe had resulted in the death, among others, of Marshal Mortier. Thus originated the famous *Messe des Morts*, one of Berlioz's greatest works. It was, however, attended by the ill-luck that seemed to pursue all the composer's achievements. A few days before the anniversary it was officially announced that the religious ceremony would not take place, and for a time it appeared as if Berlioz had laboured in vain. But in October news reached Paris of the fall of Constantine, Algeria, which had cost the lives of General de Damrémont and many officers and men. The King ordered that the General should be buried at the Invalides and that the ceremony should commemorate the brave men who had fallen with him. The Requiem being ready, it was performed on 5 December 1837. Even then Berlioz experienced some difficulty in obtaining payment.

On 10 September 1838, after many set-backs, at last *Benvenuto Cellini* was produced at the Opéra where it achieved what the composer ruefully called *une chute éclatante*. The overture was received with acclamations, but there success ended, though an analysis of contemporary reports shows that the reason lay rather in the libretto, the stage production and the performance than in the music itself. But the nature of these reports was such as to keep away the public, and for the time being *Benvenuto Cellini* shared the fate of many operas that have failed because they were not given the time and support needed for success. The overture, however, quickly established itself in the repertoire. To Berlioz this failure to win the opera public was a cruel blow. He had counted upon *Benvenuto Cellini* to give his reputation the lustre that in the France of his day only a successful opera could bestow.

Four performances were given of the opera. The last having been delayed by a change in the cast, Berlioz was not left disconsolate at its withdrawal, for it was then that the concert took place which prompted Paganini's munificence. This enabled him now to begin immediately his next important work, the vast symphony *Romeo and Juliet*, a project that had haunted his imagination ever since the first days of his Shakespearean enthusiasm. He began it on 24 January 1839, and by 8 September the score was completed. The first performance took place under his direction in the Hall of the Conservatoire on 24 November with an orchestra of 160 players, besides three soloists and a chorus of ninety-eight for the vocal sections. Two further performances followed in rapid succession, which is no mean tribute to a work of this character.

Throughout his career Berlioz formed vast projects and had to wait for the opportunity to present itself for their realization. Sometimes the opportunity came, as with the Requiem. But more often than not he was disappointed. One such project was the music of a huge commemorative festival in honour of France's famous men. Two sections of it were already in existence in 1835, and the *Te Deum* of 1849 is said to have been a tardy contribution to the realization of the same cherished idea. Officially, however, it is represented by the *Symphonie Funèbre et Triomphale* for chorus and orchestra, commissioned by the Ministry of the Interior for the inauguration, on 28 July 1840, tenth anniversary of the revolution of 1830, of the column erected on the Place de la Bastille. At the original performance the orchestra of 200 was of wind instruments only, but at a subsequent concert it was performed by a combined military band of 120 and symphonic orchestra of 130. This is the work of which Wagner, who was then living in Paris, speaks so highly in his autobiography. It is also the last work of any importance that Berlioz composed before he entered upon the wanderings that occupied his later years. Towards the end of 1841 he formed the liaison, mentioned above, with Marie Recio. She was engaged at the Opéra – it is said, on Berlioz's recommendation – but without much success. If ever he had any illusion concerning her talent as a singer it was soon dispelled, for we know on the authority of Hiller that her ambition to sing at his concerts was a sore trial to him. But his critical susceptibilities did not moderate his ardour. Harriet, his first wife, died on 3 March 1853, and on 19 October 1854 he married Marie Recio. It does not seem that this second marriage proved any happier than the first. If, however, contemporaries do not speak well of the second Madame Berlioz, they have nothing but praise for her Spanish mother, Mme Martin, *née* Sotera de Villas, who would appear to have flown in the face of all 'mother-in-law' tradition by watching with devoted care over Berlioz's welfare. If we have taken a leap forward in Berlioz's biography, it is because it is the last occasion on which we shall have occasion to refer to his domestic life.

A Musician's Wanderings

Berlioz's first spell of foreign travel opened with a visit to Brussels in September 1842, when he conducted several of his works. He had already planned his German tour, but returned first to Paris for a great farewell concert, which took place on 7 November. The same month an election was held at the Académie des Beaux-Arts to fill the vacancy created by the death of Cherubini, the preceding March. There were five candidates: Onslow, Adam, Berlioz, Zimmermann, and Dourlen, of whom Adam complacently records that only the first two merited serious consideration. Of these Onslow proved successful, which must have been a bitter disappointment to the composer of *Giselle*, the successful ballet produced a year earlier. Berlioz left Paris again in December and travelled to Germany via Brussels. He was unable to give the projected concerts at Mainz or Frankfurt and continued his journey to Stuttgart where, on 29 December, he conducted a programme of his symphonic works in the presence of the King and the Court. This was followed by concerts at Weimar, Leipzig, Brunswick, Hamburg, Berlin, and Darmstadt, whence he returned to Paris at the end of May 1843.

One of the works he had taken with him on his travels was his unfortunate opera *Benvenuto Cellini*. Turning over the pages he concluded that there were ideas in it worth saving from the wreck. With that end in view he wrote a new '*ouverture caractéristique*', intended to be a separate work, which he entitled *Le Carnaval Romain* and dedicated to one of his new-found German patrons, the Prince of Hohenzollern-Hechingen. Eventually, however, it became a second overture to the opera, in which it precedes the second act. That winter and the following spring Berlioz conducted several concerts in Paris, at one of which, on 3 February 1844, he conducted the first performance of *Le Carnaval Romain*. The principal composition upon which he was then engaged was an opera, *La Nonne Sanglante*, begun two years earlier and intended for the Opéra, but destined to remain unfinished. In August 1844, however, he went to Nice to recuperate after the fatigues of the season and occupied a tower near the Rocher des Ponchettes; possibly the scene recalled his experiences of 1831, when he was weatherbound in sight of Nice on his way to Rome, for he rewrote the overture, *The Corsair*, in which he had recorded his impressions. This new version was entitled *La Tour de Nice* and performed on 13 January 1845, at the first of four concerts arranged by Franconi at the Cirque des Champs-Élysées, when it proved a failure. He destroyed the score, but evidently still possessed the original version, for ten years later he again rewrote it. This final version was first performed by the Société Sainte-Cécile, on 1 April 1855. It was then announced as *The Red Corsair*, but on publication the adjective was dropped and the original title restored. Though well received at the time, this work afterwards suffered neglect until it was taken up by Hans von Bülow, who included it in his programmes when touring with the Meiningen Orchestra. After the spring season of 1845 Berlioz again recuperated in the South during June and July. In August he attended the unveiling of the Beethoven monument at Bonn, returning to Paris almost immediately to prepare for his second extended tour.

Faust

He left at the end of October and arrived in Vienna on 3 November. As on his former journey he was accompanied by Marie Recio, but he appears to have subdued her determination to sing, for the programme of one of his first concerts in Vienna shows another artist singing *Le Pâtre Breton*, which on the previous tour she had considered as reserved for her. What is, however, more important, is that on this journey he took with him his *Eight Scenes from Faust*, which were to be incorporated in a larger work. In the Memoirs he writes: 'Whilst trailing round Germany in my old postchaise I composed my *Damnation of Faust*. Each movement is punctuated by memories of the place where it was written. For instance the Peasants' Dance was jotted down by the light of a shop gas-jet one night when I had lost myself in Budapest, and I got up in the middle of the night at Prague to write the song of the angelic choir.' Other portions were composed on the Danube steamers. At Vienna Berlioz met many friends, one of whom – possibly Liszt – lent him a collection of Hungarian national airs, among which was that of the *Rakoczy March*. He was so attracted by the tune that in one night he made the now well-known orchestral version subsequently incorporated in *Faust*. He had it with him when, after directing concerts at Vienna and Prague, he proceeded to the Hungarian capital. At that time, in the restless forties, the atmosphere there was heavily charged with political electricity. A storm was brewing which was to burst out later. In the circumstances it is not suprising to read in the composer's Memoirs that the first performance of this march made a volcanic impression on an audience of patriots. The occasion became, in fact, a patriotic demonstration. He records: 'The extraordinary effect it produced at Budapest induced me to introduce it in *Faust* by taking the liberty of placing my hero in Hungary at the beginning of the action.' The next stage of the tour was Breslau, after which he conducted another concert at Prague, revisited Brunswick, and returned to Paris at the beginning of May 1846.

Back in France, and whilst still engaged upon the last remaining portions of *Faust*, he composed a choral work, *Le Chant des Chemins de Fer*, which was performed at Lille, 14 June 1846, the occasion being the inauguration of the railway still so well-known to English travellers, the Chemin de Fer du Nord. *Faust* was finished on 19 October and performed for the first time on 6 December at the Opéra Comique, which was not more than half-filled. A second performance fared no better, and Berlioz found himself seriously in debt. Friends, however, came to his aid and he was able to leave Paris, on 14 February 1847, to make his first visit to Russia, where he gave successful concerts at St Peterburg, Moscow, and Riga. He broke his homeward journey at the request of the King of Prussia, who wished to hear his *Faust*. He reached Paris on 4 June and in August received an offer from Jullien, who had just taken Drury Lane Theatre, to come to London and conduct the opera. He arrived on 5 November, and stayed at 76 Harley Street. The opera opened on 6 December with Donizetti's *Lucia di Lammermoor*, but only two other works were presented, and the undertaking failed at the end of four months, owing chiefly to Jullien's extravagance. Berlioz gave two concerts in London, one on 7 February, the other on 29 June 1848, but the receipts did not go far to compensate him for Jullien's failure. He left London on 16 July, bringing back with him the first instalment of his Memoirs and a version for female chorus of his *Ballade sur la Mort d'Ophélie*, dated 4 July. Soon after his arrival in Paris his father died, on 26 July, and he had to journey to La Côte to settle up his affairs. While there he visited all the familiar places haunted with memories of his childhood and learned that his once-beloved Estelle was now fifty-one, a widow with a grown-up son at the Bar. Returning to Paris he composed, on 22 September, the impressive *Marche Funèbre* for the last scene of *Hamlet*.

The Te Deum *and* L'Enfance du Christ

Meanwhile the revolution of February had resulted in the abdication of King Louis-Philippe and the establishment of a Republic. On 20 December Prince Louis Napoleon was elected President. It was at this time that Berlioz planned another large work, in honour of the first Napoleon. It was to be entitled *Le Retour de la Campagne d'Italie*, and at the entrance of the victorious general Bonaparte into the cathedral a *Te Deum* was to resound through the sacred building. Thus originated another of those works for State occasions which Berlioz found so hard afterwards to place. When in 1852 Louis Napoleon abolished the Constitution and became the Emperior Napoleon III, the composer hoped that this *Te Deum* might be used at his coronation. The following year he hoped it might be used for his wedding. Again disappointed, he tried to have it commissioned for the opening of the Paris Exhibition of 1855. That it was performed on the eve of that event was, however, due not to the Government, which again failed him, but to Ducroquet, the organ builder, who had installed in the previous year a new instrument at the Church of St Eustache and persuaded a few friends to join him in guaranteeing the expenses. The *Te Deum* was then published, with a dedication to the Prince Consort. It is one of Berlioz's greatest works, but it had to wait nearly six years for a performance.

In January 1850, Berlioz founded the Société Philharmonique of Paris, which gave its first concert on 19 February and, alas, its last on 25 March 1851. At one of the concerts of its second season, on 12 November 1850, it gave the first performance of *La Fuite en Égypte*, fragment of an oratorio ostensibly by Pierre Ducré, *maître de chapelle* at the Sainte Chapelle in 1679, but in reality by Berlioz himself and destined to become the central portion of his sacred trilogy, *L'Enfance du Christ*, afterwards known in England as *The Holy Family*. The two sections that were added later are the first, *Le Songe d'Hérode*, and the third, *L'Arrivée à Sais*. The completed trilogy was performed for the first time on 10 December 1854. It bears a dedication to John Ella, founder and director of the Musical Union in London, which the composer had visited three times in the interval since the trilogy was begun. The first occasion was an official one in connexion with the great Exhibition of 1851 in Hyde Park. He left Paris on 9 May and stayed at 27 Queen Anne Street, Cavendish Square. It was then that he first became associated with Dr Henry Wylde, professor at the Royal Academy, and T. W. Beale, a partner in the firm of Cramer, who secured his services for their projected New Philharmonic Society, which was founded in January 1852. He returned, and conducted the first concert of the society on 24 March, four days after Liszt had presented, and incidentally rehabilitated, his *Benvenuto Cellini* at Weimar. Six concerts were given that season, the last on 9 June. The financial outcome was unsatisfactory and Berlioz was not re-engaged until 1855, but the guarantors persevered and the society lasted until 1879, when its concerts were taken over by Wilhelm Ganz.

More Wanderings

November 1852 found Berlioz at Weimar, where a week's festival was held of his works, including the performances of *Benvenuto Cellini*, which was produced by Liszt on 20 March. It was one of Berlioz's greatest triumphs. The following spring he returned to London and there conducted his *Harold in Italy* at the sixth concert of the (now Royal) Philharmonic Society; a fortnight later, on 25 June, his *Benvenuto Cellini* was produced under his direction, for the only time at Covent Garden. According to Spohr, who was present, the audience 'broke out into one general storm of hisses and whistling, a circumstance never before known to have occurred at the Italian Opera in London in the presence of the Queen.' For some of this an Italian element in the audience appears to have been responsible. A supper had been arranged to take place after the performance and many distinguished guests were invited, but after the catastrophe they were reluctant to meet the victim and failed to attend, with the exception of J. W. Davison, musical critic of *The Times*, with whom Berlioz dined in what his companion afterwards described as a sentimental *tête-à-tête*. Efforts were made to atone to him for this failure, but the mischief was done and the opera seems never again to have been performed in London.

A month after his return from London, Berlioz left for Baden-Baden on the invitation of Bénazet, the lessee of the Casino. It was the first of a series of visits that were to continue annually and lead eventually to the composition of an opera, his last, *Béatrice et Bénédict*. In 1855 he paid another visit to London at the invitation of the New Philharmonic. This was the season when Wagner conducted the concerts of the senior Philharmonic. He also paid repeated visits to

Weimar and occasionally to other German cities, but his attention was soon to become absorbed in another great work, *Les Troyens*, in which his devotion to Virgil was to find expression. Whilst at Weimar in February 1856 he discussed the plan of this work, based on the second and fourth books of the Aeneid, with the Princess Sayn-Wittgenstein, who gave him every encouragement. He kept her informed and reported to her on 24 June that the libretto was nearly ready. Two years later the music was completed. It is a vast opera, in two parts, *La Prise de Troie* and *Les Troyens à Carthage*, of which the latter was produced separately at the Théâtre Lyrique on 4 November 1863. The first part was not performed in the composer's lifetime, and the first integral performance of the whole work did not take place until Felix Mottl gave it at Karlsruhe on two evenings, 6 and 7 December 1890.

The Last Work

In August 1858, Bénazet told Berlioz of his intention to build a theatre at Baden-Baden. He wanted to commission an opera on an episode of the Thirty Years War, but the subject bore too much resemblance to *Les Francs Juges* and the composer suggested *Béatrice et Bénédict*, based on Shakespeare's *Much Ado about Nothing*. The composition was begun towards the end of 1859 and completed early in 1862. The opera was produced in the new theatre on 9 August 1862, and eight months later at Weimar, but not in Paris until after the composer's death. It was to prove his last work. He paid a few more visits to Germany and Austria, and one to Russia in the winter of 1867–8, at the invitation of the Grand Duchess Helena. It was another great triumph, culminating in a banquet on his birthday which was attended by five hundred people. But he was already a sick man and his death, on 8 March 1869, occasioned little surprise. His only son had died at Havana, of yellow fever, in 1867, his second wife five years earlier. During those last few years he found solace in corresponding with the Estelle of his youth, now nearing seventy and a grandmother, and even tried to persuade her to marry him. To the end a Romantic! Perhaps one should say *the* Romantic, for it is difficult to name another artist as completely representative of all that is meant by the Romantic Movement.

JOHANNES BRAHMS

1833–97

F. BONAVIA

Origins and School Days

Most biographers of Johannes Brahms are agreed in regarding his life as uneventful – as the record of work accomplished and little else. There is a very real difficulty in reconciling the man and the artist in retrospect – the undistinguished domestic individual with the inspired composer. Some biographers, trying to discover a link between the two images, have found it by distorting and enlarging the man until he acquires the glory of Brahms the artist. Richard Specht, for instance, describes Brahms in terms applicable to a Wagnerian hero, using the language of a Houston Stewart Chamberlain portraying Tristan. Although, unlike Lohengrin, he has no kingly ancestors, Brahms is a man of privileged race, his father being 'of that straight-grown, gnarled and healthy humankind found in the soil of Hylstein'. He goes to Liszt's house like Tannhäuser to the Venusberg; his friend Max Kalbeck is called 'the master's Kurwenal'. His notorious rudeness becomes playful humour; his shortcomings, the amiable weaknesses common to the noblest natures. His very passion for tin soldiers is recorded as an heroic trait.

This may be creditable to the biographer's capacity for sympathy, but it does not tally with the recorded facts. The huge, distorted, magic lantern image of the composer has no correspondence with the unheroic reality. It is probably true that Brahms was of 'Aryan' stock (there seems to be no foundation for the suggestion that the family name was once Abrahams), but there are many incidents in which he did not behave like the perfect opera hero. Indeed little in him was truly heroic. He was a blend of noble and ignoble instincts, and it was not the higher instincts that were always most apparent. Like all great artists he was endowed with keen sensibility and had to pay the price the artistic temper exacts. In other respects he was unusually fortunate. He won recognition at a much earlier age than Beethoven or

Schumann, and his last years, unlike Mozart's, were spent in comfort. Specht finds it heartrending that Brahms should have died weeping. Few men who reach the end of a full life have any tears left for their own deathbed.

Johannes Brahms was born in 1833, at Hamburg, where his father played the double-bass in an orchestra and played it, according to his own confession, none too well. His mother appears to have been of a different stamp. It is said of her that she knew the whole of Schiller by heart – a feat the more remarkable considering all the household cares that must have fallen on her shoulders. Johannes learnt the rudiments of music at a very early age. At school he does not seem to have distinguished himself. He was teased, says Specht, and suffered cruelly under the officious sadism of spiteful school beadles. He was taught French and hated it; dislike of the French language brought about dislike of the French nation and, according to his biographer, awoke in him proud patriotism and heroic Germanism. It must have been some comfort to the little patriot to know that his sadistic tormentors probably detested the French as heartily as he did himself.

If his progress at school was unsatisfactory, his progress in piano playing was rapid. He was first taught by his father, whose place was taken later by Otto F. W. Cossel and, still later, by Edward Marxsen. It is difficult to know exactly how much Brahms profited under his teachers. We are told that he showed his gratitude and devotion by dedicating to Marxsen the *Piano Concerto in B flat* and by persuading the publisher, Simrock, to issue a set of variations composed by Marxsen. We are also told that he spoke of him as the most inartistic musician in Hamburg. Cossel, who ignored Schumann and Chopin and founded his teaching on Bach and Beethoven, he remembered with affection and regard. In these early years he composed a good deal, but he could not be induced to publish these youthful works, which he later destroyed. His teachers thought highly of him and, at the death of Mendelssohn, Marxsen is reported to have said: 'A master has gone; a greater master arises in Brahms.' The boy helped his family by doing hackwork for publishers, playing in dance-halls, and teaching. He read a good deal, dividing his allegiance between Heine and the Bible.

In 1853 he met the Hungarian violinist Remenyi and the meeting marked an epoch in his life. Remenyi was a violinist of a wandering disposition, a musician by nature more than by education. He proposed a joint tour, and Brahms, glad to break the deadly routine of his Hamburg engagements, accepted. They wandered, mostly on foot, through North Germany, ending at Hanover, where Joachim lived. Remenyi, who knew him, called and introduced the young pianist. Joachim was immediately struck by Brahms's piano playing. He listened with delight to some of his compositions and at once took the composer under his wing. He suggested visits to Göttingen and Weimar, wrote to Schumann at Düsseldorf, and urged Brahms to visit the Schumanns there.

Liszt and the Weimar School

No other composer ever saw so rapid a change in his fortunes. One day Brahms was unknown; the next, he was introduced to the most influential musicians of his time. In recommending his new friend, Joachim described him as 'pure as a diamond, soft as snow'. The future proved how accurate that description was. Brahms himself was delighted with the prospect of visiting Weimar, where Liszt held court like an emperor. In Remenyi's company he set out on a visit that was destined to make history. Liszt welcomed Remenyi and the young composer of whom Joachim had spoken so highly. He invited them to stay with him at the Altenburg house; he arranged an evening party for their benefit and asked some of his friends to meet them, Joachim Raff and Klindworth among them.

Brahms, obviously ill at ease in the society of the urbane and plausible Liszt, refused to play. Liszt, all affability and condescension, took the manuscript and proceeded himself to play the *E flat minor Scherzo* and some pages of the *C major Sonata*, delighting his guests, including Brahms, by his inimitable performance. Then, having congratulated the composer, he proceeded to play his own *Sonata* in B minor, which he had just finished. At a certain point, expecting to see signs of emotion in the countenance of his youngest colleague, he turned to him as if to indicate that this was the language they alone, brother composers, spoke and understood, when he discovered that the brother composer was fast asleep. Liszt quitted the room in displeasure and left his friends to unbraid Brahms for his breach of manners; he did not refer to it the next day, when he behaved once more like a perfect host; he did not allow Brahms to curtail his visit and when they parted he presented him with a cigar case. Brahms's apologist describes the incident as incomprehensible and unpardonable but adds 'that it was here a question of one of those very healthy but very susceptible and hyperaesthetic artists' constitutions which are often violently assailed and made defenceless by sleep'. One wonders if the hyperaesthetic constitution had showed itself in Brahms's school days. It would explain to some extent the sadism of the beadles and the hatred of French grammar. There is other evidence to show that he was one of those who can fall asleep at any moment they choose, but it is unlikely that he exercised this enviable power deliberately in Liszt's company.

Liszt, in time, forgot the episode altogether. Not so the offender, who from that moment looked upon Liszt as an enemy to be fought at any time and with any weapon. If the first offence can be excused on the ground that tired nature will not be denied, there is no excuse for Brahms's subsequent conduct, for the hostility he showed towards a man who was a great artist and wished to be a friend. 'The noblest natures,' we are told, 'and particularly those who conceal great sensitiveness under a robust exterior, are capable of behaving in an unjust, even hostile, manner precisely towards those whom they have injured.' It is a curious form of partisanship that can mistake unjust hostility, the adding of injury to insult, for the proof of a noble nature. But for Brahms's determined hostility, the discreditable controversy between the Wagnerians and their opponents would have been healed in time to prevent its becoming the laughing stock of posterity. But Brahms's enmity could not be placated. When a newspaper reported that the whole of North Germany was converted to the Weimar School, he persuaded his friends to join in a protest, which turned out to be a boomerang. While Brahms was still collecting signatures, the protest fell into the hands of a mischievous opponent who immediately published it in the Berlin *Echo* with only four signatures attached to it. The outcome was that the signatories – Brahms, Joachim, Grimm, and Scholz – looked extremely ridiculous, for, of course, it was concluded that two signatures were all that Brahms and Joachim could obtain besides their own. Still later Liszt made an attempt to get into touch with Brahms, with the object, it is said, of bringing him to the side of the Weimar School. Liszt had no need of Brahms; with Wagner at his side he was quite strong enough to fight any battle. But as a man of the world he must have known that the controversy could only discredit all concerned. Brahms did not accept the olive branch. When he met Wagner in 1868, he seems to have made a good impression, and the two dictators parted, apparently on friendly terms. Wagner's enmity later broke out afresh – no one knows why. The only possible explanation is that some ill-chosen jest of Brahms or of one of his adherents must have fanned the embers into flame.

The Schumanns and Düsseldorf

The galling consciousness of having behaved badly at Weimar made Brahms hesitate to accept Schumann's hospitality at Düsseldorf. He had felt a provincial by the side of the cosmopolitan Liszt and he dreaded a repetition of such an experience. On the way there he stayed some time at the house of friends who were also great admirers of Schumann. Encouraged by them and fortified with the reading of some of Schumann's works he had not known before, he set out again to meet the second crisis of his life. Schumann was at the height of his fame. It is probable that his wife had already noticed some sign of the illness that shortly afterwards blighted every prospect. Brahms saw no sign of it in the warm welcome that was given him. He was asked to play and Schumann at once hailed him as the heir to the great German tradition. The visit was prolonged and a happy intimacy was established between the young composer and the Schumann family. Clara Schumann shared her husband's admiration; her maternal instincts were also aroused by the spectacle of a young man so gifted, so modest, so unlearned in the ways of the world. In Brahms, who had never before known such kindness and who least expected it after the ordeal of Weimar, the friendship of the Schumanns worked a wonder; the world seemed a fairer place since they were of it, and the youth who had been dumb began to speak. A flood of words came from his pen whenever he mentioned his kind friends, words that testified to a sentiment partly affection, partly reverence. Robert he worshipped because of a knowledge so much greater than his own, because of his work, and because in a remarkable article entitled 'New Ways' (written after a critical silence of ten years) he had proclaimed Brahms 'one of the elect' to be hailed on his first progress through the world 'with laurels and palms'. For Clara he had a still warmer feeling; she was the first to show him what a woman's care and kindness can mean to a man. They had met in September 1853, and Schumann's article, written a month later, secured the publication of two *Piano Sonatas*, a *Scherzo*, and a book of songs acquired by Breitkopf and Härtel for forty louis d'or. After leaving Düsseldorf, Brahms went on to Leipzig, where he played with Ferdinand David and met Clara Schumann's father, Wieck, and Moscheles, Berlioz, and Peter Cornelius. He returned to Hamburg at Christmas, a happy man. He had left his native city a promising student; he returned nine months later, a man honoured by the great. Hamburg was not impressed; but Brahms surely knew that the gods had been kind to him and that such boons are not given twice in a man's lifetime.

A few months later Robert Schumann in a fit of madness threw himself into the Rhine. He was saved from drowning but had to spend the two years of life that remained to him in an asylum. When the news reached him, Brahms was thunderstruck. He had seen in Schumann's home family life such as he had never thought of – husband and wife joined by community of interest as well as by affection. He had seen for the first time educated people who had none of the affectation and artificial polish that had made him feel a stranger at Weimar. He had shared their life, their thoughts, and it seemed to him as if that perfect world had suddenly been blasted by a calamity that robbed existence of all its promise. He hurried to Düsseldorf to share the sorrow and to help, as far as he could, in alleviating the pain. He was received with thankfulness by Clara Schumann, glad to see the man her husband had loved. Her plight called out all that was chivalrous in him; he stood on guard over her; he prevented unwelcome visitors from annoying her, looked after her, and after her children. In that atmosphere of disaster the friendship ripened and became an affection that, it is said, developed into love on the part both of Clara Schumann and of Brahms.

Clara

There exist some letters which at first sight seem to confirm this view. They are all written by Brahms, who uses every form of endearment and, after addressing a 'Dear Frau Schumann', ends by calling her 'adored' and 'most beloved being'. But before accepting the evidence as final we must look a little deeper into the character of the man and his circumstances. The fact that, after addressing Clara in the third person (*Sie*), he gradually turns to the intimate *du* in his letters has no importance whatever, since both Robert and Clara Schumann had so addressed him long before. The Schumanns must have looked upon him as a son, and now, in the terrible crisis, Brahms actually did behave like one. That he should be dearer to Clara, now that she had no other man to support her, was inevitable, and it is equally natural that the sight of a woman in her sorrow and distress should reveal depths of feelings the existence of which Brahms had not suspected. He had never had occasion before to use words for the expression of a deep emotion, and now they poured from him in spate. His restraint, his shyness gone, he gave vent to his feeling through a medium that was new. That there was deep affection in that emotion is undeniable, but how much of it was pity, how much friendship, and how much veneration is impossible to say. When he speaks of 'the old love and the new', does he mean the love of a lonely youth for those who had befriended him and the love for the woman robbed of her husband, or does he mean the lover's distant worship and the lover's overwhelming passion?

For all that has been said to the contrary he was not temperamentally inclined to passionate love. He had admired from a distance an actress at Hamburg – a mild infatuation that in vanishing left no scar; he had not been attracted by other women. His letters to Clara Schumann are not those of a lover. In one of them, after protestations of affection, he writes at length about the weather. It is possible that he resorted to commonplaces as a cloak for his real feelings. But the argument would have greater force if the letter had begun by seeming indifference, and later, the writer, unable to restrain himself, had given free rein to emotion.

Clara Schumann was older than Brahms by a good many years. She had been deeply in love with her great and unfortunate husband, to whom she had borne six children. The birth of the last of these was expected when the disaster occurred. She knew the world. She had had to fight to obtain her father's consent to her marriage; she had come into contact with men and women of all conditions. She was as shrewd a judge of men as of music. Many years later Brahms said to a poet: 'Whenever you write, ask yourself if a woman like Clara Schumann would look upon it with approbation. If you have any doubts, cross it out.' In the whole of their correspondence it is always Clara who has the upper hand. She is the predominant partner, she commands; he asks counsel and obeys. And there is nothing to show that she loved Johannes otherwise than as a mother might love a son. That love she acknowledged with pride.

Brahms left Düsseldorf after Robert's death. Then, had they desired it, nothing stood in the way of a union. His departure took Clara by surprise but did not affect their friendship, which remained unbroken to the end of her life.

They corresponded till Clara's death in 1896 and their letters are more revealing than any single fact in their lives. Brahms hides from her little about his own life, nothing that concerns his work. His curious distrust of himself is again and again shown by the way in which he announces the completion of a new work and by the way in which he acquiesces in her criticism.

There is a touching letter written after a visit to Robert Schumann in the asylum which casts light on the spiritual bond between the three. Brahms was 'almost intoxicated with happiness'. He had placed in Schumann's hand Clara's portrait, which Robert, who had long wished to possess it, kissed and put down with trembling hands: 'the most beautiful side of it I cannot describe – his fine, calm demeanour, his warmth in speaking of you and his joy over the portrait. Just picture all this as perfectly as you can.' When alone with the children at Düsseldorf he gravely writes to Clara details of intimate family life; the alphabet is not being learnt in spite of great quantities of sugar offered as a reward; his concern about a cold; he tells her he has bought a bottle of punch-essence to drink her health every night at supper.

Here is not an opera hero but a much simpler and much more lovable being of homely virtues. It was odd that such a man should come in an age which, unable to conceive artistic greatness apart from stirring events, tried to make him into a hero *malgré lui*.

Brahms and England

In the letters to Clara Schumann there is also a first hint of that dislike of England which caused many a rift between him and Joachim. 'Another letter has come from England,' he writes. 'Oh, if that fatal journey were not to be!' To Joachim he wrote on another occasion: 'You know once and for all I cannot reconcile myself to your English tours.' His prejudice had no other grounds than the instinctive dislike of an ignorant man for a place he has never seen and for people with whom he has never come into contact. Even homage from England was unwelcome, and he suspected Joachim of travelling abroad merely to earn large fees. It never struck him that Joachim could have friends in England of whom he was genuinely fond or could admire anything English apart from an English cheque. When he was famous he was visited by Stanford, who greatly admired him and who was accompanied by Richter. Brahms offered Richter a cigar, but instead of offering Stanford one, he closed the box, remarking curtly that Englishmen did not smoke. Stanford's Irish wit was quite equal to the occasion. He grabbed the box, helped himself to a cigar, and coolly remarked that Englishmen did smoke and even wrote music.

Brahms refused to come to England to receive the honorary doctor's degree, which the University of Cambridge meant to confer upon him. It is said that he would have accepted it if the Crystal Palace authorities had not announced without authority that he would conduct one of their concerts. It is difficult to see any connexion between the two events and the only reasonable explanation for the strange refusal is that he did not wish to come. We may be sure that Joachim, who knew and loved England well, did his utmost to persuade him to change his mind, but Brahms could not be induced to alter his decision.

After the Schumann catastrophe he was long uncertain as to the choice of a city where he could settle and work in quiet seclusion. Hamburg attracted him, but his fellow townsmen were indifferent to his fame; he thought of Hanover where Joachim was; Düsseldorf had lost all attraction after Clara Schumann accepted a post in Berlin. A first invitation to visit Detmold in 1856 had been put aside owing to Schumann's death; but when a second invitation came from the Princess Frederike, the sister of the reigning prince, who wished him to become her teacher and director of music at her brother's court, he accepted.

Agathe von Siebold

The engagement lasted three months, and in that time he appears to have made himself respected as a musician, if not much liked as a man. The 'free son of the Hansa city' had no regard for noble birth and made no secret of it. At the conclusion of the engagement he returned to Hamburg to pass the winter, then moved on to Göttingen for the summer and in Göttingen met his love only to part from her without an avowal.

His feelings for Agathe von Siebold are expressed in the songs he then wrote and in the G major *Sextet* in which the letters of her name are somehow made to form the second subject. But although he was sure of the nature of his own feelings and had no doubt that they were reciprocated, he dared not take an irrevocable step. Agathe passed from his life, leaving behind regrets and a little remorse. He tried to justify his conduct in various ways. The coldness of the public had sapped his courage: 'When I entered my lonely chambers after such failures, they did not hurt me. But if I had been obliged to meet the questioning eyes of a wife and to tell her that once again I had failed – that I could not have endured.' This sounds well. But he might at least have given the girl an opportunity to accept or refuse. Had he been younger and unknown, or older and without hope of recognition, his fears might have been justified to some extent. But he was in the full pride of young manhood; he was known throughout musical Germany; his compositions were being published and bought. He must have been a laggard if he dare not ask Agathe to wait until his prospects grew brighter. He has been held up to our admiration because he never risked either marriage or opera. He might have been a greater man if he had had the courage to undertake the responsibilities of either, or both.

Diffidence, want of faith in his own strength, were characteristic of the man who would rather trust to Joachim's approbation than to his own artistic conscience. There is something inexplicable in the spectacle of an artist whose conceptions are greater than he can well manage. He envies Joachim, 'whose compositions stood so firmly on their legs' while his own 'required an orthopaedic institute'. Like most great composers, he was not a good judge of other people's work. After listening to a Schumann symphony he could not stay for Beethoven. He saw nothing in Tchaikovsky but discovered in Joachim 'gigantic Shakespearean imagination' and to Joachim he turned whenever a new work was completed. He sent him the D minor *Piano Concerto* in so many revised versions that Joachim lost patience and urged him to send the work to a copyist at once so that it could be tried. Brahms did so and the first performance was given in Hanover, Joachim conducting while Brahms played the solo part. Clara Schumann was in the audience. She had arrived from Cologne, where she had won a great success with his *Hungarian Dances*. The new concerto was well received at Hanover and the performers were encouraged to make a more decisive test by playing it before the audience of the Gewandhaus at Leipzig. Leipzig did not ratify the verdict of Hamburg. The concerto was declared to be dull and was actually hissed. Two reasons have been given for the failure – the innate conservatism of the Leipzig public and the intrigues of the 'New German' (Liszt's) party. How much of truth there is in these allegations it is impossible to discover. It must be admitted, however, that the concerto is not the kind of work to appeal to a vast public at a first performance – especially with an indifferent interpretation, as the Leipzig performance most probably was.

Hamburg Again

The set-back had little effect on Brahms. 'I believe this to be the best thing that could have happened,' he wrote. 'It forces one's thoughts to concentrate properly and enhances one's courage.' He returned to Hamburg, where the concerto was played once more and applauded. Another concert, given by him with the collaboration of Joachim and Julius Stockhausen, was financially successful and the means of introducing him to the greatest interpreter his songs ever had. A chance meeting with some ladies from a vocal academy led to the creation of the Hamburg Ladies' Choir, whose statutes were drawn up after the manner of a medieval charter by Brahms himself. Hamburg seemed just then inclined to make amends for past neglect. His compositions were sought and studied, the choir made progress under his direction; when he returned once more to Detmold he found himself longing for the more capable singers of Hamburg.

An event occurred, however, that was to show that if the people of Hamburg flocked to his concerts, if the amateurs bought his music, the intelligentsia of the city were not to be won so easily. The conductor of the Philharmonic concerts had been obliged to retire owing to old age and ill-health, and Brahms applied for the post. He had a better title than any other likely candidate. He was a Hamburger; he had given proofs of undoubted talent in composition and piano playing; he had conducted a choir successfully; he knew the organization of an orchestra. He was supported moreover by Joachim and other notabilities of German music. He had hence every reason to anticipate a favourable result to his application. The Hamburg authorities were slow in coming to a decision. When they did, the choice fell not on Brahms but on his friend, the singer Stockhausen. Brahms was bitterly disappointed. Stockhausen probably did not know that Brahms was one of the aspirants and the appointment did not result in strained relations. But Brahms felt that a slight had been put on him by the preference given to a man who, however admirable as a singer, had almost as little practical experience of conducting as himself, while in theoretical knowledge he was distinctly his inferior. Stockhausen had not an easy time at Hamburg, according to Clara Schumann's reports, and perhaps Brahms was well out of it. He did not allow his disappointment to interfere with his composition. He had already sketched the *First Symphony* and the *German Requiem*. The two *Piano Quartets* in A major and G minor were almost finished and he had started on the *Magelone* romances. Publishers, who after the ill success of the Gewandhaus concert had become chary of accepting his work (Breitkopf and Härtel refused the *Piano Concerto*), began to take a new interest in him. The first concerto was published by a Winterthur firm, and Fritz Simrock gave practical expression to the admiration he felt for Brahms's compositions by seeking him out and opening relations that ended in Simrock's becoming Brahms's sole publisher. He was still waiting to hear the result of the Hamburg appointment when he decided to follow Joachim's advice and visit Vienna. Armed with his savings and two *Piano Quartets*, he reached the Austrian capital in September 1862.

Vienna

Vienna, always alive to artistic interests, had not forgotten Schumann's article. A warm welcome was given to its hero and curiosity was aroused by the announcement that Viennese criticism would be challenged with a number of new compositions. A concert was organized, with the co-operation of Hellmesberger, in which Brahms appeared as composer and performer; it proved an unqualified success. A second concert was hardly less satisfactory. If Hanslick was cautious in his criticism, if he had doubts, he frankly admitted that it was hardly possible to give a considered opinion of important music after a single hearing and spoke of Brahms with the regard due to a master.

Brahms was delighted in the genial warmth of new friendships, the deference that was paid to him, the walks he could take undisturbed in the early hours of the morning, the jovial trivialities of the Prater, where the composer of the *German Requiem* could be seen sometimes taking a ride on a roundabout. He attended concerts and was present at three given by Wagner in Vienna at this time. In his admirable biography, Mr J. A. Fuller Maitland goes so far as to say that Brahms was a devoted admirer of his supposed rival. Specht, on the other hand, relates that when Brahms noticed a friend frantically applauding a

Wagnerian piece, he turned to him and said: 'But, my dear X, you are tearing your beautiful gloves!' Whether he admired Wagner or not, it is certain that he was shocked by the peurilities of the anti-Wagnerians. He wrote at this time to Joachim: 'I shall be called a Wagnerian simply because I cannot stand the shallowness of his opponents.' There was another attraction in Louise Dustmann, a singer of the Vienna opera whose charms made some impression on the susceptible composer. But the affair had no opportunity to develop. Joachim wrote announcing his engagement to Amalie Weiss and Brahms was as upset as a mother might be who unexpectedly hears of the engagement of her only son. He wrote Joachim a letter of congratulation not very different in tone from a letter of condolence. No one could wish Joachim happiness more sincerely; his letter, however, had 'frozen him into a state of utter dejection.' He looked forward to the time when he could 'bend over a cradle in Joachim's house and forget to indulge his own thoughts.'

He stayed on in Vienna till the appointment of Stockhausen was made. Then he returned to Hamburg, calling first on Joachim at Hanover. Family quarrels made his stay in Hamburg less pleasant than he had anticipated; when the conductorship of the Vienna Singakademie was offered to him, he eagerly accepted the opportunity of returning to the Austrian capital. Hamburg had slighted him – a more important musical centre sought him. He would go where Mozart and Beethoven had lived and worked before him. If he had any doubts about his abilities as a conductor, the opportunity to perform his own choral works as soon as they were written was not to be resisted, and he hoped that the attraction of new music might make up for any deficiency in conducting.

There was in Vienna besides the Singakademie a rival organization, the Singverein, whose conductor, Johann Herbeck, appears to have been a master of his craft. A performance of Bach's *Christmas Oratorio* under Brahms by the Singakademie met with lukewarm approval, while a performance of the *St John Passion* by the Singverein under Herbeck made a profound impression. Brahms, unconcerned at first, gave concerts of his own compositions, where he had the field to himself, but his friends were obviously alarmed. In the end he himself found that conducting was not his vocation. In May 1863, the Singakademie re-engaged him for a term of three years; a few months later he sent in his resignation, which was accepted.

Leaving Vienna at the conclusion of the engagement, he went to Hamburg, where his mother was dying. She had not been treated well by her husband. The 'straight-grown, gnarled, and healthy' man of Holstein had left her and refused to support either wife or daughter. Clara Schumann found them in serious want. The husband not only refused to pay, but also threatened legal proceedings, trusting, no doubt, that the fear the very name of the law has for ignorant people would keep his victims silent. 'If he does go to justice,' said Clara, 'it will end in his having to support them, as no court could give a different decision.' Death came to solve the tangle and carried off Brahms's mother in February, her son arriving in time for the funeral. Saddened by the event, his thoughts turned once more to the *German Requiem* he had left unfinished. He set about its completion and revision; three movements were sent to Herbeck, who performed them in Vienna in 1867, where they made little impression. The whole work with the exception of one movement was given a year later in Bremen Cathedral, where it at once established itself as one of the masterpieces of our time.

Wit and Some Opponents

Back amongst his Viennese friends Brahms found life attractive. He was accepted as a composer; his oddities surprised no one; he was sought after and lionized; his bad manners were looked upon as a sign of the artistic temperament. He could afford to show himself as he was, a lover of good living, not above courting the favours of chambermaids and others of easy virtue. Woman was either above him and beyond his reach or below and negligible. In his associations with men there were other difficulties, for his wit was quick, but caustic rather than brilliant. A singer whom he accompanied loudly complained that he could not hear his own voice. 'You lucky man!' retorted the composer. To the leader of a quartet who, after playing the C minor, asked the master how he liked the tempos, Brahms replied: 'Tempos? I liked them all; especially yours.' He welcomed new pupils with the assurance that they would never get a word of praise from him. He wounded Goldmark deeply by accusing him of irreverence because he, a Jew, had dared to write music for a Lutheran Psalm. He insulted Herman Levi, it is said, because Levi upheld the Wagnerian cause. In this case the excuse must be rejected, for Hans Richter was also one of Wagner's staunchest supporters and yet no cloud ever darkened the relations between Richter and Brahms; the conductor who had been entrusted with the opening performances of *The Ring*, at the first Bayreuth festival of 1876, was also chosen to conduct this first performance of Brahms's *Second Symphony* in Vienna in 1877. Clearly the reason for the rupture must be sought in Brahms's ill-humour and biting tongue. A misunderstanding marred his long friendship with Clara Schumann. A more serious quarrel put an end to the long intimacy with Joachim.

It appears to have arisen first when Brahms suggested that his *Requiem* should be given at the Schumann commemorations at Bonn. The committee did not accept the suggestion and Brahms blamed Joachim for the rejection. Clara Schumann intervened and for the time being the quarrel was patched up. It broke out afresh when Brahms took the side of Amalie Joachim in the divorce proceedings her husband had started. For two years Brahms and Joachim never met. A reconciliation of sorts was made by the intervention of common friends, but the old tie had snapped; they became admirers of each other's accomplishments – not friends. Perhaps some of the blame rested with Joachim. It was a friend's part to attempt a reconciliation between husband and wife, especially since the friend believed, as the court did, that the wife was in the right. Probably Brahms's outspoken remonstrances surprised as well as irritated Joachim, who before had always found the composer most complaisant. But in that matter Brahms showed a firmness and vigour that vanished when the two were brought together again. When he has to tell Joachim that he has written a *Double Concerto*, he begins by inquiring whether his 'honoured friend' would care to hear news of an artistic nature. When Joachim assents, he makes 'his confession more cheerfully'. The concerto is supposed to have brought the two together again. It should have widened the gulf between them. Joachim played it, but made no mystery of the fact that he considered it one of Brahms's less inspired efforts – an opinion that has militated against the double concerto ever since.

A man of Brahms's temper was bound to make enemies. One of them was Wagner, who quarrelled with Nietzsche because the latter wanted to show him 'some songlet of triumph or destiny' by Brahms. Another was the peace-loving Bruckner, whose music excited Brahms's scorn. 'Bruckner,' he said, 'is a swindle that will be forgotten a year or two after my death.' A more determined opponent was

Hugo Wolf, who attributed his own ill-success to the intrigues of Brahms's friends, including Richter, though he, if Brahms's friend, was also the friend of Wagner, whom Wolf revered. Nietzsche, on the other hand, detached himself from Brahms as he did from Wagner.

Rising Reputation

Brahms's apologists point to his early upbringing as an excuse for his bad manners and quote Brahms himself, who is reported to have asked: 'Where should I have learnt tact? In my youth I was obliged to play in sailors' taverns to keep alive; one does not learn good manners there.' Upbringing may explain his deficiencies up to a point. But something else was surely wanting in a man utterly unable to put himself in another's place, to sympathize with others' feelings, to imagine the effect of his taunts on those who suffered them. Something was lacking in his capacity for understanding men as for understanding the average woman. By all means let us praise him for having shown sympathy and consideration for others, for a love of children that was almost feminine in its tender anxiety, for taking holy water on entering a Catholic church, for asking the ladies' permission before venturing to light a cigar, for taking off his shoes when returning home late lest the noise should wake sleepers. These admirable traits do not amount to heroism. There was a story, current in Vienna, of an encounter with a landlady awakened by the returning lodger, after a jolly party, at an early hour; the story is probably an invention of his enemies. If true, it would be inconsistent with the Tannhäuser-Tristan version of Brahms's character – but how much more human!

His less amiable qualities could not affect a reputation that grew with every new work published, rising to the highest pinnacle with publication of the *Symphonies*. The first was given in 1877; the second came out the following year. An interval of six years separates the second from the third; then came the fourth in 1886. Brahms's individual treatment of the orchestra was a surprise to his admirers, for before the symphonies he had written only the *Serenades* and the *Haydn Variations* for this medium. It is impossible here to discuss his great output of music – the *Violin Concerto* which Joachim played first to an admiring Gewandhaus audience in '78, the second *Piano Concerto* which Brahms played first at Meiningen in 1882, the *Academic Festival Overture* written the year before to celebrate the conferring of the Doctorate of Philosophy upon him, or his inestimable contributions to chamber music – nor does it seem necessary in view of its even qualities. Schumann was right when he said that Brahms had come into the world fully armed. Experience had little to teach him. Nor did his outlook change, once he had passed the critical period of youth. He hardened a little in his attitude towards men and he definitely refused to contemplate marriage when friends who pitied the lonely bachelor suggested it. But he appears to have been attracted by various women with whom he came in contact. It is difficult to take his passing fancies seriously. He doubtless admired Elisabeth von Stockhausen, but never let her marriage with Heinrich von Herzogenberg disturb his peace of mind. Herzogenberg was a composer of the minor variety, and Brahms could not but feel that in choosing him Elisabeth had accepted a good deal less than he had to offer. They met and corresponded frequently. Elisabeth was always full of admiration for the man whose music she interpreted well. Brahms was always friendly but rather patronizing when Heinrich's work came in question.

Some Passing Attachments

He is said to have fallen a victim to the charms of Clara Schumann's daughter, Julie, because when her engagement was announced he could hardly stammer out a few words of congratulation. Somehow Brahms does not fit in the character of a male Phædra, as the lover of both mother and daughter. His perturbation may have had other causes; it may have been the pang he felt whenever one of his closest friends entered the matrimonial state; it will be remembered that he was in the depth of misery when Joachim announced his engagement. It may also have been a sudden recollection of the days when first he had seen Julie and her family, days that closed with the never-forgotten tragedy of Schumann's death.

He also admired two singers – Hermine Spies and Alice Barbi – probably more for their talents than for their prettiness. He was deeply moved by Barbi's singing of his songs, which, after the recital, he declared he had really heard for the first time. He never uttered a word that might lead us to suppose he thought of her with warmer sentiments. His 'intimates' are said to have 'suspected a serious passion'. No case can rest on such slight evidence. The Spies affair rests on the still more slender report of an after-dinner jest. When the moment for toasts had arrived Brahms asked Hermine Spies before all the guests to drink the health of her future father-in-law. When the embarrassed lady hesitated, Brahms, turning to the company, remarked mischievously: 'She is wondering whether Brahms has still a father.' Had his feelings been deeply engaged he would hardly have ventured a jest in such questionable taste. Amongst Brahms's friends must be reckoned Hans von Bülow, the conductor of the Meiningen orchestra, which, although but half the strength of our modern orchestras, was long considered the best in Germany and the most authoritative exponent of Brahms's compositions. The clarinettist of the orchestra was Richard Mühlfeld, 'the Joachim of the clarinet', whose exquisite art inspired the *Sonatas* for clarinet and piano and the *Quintet* for clarinet and strings – this last unquestionably one of Brahms's loveliest creations. Von Bülow and his orchestra toured Germany, kindling everywhere a new interest in Brahms. With von Bülow, too, there was a misunderstanding, due entirely to the composer's lack of tact. It was fortunately smoothed over and complete harmony was restored.

Clara's End

Late in the correspondence between Brahms and Clara Schumann there is mention of one of her pupils which should interest English readers. Leonard Borwick had delighted his teacher by his talents and aptitude, and Clara was anxious to ascertain Brahms's opinion of the pianist who later did so much to popularize his work in this country. Brahms at first was inclined to be critical; he found much to admire in the 'handsome Englishman's' playing, but missed a personal touch. After hearing Borwick a second time his praise is full and no longer qualified: 'I am writing to tell you with very great pleasure that Borwick played quite excellently, with the most perfect freedom, warmth, energy, and passion, in short, everything that one could desire.' He concludes: 'One could not have wished for anything better and you may readily believe all that your lady friends will tell you about it.'

With Vienna as his home he travelled about a good deal, conducting sometimes, more often playing, spending the summer months in some quiet mountain retreat, the spring frequently in Italy. His last years were happy. His position was secure; he was a well-to-do man; he had no anxieties and he does not seem to have been too much perturbed by the obvious signs that his generation was gradually disappearing. Letters from Clara Schumann often brought news of the illness of one friend or another. Stockhausen had become an invalid; Liszt had died in 1886; Wagner in 1883; Elisabeth von Herzogenberg in 1892; Theodor Billroth, one of his closest friends, two years later in Vienna. There were no compensations for these losses in the tributes that came to him from all civilized countries. Leipzig had made amends for hissing the first *Piano Concerto* and its cool reception of the *Academic* and *Tragic Overtures* with a Brahms concert that had been the source of great pleasure to the composer. The hotel-keepers had treated him like a prince and charged him as if he had been a needy peasant; he had expected a small fee for expenses and was presented with two thousand marks; no one in the audience had left the hall before the last note was played and, lastly, there had been a banquet which, he wrote to Clara, 'put in the shade the function you and I attended at Limburger's'.

This was in 1895. Early in the next year Clara was feeling ill and depressed; her illness gave rise to anxiety; her letters became short messages. In April she seemed to improve a little, but there was little strength left in her. On 7 May her grandchild reminded her that Brahms's birthday fell on that day. The invalid found enough strength to scribble a few words of greeting. Three days later she had another stroke. On 20 May she was dead. Brahms had been kept informed of the course of her illness and the end was not unexpected. He left Vienna to attend her funeral and walked at the head of her friends behind the coffin. Back in Vienna he took up the pen to write to Marie and Eugenie Schumann to offer all he had, if it could be of use to them. In the whole collection of the Brahms-Schumman letters there is not one that does him greater honour. He is deliberately formal in order not to distress his correspondents; he chooses words that by constant use have lost their expressiveness; he makes his offer with an air of apology as if it were what a thousand others were ready to do. But in those simple phrases all that was fine and compassionate in the man's heart can be read as it never could be in a document of literary pretensions.

Finale

He wrote to them again when sending a copy of the *Four Serious Songs*. He had composed them early in May when there was still some little hope of Clara's recovery. 'But deep in the heart of man' he wrote, 'something whispers and stirs. . . . You will not be able to play them . . . but I beg you to lay them aside and regard them as a death-offering to the memory of your dear mother.' Thus was broken the last earthly tie with his youth, with the early days when he had left Hamburg, light of heart and lighter of purse, hoping to improve his condition, and had suddenly been placed on a pinnacle by Robert Schumann. Clara Schumann had been his constant friend and his most enlightened critic.

A cold caught at Clara Schumann's funeral perhaps hastened the course of the disease from which he was suffering. To use his own phrase, something 'whispered in his heart' that his own end was not far, and the knowledge dismayed him. He found no comfort in the religion that had inspired the *Requiem* and the *Four Serious Songs*; his fears were not allayed because those he had loved most had preceded him on the journey from which no traveller returns. He would not think of his disease as serious and clung to life desperately. But he destroyed a vast number of letters and manuscripts which he would not have wished to fall into a stranger's hands. He made a Will leaving 400,000 marks, the bulk of his fortune, to the Gesellschaft der Musikfreunde and delayed signing the last draft until too late, causing endless legal trouble to his executors. He was persuaded to go to Carlsbad in September 1896; he returned worse than he had been before. He still went whenever he could to concerts and to the opera. He went to hear an operetta of Johann Strauss and had to leave after the first act. The disease was gaining; the doctor who attended him saw to it that he never suffered pain. It was all that could be done. In the morning of 3 April 1897, the landlady entered the room and, seeing the emaciated condition of the invalid, burst into tears. The dying man opened his eyes, made a movement as if to rise, then fell back. He died a little less than a year after his one staunch and ever affectionate friend, Clara Schumann.

Evaluation

Fear of death seems strange in one who had fought a long battle alone, who had given artistic expression to religious thoughts and faith with a sincerity unsurpassed by Palestrina or Bach. It may be that he felt that life had been very different from what he had once hoped it might be, that he had other things to say and do, which he could not accomplish while the shadow of death was on him. It is even possible that he regretted the comforts he could indulge in after the stormy years of young manhood, the harvest of his fame. It would be more charitable to suppose that illness had sapped his strength, for no matter how strong and brave the man, death and her attendants are stronger still. But it is undeniable that he did fear death, and the phenomenon seems to fit in with that strange diffidence he showed so often in his life and with the dualism seen in his works. The greatest modern master of contrapuntal art submitted his essays in counterpoint to the judgement of Joachim, who was at best a mere scholar. But he would not listen to Joachim when the latter advised him on the marking of string music – a department in which Joachim was the absolute master and Brahms the apprentice. He had a feminine tenderness for children and a very masculine want of understanding and consideration for grown men. Women were either worshipped from afar or regarded by him as pretty fools who could contribute to his pleasure. In the great patrimony he left, the romantic and the classical elements are found side by side and often mixed inextricably. He produced his compositions in pairs and, as with the first and second symphony and with the two overtures, the general character of the one differed entirely from that of the other.

He was a great artist and like all such was endowed with an imagination that made him see things in a proportion not in strict accordance with reality. The so-called unworldliness of certain men of genius springs entirely from a too generous fancy. Those who look at the sun can no longer distinguish clearly the outline of near objects. They are apt to see that which is not and to ignore that which is. Certain peculiarities in Brahms's temperament may be thus explained, and it is also probable that what he saw and heard in the sailors' haunts at Hamburg as a half-grown lad affected his whole outlook. Those who allowed it, those who were responsible for it, have a good deal to answer for. His pathetic reliance on Joachim's opinion, his deliberate refusal to accept credit or praise for a happy, inspired thought, his determination to deserve approval by sheer hard work, may all have their origin in some injury done to his mind at an age when he was physically and morally defenceless. His nature as an artist was incomparably greater than his stature as a man. But a great artist has no need to be also a great hero.

ANTON BRUCKNER

1824–96

RALPH W. WOOD

Clean Beginnings

It is usual for an account of a composer's career to begin with details of his training. After his showing an unmistakable bent for music at a precocious age has been mentioned, together with the first lessons given by mother or father, his various subsequent sources of tuition – places and people – are enumerated. It is generally a concise paragraph or so, bristling with names and dates, and finishes half-way down the first column, with the composer somewhere around twenty.

Anton Bruckner's specific training as a musician lasted rather more than half his life-time, and he did not die young. His father and grandfather no doubt had both, being village school-teachers, to some degree functioned as organists and choir-masters. The father, it is known, also played the violin. Whether or not his duties as teacher, organist, choir-master, sexton, assistant to the priest, not to mention fiddler (at local festivities), left him time to give his son any musical grounding, and whether or not that son, his first-born, was precocious, it is certain that Anton Bruckner senior packed the boy off at 10½ to a cousin, Johann B. Weiss, who was known as an excellent musician, and that as a sequel the boy was able, when aged 11, to accompany at the organ on choral occasions. So the composer's beginnings were sufficiently orthodox. Incidentally, he had already then begun to compose.

Choral Training

There was a short break when, after eighteen months with cousin Weiss at Hörsching, Bruckner had to go back to Ansfelden. Hörsching (close to Linz) and Ansfelden are villages in Upper Austria. As eldest son he would anyhow probably soon have been called on, to lend a hand, for instance, in looking after the smaller school-children. But his father, as well as being a busy man, was now a sick one and shortly died (June 1837). The family split up (the school-house no longer their home), and the twelve-year-old returned to Hörsching – whence Weiss managed a couple of months later to get him off into the near-by Chorherren Stift of St Florian (see below) as a choir-boy.

During four years at St Florian the youngester had lessons in thorough-bass, organ, and violin, as well as singing in the choir. It was really just part of the preparation for his becoming an assistant school-teacher, and in the last year of the four, before sitting for the final examination, he took a special ten-months' course conducted for that purpose at Linz, with music more prominent than ever.

The examination passed, his future secured, he went back into the world – as a 'school-helper'. Back into the world of tiny Upper Austrian villages. Two years he spent drudging at Windhagen-on-Maltsch, and one at Kronstorf-on-Enns. The former was in any case, drudgery apart, too remote for him to be able to obtain any musical instruction; but at Kronstorf, which was close to civilized centres, he was able to resume lessons. He went to L. E. von Zenetti, organist and choir-master, three times a week for tuition. He managed to borrow a piano and put it in his school-room. Henceforward he seems never to have ceased studying at all, studying quite formally with lessens and courses and examinations and certificates, for twenty years.

Organist, Theoretician, Composer

In 1845 he became 'First School-helper' at St Florian itself. Over the signature of Kattinger, one of his previous tutors there, he gained further certificates covering the musical requirements of the school-master's calling to which he was still dedicated. Actually he followed Kattinger, who left in 1848, as the Stift's organist and choir-master. In 1850–1 he took a new course in Linz, culminating in more certificates. In 1854–5 he was in contact with Assmayer and Sechter at Vienna, passing examinations and obtaining a promise to be accepted as a pupil by Sechter. Later in life he said that at St Florian he had practised on organ and piano thirteen hours a day.

As Linz cathedral-organist, just into his thirties, he at once proceeded to broaden and intensify his musical studies. Between 1856 and 1861 he undertook courses in thorough-bass – single, double, and triple counterpoint – canon and fugue, subjects in which, as also in organ-playing and 'practical composition', he procured additions to his store of certificates. He was now for several weeks each year, with the sanction and encouragement of his Linz bishop (Franz Jos.

Rudigier), paying visits to Simon Sechter at Vienna. Sechter was a renowned master of academic theory, the sort of man of whom it could be (and was) said by some that a text-book of his was already obsolete when it was published.

Only in 1861 did Bruckner look about him in Linz and fasten on Otto Kitzler, the conductor at the theatre, to be his guide in more up-to-date aspects of music. Kitzler had studied at Brussels, had been a cellist, was emphatically a man who had seen the world, although he was ten years Bruckner's junior. Under him Bruckner found new eyes with which to look at the works of Beethoven, surveyed the achievements of, for instance, Schumann, Mendelssohn, and Meyerbeer, and at length reached Wagner – *Der Fliegende Holländer* and *Tannhäuser*. He perused the score of *Tannhäuser* in December 1862, and the following February saw a performance of the work in Linz. The symphony in F minor, which he composed between 15 February and 26 May 1863, and later referred to as 'school work', severely described by Kitzler as not very much inspired, was the last thing he wrote while receiving any form of instruction.

It will perhaps have been noticed that at the very period of life when the more fortunate majority of composers have been receiving important tuition, from 17 to 19, Bruckner was receiving none at all. At that time he was working as 'school-helper' in an out of the way hamlet of 200 souls near the Bohemian frontier. Dependent on the village school-master for meals and for a salary of twelve gulden a year, he had to handle by himself the school and church services, to work in the fields, in the early morning to perform the ceremony of sounding the church bell to announce the start of day (summer 4 a.m., winter 5 a.m.), to dress the priest, after school to make hay, dig potatoes, thresh and plough, and ring the evening-prayer bells (the last at 9 p.m.). In 1840 the miserable school-teacher's quarters at Windhagen had been closed down on account of dilapidation, and he had the additional pleasure of doing his school work in an only half-finished new place. And he was playing the violin for dances at weddings, fairs, and the like, to augment his earnings.

Still Groping

Even when he was, before and after that wretched interlude, undergoing musical training, he seems neither to have realized for himself nor to have had anyone at hand to tell him, and help him to obtain, the sort of tuition and experience that his obvious talent cried out for. Or perhaps, rather than against the actual instruction he obtained, our criticism should be directed against the lack of any clear understanding of his vocation, against the unhappy circumstance that at no time during the long series of study-courses described above was his career even settled on as that of a musician. Left to himself, all Bruckner at first thought of was to follow the examples of father and grandfather as village pedagogue, and no better suggestion seems to have been offered by his priestly benefactors – as in many ways they undoubtedly were – at the Chorherren Stift of St Florian. At that institution, with its massive buildings, the imposing baroque minster, the famous organ, and its fair precincts, that world apart – calm, secure, powerful, splendid – rooted in the twin mights of church and riches, was consolidated for Bruckner the profound, unquestioning acceptance of the Roman Catholic dogma that could already have had its lines set pretty firmly in his village childhood (where the centre of power and authority was the priest) and that was to remain the governing element of his heart and brain alike throughout his days. There, it is true, and in a tranquillity and comfort that must have contrasted almost miraculously with everything he had otherwise experienced, his musical education was unflaggingly sustained. But there he was, primarily, put in shape for becoming a school-teacher; from there he 'graduated' into the job at Windhagen, by the kindness of Prelate Michael Arneth there he was removed to Kronstorf when he rebelled at being required by his Windhagen boss to transport manure, and to there still as a 'school-helper' he presently returned. During the ensuing eleven years he continued to be tutored principally for advancement on the school-teaching road; he studied the organ and the craft of choir-training and Latin (but not history or natural science), all equally with that end in view. The only alternative hint we hear of was when he did some work, during one period, at the District Court of Justice, partly to supplement his income and partly with the idea of turning to a career as an official in such a place. He merely, as it were, incidentally stepped into Kattinger's shoes as the Stift's organist and choir-master. Only when the organist of Linz cathedral happened to die and Bruckner was pushed into competing for the vacancy was his main line more or less accepted as being music. In the very same year (1855) he passed a *Hauptlehrer* (head-teacher) examination, and it was not till 1856, and after another competition, that the Linz organistship was confirmed.

Music as Career

The remainder of Bruckner's life was spent in an almost equal uncertainty about precise means of existence, though at any rate the sphere was always now to be musical. While still organist at Linz he began to feel (above all, no doubt, as a result of his eye-opening studies with Kitzler and his introduction to the music of Wagner) that he needed a less provincial milieu. An application that he made to *Hofkapellmeister* Johann Herbeck in Vienna, 1866, bore fruit in 1868 when by Herbeck's influence he was installed as teacher of thorough-bass, counterpoint, and organ at the Vienna conservatoire, in place of Sechter, his earlier tutor, who had died in 1867. In 1867, while the negotiations for this post were going on, he wrote to the University of Vienna asking for a position as a lecturer, but without success. He was, in fact, rather chary of leaving his organist's job, which was not only worth 448 gulden per annum plus certain perquisites but also carried a pension; when he at length did go to Vienna he had managed to obtain a promise from the Linz cathedral authorities that it should for a time be kept open for him. He also, while at Linz, applied unsuccessfully for work as conductor at the Salzburg Mozarteum.

From 1869 he was associated with the Court Chapel, though it was only in 1875 that he became vice-librarian there and also second singing-master of the choristers. In 1875 too he did become a lecturer, on harmony and counterpoint, at the University. Between 1870 and 1874 he was an assistant teacher at a seminary. As late as 1877 he was applying, unsuccessfully, for a job as choir-master, at the church Am Hof. The following year he became a 'real member' of the Court Chapel, which gave him once more a position with a pension. He was not altogether comfortable there, being looked on with little favour by the Hofkapellmeister, Hellmesberger (Herbeck had died in '77), but he was very pôpular with the imperial family, and particularly with the Emperor's daughter, the Archduchess Valerie.

Retirement

He retired from the conservatoire in 1891 and from the Court Chapel a year later. In 1894 he gave his last lecture at the University, and went into retirement at the Lustschloss Belvedere, which had been offered to him by the Emperor. By then he had been the recipient of numerous honours, from home and abroad. By then, too, his health was failing. When he died he was given a funeral in Vienna at which not only all the musical world but also all the laity of consequence and high degree were represented.

It is important to remember that Bruckner's hours of practice were not fruitful merely to the extent of the posts he held as organist. In 1869 he travelled to Nancy to perform, together with other famous players, on the new organ at St Épure, and after that there came an invitation to Paris, where he played in Notre Dame and in the atelier of the organ firm Merklin. His playing and especially his improvising were everywhere much admired. Two years later he was sent by the Viennese Chamber of Commerce – after a test-playing of a number of organists – to the World Exhibition in London. He performed on the new organ at the Royal Albert Hall and afterwards in two concerts at the Crystal Palace. In 1880, going for a holiday to Switzerland, he appeared as organist at all the principal towns en route.

And equally significant is the fact that, having already in Kronstorf formed a male-voice quartet (himself singing first bass), he was in Linz librarian, singing member, and finally conductor (1860–1, in succession to A. M. Storch) of a men's choral society – named 'Frohsinn'. Under him it had successes in festivals at Krems and Nürnberg. He had another spell as conductor of this choir later and kept in touch with it throughout the last forty years of his life.

Compositions

Bruckner's first recorded compositions are four preludes for organ, from his eleventh year. He produced at least two works, a *Mass* and a *Pange lingua*, at Windhagen. He never really stopped composing thereafter; and he was engaged upon his *Ninth Symphony* on the morning of his death. Up to the time with Kitzler he wrote practically nothing but choral music, sacred and secular; but he then plunged straight off with four orchestral pieces, followed in 1863 by the *F minor Symphony* (see above) and the *Overture in G minor*. His proper *Symphony No.* 1, in C minor, dates from 1865, and in fact the last thirty years of his life were continually occupied with the production or revisions (frequent) of his symphonies. It is interesting that the overwhelming impact of Wagner's music was responsible for that critical change in his output, but appears never to have given him any desire himself to write for the stage. Of course the latter half of his life was also devoted to an undiminished stream of choral music, notably the great *Masses*, the *Te Deum*, and *Psalm CL*. Those works also were some of them subjected to revision. From the exact point when Kitzler and Wagner had their effect upon him his music, while for the first time making its way, though very slowly, all over the world, encountered much opposition from both critics and public – some of it on account of his known Wagnerian sympathies but much arising out of genuine incomprehension of the music itself. (Even Hugo Wolf declared that when he first heard Bruckner's *Symphony No.* 1 he made practically nothing of it.) He was an intense devotee of Wagner – went to the première of *Tristan* at Munich in 1865, made pilgrimages to Bayreuth in 1873 and 1882, gave a performance at Linz of the final chorus of *Meistersinger* in 1868 when the work was still in the press, dedicated one of his symphonies to Wagner, and so on....

The Man

It is known that Bruckner on several occasions was much attracted by some woman; each time some young, fresh person whose difference in age from himself made him a hopeless suitor from the start. He did not care at all from what class of society the girl came – a merchant's daughter, a lawyer's daughter, a high official's daughter, a girl at Oberammergau, or finally (when he was nearly 70) a chambermaid in a Berlin hotel. But the question of religion, dominating as it did his life, was crucial. He gave one girl a prayer-book. Another, a Protestant, would perhaps have accepted him; at any rate she did not object to the difference between them in religion; but that was something that he himself could not get over. In middle life he had a nervous breakdown. It began with letters to various acquaintances (e.g. Storch) in 1866, referring to great depression. Before long he was suffering from fixed ideas and from a 'counting mania'. Waldeck, his pupil and his successor at Linz, tells how whilst out walking he would stop to count the leaves on a tree. In the summer of 1867 he took a 'cold water cure' at Bad Kreutzen, and before the end of the year he was quite recovered. His profound religiousness has already been mentioned more than once; it cannot be mentioned too often; it coloured his whole life, and together with his organ-playing it coloured, directly, his whole creative output. His *Ninth Symphony* (unfinished) was dedicated to '*dem lieben Gott*'.

He took his work as a teacher very seriously, several times suggesting radical alterations in the syllabus, so far as it affected him, at the Conservatoire, and was popular with his pupils. He was always on the side of youth and always rather needing their sympathy and affection. Though ready enough to stand up for himself as an artist, he had till his dying day a certain humbleness, almost a tinge of servility, in his personal manner, no doubt attributable to his early years. He worked very hard indeed all his life.

In accordance with a request in his will he was buried under the organ at St Florian.

FRÉDÉRIC FRANÇOIS CHOPIN

1810–49

HERBERT HUGHES

Poland and Lorraine

There are people, some of them solemn musicologists, who regard Chopin as a creative artist of the second rank. He is not, they say, colossal; therefore he cannot be ranked with composers of the calibre of, for example, Bach or Beethoven. That is a questionable sort of estimation. Aesthetic values have surely nothing to do with size, though quantity may imply influence, as influence implies power. Must one be impressed by the Pyramids of Gizeh? I do not intend to discuss here the paradox that colossalism is often an expression of the little mind, but to suggest that the relatively frail, sensitive Chopin, expressing himself in unpretentious forms, less ostensibly intellectual than the symphonists, less spectacular than the composers of opera, was one of the greatest forces in modern music and probably not less vital than his great contemporaries, Beethoven and Schubert. It is not merely that the influence of his original mind can be traced in the music of Liszt, Wagner, Schumann, Tchaikovsky, Grieg, Wolf, Scriabin, Debussy, Delius, and a host of smaller writers in between, but that it is to be found in the music – good and bad – that is heard on the radio every day of our lives. That influence has been not merely academic, not merely world-wide, but domestic, and it remains incalculable.

His ancestry was mixed, French on his father's side, Polish on his mother's. It is now established that his father Nicolas (born in 1771), his grandfather François (a wheelwright who became a vine-grower) and his great-grandfather Nicolas were natives of Lorraine. At his father's baptism in the parish of Diarville one of the witnesses was Thérèse Chopin, of Xirocourt, a spinster and presumably a relative, who was unable to write and observed the regulations by marking with a cross the entry in the parish register.

Modern Lorraine is but a fraction of that 'Lotharii regnum' (Lothringen), a vast territory extending from the shores of the North

Sea to the centre of Italy, taking in the Netherlands, Rhinelands, Switzerland, and Lombardy, which by the Treaty of Verdun, A.D. 843, was allotted to the eldest of Charlemagne's grandsons, Lothaire II. Celtic, Roman, and German blood had contributed to the main stream of Lorraine's population through a long period of history. The overlordship of the province itself had been disputed over and over again; German and Frankish kings had fought for possession; and there followed by the successive treaties of Cateau-Cambrésis 1559, Westphalia 1648, Pyrenees 1659, Nymwegen 1679, Ryswick 1697, and Vienna 1738 such an international buffeting that it would be unnatural if partisanship had not coloured its historical records and literature. After the Franco-Prussian war of 1870–1, German ethnologists were found to stress the Germanic influences that had persisted since Caesar's time, while French scholars dwelt on qualities of non-Teutonic character. In the circumstances it may well be left to later writers, with possibly more material than is now available, to discuss the various spellings of Chopin, Choppen, and Schopen, and to delve further into the family history of a composer whose paternal ancestors came from such an epic battlefield.

A Lorrainer comes to Poland

It is known that the composer's father, Nicolas – brown-eyed, intelligent, vivacious – was about seventeen when he was persuaded by a friend in Warsaw, who owned a small tobacco and snuff manufactory, to emigrate thither and take a post in the counting-house, an apprenticeship that was probably humdrum enough until political upheaval brought it to an end. Nicolas was in his twenty-third year when Poland, in 1794, went through another paroxysm of her turbulent history. Koscisuzko called his compatriots to arms; trade was upset; and the tobacco and snuff establishment had to close down. Nicolas, although not robust, was spirited enough to join the National Guard and was soon promoted captain. In November the Russians made a furious and successful assault on the suburb of Praga, which had been in a state of siege. Captain Nicolas Chopin and his company happened to be relieved a few hours before the collapse of the position, to which providential circumstance he, no doubt, owed his life. But Warsaw fell and the career of Nicolas as a temporary officer came to an end.

On two occasions Nicolas was on the point of returning to his native

Lorraine, and on each he was deflected from doing so by indifferent health. Then there came a day when he met the Staorcina Laczynska, who was so struck by his intelligence and character that she immediately engaged him as tutor in the French language to her four children. That engagement lasted until the children had grown up, and was succeeded by another similar post in the family of the Countess Skarbek at Zelazowa Wola, an estate about twenty-eight miles outside Warsaw. There he met and loved Justina Krzyzanowska, companion and lady-in-waiting, and married her with the blessings of the Countess. Justina, we are told, was twenty-four and the daughter of a noble Polish family that had suffered impoverishment; but of the family history little or nothing appears to be known. The marriage, however, was a happy one, and on 22 February 1810, the composer was born, the second of four children and the only son. He was baptized Frédéric François, his godmother being Countess Anne Skarbek and his godfather her brother, Count Fryderyk Skarbek, a youth of seventeen.

The composer's close association with the aristocracy, begun thus early, was to continue throughout his life and to have a profound effect upon his work and his outlook. Shortly after he was born his parents transferred their home to Warsaw, where his father was appointed to a professorship of French in the newly opened Lycée; and while he accepted other similar appointments at the School of Artillery and Engineering, at the Preparatory Military Academy, and at the Academy of the Roman Catholic Clergy, he set up a boarding school 'for the sons of the Nobility and Gentry'. This last was Frédéric's only 'prep.' school, and he spent some years there before proceeding to the Lycée. Poets, artists, men of science were among his father's intimates, and it was in an atmosphere of culture and refinement that he spent his first impressionable years. Of the composer's mother little is recorded. George Sand, who never met her, said in her sententious way that she was Chopin's only passion. Karasowski, who must have known her well, described her as being particularly tender-hearted and rich in all fine womanly qualities, finding the greatest happiness in 'quietness and homeliness'. Niecks recorded the remark of a Scots lady who had seen Justina Chopin in her old age, and talked with her in French, that she was 'a neat, quiet, intelligent old lady'. A prosaic phrase that carries in it – when one considers to whom it was applied – the whole mystery of motherhood, the motherhood of genius.

The Wand of Youth

No creative artist who ever lived had a happier childhood than Frédéric Chopin. The atmosphere of his home was serene and sympathetic; there was no element in it that could be regarded as antagonistic to the free development of his mind. He was not robust, neither was he remarkably delicate; he played games and was, of course, somewhat precocious in his flair for music, though not exceptionally so. When he was an infant the sound of music made him weep, yet before he could read or write he had already begun to take pianoforte lessons from a Bohemian fiddler and pedagogue, Adalbert Zywny. Before he could handle a pen he had begun to compose, his master writing down his childish efforts, putting them straight and telling him of a composer called Bach, whom he worshipped – whom Frédéric, too, was soon to worship. The boy was boisterous and dreamy in turn, droll, high-spirited, delighting in mimicry. And his musical gifts developed apace. Practical jokes and private theatricals alternated with the creation of little valses and mazurkas and polonaises. By the time he was eight years old his talents were discussed beyond the family circle.

On the eve of his ninth birthday Frédéric was waited on by Niemcewicz, the illustrious statesman and *littérateur*, on behalf of several leaders of Warsaw society inviting him to take part in a concert that was being organized for charity. At this début – for it was his first public concert – he took the solo part in a piano concerto by the eminent composer, Adalbert Gyrowetz, and with such success that the leaders of Warsaw society were soon in open competition to pet and entertain, and be entertained by, such a wonder-child. The calm mental discipline of his methodical home and his already acute sense of humour – humour that in later life was to become bitter and sardonic on occasion – prevented such praise and adulation going to his head. Invitations came from the princely houses of Czartoryski, Radziwill, Sapieha, Lubecki, and other of the local aristocracy. The Princess Czetwertynska, whose drawing-room was a particular rendezvous of artists and elegant amateurs, took him to the Princess Lowicka, the Polish wife of the Grand Duke Constantine, the 'Napoleon of Belvedere', and Frédéric was soon a familiar little figure at the ducal palace as playmate to Paul, the Grand Duke's son, a boy of his own age.

When he entered the Lycée at the age of fifteen his music had to be studied outside school hours and under the guidance of Joseph Elsner, Director of the Conservatoire. Elsner, famed as a church musician and teacher, at once perceived the rare qualities, expressed and latent, in the poetic boy who came to him for lessons in harmony and counterpoint – a boy with silken auburn hair, beautiful hands, and the sloping shoulders of a girl. He put Frédéric under no restraint that could curb his imagination; rather did he show him – if that was necessary – what it meant to be exacting to oneself. Frédéric's schooling had sharpened a naturally keen intelligence, and Elsner found a disciplined and lively young mind to work upon, a mind surprisingly radiant under the veil of languid eyes.

Early Influences

To an intelligent and imaginative boy with such an upbringing in such surroundings it was inevitable that the literary movements of the day should be familiar at least by repute. The classicism that had survived the eighteenth century was in decay, though dying hard. Poland was in a state of intellectual renaissance. Romanticism was almost in full flower, already tingeing the study of political history and folk-lore. Now and then Frédéric would join his father on excursions into the country, and it may easily be assumed that into their conversations would slip the names – often discussed by his father's guests – of Mickiewicz (whose verse was bringing a new note into Polish literature) and Goethe and Jean-Jacques Rousseau, of Schiller and that young Englishman, Byron, who had joined the Greek army and had lately died at Missolonghi; name strangely mixed, maybe, with those of Bach and Mozart and that excellent pianist, Carl Maria von Weber whose *Freischütz* had been seen in Warsaw. With the widespread and deliberate cult of nationalism went naturally the collection and preservation of folk-songs; and Frédéric took delight in listening to these in their native environment. Art-music, a thing of the cities and the courts, had not yet affected the traditional music and dances of the country-side; and the mind of the adolescent student was strangely moved when he became aware that all that enchanting beauty of rhythm and melodic line was the ancient and expressive birthright of a peasantry incredibly ignorant and superstitious. And in his attic at dead of night, while improvising mazurkas and krakowiaks and polonaises on the piano in rhythms that had been beating into his brain all day, he would make experiments in touch and in the fingering of broken chords, that were to crystallize later on into a technique inseparable from his art, a technique that was to revolutionize the whole of piano music.

Meanwhile Frédéric's circle of friends and acquaintances was widening and there was little likelihood of the wheelwright's grandson developing into a type of the raw provincial. In this third decade of the nineteenth century the salons of the Polish nobility were at the zenith of their brilliance. Many of the families were rich and powerful, the political connexion with France during the first Empire to some extent influencing the manners and literary taste without destroying the national distinctiveness of class or loosening the conventions of etiquette. The noblesse, while insisting on the proprieties, were far from being stiff-necked; any kind of hard artificiality was antipathetic to their Slavonic caste. Gallantry and good manners, conviviality and a deep love of music and of their national dances were outstanding qualities. It was in frequent contact with such an *ambiente*, blended with that of the Conservatoire, that the youthful mind of Frédéric Chopin was being formed and the innate characteristics of his own already sensitive nature developed and expanded. He was happy in the companionship of his school days. Juljan Fontana, Counts Antony, Casimir, and Felix Wodzinski, Titus Woyciechowski, and John Matuszynski were among his closest friends. To Titus and to John in after years he was to write some of his most intimate, self-revealing letters.

Frédéric Abroad and in Love

When he left the Lycée at the age of eighteen Frédéric made his first considerable trip abroad. This was brought about by his father's friend, Dr Jarocki, zoologist and Professor at the Warsaw University, who suggested that Frédéric should accompany him to a conference of experts in Natural Philosophy which was to take place in Berlin, a five days' journey by coach. Frédéric, with the curiosity of youth, missed little of the parade of life in the German capital; its motley interested him; he haunted the Singakademie and the Opera and 'discovered' Handel; and his letters to Titus and his family were buoyant and amusing. At the age of 19, accompanied by three friends, he went to Vienna and, unperturbed by that critical public, gave two concerts, visiting Prague, Dresden, and Breslau on the way home. At the age of 19, moreover, he was in love, and from the 'loneliness' of an adoring home circle he unburdened himself to Titus, from whom he could conceal nothing.

> You cannot imagine [he wrote on 3 October 1829] how sad Warsaw is to me; and if I did not feel happy with my people I should not like to live here. Oh, how bitter it is to have no one with whom one can share joy and sorrow, how dreadful to feel one's heart oppressed and to be unable to confide in one human being. You know well what I mean. How often do I tell my piano all that I should like to tell to you! Six months have passed and not yet have I exchanged a syllable with her of whom I dream every night. Whilst my thoughts were with her I composed the Adagio of my Concerto, and early this morning she inspired the Valse which I send along with this letter.

And the more or less unconscious cause of all this emotional disturbance was the charming Constantia Gladkowska, a pupil at the Warsaw Conservatorium.

At that period, on the threshold of manhood, he was obsessed by three great passions; his art, Constantia (whom he did not yet know), and Titus. His passionate friendship for Titus was covetous and jealous as any lover's; no mistress could be more exacting. To the ordinary West European, knowing neither Titus nor Chopin, certain letters to his beloved friend would appear as the epistles of a homosexual or at any rate of a youth in whom feminine qualities were predominant.

> If I scrawl to-day again so much nonsense it is only in order to remind you that you are as much locked in my heart as ever and that I am still the same Fred. You do not care to be kissed, but to-day you must permit me to do so. . . . I embrace you heartily and kiss you on your lips if you will permit me. . . . Time passes, I must wash myself . . . do not kiss me now . . . but you would not kiss me now in any case – even if I anointed myself with Byzantine oils – unless by magnetic means I forced you to do so. . . . You, my dearest one, do not require my portrait. Believe me, I am always with you, and shall not forget you until the end of my life. . . . You have no idea how much I love you. If only I could prove it to you. What would I not give if I could once right heartily embrace you! . . .

Nevertheless, the love-lorn youth did not find life insupportable. He protested that he would not spend the winter in Warsaw, having Vienna in mind; but he did. Prince Radziwill and his wife invited him to Berlin, offering him apartments in their palace; but Constantia, the Ideal, evidently held him in thrall for the time being. Later, having sung for him at a local concert, she slipped into marriage with someone else and, it is said, suffered the misery of blindness.

In November 1830, after much vacillation, he said good-bye to Warsaw, being accompanied as far as Wola by Elsner and a number of intimate friends. Elsner had written a cantata for the occasion and had secretly rehearsed it with pupils of the Conservatorium. At Wola Frédéric found a banquet prepared in his honour; the cantata was sung and a silver goblet filled with Polish earth presented to him. 'May you never forget your native land wherever you may go,' someone said to him, handing him the goblet; 'may you never cease to love it with a warm and faithful heart.' And as the carriage rolled away Frédéric Chopin knew he was never to see Warsaw again nor set foot on Polish soil. But that goblet and the earth in it he was to keep faithfully to the end, as he kept the letters of Constantia Gladkowska.

Titus accompanied Frédéric to Vienna, but revolution broke out in Poland on 30 November and Titus at once departed to join the insurgents. With dramatic suddenness Frédéric found himself alone and homesick. What should he do? Should he follow Titus? In a letter to his family he laid bare his soul; but they urged him to stay where he was, saying that he was 'not strong enough to bear the hardships and fatigue of a soldier's life'. His loneliness and homesickness together became unbearable; and impulsively he hired a carriage and pursued his friend several stages along the road to Warsaw. Yet his mind was not made up; he was irresolute, his courage gave way, and he returned to Vienna. In the following July (1831) he left Vienna, gave a concert in Munich, and was in Stuttgart on his way to Paris when he learned to his horror that Warsaw had fallen to the Russians on 8 September. 'Who could have foreseen such a calamity?' he cried. Out of the agony of his mind he poured forth the *Étude in C Minor* – No. 12 of Op. 10 – 'La Révolution'; and in his notebook he wrote: 'The faubourgs fired! Titus and Matuszynski killed, no doubt! Paskewitsch and that dog from Mohilew seizing the town ... Oh, God, where art Thou? Art Thou there and dost Thou not avenge Thyself? Art Thou not sated with murder? Or art Thou indeed a Muscovite? ...'

Early Days in Paris

On his arrival in Paris Chopin took rooms at 27 Boulevard Poissonnière, opposite the Cité Bergère. He carried with him letters of introduction, and it was not long before he met Cherubini, head of the

Conservatoire and the greatest musical influence in France. Cherubini was seventy-one and kept open house. At first he considered the old pedagogue to be expressionless and cold; in one letter he referred to him as a mummy, but changed his mind as acquaintance ripened. Cherubini's Monday evening salons were crowded, and there one would meet Meyerbeer and Rossini, Auber and Halévy (his favourite pupils), Hummel and Kalkbrenner and Liszt, stars of the platform and the stage. There was something in the austerity of the Italian, in his calm, severe idealism, which soon appealed to the young Franco-Pole, who became so far devoted that he wrote out a fair copy of one of Cherubini's fugues. He made the acquaintance of Mendelssohn, who affectionately dubbed him Chopinetto; of Ferdinand Hiller, Hummel's pupil, who was the first to play Beethoven's *E flat Concerto* in Paris; of Baillot, whom he called the rival of Paganini; and of many others. He was so impressed by the smooth dexterity of Kalkbrenner's piano-playing that for a time he considered taking a course of lessons (at Kalkbrenner's suggestion), but abandoned the idea (to Kalkbrenner's disgust) and prepared himself for a public concert. After two postponements, this took place on 26 February 1832, in Pleyel's Rooms. It was a failure financially; the public knew nothing of Chopin, and the receipts did not cover the expenses. He played a *Concerto*, some *Nocturnes* and *Mazurkas*. He took part in Kalkbrenner's new work, a *Marche suivie d'une Polonaise* for two pianos (a very large one for Kalkbrenner and a little one for himself) with accompaniment for four others, 'as loud as an orchestra', played by Hiller, Osborne, Sowinski, and Stamaty. Chopin was partly amused, partly disgusted at the sextet of pianos, accepting it as the price paid for his début. ('An altogether mad idea' was his comment beforehand in a letter to Titus.) Liszt and Mendelssohn were present, both already eminent personages and both greatly impressed by the young man's individuality. Liszt perceived that in his art he combined a new phase of poetic sentiment with 'happy innovations' in form; Mendelssohn, who had heard all about Kalkbrenner's designs upon Chopinetto's career, was delighted with the playing and applauded vigorously; Hiller declared that now there would be no more nonsense talked about the want of technique. The *soirée musicale*, in fact, if not the talk of the town, was a new topic of conversation in the drawing-rooms – for the moment. And the influential Fétis, in an elaborate report in his *Revue Musicale*, remarked, while objecting to 'too much luxuriance in the modulations, disorder in the linking of the phrases', that there will be found in M. Chopin's inspirations the indication of 'a renewal of forms which may exercise in time a great influence over this branch of the art'.

After a very short period when he was threatened with desperate penury, good fortune smiled upon him, and Chopin began to make a remarkable reputation as a teacher, his pupils almost without exception being aristocratic young ladies moving in the most exclusive society. His life was now practically the life of the salon; bohemianism was antipathetic to him; any deep literary or political discussion he avoided; and the only fellow-artists in whom he showed the slightest interest were those, like Liszt or Franchomme or Delacroix, who happened to move in the same restricted circles. He showed the same fastidiousness in the choice of clothes, in the decoration and arrangement of his rooms, as in the composition of some exquisite *fioriture* for a Nocturne – and over these we know he would spend hours and days altering, restoring, correcting, before he was really satisfied.

I move in the highest circles among ambassadors, princes, and ministers [he wrote to his friend Dziewanowski in January 1833], and I know not how I got there, for I did not in any way thrust myself forward. But at present it is for me an absolute necessity, for thence comes, so to speak, good taste . . . To-day I have to give five lessons. You will imagine that I must have made a fortune by this time; but the cabriolet and the white gloves eat the earnings almost entirely, and without these things people would deny my good form. I love the Carlists, hate the Philippists and am myself a revolutionist. Therefore I don't care for money, but only for friendship – for the preservation of which I earnestly entreat you. . . .

How characteristic of the man, of the still young man, was this! In spirit a revolutionist, actually something of a sybarite, dependent on the hated Philippists; caring for friendship, loyal, yet by nature eclectic and hypercritical, having only the most theoretical care (and little of that) for the world outside. With Fédéric Chopin the cabriolet and the white gloves were as much a natural inclination as a conscious investment.

In the summer of 1835 Chopin journeyed to Carlsbad to meet his parents, whom he had not seen for five years; in September he proceeded to Dresden at the invitation of the Wodzinski family and fell in love with Marie, then nineteen years of age. The following summer he joined the Wodzinskis at Marienbad, and his love for Marie was intensified; but Count Wodzinski's domain of fifty thousand acres no doubt represented in Chopin's mind an obstacle of social rank he could not hope to surmount by the simple process of proposing to the owner's daughter. At any rate, he was gently dismissed, and the world was the richer for at least one perfect *Valse* dedicated to the insincere Marie.

George Sand

Early in 1837 Chopin first encountered George Sand, one of the most remarkable women in history, and life immediately became complicated. He was in his twenty-eighth, she in her thirty-third year – the most conspicuous figure in a *galère* that included Balzac, Heine, Sainte-Beuve, and other men distinguished in literature and the arts. The most intemperate fiction could hardly have produced such a type: a voluptuary without vice, who could take delight in recording her erotic impressions; a woman in whom the qualities of compassion, of hypocrisy, of pure motherliness, and of the vampire were grotesquely mixed. Through her veins coursed the blood of kings and courtesans; lights o' love and aristocrats had collaborated in her pedigree; generations of unsanctified unions had brought her into being. She had had many lovers after her unfortunate marriage to Casimir Dudevant: Jules Sandeau (with whom she co-operated in her first novel), Prosper Mérimée, Alfred de Musset, Dr Pagello, the tutors Pelletan and Malfille, Leroux – and then Chopin. Let those who would understand this tragic liaison, and the contrapuntal character of the quarrel that ended it, read the lady's *Un Hiver à Majorque*, her *Histoire de ma Vie*, and her published Letters, and discount much that is obvious embellishment. George Sand saved Chopin's life during those dreary winter months in Majorca, nursed and watched over him with consummate care in circumstances of unusual difficulty. But tuberculosis had set in; and thereafter, at the château of Nohant and in Paris, with intermittent periods of comparative happiness, the composer's life was in decline. Two visits to England were undertaken in misery. He played to the Queen at the Duchess of Sutherland's in 1848; appeared at other important London houses; underwent the indignity of being treated as a mere touring pianist of no account; suffered a complexity of boredom with country-house visits in Scotland, recitals in the provinces, and a certain amount of indifferent criticism. Illness, loneliness, and the fogs of London drove him back to Paris, there to die on 17 October

1849. His grave is in Père-Lachaise, close to Bellini's. His heart is in Poland.

Chopin's Bequest

I know of no more futile occupation than an attempt to make a formal analysis of any work of Chopin, pointing out here the influence of Hummel or Weber, there his devotion to Bellini. He was no orchestrator, and the two *Concerti*, with all their charming touches, are of secondary importance. Apart from the three *Sonatas*, the most highly organized works are the four *Ballades*, for the 'programmes' of which the reader may be referred to M. Cortot's edition and take with a grain of salt what that eminent pianist has to say about them. The two books of *Études* remain unapproached for the unusual combination of technical virtuosity and sheer beauty; these alone make most subsequent writers for the piano appear as pygmies. Brahms only is comparable, technically. The presto Finale of the *Sonata in B flat Minor*, which has baffled so many commentators as being unorthodox and formless, stands to-day as one of the most astonishing pieces of impressionist writing in the whole literature of the piano. The *Nocturnes* and *Valses* are unequal in merit, but include some that belong to the heritage that has survived a century of development and change. The Slav element in Chopin would appear to be more subtly expressed in the *Mazurkas* than in anything else, and a proper estimate of their essence can, I feel, only be realized by those who have an intimate knowledge of the traditional folk-music of that part of Poland which gave inspiration to the composer.

It is possible that the low dynamic plane of Chopin's piano-playing may have been originally suggested to him by the technique of the clavichord. In this connexion it is worth noting the remarks of A. J. Hipkins, who knew Chopin well and heard him play many tunes when he was in England in 1848. (The remarks appear in a letter quoted by Miss A. M. Diehl in *Musical Memories*, 1897.)

His fortissimo was the pure full tone without noise, a harsh inelastic note being to him painful. His nuances were modifications of that tone, decreasing to the faintest yet always distinct pianissimo. His singing legatissimo touch was marvellous. The wide-extended arpeggios in the bass were transfused by touch and pedals into their corresponding sustained chords, and swelled or diminished like waves in an ocean of sound. He kept the elbows close to his side, and played only with finger-touch – no weight from the arms. He used a simple, natural position of the hands as conditioned by scale or chord-playing, adapting the easiest fingering – although it might be against the rules – that came to him. He changed fingers upon a key as often as an organ-player.

In our own day the tradition of Chopin-playing was probably best exemplified in the interpretations of Moritz Rosenthal; he was a pupil of Mikuli, who had studied with the composer himself. According to Rosenthal, the composer confined himself in his lessons strictly to the playing and did not, like Liszt, dwell upon the music itself; he was always disinclined to discuss the merits or shortcomings of his own or other people's music. And it was à propos of pure technique that Chopin, in the last year of his life, wrote so whimsically: 'Nothing has come from my efforts except my long nose and my badly cultivated fourth finger.'

CARL AUGUST PETER CORNELIUS

1824–74

RALPH W. WOOD

Early Plans

Arnold Leonhard Ignaz Cornelius, a Düsseldorf copper-engraver, took to the stage when in his thirties. Of his three children only one survived, and that one, Carl Josef Gerhard, had an extremely unhappy and stormy youth. He was apprenticed to a goldsmith, but presently ran away to become, in his turn, an actor. He married an actress, his manager's step-daughter, and they had seven children. Not wishing their nomadic actors' life to cause the children to have a different school every six months, they left them in a boarding establishment at Mainz (the birthplace of five of them, including – 24 December 1824 – Carl August Peter). They visited the children as often as they could. The father is described as 'a great idealist' and 'of rare kindness of heart'. The mother was a woman of limitless industry – religious, sincere, placid. Peter's letters contained enthusiastic references to her, full of admiration and love.

So much for factors fundamental in their influence on the composer Cornelius's character, quite apart from what direct material bearing they may have had on his career. It may be worth remembering too that he was related to a famous painter, of the same name as himself, and that another relative, besides also painting, was a dignitary in an art gallery.

Carl Josef Gerhard's idea was to make son Peter into an actor. The youngster early showed a gift for music, and at school he revealed a bent for foreign languages and for poetry. In addition to the usual elementary syllabus he was taught French and English, had singing lessons with a formerly well-known vocalist, Scharrer, and studied violin and musical theory with a Hungarian named Panny. Presently his instruction was taken over by the director of a local choral society, and later still by *Hofkapellmeister* Heinrich Esser (by then he was well into a stream of tyro composition).

His father did go so far as to combine with his plan of turning him into a master of the histrionic art an affection for music and also a belief in its usefulness as a money-producer if necessity arose. In 1836, aged 11, the boy began his first composition; in 1838 he left school; in 1840 he visited London with the Mainz Orchestra as 'last second fiddler'. The succeeding years found him continuing to study both music and acting and making his first stage appearances. Though not untalented, he did not seem quite cut out for an actor. So at least he himself decided. A talk he had one day with his father about a possible comic-opera subject showed where his thoughts were already running.

Study and Teaching

His father died in 1843, and for the best part of a year Cornelius worked at music-teaching for the support of his mother. His systematic education had ended early and he was now quickly discovering the gaps in his knowledge, which he did his best to fill by private study. A good musical foundation he had; an acquaintance, promoted by his father, with Goethe, Shakespeare, Lessing; and a knowledge of the life of the theatre. . . .

In September 1844 he got to Berlin, where his relative, the famous painter, took him under his wing and helped him to start a course of study with Dehn, famous theoretician. Counterpoint occupied him four to five hours daily, and as he was also learning Spanish, Italian, Old French, and Provençal, not to speak of writing 'notices' for a newspaper and giving music-lessons, he was often at his books till 3.0 a.m. It hurt him to earn money by music, which he regarded very idealistically; and to that chagrin was presently added the smart of an abortive love-affair. In 1846 began his friendship with the poet and novelist, Paul Heyse. He composed a good deal, choral and chamber works and sonatas (a large-scale *Miserere* was performed at a soirée given by his cousin in 1847), wrote two libretti for comic-operas and began sketching music for one. He also wrote poetry. Overwork presently caused him to fall ill for several weeks (all the time he had to be on guard against a consumptive tendency).

He was in Berlin, his mother now with him, until 1852 and during the last few years earned a tolerable livelihood by his teaching. As well as composing, and writing about music, he translated some Victor Hugo and some Old French poetry. It was curiosity about Wagner, and a desire to consult Liszt (whose interest had been attracted by his excellent articles) about himself, that led him, when his mother went away on a visit, to seize the opportunity of making an expedition to Weimar.

Weimar and Liszt

The artistic coterie gathered round Liszt, Weimar *Hofkapellmeister* since 1842, acted like a spell on Cornelius. He was fired with an ambition to study all over again and to find a place in that circle. He had a friendly reception by Liszt and by Hofrat Schöll, to both of whom his cousin had given him letters of introduction, went off after a few days to join his mother for the Easter at the Bernhardshütte (near Sonneberg) with his married sister and then was back to Weimar. Liszt only really liked his sacred compositions and advised him to stick to church music. In a rather pessimistic mood he retired once more, for the summer, to the Bernhardshütte, where, however, he did write several large church works, which were duly submitted to Liszt. Liszt was encouraging, but Cornelius himself was far from satisfied. The impact of the music of Berlioz had been for him one of the most important consequences of his coming to Weimar, and he was eagerly studying *Benvenuto Cellini* and its forerunners, but missed a Berlioz festival because of spending the winter at Soest, where his brother Carl knew influential people. More church compositions were brought back to Liszt the following spring.

An attempt to obtain a position in a Jesuit college was unsuccessful. So was his entry in the competition for the conductorship of the Mainz choral society, whose director at the time had been one of his boyhood tutors (and letters to Schöll reveal that this must have been a disappointment). For a fortnight he was a guest first of Liszt and then of the Princess Wittgenstein, in the Altenburg.

In October 1853, he went to Basel with Liszt to visit Wagner. Just before they had been in Karlsruhe, Liszt directing a music festival that amounted to the introduction to Southern Germany of the 'New German Music'. These events set Cornelius writing articles that, in their turn, demanded of him special intensive studies of his material. Of his many friends among Liszt's pupils H. von Bronsart and Tausig were the closest. He tried to get a steady income by translating (e.g., French articles, prefaces to Liszt's symphonic poems, Berlioz texts) and teaching. Also he wrote for a Berlin paper. On a visit with Liszt to Leipzig he met Berlioz. He was full of plans for a comic opera, but had no time to compose. At the Bernhardshütte for his mother's birthday, he did produce a song and later some duets as a Christmas gift for his sister Susanne. He was hard-up that winter (1854-5), and his family pressed him to get a permanent post. But he could not be happy unless he was living primarily for rather than by his art. He was intent on what he saw as his destiny – writing operas. An unwilling journey to try for the again vacant Mainz conductorship succeeded only in emptying his purse.

Success

At this point Liszt intervened with a providential offer of a permanent situation as translator and secretary and of a place to live in, in the Altenburg. Thus Cornelius stayed on in Weimar. He soon now achieved his first real success, both in performance and by publication, as composer – with some of his songs. He had pupils. He was better off than ever before.

During the past few years he had continued to write poems but had composed hardly at all. At last he now found, in the *Thousand and One Nights*, the subject for his comic opera. Between October 1855 and September 1856 he wrote the libretto of *The Barber of Bagdad*. To be undisturbed he spent the ensuing winter at the Bernhardshütte, whence came reports to von Bronsart of the first attack on the music. (He also wrote at that time the first version of his *Christmas Songs*, Op. 8, a present for his sister Elise.) After intensive work on the opera at Weimar through the spring and summer, he retired in the autumn again, to a little house at Johannisgrund (Rhineland) put at his disposal by an old friend of his father's, where he worked for some months in solitude. To Mainz, zestful, in the new year, and in April to Weimar. There Liszt, though first disliking his subject, became approbatory after going through the score.

Cornelius began already to be full of ideas about a new 'great, beautiful German opera'. Meanwhile he finished off the *Barber;* it was enthusiastically rehearsed and was performed under Liszt's baton at Weimar in December 1858. In Weimar itself, though Liszt was so leading a figure there, the Intendant of the Court-theatre led a strong party of opposition to the 'new music'. Perhaps Liszt and all he stood for, as much as this particular disciple-work, was the object of the organized hostile demonstrations that wrecked what could have been a successful première. Cornelius remained cheerful and pleased with his work; but Liszt was so offended that he resigned his conductorship of the Court-opera, refusing to be mollified when his rather staggered adversaries climbed down even to the extent of offering to have the Intendant removed. Only two days after, Cornelius received 'stormy ovations' at a Beethoven festival when a prologue written by him was recited.

Cornelius felt himself a composer on the way to becoming known farther afield. At all events this was the end of his Weimar days. He went back to Mainz, and then (April 1859), piqued by a letter from his brother urging him to become self-supporting, to Vienna, long the city of his desire. He felt very lonely after Weimar. Soon, indeed, there was a fruitful friendship with the poet Hebbel, and presently he came in close contact with Wagner. Through the latter, too, he met a Dr Standhartner, at whose home his soul found much comfort. Partly owing to his own carelessness he was often short of money. However, his nose was pressed fast to the trail of the ideas he had already formed at Weimar for his next opera. He prepared in fact three separate texts, as well as toying with yet a fourth subject. The actual poem of *The Cid* was completed in August 1860, and he began on the music in September. This would be a little before he heard *Tristan* for the first time.

Wagner

And now began the great friendship that bore fruit three years later in an invitation to join Wagner at Munich, under the patronage of Ludwig II (with a salary of 1,000 gulden). Cornelius published in 1861 a selection of his poems, Op. 5 and Op. 6, and other songs were composed in Vienna. Also he was writing regularly all the time for the *Neue Zeitschrift für Musik* and turning out fine essays on the 'new school's' principles. In November 1864 *The Cid* was finished, but for the overture. After some hesitation, due to fear of being 'swallowed up by W.'s magnetic nearness,' Cornelius went to Munich.

His first activity there was to compose the prelude to *The Cid*, after which he was off to Weimar, where the Grand Duchess had long ago suggested that the new opera should be produced. The first thing he did in Weimar was to get engaged (to a Frl. Bertha Jung), having now a solid position. By patrons and artists alike he was honoured, and in

May *The Cid* was staged – and some satisfaction given for the wrong of 15 December 1858.

Already he was beginning to be preoccupied with new operatic plans. By the time the poem of *Gunlöd*, the subject taken from the Edda upon which his choice at length fell, was finished practically two years had passed. Upon the music he was engaged during a further seven years, for just before that his hitherto free disposal of his time at Munich was halted by his appointment as a teacher of rhetoric and harmony at the reorganized conservatoire, and also meanwhile (as well, it is true, as composing some smaller things, among them a series for his friend Riedel, choral conduct or in Leipzig) he revised old works, wrote, translated, studied languages . . .

In March 1867, on the suggestion of the Princess Wittgenstein, he made a translation from the Polish of sonnets by Miskiewicz. That month his mother died. The composition of *Gunlöd* began during a stay with his fiancée and some relatives of hers at Feldafing on the Starnbergsee (Bavaria) that summer. His salary for the teaching job now begun was 1,200 gulden a year. He was learning Greek, and conjugations of Greek verbs alternated in his note-book with sketches for harmony exercises. In September he got married.

Journalism

His journalism continued. In fact, in 1869 he looked rather longingly towards the editorship of the *N.Z.f.M.*, then vacant. Moreover he was asked by a publisher to edit a new paper and by a Berlin editor to become his opera critic. But as the teaching job was safe, and as von Bülow (the director of the School of Music) was anxious to keep him and raised his salary, he stayed in Munich. An expedition with his brother that spring to Paris, where he heard much music, may be worth mentioning. His second child, a daughter, was born in the autumn (his first, a boy, had arrived in July 1868).

During the following year much of his composing for Riedel's choir, and correspondence arising therefrom, took place. A year later still, on an autumn holiday-tour with his wife and children (another son had been added to them in December 1870), he met Riedel at Rüdesheim, having suggested the rendezvous to him in a humorous poem. He remained always on very good terms and in close touch with Wagner, on whose work he wrote yet another essay at the end of 1871, for the *Wiener Neue Zeitung*.

He was present at the foundation-stone ceremony in Bayreuth in May 1872. From Bernau-am-Chiemsee on holiday in the summer he was able to report to Riedel a good recent output, quite apart from *Gunlöd* and from literary work. The autumn brought a commission from Paris à propos of a revised edition of Gluck's operas. He made new Gluck translations and was altogether exceedingly busy. When Riedel asked him to write some chamber-music he pleaded lack of time and lack of vocation and ended '. . . back to the drama! Back to the drama, to the damned boards. . . .'

In 1873 the male-voice choruses, Op. 12, were born: also Cornelius's fourth child, another son. He took to Bayreuth for Wagner's sixtieth birthday a *Festspiel, Künstlerweihe*. A batch of his compositions was published late in the year, the while he was himself engaged in revising the *Barber*. He did various small jobs of composing or revision (he was always one to revise works, often long after their original appearance), published an *Autobiography*, made plans, wrote his charming letters to old friends like von Bronsart, continued busy on *Gunlöd*, through to the following summer. The heat of that season made him suffer more than usual this year. At the beginning of their holiday the family went to Mainz, where they called in a doctor because of a slight indisposition of one of the children. The doctor at once saw that Cornelius himself was gravely ill. He must in fact have had the beginning of diabetes mellitus in him long before. He went straight for a cure at Neuenahr (he wrote a small choral piece there) and seemed to improve. But back in Mainz came a violent resurgence of the disorder, and on 26 October he died – two months before the fiftieth anniversary of his birth in that same place.

Gunlöd had to be completed and orchestrated by other hands.

The Man and the Catholic

Cornelius was said to combine with his flair for letters and for music a sort of alienness from everyday life. He was very sensitive and utterly sincere – alike towards himself and towards others. The warm kindness of his heart, his humour, his great modesty, were as evident as his religiousness. Despite the existence of sympathetic friends, the equation with life that wide culture should connote, and eventually the resource of a loved and loving woman, he could write to her (when he was 41 – two years before his marriage): 'I see myself helplessly abandoned in a deep abyss', and again 'Once more I feel so very much alone and find that I do not fit at all into this world.' Against his sensitiveness he fought and was helped in the fight by his honesty, the candid critical sense that, as well as being frankly directed upon others, even those he most admired, was before all directed upon himself. In a letter to his sister Susanne, when he was nearly 46, he said: 'I am always starting again to learn from the beginning. I have a terrible urge to educate myself.' Intensely pious, he was a Catholic not too narrow to be able to live in great happiness with a Protestant wife. Of a man so modest, so unspectacular, so far the reverse of prominent, established or (except with his pen) forceful, it is well to remember that he consistently stood up with complete boldness for the music of Wagner, Liszt, and Berlioz during a period when it was provoking doubt, misunderstanding, and bitter opposition.

KARL CZERNY

1791–1857

MAX PIRANI

A Link between Eras

If the popularity of a composer were measured by the frequency with which his music is played, Karl Czerny would be well in the running as a favourite, for it is quite possible that notes written by him have been the subject of more practice-hours during the past hundred years than those of any other musician. His *Exercises*, his *School of Velocity*, and his many other collections of technical studies have been the daily task of countless pianoforte students wherever music is taught, from Montevideo to Manchester, from Melbourne to Madrid.

Apart from his claims as a composer, he merits attention as a link between two musical eras, and he could have answered most impressively those two questions so frequently asked of musicians, 'With whom did you study?' and 'Have you any interesting pupils?', for his replies would have been, 'Beethoven' and 'Yes, Liszt among others.'

Karl Czerny was the son of Wenzel Czerny, a pianoforte teacher from Bohemia, who migrated to Vienna in 1786. Five years later, on 20 February 1791, Karl was born. Wenzel's aim, to establish himself in a wider field of culture, seems to have been unfulfilled, for a few months after Karl's birth the family, consisting of father, mother, and baby, changed its home again and left Vienna for Poland, where Wenzel had obtained a post as music teacher in a nobleman's household. From his earliest years Karl showed musical aptitude; he writes in his autobiography 'I must have been a very lively child; I was able to play little pieces on the piano to my parents when I was three years old.'

Back to Vienna

In 1795, unhappy Poland was in a state of political instability, a situation so often repeated in its history, and father Czerny, deciding that economic uncertainty was preferable to the risk of being involved in a revolution, returned to Vienna in that year to try his fortune once again. This time his star was luckier; the family formed many musical friendships and gradually became identified with musical life in Vienna. For the next four years Karl was his father's pupil. Brought up on whatever may have been the orthodox method of training prodigies, Karl developed into a public performer by the time he was nine.

Beethoven

Among the musicians in the Czerny's circle was a violinist named Krumpholz, who played in the Hoftheater orchestra. (Incidentally, Krumpholz's brother was the inventor of the pedal-harp.) Krumpholz was a passionate admirer of Beethoven, who by 1800 had made his name both as composer and as pianist. It was arranged that the wonder-child should play to the Master; following this introduction, Beethoven, on his own initiative, offered to take Karl as a regular pupil. In 1801 a performance of Mozart's *C minor Concerto* with Karl as soloist met with Beethoven's approval and the way seemed clear for Czerny to follow the strenuous life of a virtuoso. The social aspect of a projected career was not forgotten. Beethoven took the young Czerny to play to Prince Lichnowsky, a visit that was repeated many times; on such occasions Czerny sometimes gave to the Prince and his friends first performances of pianoforte works that his master had just completed. Some instruction from Hummel tided over the period 1804 to 1806, when the lessons with Beethoven were interrupted, owing to an argument between the master and father Czerny. When they were resumed, Beethoven was even more enthusiastic about his pupil's talent than before.

It is not clear why these promising beginnings did not have their anticipated sequel; perhaps the unsettled state of Europe in the epoch of the Napoleonic wars contributed to the decision to abandon a concert career, perhaps Czerny found himself temperamentally unfitted to become a virtuoso. His only recorded concert tour was in 1804, and by the time he was fifteen years old Karl had already embraced the profession that was to predominate for the rest of his life and had begun to teach confidently and successfully. Beethoven had grounded him in the method of Karl Philip Emanuel Bach. Association with Clementi in 1810 broadened his pedagogical outlook, and it was at about this time that Czerny turned his attention towards the composition of studies and exercises, though the first publication of these did not take place until he had further established his reputation as a teacher.

Other compositions were also taking shape in his mind. His Opus 1, *Concertante Variazionen für Klavier und Violine über ein Thema von Krumpholz*, 'a youthful tribute to a valued friend', had appeared in 1805, but it was not until 1819 that Opus 2 was published. From this time onward, however, a continual stream of his works flowed from the press, a catholic collection in almost every musical form, opera being the only major exception.

By 1815, Czerny's renown as a teacher had mounted to considerable proportions, and he watched over his pupils paternally. Father and mother Czerny added the grand-parental touch by giving weekly parties and recitals in their house, at which the students showed their abilities. It was in 1815 that Beethoven entrusted his nephew Karl as a pupil to Czerny. Beethoven and the Czernys had formed a lasting friendship; the former even proposed that he should make his home in the Czerny household but, perhaps fortunately for their future amity, this project was never realized. Czerny took lessons from Beethoven until he was over twenty years of age and he writes in his autobiography that 'even in 1812 Beethoven corrected me with the greatest precision, just as he had done ten years earlier.' The following extract from a letter, written after a private performance of Beethoven's *Wind Quintet* in which Czerny played the pianoforte part, indicates that the relation of teacher and pupil was still maintained, in spite of growing intimacy.

Dear Czerny,

I cannot see you to-day, but to-morrow I will come to your house myself and talk to you. I exploded yesterday and I was very sorry after it happened, but you must forgive this to a composer who prefers to hear his work played exactly as it is written. Otherwise you played so beautifully. . . .

Your true friend,
Beethoven.

Later, Beethoven showed his continued confidence in Czerny's ability by allowing him, in one of his rare public appearances, to give the first performance in Vienna of the *Emperor Concerto*.

Liszt

In 1816, Czerny became the teacher of an eight-year-old prodigy, Ninette de Belleville, 'a rare talent', who lived with his parents for three years. Making an extended concert tour in 1819, she covered both herself and her teacher with glory, bringing his teaching genius to the attention of musicians in many European countries. The next pupil of note was ten-year-old Franz Liszt, of whom Czerny wrote 'Here one sees that nature herself has educated a pianist', foreshadowing another great pedagogue's dictum, Leopold Auer's remark that there are no best teachers, only best pupils! Later came Thalberg, Döhler, and a host of others, their names making a catalogue of most pianist-celebrities of the early nineteenth century.

By 1820 Czerny's fame had reached its peak. Supported by his adoring parents and surrounded by faithful pupils, his life's routine had become established. After a day's teaching he would compose throughout the evening, and his output of compositions gradually reached heroic proportions. It included twenty-four Masses, four Requiems, numerous symphonies and string quartets, exercises, studies, and pieces of all kinds for the pianoforte, as well as many arrangements. He made piano scores of contemporary operas, among the first of which was a transcription of Beethoven's *Fidelio*. He writes in his autobiography that Beethoven's comments and encouragement while this was in preparation helped him to acquire a skill of which he made great use in later life.

Composition and Teaching

In all, Czerny's works exceeded a thousand, and many of these contained fifty or more separate pieces or studies. Though he cannot be classed among the great composers, his works very often have charm and considerable musical interest. There is no doubt as to the technical value of his *Studies*. Though they have passed through phases of belittlement, they are revived again and again, because they are based on the essentials of pianoforte passage writing, and very often their patterns are prophetic of the work of composers yet to come.

It is not surprising that, with such a programme of teaching and diligent composition, Czerny found himself 'settled down' in a very full meaning of that phrase. After 1804 he made only three journeys from Vienna, including one in 1837 that brought him to Paris and London. Outside his limited circle he made few social contacts and, though he has been described by an anonymous biographer as 'simple and undogmatic, friendly and pleasant towards all who met him', his life became more and more circumscribed as time passed. He never married and had neither brothers nor sisters. There is no record of personal intimacies beyond his attachment to his parents.

Retaining Beethoven's friendship until his death, Czerny visited him in 1823 and 1824 in Baden-bei-Wien. He writes sorrowfully of the Master's deafness and the difficulty of communication. Czerny kept abreast of musical thought and was one of the first to appreciate the compositions of Beethoven's final period. Indeed, he was a sensitive musician, and one is apt to get a false impression if one takes his *Studies* as the complete expression of his personality. In his *Letters on Teaching the Pianoforte* he wrote an appendix on 'The Higher Branches of Musical Execution and Expression'. In this he emphasizes the importance of tone variety and the vital necessity of good pedalling. He shows a great concern for sonority and stresses the need for acquiring a sense of style. He advises his reader (a lady whom he addresses formally as 'Madam' in each letter) to study melodic playing intensively, to learn to sing if she has any voice or, alternatively, to listen to artistic singing in order to obtain a vocal line in phrasing.

His own words on the subject of tonal and stylistic restraint, as translated by J. A. Hamilton in an English edition of about 1840, could hardly be improved by paraphrase: 'When a player by monstrous passages produces only a loud and often a discordant noise, and then dignifies this hubbub with the appellation of an impassioned, romantic and characteristic style of execution, his auditors, at the end of his performance, will applaud only because he has at length come to a close and they are no longer obliged to compassionate his convulsive agonies.' These words are as apt to-day as when they were written.

Other literary works included a *School of Practical Composition* (and who could be better qualified to write one?) and a *Chronological Sketch of the History of Music*. Czerny seems to have been indefatigable and, though from his fiftieth year his health declined, he kept at work until a few weeks before his death on 15 July 1857, in the Vienna where he had been born and where he had spent practically the whole of his life.

Fifty years of successful teaching and the composition of remunerative Gebrauchs-Musik enabled Czerny to accumulate a large fortune; part of this he left to the Vienna Conservatoire and the remainder to various benevolent institutions. But his indestructible legacy is the influence he has exerted on the piano-playing of every succeeding age.

Towards the end of Liszt's life, Leschetizky visited him in Vienna and admired the way in which he had retained his technical dexterity. Liszt said 'I practise Czerny exercises for half an hour every day.' And, in spite of changing fashions, so do many of us still!

GAETANO DONIZETTI

1797–1848

DYNELEY HUSSEY

The North Italian

'My friend had, among many original relics . . . two or three reproductions of the finest bronzes in the Naples Museum, the work of a small band of brothers whom he had found himself justified in trusting to deal with their problem honourably and to bring forth something as different as possible from the usual compromise of commerce . . . I am not sure it was not the conversation and the beautiful manners of these obscure young men that most fixed in my mind for the time the sense of the side of life that, all around, was to come out strongest. It would be artless, no doubt, to represent them as high types of innocence or even of energy – at the same time that, weighing them against *some* ruder folk of our own race, we might perhaps have made bold to place their share even of these qualities in the scale. It was an impression indeed never infrequent in Italy, of which I might, in these days, first have felt the force during a stay, just earlier, with a friend at Sorrento – a friend who had good-naturedly 'had in', on his wondrous terrace, after dinner, for the pleasure of the gaping alien, the usual local quartette, violins, guitar and flute, the musical barber, the musical tailor, saddler, joiner, humblest sons of the people and exponents of Neapolitan song. Neapolitan song, as we know, has been blown well about the world, and it is late in the day to arrive with a ravished ear for it. . . .

'The personal civilization, for intercourse, of the musical barber and tailor, of the pleasant young craftsmen of my other friend's company, was something that could be trusted to make the brooding tourist brood afresh – to say more to him in fact, all the rest of the second occasion, than everything else put together. The happy address, the charming expression, the instinctive discretion, the complete eclipse, in short, of vulgarity and brutality – these things easily became among these people the supremely suggestive note, begetting a hundred hopes and fears as to the place that, with the present general turn of affairs about the globe, is being kept for them.'

That is how it struck an intelligent and sensitive observer from across the Atlantic half a century ago. And it is not to be supposed that the Naples and the Neapolitans of fifty years further back differed much from those of the eighteen-nineties. The beautiful manners of 'these obscure young men, whom it would be artless to represent as high types of innocence or even of energy', which so impressed Henry James, were evidently not absent from the make-up of Italians a century ago. How else are we to explain the creation, upon a basis of little more than instinctive good taste, of works so devoid of vulgarity and brutality that one must perforce call them aristocratic – of *Lucia di Lammermoor* and *Don Pasquale*?

Although Naples was the scene of one of his chief successes and Neapolitan melody formed the basis of much that is most characteristic in his music, Gaetano Donizetti came from Northern Italy. He was born on 29 November 1797, in Bergamo, a provincial city on the northern verge of the Lombard plain where the foothills begin to rise towards the Bergamask Alps and the massif of Piz Bernina. He came of humble stock, his grandfather being an employee in the textile industry, which is one of Bergamo's chief resources, and his father was probably also a weaver until in 1800 he was appointed to the post of porter at the municipal pawn-shop. Gaetano was the youngest of four sons, two of whom became military bandsmen. Like many a father before, Andrea Donizetti hoped to see his children in better circumstances than his own. But, like other fathers, he came to differ from his son as to the best means of obtaining that desirable objective. As Gaetano showed some early talent for music, he was sent to the local conservatoire and subsequently to the Philharmonic Lyceum at Bologna, where the high traditions of Padre Martini were maintained by Stanislas Mattei. Donizetti's father hoped that his son would follow in these respectable footsteps and become a learned teacher and a church musician. But the boy took no interest in counterpoint or musical scholarship. The theatre was his goal, and for that all he would need was the ability to harmonize a tune in the simplest fashion, coupled with a sense of theatrical effect, which could be acquired by experience, and, of course, a natural gift for melodic invention. Donizetti had that gift.

The Influence of Mayr

His attraction to the theatre may, one suspects, be traced to the example, if not to the positive precept, of his first master at Bergamo. Johann Simon Mayr, the professor of composition at the conservatoire, was a Bavarian musician who had been appointed organist and choirmaster of Santa Maria Maggiore in Bergamo, on the strength of a number of masses and oratorios produced mostly in Venice. This excellent man, who allocated a large part of his savings to the foundation of two hostels for aged musicians and their dependants, was also in his spare time the most successful composer of Italian operas during the first decade of the nineteenth century. Mayr was no genius and his works are all forgotten; it was the case of the one-eyed man in the country of the blind. So soon as the young Rossini began to compose, Mayr suffered a rapid and total eclipse. It is reasonable to suppose, then, that Gaetano Donizetti acquired his taste for opera from the celebrated composer of *Lodoiska* and *Ginevra di Scozia*.

His schooling ended, Donizetti flatly declined his father's proposals for a scholastic career. He is commonly supposed to have taken the course traditionally adopted by romantic schoolboys dissatisfied with parental designs and, in default of an Italian Navy to which he might run away, enlisted in the Austrian army. The story then goes that, after producing a number of operas, of which the first, *Enrico di Borgogna*, was given in Venice in 1818, he had such a success with *Zoraide di Granata* in Rome four years later that he was promptly released from the army. His latest biographer, however, avers that Gaetano was exempted from military service, in view of the fact that he had two elder brothers already serving. This seems to accord more closely with the probabilities. This consideration need not throw discredit on the tradition that the Romans carried the young composer in triumph to the Capitol with a laurel wreath upon his handsome head.

He was indeed a good-looking young man, with the ambrosial curls and whiskers familiarized in the portraits of our own Prince Consort and a moustache neat, not effusive. In the portrait by Kriehuber done in Venice in 1842 he is shown to have had a humorous twinkle in his eyes. And, as one might expect, he presents an altogether more masculine appearance than his younger contemporary, the almost effeminately beautiful, consumptive Bellini.

Two Operas a Year!

On the strength of Donizetti's successes in Rome and Naples, where a couple of light operas were produced shortly before *Zoraide*, Simon Mayr, who apparently had supported his pupil in opposition to his father, wrote a letter recommending him to the directorate of the Scala Theatre in Milan. This letter is dated 29 August 1828, and just two months later *Chiara e Serafino ossia i Pirati* was given its first performance on the premier stage of Italy. Donizetti was already a quick worker. For the next eight years he was occupied with the production of at least two operas a year. In 1828 he was particularly fertile, composing five operas, including one about Queen Elizabeth at Kenilworth. The year 1830 opened with an oratorio, *The Universal Deluge*, after which there were five operas, the last of which dealt with the tragedy of Anne Boleyn.

In the meantime, Donizetti had married in 1824 Virginia Vasselli, a girl of sixteen, who seems to have come from a socially higher class than Donizetti himself. She was intelligent, well educated, and a good musician. Although the marriage took place in Bergamo, Donizetti's father was not invited to be present. The disagreement about his career seems to have died down, and in the years following his marriage we find Gaetano writing most affectionately to his father. We must suppose, therefore, that he was ashamed of his humble parentage.

Anna Bolena was Donizetti's first international success. Composed for Pasta and Rubini, the most famous soprano and tenor of the day, it was produced in Milan in December 1830, in Paris six months later, and then at the King's Theatre, London, where Lablache, the bass, made one of his greatest hits in the part of King Henry VIII. Rossini had just retired from the composition of operas in a dudgeon (or from sheer laziness) after the production of *William Tell* and the field was clear for his younger rivals.

The libretto of *Anna Bolena* was by Felice Romani, a poet of distinction, who supplied Rossini and Bellini with books for their operas, notable among them being *Norma*. He also adapted Victor Hugo's *Lucrezia Borgia* for Donizetti, whose opera was produced in Milan in 1833. Hugo was, however, not pleased at the way his tragedy had been treated by the Italian poet and, when the opera was given in Paris, the title had to be altered to *La Renégate* and the Italians of Alexander VI's time were transformed into Turks.

An even more resounding success was achieved in 1835 with *Lucia di Lammermoor*, adapted from Scott's novel by Cammarano, later to be the librettist of *Il Trovatore*. *Lucia* was composed for the San Carlo Theatre at Naples, then under the management of that remarkable impressario, Domenico Barbaja. Barbaja began life as a café-waiter in Milan, where he invented that mixture of whipped cream and coffee known in modern times as 'café viennois'. This stroke of genius brought him sufficient money to set up a gambling saloon near the Scala Theatre. Being a natural financial genius, he was soon wealthy enough to be able to rebuild the San Carlo Theatre after its destruction by fire in 1816. He was simultaneously director of this theatre and of the Scala, and, despite his complete illiteracy, possessed a remarkable flair for artistic merit.

Naples

The success of *Lucia* established Donizetti for a time in Naples, for he was appointed to a professorship at the Royal College of Music and a year later succeeded to the post of director. Soon after his appointment he was approached by a singer at one of the other Neapolitan theatres, which was in difficulties, with a request for a comic opera. Within a week he had written and composed *Il Campanello di Notte*, based on a vaudeville he had seen in Paris. He had acquired a considerable literary ability and himself designed the last acts of *Lucia* and *La Favorita* (1840), besides making the Italian translations of some of his French operas.

In 1837 Donizetti suffered the loss of his wife, who died from cholera on 30 July. A week earlier she had given birth to a still-born child. Donizetti, who was deeply devoted to Virginia, was overcome with grief. He had lately lost his parents and none of the children of his marriage had survived. He was left a very lonely man.

Donizetti remained in Naples for four years, his stay being brought to an end by a conflict with the censorship concerning an opera on the subject of Polyeucte, which was considered too sacred for treatment on the stage. The composer departed, therefore, to Paris, where *Poliuto* was produced in 1840 under the titles of *Les Martyrs*, with a French libretto by Scribe. With his astonishing facility he proceeded to follow up *Les Martyrs* with two further successes, *La Fille du Régiment* and *La Favorita*. The one is a light and delightful comic opera, the other a tragedy upon a highly dramatic subject whose final act, for which he supplied the words, is the best thing in all his serious operas. The whole of the music of this act, excepting two movements that were added during the rehearsals, is said to have been composed in four hours. No wonder that, when he was told that Rossini composed *The Barber of Seville* in thirteen days, he exclaimed, 'Yes, yes, he was always notoriously lazy!' It is of interest to note that the pianoforte reduction of the score of *La Favorita* was made by a young German named Richard Wagner.

Still more Operas and the End

Visits to Switzerland and Bergamo, to Rome and Milan, and finally to Vienna, followed in 1841, and still the operas came at the rate of two or three a year. There was an unfortunate first night for one of them, when more tickets were sold than there were seats available and the evening ended with a riot in the theatre, the arrest of the manager, and the seizure of the cash-box by the police. But life generally proceeded prosperously. In 1842 Rossini invited Donizetti to conduct his *Stabat Mater* at Bologna and tried to induce him to accept the directorship of the Liceo Musicale, but Donizetti was unwilling to give up his career as an operatic composer. He did, however, accept the more or less honorary appointment of Hofcompositeur to the Austrian Emperor, and in that capacity composed some sacred music in a strict style, which purported to be in the tradition of Palestrina. He also produced in Vienna the romantic opera, *Linda di Chamounix*.

In 1843 he returned to Paris and wrote his most brilliant comedy, *Don Pasquale*, a masterpiece in the buffo style, which immediately delighted the Parisians and has continued to charm and amuse its audiences ever since. Its companion tragedy, *Don Sébastien*, was a failure, and it would seem that Donizetti's health was already beginning to decline by the end of the year. He wrote only one more opera, *Catarina Cornaro*, produced in Naples in 1844.

During the remainder of his life, Donizetti became increasingly subject to fits of melancholia, until eventually general paralysis of the insane set in. It is probable that he had contracted syphilis early in life, which would account for the succession of still-births and deaths in infancy during his marriage, and in 1845 the dreadful ultimate consequences of the disease overtook him. As a result of consultations between his family, represented by his nephew, Andrea, son of the bandmaster in Constantinople, he was taken to an asylum near Paris.

Later it was decided to move him to Bergamo, and this was at last arranged, despite the opposition of the Parisian doctors, who appear to have wished to retain so distinguished a patient, through the instrumentality of the Austrian ambassador who took an interest in the Imperial *Hofcompositeur*. So the poor, helpless man, who had been so handsome and so amiable and free from spite or jealousy, was brought home to his native city, where he lingered on until 8 April 1848. He was buried outside the city, but in 1875 his body was exhumed and re-interred in the church of Santa Maria Maggiore, where his master Mayr had served and where he had been married.

JOHN FIELD

1782–1837

ROBERT ELKIN

Boyhood

The city of Dublin, in which John Field was born, was in the eighteenth century one of the most musical centres in Europe. Composers and performers from England were in the habit of paying visits which ran into several weeks or even months – Handel, it will be remembered, was there for the best part of a year, in the course of which he directed the first performance of his *Messiah*; many musicians from abroad found it congenial and lucrative to settle there for good. It is worth noting, too, that until Queen Victoria's time the only knighthoods bestowed on English musicians were those conferred by the Lord Lieutenant of Ireland. It was therefore in a thoroughly musical atmosphere that Field spent his early boyhood; music was in his blood too, for his father was a violinist in the orchestra of the Theatre Royal and his grandfather was organist at one of the Dublin churches. Father and grandfather lived in the same house, which they used as a kind of musical academy, the father teaching violin and the grandfather pianoforte. At the age of seven young Field showed signs of a taste for the pianoforte, and his grandfather took his musical education in hand, while his father with some severity superintended his practising. The lad was not by nature a hard worker; he so much resented the drudgery of practice, and the thrashings which were the sequel to any signs of idleness, that he ran away from home. Where he went to, or how long he stayed, is not exactly known; but in the spring of 1791 we find him sent for 'finishing lessons' to Tommaso Giordani, one of the most popular teachers in the city and a brother of the composer of the well-known air 'Caro mio ben'. By the time he had reached the age of nine he displayed unusual talent, and in the spring of 1792 he was billed as one of the principal attractions at a series of concerts given by Giordani at the Rotunda. In the following year he made his first attempts at composition, including some pianoforte variations which were much admired.

In the summer of 1793, Field *père* left Dublin to assume the position of leader of the orchestral concerts at Bath, and he took his family with him; but he had only been there six months when he secured a better engagement in the orchestra of the Haymarket Theatre, London. To London, therefore, the Field household removed; and John was now apprenticed, at a fee of one hundred guineas, to Muzio Clementi, by common consent the greatest pianist of his time. In April 1794 Field was publicly announced as Clementi's pupil, and in the following month he played one of his master's sonatas at a concert given by the violinist Barthélémon. He was heard by Haydn, Dussek, and J. B. Cramer, all of whom predicted a great future for him; but for a number of years Clementi, who had an interest in the publishing and pianoforte manufacturing business of Longman and Broderip, used him principally as a hack for demonstrating his firm's instruments to potential purchasers.

By the time he was seventeen, Field had so far progressed in the art of composition as to produce his first pianoforte concerto, which he played at the Haymarket Theatre at a benefit concert arranged for the young violinist George F. Pinto. Parke, in his *Musical Memories* (published 1830) says that the concerto was 'more remarkable for rapidity than expression'; but this looks suspiciously like a careless and misleading transcription of the concert notice in *The Morning Chronicle*, which was as follows:

> The chief source of admiration in the course of the evening was a Concerto on the grand piano forte by Master Field, a pupil of Clementi's . . . The Concerto was, we understand, wholly of his own composition, and one more calculated to display rapidity of execution, attended with characteristic musical expression, we never heard.

A year or two later we find Field creating something of a furore by a performance of the same work at the 'Lenten Oratorios' at Covent Garden Theatre; towards the end of 1801, Clementi (who had now gone into business on his own, in consequence of the failure of Longman and Broderip) writes to Pleyel of Paris announcing the publication of three sonatas and various other compositions by Field, whom he describes as 'a very promising genius, and already become a great favourite in this country both in respect to composition and performance.'

Master and Pupil go Abroad

In the summer of 1802, master and pupil visited Paris, where Field's playing of Bach, Handel, and Clementi excited great admiration. A similar success was achieved in Vienna; there Clementi had intended to leave him, under the care of Albrechtsberger, while he himself went on to St Petersburg, but when the time for parting arrived Field was so miserable at the impending separation that Clementi was moved to compassion and took him to Russia with him. Arrived in St Petersburg, Clementi lost no time in opening a showroom for the display of his firm's pianos, and once again Field was used as a demonstrator. Spohr, who was in Russia at this time, paid several visits to the showroom, and in later years he retained a vivid recollection of that 'pale, overgrown youth', whom he never met again: 'When Field, who had outgrown his clothes, sat down at the piano and stretched out his arms over the keyboard, so that his sleeves shrank nearly up to his elbows, his whole figure appeared awkward and stiff in the highest degree; but as soon as he began to play, everything else was forgotten, and *man war nur ein Ohr*.' It was generally believed, Spohr adds, that Field was kept on a very meagre allowance and was obliged to suffer many privations for the privilege of having such a distinguished teacher.

Success in Russia

In the summer of 1803 Clementi left Russia. Field stayed in St Petersburg and soon formed a large and remunerative teaching connexion, besides being much in demand as a concert pianist. He began to move in aristocratic circles, had his head somewhat turned, became lazy and absentminded, embroiled himself in various love affairs, and in 1808 married a young French actress from whom he subsequently parted after five years of disharmony. In 1814 he composed the first three of those *Nocturnes* which are his outstanding contribution to the art of music and in which he embodied an entirely new style of writing for the pianoforte. It was left for Chopin to bring this new genre to perfection, but it was quite certainly Field who invented it; and indeed Anton Rubinstein, who devoted the last years of his career to a series of 'historical' pianoforte recitals in the principal cities of Europe, used to maintain that Field was the founder of modern pianoforte music and pianoforte playing. At about the same time, Field produced some more concertos and a *Rondo Écossais*, which became very popular. Further Nocturnes appeared in 1817 (including the example in A major which Dr Ernest Walker, in his *History of Music in England* declared to be Field's masterpiece), besides four concertos and several miscellaneous compositions. Meanwhile, in spite of his unreliable habits, his reputation as pianist and teacher continued to expand; among his pupils at this period was Glinka, the 'father' of modern Russian music, who in later years wrote of him: 'Field's playing was at once sweet and strong and characterized by admirable precision. His fingers fell on the keys as large raindrops which spread themselves like iridescent pearls . . . I do not share the opinion of Liszt, who told me once that he found Field's playing "sleepy". No, it was not sleepy; on the contrary, it was vigorous, capricious, and spontaneous. In particular, he never descended to charlatanism to produce his effects.'

In 1822 Field moved from St Petersburg to Moscow, where he was again highly successful both as pianist and teacher. Among his pupils at this time was the English pianist Charles Neate, who was one of the original members of the Philharmonic Society of London (now the Royal Philharmonic Society) and had the distinction of giving the first performance of a Beethoven concerto in this country. In the following years Field allowed himself to drift into slovenly and intemperate habits; his health suffered in consequence, and he was twice reported to be dead. On the second occasion, anticipating Mark Twain's famous cable to the Associated Press ('the reports of my death are greatly exaggerated'), Field issued a denial of the rumour; the London musical journal *Harmonicon* published the following paragraph in June 1831:

The report of the famous John Field's death at the beginning of the year is unfounded. This great virtuoso on the piano-forte still lives; and if his love of retirement can be conquered, Europe need not yet renounce the expectation of being gratified by hearing him; but it is with difficulty he can resolve on any exhibition of his powers.

London Revisited

Towards the end of 1831 Field's alleged 'love of retirement' was so far overcome as to induce him to accept an invitation from the Philharmonic Society of London to play at one of their concerts in the following February. Among the Society's archives is a letter, written by Field to the Society's secretary a fortnight before the concert, from which one may infer a certain nervousness whether he could be relied upon to fulfil his engagement:

J. Field presents his Compts. to Mr Watts, and begs to state that nothing in his power shall prevent his having the honor of playing at the Philharmonique (*sic*) Concert of the 27th inst.

Field duly appeared on the appointed date. His contribution to the programme was his own concerto in E flat, of which the *Harmonicon* gives the following account:

His concerto in E flat differs materially from the more prevailing style; it is clear, melodious, and not so overloaded with what are called brilliant, but are in fact confused, passages, as we are now so much accustomed to hear. The middle movement, a *pastorale*, is exceedingly delicious, and excited a unanimous encore. The finale is very lively, though the whole was, perhaps, rather too long, the first movement particularly, which admits of abridgment. Mr Field has a rapid finger, and executes with the utmost degree of neatness. His taste is pure, and in expression he now and then reminds us of the great master of this style, Cramer.

About a fortnight after this event, Field's old master, Clementi, died, and Field was one of the chief mourners at the impressive public funeral organized by the Philharmonic Society. A little later in the same year Field was one of the principal guests at a reception given in London by Moscheles, where he met Mendelssohn, who was much charmed by his playing.

Last Years

In the winter of 1832–3 Field was persuaded to give some recitals in Paris, and there his reception was even more enthusiastic than in London. Those who heard him at his first recital (at the Conservatoire, on Christmas Day, 1832) and on subsequent occasions spoke of the marvellous mechanism of his fingers, his command of infinite nuances, his easy mastery of the greatest difficulties, his completely natural and unaffected demeanour at the pianoforte. 'As a pianist,' wrote Joseph d'Ortigue, 'Field has no rival, whether as regards genre or method. He has no adopted system and is of no school . . . Field is Field – a school of his own . . . His music is the music of the fairies.'

After leaving Paris in the spring of 1833, Field embarked on a European tour, including Brussels, Toulouse, Marseilles, Lyons, Geneva, Milan, Florence, and Venice; everywhere he was received with the greatest enthusiasm. In May 1834, he arrived in Naples; and there the strain of overwork, coupled with his unwise mode of living, brought its penalty in the shape of a serious illness. An operation was necessary, and for nine weeks he lay ill in hospital, reduced to a wretched condition and too proud to seek aid from his friends in Moscow. Ultimately he was discovered and rescued by some Russian noblemen who happened to be visiting Naples, was taken by them to Ischia for a few weeks' convalescence, and thence *via* Venice to Vienna, where he was the guest of the famous teacher, Karl Czerny. In Vienna he was sufficiently recovered to give three concerts before fashionable and admiring audiences, also to compose a new concerto and a new nocturne. Towards the end of August 1835, he returned to Moscow, but a few months later he again fell desperately ill, and in the following January he died. It is related that, a few days before his death, his friends, thinking that he might appreciate a visit from a minister of religion, asked him whether he was a Catholic, a Protestant, or a Calvinist. 'Neither of them,' said Field; 'I'm a Pianist.'

ADOLF FERDINAND FRIEDRICH VON FLOTOW

1812–83

JOHN S. WEISSMANN

Childhood

The surprising fact of Adolf Ferdinand Friedrich Freiherr von Flotow's life is that he was almost entirely contemporary with Wagner; he was born one year earlier than his illustrious colleague, in 1812, and both of them died in 1883. Flotow came from an ancient landed Prussian family, whose forefathers could be traced back to the twelfth century. Of the several branches of this family the composer comes from the so-called Wildkühl lineage, residing in Mecklenburg-Schwerin. They were usually high Court and State officials or officers in the Army. Our composer was born on 27 April 1812, in Teutendorf, the family estate in Mecklenburg. His father, Johannes Adolf Wilhelm von Flotow, a captain of the horse, was compelled to do some hard work in order to put the heavily mortgaged land on a basis that would secure a comfortable living for the family; little by little he was able, through his diligence, not only to repay his creditors, but also to increase his domains by the purchase of some additional properties, among them Wutzig, a rather large estate in Pomerania. Yet he found time to enjoy music: he was a passable flute-player. One is tempted to think that his predilection for the flute originated not so much in the intrinsic merit of the instrument as in the fact that it had been the favourite instrument of Frederick the Great, King of Prussia, idolized by a few, hated by many, but respected and imitated by all his subjects.

The father, however, looked upon music merely as one of the noble and harmless pursuits that refreshed mind and body during the all too short hours of leisure. Having arrived at this fixed conclusion, he stuck to it with determination, much to the later despair of his son. His mother on the other hand was of less stern nature; she played the piano and sang tolerably. The children, Frederick and his sister Bernardine, were under her care. It was she who noticed that little Frederick, barely four years at that time, could recognize every note played on the piano; also, whenever father betook himself to playing the flute, the boy could not be enticed away from the room and would listen enraptured to the music.

When the boy reached his tenth year, it was decided to place him under the care of a parson in a nearby town. His mentor, however, proved to be a devotee to Bacchus and therefore the boy's studies lagged behind. But the parson was a good musician and so young Frederick made headway in his piano-playing. This fact was not altogether to his father's liking, and – after keeping the boy at home for some time – he found near Güstrow a place for his son where, at a curate's dwelling, lodgings and tuition were provided for scions of noble houses. Thanks to his mother's intervention it was also arranged that young Frederick would take music lessons with the organist in Güstrow. He would go to the town on Saturdays and spend the rest of the day and Sunday at his uncle's. Uncle Gabillon, husband of the sister of Frederick's mother, had a job at the office of taxes and was an enthusiastic music-lover. Unlike the amateurs of the present era, he was not content with a passive interest in it, but spent most of his time in organizing and leading the local choral and orchestral society.

All this of course was a heaven-sent opportunity for Frederick. As he possessed a good voice, it was not long before he was regularly attending rehearsals, thereby gaining invaluable experience which no text-books of that time could provide. It may be surmised that his music-studies had brought some fruit at about that time; yet definite proof of his creative activity exists only in the form of a letter dated 1826. In this letter, sent to his mother after a further change of address and mentor, he refers to a sonata nearing its completion.

Mention has already been made of his father's unwillingness to consider music as a suitable career for his son. He gave him a careful education and visualized the civil service, leading eventually to a diplomatic post, as an occupation for him. But all his plans were shattered when Frederick presented his case, saying that he had seriously resolved to make music his profession, and asked his father to consent to his studying with this end in view. He could not resist his inner impulse, he declared, yet would not like to be disobedient. It was not so much the social unsuitability of music as an occupation that caused Flotow senior's misgivings as the fact that he was not convinced of his son's talent. Here at length the opinion of Müller the clarinettist – combined with Uncle Gabillon's eloquence – proved to be decisive, and a journey to Paris was resolved on.

Paris, July Revolution, Flight, Return to Paris

In 1828, then, Flotow arrived in Paris, found quarters at the home of a major who also shared his table with him and strove to provide a substitute home-life for the youth. As for his music-studies, he took lessons in composition from the famous Anton Reicha, one of the foremost teachers of his time, writer of several text-books and himself a composer. In piano he enjoyed the tuition of Johann Peter Pixis, equally renowned in the field of piano-instruction.

Flotow set to work with Teutonic thoroughness and determination: at that time he cared little about the brilliant social life of Paris. His teachers were completely satisfied with his progress – especially in composition – which only a serious attack of smallpox checked for a while; but even in the hospital he was full of plans and looked forward to resuming his studies. The year of 1830 was a fateful one for young Flotow. First, in March, his host, the major with whom he stayed, committed suicide. Flotow now stood alone in the great city; undismayed he took a small room in the Quartier Latin. In addition to this, the outbreak of revolution, which he witnessed, affected him profoundly. Charles X, king of France, an autocratic ruler, took the return of a liberal administration by a recent general election as a personal affront. On the instigation of Polignac he issued an ordinance suspending most of the hard-won civil liberties of the nation. This was the signal for the July revolution of 1830. There was street-fighting, but the National Guard went over to the people after a few days' resistance, and Charles X was driven away.

How did these events affect our composer; what did Flotow do? His attitude could not be called heroic; not even courageous. One must admit, however, that Flotow had hardly any connexions with the 'life' of Paris; he lived for his studies only. There is a description in his posthumous papers of the eventful 27 July. As he left his abode to have some dinner, he found 'to his surprise' the restaurants closed. Alarmed by the noise of shooting in the distance, he took refuge in the house of some acquaintances nearby, and after a restless night and exciting day he thought it wiser to return home to Teutendorf; which demeanour did not exactly conform to the family traditions of army officers.

Arrived home, he looked forward to meeting Uncle Gabillon and showing him the results of his studies. In fact, the idea of a performance of Flotow's compositions was very welcome to the uncle. The society of which Flotow used to be a member was suffering from a growing material loss, and Uncle Gabillon hoped that young Flotow would prove a 'sure draw'. One of his two *Overtures* and his *Concerto for Piano* were included in the programme. The performance proved to be a great success, Uncle Gabillon scored a personal triumph, and the finances of the society were improved beyond expectation.

During the winter he stayed at home and finished his first opera, *Pierre et Cathérine*, on which he had begun work in Paris. The text came from Vernoy de Saint-Georges, a successful and prolific librettist and playwright, who collaborated with nearly all opera-composers of his day. In the spring of 1831 Flotow returned to Paris, this time however in different circumstances. Now he could afford to move in society; recognizing this to be the surest way to success, he frequented those places where he could meet influential people: salons, residences of the great, theatrical green rooms, and so on. He made the acquaintance of Adam and Halévy, and Gounod, Donizetti, and Meyerbeer invited him to take part in a theatrical venture; the plan however did not materialize. By this time he was so well accepted in the salons that it was a comparatively easy matter to introduce a talented cellist, Jacob Eberst, to one of those mansions. The Countess of Bertin de Vaux was prepared to let Jacques Offenbach – for so the talented cellist called himself – play at her next reception. Flotow even collaborated in composing some suitable pieces for cello and piano for the event.

However complete his success in society, he did not neglect his compositions. He shared a flat with Edward Bergounioux, his librettist, and work went on rapidly on Flotow's second *opéra comique La Lettre du Préfet*, which was performed (privately) in 1837. The libretto seems to have been in three acts, but the performed opera consisted of one act only. He also had various plans for operas, songs, and piano pieces and even sketches for a symphony, of which he wrote in his letters. In these he also depicts the society and its personages of the period in question. At a hunt to which he was invited he made the acquaintance of Count Ribbing, known as de Leuwen, the renowned librettist and later director of the Opéra Comique. Similarly, there is a description of his meeting Chopin at the house of the Marquis Custine. Chopin's playing made a great impression on him; the more so as he was a rather inefficient pianist himself.

Pierre et Cathérine, his first work, was staged in Schwerin in 1834; although he was pleased to hear of the performance at the Court Theatre, he did not attach too much importance to it, as he thought Germany at that time to be an unsuitable place for operatic performances. In France, the residences of the aristocracy usually possessed a private stage and generally the most lavish entertainments followed one another sometimes on the same evening. The custom of the Roi Soleil, acting and dancing in person, became a fashion in these circles, and Flotow was welcome in those houses both as a nobleman of equal social standing and as a musician. It was, therefore, comparatively easy to arrange performances of his works on those private stages. One of the first of his operas so performed was *Rob Roy*, the libretto based on Sir Walter Scott's novel by Paul Duport and de Forges (Desforges), the latter's wife singing one of the parts at the Hôtel de Castellane in 1837. *La Seraphina*, with libretto by de Forges after a play by Frédéric Soulié followed, performed at the home of the Marquis Bellissen at Royaumont in October 1836, Mme de Forges again singing in it.

First Public Successes

His debut at a professional theatre took place at the Théâtre Palais-Royal on 19 November 1836. The play, *Comte de Charolais*, written by Duport and de Forges, contained some music, to which Flotow contributed a chorus and a grand waltz. He had the pleasure of seeing his name printed on the playbill, although the curious spelling 'M. de Flotteaux' may have somewhat spoiled his happiness. The one-act drame lyrique, *Alice*, performed at de Castellane's on 8 April 1837, was based on Sir Walter Scott's novel again; his *Woodstock* was adapted for the stage by Count Sussy and de Laperrière. Among the aristocratic amateurs taking part in it were Mme de Forges and Philippe Panel, a close friend of Flotow. *Le Comte de St Mégrin*, performed on 10 June 1838, at Royaumont, marks a culmination in the appreciation of his aristocratic audience.

As his name and person were by now well known in society, the great success of *Mégrin* encouraged his friends to arrange a *soirée* to which the director of the Opéra Comique was to be invited. The efforts of his friends seemed to succeed: the director promised to attend. Mr

Crosnier indeed appeared, listened for a while, and then took his leave. Next day he stated to inquirers: 'I did not hear much, but the little I did hear of the German gentleman's music did not please me at all!' Undiscouraged, Flotow tried another method, which ultimately brought him the desired success. He entered into collaboration with Albert Grisar, a composer who had a few public performances to his credit and whom he had known since his student-days at Reicha's. The collaboration depended on one condition: at the beginning the works to be performed were to appear under Grisar's name only.

The first work thus produced was *Lady Melvil*, an *opéra comique* in three acts, text by Saint-Georges and de Leuwen, performed at the Théâtre de la Renaissance on 15 November 1838. This was followed by *L'Eau Merveilleuse*, an *opéra bouffe* in two acts, the libretto of which came from the pen of Thomas Sauvage, performed at the same theatre on 30 January 1839. The partnership was, however, not to last long. Grisar's health was failing and so the bigger share of the work was left to Flotow. Indeed in the following venture, *Le Naufrage de la Méduse*, of which the first act was composed by Pilati, the second by Flotow, and the third by Grisar, the share of the last was negligible. The opera, with a text by the brothers Coignard, was first performed at the Théâtre de la Renaissance on 31 May 1839. This opera established Flotow's position in the musical world of Paris. During the same season it had more than fifty performances, an average of two nights a week – a considerable success.

In this same year he finished his first absolutely 'independent' opera entitled *L'Âme Jalouse*, for which the libretto was written by Saint-Georges. In spite of Flotow's recent successes, the performance of this work encountered many obstacles. One of the causes of delay was the impending removal of the Théâtre de la Renaissance to its new building, henceforward called Théâtre Port Saint-Martin. At this point an occasion presented itself for a production of which the success abundantly compensated him for the previous delay. The Princess Czartoryska planned an amateur performance in aid of the ubiquitous Polish refugees. Her choice fell on Flotow's *Mégrin* which, thoroughly revised and carefully prepared, also rechristened *Le Duc de Guise* for the occasion, was performed in the Salle Ventadour on 3 April 1840. The performance, besides being a great success, had some far-reaching consequences. Mlle Lagrange, the world-famous soprano – for whom Erkel wrote a special *aria di bravura* on her first appearance in Budapest

– then at the beginning of her brilliant career, sang the leading part; and a Mr Friedrich Wilhelm Riese assisted in the chorus. Known in the literary world as Wilhelm Friedrich, he was a prolific playwright and journalist (having about a hundred plays to his credit), the librettist of Flotow's two future masterpieces. He was introduced on this occasion to the composer, and Flotow mentioned the encounter in a letter: 'During our lively conversation we talked frequently of operatic librettos.'

In 1843 the Opéra in Paris produced its annual ballet-novelty with music by Burgmüller, Deldevez, and Flotow. He obtained the commission for his share by a lucky chance. In fact, the subject of this ballet interested him so much that the opera on which his fame now rests, *Martha*, is based on the same story. At last the Opéra Comique opened its doors to the successful composer and *L'Esclave de Camoëns*, a one-act opera, text by Saint-Georges, with Flotow's music, was performed there on 1 December 1843. His fame also began to spread in Germany. *Mégrin* was performed at the Court Theatre of Schwerin in 1841, and his *Médusa* was to be performed on one of the foremost stages in that country when the complete material was lost in the great fire of Hamburg in 1842. Undaunted, Flotow partly reconstituted, partly rewrote, the work to Riese's new libretto. Entitled *Die Matrosen* it was performed in Hamburg on 23 December 1845. It was, however, with *Alessandro Stradella*, a three-act romantic opera, with a libretto by Riese, performed on 30 December 1844, that Flotow reached full maturity. At the end of the performance in Hamburg copies of a eulogistic poem were showered from the balcony in a scene reminiscent of the *Fidelio* production some forty years earlier in Vienna. His next opera, *L'Âme en Peine*, transformed from the previous *L'Âme Jalouse*, was also very popular and received performances on the Continent and also in England. It was produced for the first time at the Opéra in Paris on 29 June 1846.

Germany

The great success of *Stradella* induced the directors of the Court Opera in Vienna – now known as the Kärntnerthortheater – to commission a work for their stage. The invitation resulted in *Martha or The Fair of Richmond*, practically his only opera that lives to-day. The libretto of *Martha* is based on Vernoy de Saint-George's plot for their earlier *Lady Henriette*, adapted by Riese. The music was composed partly at Teutendorf, whither he had returned from Paris, and partly in Vienna; in fact, he wrote the overture during the rehearsals. After the first performance in Vienna on 25 September 1847, it was produced subsequently all over the world.

The fact that the romantic-comic opera *Martha* was the work that endeared him with the public implies a disposition to melodious, freely accessible style, which he cultivated with such distinction. The felicity of melodic invention, almost Mozartian in its ease, the smoothness of harmonic scheme, eschewing 'experimental originality', the clearness of orchestral colouring – these are the features that predominate, especially in his comic operas. Though discriminating in his choice of librettos, he tended rather to play for applause when confronted with the alternative of dramatic fidelity or immediate effectiveness. This explains his comparative failure in more serious subjects: here his contemporaries, not always averse to exaggerated effects, scored an easy victory over his fastidious discrimination. Whenever he strove to be the learned musician, he lost his way; but listening to his particular inspiration he wrote music that remains always enjoyable.

Family Affairs

Shortly after Flotow's triumph in Vienna, his father died in 1847, and the death of his younger brother followed in 1848. These sad events necessitated his return to the paternal domain, the estate at Teutendorf. Also, the accounts and generally the management of the estates had to be attended to. The revolution of 1848, too, made him eschew the places which seemed to be dangerous to his person and career. One must state the fact that profound manifestations of the human will to liberty were not over-attractive to him! Just as he took to his heels in 1830, he repeated that performance in 1848, this time, however, with more dignity. His collaborator Riese mildly reproached him for 'sitting comfortably in Wutzig', the result of which was that Flotow turned elsewhere for the libretto of his next opera.

The book to *Sophie Catherine* or *Die Grossfürstin* came from Mme Charlotte Birch-Pfeiffer, and the work was produced in Berlin on 19 November 1850. Palpable results of this venture were his decoration with the Cross of St John and some years later his appointment to Schwerin. These years reveal him at the summit of his musical career as well as of his society success; the time seemed favourable for marriage. Accordingly, he took to wife Elisa Sophie Philippine von Zadow, the daughter of a squire whose estates lay in the neighbourhood of the Flotows'. The ceremony took place in 1849, but his happiness was painfully short: his wife died in 1851 and their child followed her the same year. Their home, now full of painful memories, was unbearable to the composer, so he decided to let it and go to visit his parents-in-law. There he made the acquaintance of a young nobleman, Gustav Heinrich Gäns zu Putlitz, a gifted *littérateur*, who later wrote a number of librettos for him. During his enforced residence in the countryside he began – and then abandoned – one opera, and another, entitled *Rübezahl*, was performed by amateurs at Retzin (in Pomerania) on 13 August 1853. Preceding his second marriage, *Indra* – a transformed version of *L'Esclave de Camoëns* – was produced at Vienna on 18 December 1852. For it, Gäns zu Putlitz, a favourite of Flotow, furnished the libretto. Apart from its success with the public, the dedication of the work to the Emperor brought him another decoration. His second marriage took place in Vienna, in 1853, with Anna Theen. He bought an estate near the Imperial city, the scene of his great success. Of the three children one boy, later the squire of Teutendorf, outlived him by fifteen years.

Opera Manager

Scarcely did the couple settle down in their new home when Flotow received an invitation to the post of Intendant of the Court Theatre in Schwerin. Having had some experience in theatrical matters, especially on their musical side, he looked forward to entering upon his duties in 1855. The post also carried the title of 'Grand-Ducal Chamberlain of Mecklenburg-Schwerin'.

He did not, however, reckon with the intrigues and wire-pullings, those exciting side-issues of the theatrical game. In 1862 he grew tired of the 'seven years' war' and relinquished his post. Yet during his arduous work, whereby he improved the general standard of performances and musical taste, he found time for productive work; the operas *Johann Albrecht* (also called *Andreas Mylius*), *Albin*; the one-act operettas *Pianella*, *La Veuve Grapin*; the pantomimes *Die Gruppe der Thetis*, *Libelle*, *Tanzkönig*; a *Jubel-Overture*; and instrumental compositions (*Fackeltanz*, *String Quartet*, etc.) were produced at Schwerin.

He became acquainted with the well-known Austrian writer Dingelstedt, who adapted *The Winter's Tale* for a production in Weimar, which should have taken place on the birthday of the Grand Duke. In fact, the performance was postponed by a few months to October 1859, owing to Flotow's delay with the music.

The same year saw the production of *La Veuve Grapin* at Paris in the theatre of his old friend, Offenbach. *Albin*, however, did not prove to be viable: it failed even in Germany, where it was entitled *Der Müller von Meran*, greatly to the mortification of Flotow, who rewrote and refashioned it up to the end of his life. The pantomime *Tanzkönig* and two other *divertimenti*, *William of Orange in Whitehall* and *Der Königsschuss*, were his last contributions to the Schwerin stage before he left for Paris, to reconquer the musical world there. *Zilda* was designed for the purpose, performed at de Leuwen's Opéra Comique on 28 May 1866. The libretto, by Saint-Georges and Chirot, was based on a story by Voltaire. Shortly before his third and last marriage *Am Runenstein*, a romantic opera, was staged at Prague. The wedding took place in Vienna on 9 August 1868, when he married Rosa Theen, a sister of his second wife, whom he divorced in 1867. Rosa Theen was a devoted spouse: she managed the affairs of her husband and at Hirschwang kept house frequented by musicians, writers, and artists. Their daughter Bernardine was still living in Innsbruck in 1940.

In these congenial and stimulating surroundings the comic opera *Die Musikanten* was finished in collaboration with Richard Genée, a musician and writer, author of popular operettas. This work, however, was not performed in Flotow's lifetime. (The first performance was at Mannheim on 19 June 1887.) During his Vienna period he was elected a corresponding member of the Institut de France. Before the outbreak of the Franco-Prussian war, *L'Ombre*, a three-act *opéra comique*, libretto by Saint-Georges and de Leuwen, was performed at the Opéra Comique on 7 July 1870. This is his most distinguished work, perhaps not even excluding *Stradella* and *Martha*. The reason for its neglect is perhaps the fact that the chorus is altogether dispensed with: there are but four principals and therefore a 'large-scale production' is out of the question.

Last Period

After the war the atmosphere was not propitious for a 'German gentleman' to live in, so he went to the family estate in Teutendorf, now managed by the son of his second marriage. His opera, *Fleur de Harlem* (libretto by Saint-Georges and de Leuwen, adapted from

Dumas' *Black Tulip* and finished while in Vienna) was produced, under the Italianized title, *Il Fiore d'Arlem*, at the Vittorio Emmanuele Theatre in Turin on 18 November 1876. Yet Paris did not remain closed to him for long. A revised version of *Indra*, now entitled *Alma l'Incantatrice*, was produced at the Théâtre Italien, with Albani in the title-role, on 9 November 1878. Shortly afterwards he migrated to his sister's residence in the Grand-Duchy of Hesse, near Darmstadt, from which place he travelled frequently to Vienna, Paris, and other places, mostly in connexion with his operas. Owing to his worsening eye-sight work was becoming increasingly difficult for him, yet he composed a series of songs and finished an opera, *Sakuntala*.

In 1882 the directors of the Court Opera in his beloved Vienna invited him to attend the five hundredth performance of *Martha* on his seventieth birthday. Shortly before his death he began work on an aria for Etelka Gerster, the Hungarian soprano. His death followed an apoplectic stroke on 24 January 1883.

CÉSAR AUGUSTE FRANCK

1822–90

W. R. ANDERSON

Origins in Liège

Though Franck was born before Beethoven died, affection for his music is a comparatively late manifestation among us. When the standard dictionary of music, Grove's, was first issued, in 1879, Franck had lived as long as the whole term of Beethoven's life, fifty-seven years; yet there was no mention of him in the dictionary. The vogue of Franck's music in England (apart from that of the organ works, earlier prized by church musicians) is practically all within the last generation – mostly after the first decade of this century, and in particular during and after the first Great War, when we found more sympathy and programme-space for French music, and for that of other allies, to replace the art of enemy nations.

During his life Franck scarcely achieved the highest recognition, though he was known as a devoted, high-minded artist. His temperament was quietist, his mind humble. D. G. Mason aptly compared him to Amiel. His Catholic piety found little favour in high political quarters in France: the ancient conflict between clericalism and anti-clericalism accounted for that.

Though Franck worked for most of his life in Paris, he was not a Frenchman. He was born in the Walloon part of the Netherlands, of an old family descended from distinguished painters, some of whom emigrated in the sixteenth century (as César did, some two hundred and fifty years later). His birthplace was Liège, a city of disturbed history, whose famous churches gave him early impressions of ancient beauty, some of which he transferred to paper, for he was fond of drawing.

Liège, seat of a prince-bishopric, had produced in the eighteenth century some writers of comic operas. Others wrote farces and burlesques which had their romantic side, in vivid and sometimes touching pictures of the country's ways and beliefs. In the mid-fifties of the nineteenth century a Society began to study Walloon literature; its success was immediate, and permanent.

Long a centre of learning, Liège had seen constant struggles for freedom from its lordly-episcopal rulers. The beginning of the seventeenth century found it in the midst of civil war. Later, the citizens lost power. The revolution of 1789 brought forth many songs, some patriotic, some satirical. In Napoleon's day the principality was annexed to France. Seven years before Franck was born it was freed by the Congress of Vienna, and before young César left it he witnessed its participation in the Belgian upthrust of 1830.

It may be noted in passing that Liège brought forth an astonishing number of fine musicians, from the fifteenth century. The best known names in recent times have been those of violinists – Massart, Léonard César Thompson, and Ysaye; of composers, the most familiar are Grétry and Jongen. It has a Conservatoire of music, which awards a Prix de Rome, with the institution at Brussels.

A perceptive musician of Franck's native land has said that the composer's music is truly Belgian, 'with the high colours of the Flemish painters and the melancholic and *tourmentée* line which is characteristic of the Walloon people'. We think of the familiar chromatic harmony of Franck: not the harmony of an ascetic, but of a romantic, mystic; and of his wrestling-Jacob melodic line, with its sense of opposition overcome, of struggle and pleading, as A. J. Hutchings has well put it: a quality also felt in his melodies' tendency first to fall back from, and then successfully to achieve, a climax note. There are debits to the account of romantic mysticism, but the attraction for congenial minds is strong.

Training

César's father, a bank clerk, showed perhaps the dourer aspects of paternal care, but he had a share of the family's artistic leanings, and saw to it that both his sons should be well trained in music. Joseph, though little known in comparison with César, became a composer of solid merit. César took first to the piano, Joseph to the violin. A course at the Conservatoire was cut short by his father's taking César on a concert tour, with the idea of his entering on the life of a virtuoso (one recalls that other less than fully wise parent, Leopold Mozart). The partial object was to earn some money for further study, in Paris. There in 1836 they went, and the youth first took lessons from the Bohemian comporer Reicha, a friend of Beethoven's, who had settled in the capital in 1808. Franck next entered the Conservatoire, where he studied composition with Leborne, a fellow-countryman, himself trained at the Conservatoire, and the successor of Reicha. Like most composers, he wrote operas, but Franck did not go the general way by attempting such works; it was only late in life that he tried that form, and then without success.

His piano teacher was P. J. G. Zimmermann (French, despite his name), a versatile musician who also wrote treatises on harmony, and an *Encyclopaedia of Pianists*, and composed concertos and operas.

The severity of outlook of the Director, Cherubini, produced a rebuke for Franck when, in competing for a prize, he was given a piece to read at sight, and, perhaps innocently showing off, played it in a different key from that in which it was written. Instead of being given extra credit for the double feat, César was refused the prize, but given a specially-created consolation award, never again conferred.

He had won prizes for writing fugues and, in 1841, for playing the organ, which he always loved. His teacher here was Benoist, himself a product of Conservatoire teaching, who also directed the choir at the Opera. Over thirty years later, Franck succeeded his former master in this teaching post. In this particular organ competition, Franck again showed his keen musicianship in a very difficult test: that of improvising a movement in sonata form, and one in fugue style. He had the wit to notice that the two subjects would combine and duly made them work together. Apparently he was rapt away (as in later years he often was when extemporizing), and his treatment exceeded the usual examination limit. The examiners deemed the exhibition unacademic, or unfitting the occasion, for they would not give him the prize. Benoist, in the end, got them to see the inequity of disqualifying his pupil, and they awarded Franck a second prize.

His ambition was to compete for the famous Prix de Rome, a scholarship allowing some years' residence in Italy, which is awarded for the best work in various departments of art, including painting, sculpture, music, and architecture. Musicians had to compose a cantata. The winner resided at the Villa Medici in Rome and was required to show progress in composition, as well as being permitted to develop his interests in other ways.

But Franck's father was again uneasy about the immediate future, and anxious to see his son set upon his career as a pianist, one which the early Belgian tour had made to seem so promising. In César's twentieth year he was removed from the Conservatoire. His father seems to have had also some hope of distinguished patronage, for he caused César to dedicate some of his early pieces to the King of the Belgians. For two years these not very fruitful methods were pursued, with violin and piano recitals by '*les frères Franck*', and César's composition of pot-pourris, fantasias, and the like, which were described on their title-pages as by 'César-Auguste Franck, of Liège'.

After this early piano writing Franck neglected such composition until much later; near the end of his life appeared the only piano piece that we now cherish. There is a gap of something like forty years between the two periods. As early as 1832 he had tried his hand in this way, his first variations on an operatic air having been written when he was between eleven and twelve, and numbered Op. 5. Three years later he conceived his first sonata, which he dedicated to his brother Joseph. There are other items in these manuscript early works, which run to Op. 18 and show that he had taken to a not very profitable pianistic path: for whoever might be a born writer of drawing-room tit-bits, it was certainly not Franck. He even wrote (as have dozens of others) a piece on *God save the King*. He was seeking, it would appear, to fall in with the habits and tastes of his audiences and showed, naturally enough, the influence of composers already familiar to him – Liszt, his countryman Grétry, the opera composer, and Weber.

Paris and Marriage

The father's chosen way of life proving unpropitious, another two years found the family again in Paris, this time for good. Life was difficult, but both sons were used to hard work. César was to devote the greater part of his life to the toil of teaching and the daily work of a parish organist. In a measure he was thus pursuing the path of one of his idols, Bach. There are few finer examplars of modest devotion to duty and the work that came to hand than Franck. The work must often have been irksome, but he had been well trained and could school his spirit.

Franck found favour from the Conservatoire for the performance in 1846 of his 'eclogue' on the Biblical subject of *Ruth*. Not all who heard it appreciated its naïve simplicity: that quality was scarcely paramount in the kinds of music that Paris was then hearing – largely the operatic splendours of Auber and Meyerbeer. Franck's interest in Biblical subjects was also marked by his composition of a symphony, somewhat in the Lisztian manner (that is, more after the style of the symphonic poem), entitled *The Sermon on the Mount*. This, which remained unpublished, was later used, in part, in *The Beatitudes*. These years, culminating in the widespread European troubles of 1838, were hard ones for the Franck family. César had fallen in love with an actress, whom his parents' strictness did not favour. The girl's mother, who was also on the stage as a tragic actress, used to express disappointment, urging that Franck ought to have become a priest; there had been many priest-musicians in the Catholic church, but the double profession, or dedication, did not notably survive into the nineteenth century, when anti-clerical forces strengthened. Madame Desmousseaux, the mother-in-law, obviously did not share her new relative's ideas about the kind of composition to which he should devote himself. She thought of profits; and Franck's shrinking from the acceptance of a possible engagement as conductor in a theatre also tended to alienate her. He had become organist at the church of Notre Dame de Lorette, and it was here, amid the revolution of 1848, that he was married, the couple having on the way to climb over the barricade manned by the citizens.

On his own side of the family, too, Franck caused disappointment in this marriage; his father saw disappearing his last hope of making a living from his chief virtuoso son. The revolution had upset teaching: there were very few pupils; yet Franck had the determination of mind to leave home and set up another with his wife. Few geniuses can have had a less promising start in married life.

From this time he accepted cheerfully much that to such a man must have been drudgery: but it is arguable that a spirit so high, modest, simple, and earnest refines the harshnesses of life and finds happiness in duty and service, giving little thought to worldly applause or profit. Without attributing saintliness to Franck, this seems to be true of him.

Organist and Teacher

Things looked dark. When they had a child, the wife had to help eke out a living by taking part in plays and even singing patriotic songs in cafés and cabarets. Perhaps the marriage was a mistake; but the child was a joy to him. So he began forty-two years of hard work:

teaching, organ-playing, choir training, and composing in the holes and corners of spare time – chiefly got by very early rising.

It was in this part of his life that Franck wrote an opera, *Le Valet de Ferme*, which was never produced or printed. This labour of 1851–3 meant late nights and morning hours stolen from rest. Harm was wrought to his nerves, and he tired easily; yet his strong constitution survived the wastage of force, and the disappointment. As with the early piano writing, here was another door that could not be forced for any prospect of profit. Franck's powers were of quite other orders, and he had to spend years in finding out where they lay.

He had improved his position as an organist, and had moved from his first church; in 1858 he moved again, to St Clotilde. His organ career expanded in 1872, when he succeeded his old teacher Benoist as professor of that instrument at the Conservatoire. He deeply loved it, unlike most other composers of his age. As he lay dying, Franck was working at the final bars of some of his best organ music. His affection for the instrument and its art was lasting and pure. St Clotilde was for him a double shrine – altar and organ – for he was a faithful son of the Church and would leave the keyboard at the climax of the service to kneel with the other worshippers.

Strength and Weakness

His pupil Vincent d'Indy has left a vivid picture of the church, the dark stairway to the loft, and Franck improvising upon an instrument that to the pupils seemed almost sacred because of his presence. Liszt came to hear him, and asserted that only Bach could have equalled his improvisation in beauty of style and perfection of form.

Franck's aspiration had long been fixed, in composition, upon what might be allowed to be a perfect subject for that meditative spirit which always brought out the best of his power: the Sermon on the Mount. In 1869 he was working, then, at *Les Béatitudes*, one of the tenderest of his testaments of beauty, an oratorio for solo voices, chorus, and orchestra, in eight parts and a prologue, which he dedicated to his wife, and upon which he spent a decade's loving thought. He had already composed a good deal of church music – motets, anthems, masses, and some organ pieces.

The Beatitudes appeals to some as being in the succession of late Beethoven. Its weakness, typical of Franck, is that simplicity sometimes fell into banality. This is true of a good deal of his other, and smaller, church pieces, some of which he wrote at short notice, to supply a choir's needs. In the midst of fervour, the romantic-mystic is apt to be too easily satisfied with a rather cheap phrase. Franck's strong sense of order, too, could lead him into using a formal phrase not always bent to high creative purpose, though unrecognized as a blemish by the composer.

Operas and Tone-Poems

Franck again attempted opera twice during his last period: with *Hulda* (1882–5) and *Ghisèle* (1888–9). These were not produced in his lifetime: he had of course no reputation in that line of work, and little influence; they appear to have been given, once each, at Monte Carlo – an odd place to associate with the name of Franck.

Hulda, based upon a play by the Norwegian Björnson, deals with racial feuds in eleventh century Norway. Only the ballet from it, *The Contest between Winter and Spring*, has been heard in concert performance. *Ghisèle*, which has something of the same pagan-versus-Christian motivation, was left incomplete as to the orchestration and finished by some of Franck's pupils. The plot is akin to that of *Aïda*, the period being the middle of the sixth century. Those who know this score declare that for once Franck, who in other works had failed in depicting evil (Satan in *The Redemption*, and *Le Chasseur Maudit*, for instance), had succeeded therein.

A few tone-poems, besides *The Accursed Hunter*, figure in Franck's output. That one is most often heard; but there are *Les Éolides, Les Djinns* (with pianoforte), and *Psyche* (with chorus). On the whole, Franck's part was that of a creator of non-programme music: he could leave the tone-poem to men like Liszt and Strauss. Franck's influence was of a wholly different kind. He avoided the weaknesses into which French music fell after Berlioz. In that time one finds the mingled classicism and rather superficial sentiment of a Saint-Saëns, and the melodrama of a Gounod. Wagnerian influence, when the effects of 1870 had somewhat worn off, was powerful. Later an anti-Wagnerian cult developed, and French individualism asserted itself: naturalism and Symbolism flourished, and Chabrier and Fauré extended and widened the work of Franck; but no composer has deepened it, if we take it at its best.

Latest and Best Works

Franck's biggest works came in his final years: in his last decade flowered the symphony, the exquisite symphonic variations, the too few best organ and piano pieces, the violin sonata, the quartet and quintet: mostly single works, one in each form or style, masterly, individual, climatic blooms of late maturity. Franck was the kind of creator who must brood and meditate long. In his later years he had clouds of witness in his pupils, adoring 'Pater Seraphicus'. Among them – either pupils or men strongly influenced by Franck – were the bulk of the best men at the end of the century: d'Indy, Duparc, Chausson, Pierre de Bréville, Bordes, Pierné, Guy Ropartz, and many another.

Franck had no talent or spirit for the pursuit of official honours. He was made an Officer of the Academy, but was not created a Chevalier of the Legion of Honour until he was within five years of his death. A would-be celebratory concert of his works, upon that event, was under-rehearsed and poor in effect; yet when his friends deplored this, Franck, ever easily pleased by the efforts of others, though not by his own, murmured, 'My dear friends, you are too exacting, I am quite satisfied.'

It was while pursuing his faithful way as a teacher, going along the street on his way to give a lesson, that Franck was struck by the pole of an omnibus. From this apparently slight mishap pleurisy developed and six months later he was dead. His last act of creative faith was the completion of his *Chorales* for organ.

The burial was at Montrouge, the bearers including a cousin, with Saint-Saëns, Delibes, and a representative of his organ pupils, Dallier. But the Conservatoire was not officially represented by any professor. The last words were spoken over the grave by his friend and pupil Chabrier, who paid tribute to a great artist and an 'incomparable teacher, whose wonderful work has produced a whole generation of forceful musicians, believers and thinkers, armed at all points for hard fought and prolonged conflicts. We salute also,' he said, 'the upright and just man, so humane, so distinguished, whose counsels were sure as his words were kind. Farewell!'

Recognition came slowly, and late; but to-day Franck's best work has a permanent place in the affection of nearly all music-lovers, who like to think of his gentle spirit's benediction as a comfort in a bitter world.

NIELS WILHELM GADE

1817–90

NILS L. WALLIN

Childhood and Youth in Copenhagen

Niels Wilhelm Gade was born on 22 February 1817 in Copenhagen. He was the only child of Sören Nielsen Gade, a joiner, and Marie Sophie Hansdatter Arentzen Gade. His father was a frank, lively man of a somewhat romantic and dreamy character, but his mother – although a little nervous – was a practical woman, attending strictly to her duties. 'As to Father I have no fears at all, he has always a good humour, but my dear Mother must learn to see the world from its bright side,' Niels Wilhelm writes in a letter to his parents in April 1847. His father bought a workshop for musical instruments. He was a dilettante in music, but not altogether lacking musical talents. He gave his son a small child's guitar and was able to teach him the simpler chords.

The boy's greatest interest during his earlier years was the theatre. His neighbour and best friend, Frederik Hoedt, had a great enthusiasm for the theatre, which could not but influence the young nimble-minded and imaginative guitar player. Hoedt was later to become one of Denmark's most famous actors with Hamlet as his most prominent character. Niels Wilhelm had ample time to dream and fancy, as he was not sent to school until the age of ten. At the same time he also began to study the violin, his teacher being a viola player by name of Moeller, a second-class musician both as artist and as teacher.

When after confirmation a profession was to be chosen for the young man, there was no thought of either theatre or music. Such plans were regarded as too expensive altogether. It was decided, therefore, that he should become an honest joiner, and he was accordingly taken into his father's workshop as an apprentice.

Studies – First Compositions

Here he worked for a year and a half, but then, having had enough of it, he openly revolted against his parents. He told them that he had made up his mind to become a musician and not a joiner. His parents understood him. They gave him the best violin teacher at that time to be found in Copenhagen, Wexschall, a member of the Royal Orchestra, and from him Niels Wilhelm Gade began to take lessons in October 1832. At the same time he carried on theoretical studies, his teacher being A. P. Berggreen, who certainly also taught his pupil to play the organ and the piano. In February 1834 Gade began studies of the violin at the music School of the Royal Orchestra, the best way for a violinist to make a career being to get an engagement as a member of this orchestra.

By this time his studies of composition began to bear fruit. Berggreen, his teacher, was the editor of a musical review in Copenhagen, and in this was published a song composed by Gade to Goethe's poem, 'Lebet wohl, geliebte Bäume'. Gade also tried his ability at greater tasks. He succeeded in persuading the members of the Royal Orchestra to play his overture to Oehlenschläger's tragedy, *Socrates*. The result, however, was a disappointment to young Gade, and he burned the composition at once. It did not sound as he had thought it ought, and he realized that he had to sit in the orchestra and learn more about this complicated instrument. But he was too impatient. Only for a short time did he play in the orchestra as a pupil with a very small salary. He then applied for his discharge, saying that he wished to see the world. Probably he planned to go to Ludwig Spohr in Cassel, his ambition being to be a composer and a virtuoso at the same time. Fate had, however, intended that he should go in the opposite direction. In the company of another musician, he set out on a tour to Sweden and Norway, but the trip was not a great success. In Stockholm he played at the opera during the intervals between the acts. His visit to Norway, we may suppose, must have made a very strong impression on him, for here he encountered scenery that fascinated him and spoke to his imagination. It is difficult to say how much these impressions inspired his later *Ossian* music, but it seems certain that they were not without importance. From an economic point of view the tour was a failure. To be able to get home again Gade had to write to his father and ask for money; when he got back to Copenhagen, he resumed his place as a pupil at the Royal Orchestra school as if nothing had happened.

By and by, however, he succeeded in making people believe in his talents as a composer. In 1839 he wrote for Det Konglige Teater (the Royal Theatre) the music to *Aladdin*, and some of his songs were published in a book of patriotic songs, which meant a Scandinavian reputation for him. At this time he also composed the piano sonata in E minor, later dedicated to Liszt. In the circle of his friends he devoted his time not only to the classics but also to the 'modernists', Mendelssohn, Schumann, and Chopin. In 1842 Clara Schumann writes in a letter to her husband: 'He (Gade) is an ardent admirer of yours, he knows everything you have written, and he plays it to the best of his ability.'

When Clara Schumann wrote this letter, Gade had, however, already laid the foundations of his reputation as a composer. His earlier compositions had been strongly influenced by Mendelssohn and Schumann. But in 1840 he had found his own personal line. The Musical Society of Copenhagen had announced a competition for the best concert overture. The most famous musician in the jury was Ludwig Spohr. The prize was awarded to Gade for his *Ossian Overture*, with which composition he had certainly created something new of his own production and, moreover, one of the most prominent musical works in the history of Danish music. The overture is a typical romantic piece, distinguished for poetic inspiration, but at the same time somewhat weak in form. As a motto for his work Gade had chosen two lines from *Freie Kunst*, a poem by Uhland. 'We are not bound by any formula; our art is called poetry.' At the first rehearsal the members of the orchestra praised him highly for the work. Shortly afterwards it gave him another distinction: he was elected a deputy of the Musical Society. This was the beginning of a collaboration that was to continue with short interruptions to the end of his life.

Intermezzo at Leipzig

Soon Gade had finished his first symphony. He presented it to the Musical Society, but its orchestral conductor disapproved of the performance, since – according to his opinion – the work had too many imperfections. Gade thought of sending the symphony to Mendelssohn in Leipzig, but his caution prevented him, until his friend Hoedt persuaded him to do so. The answer from Mendelssohn soon came, and it contained so much praise that Gade said to his mother: 'Someone must be mocking at me.' It is, however, evident that Mendelssohn's praise was sincere, for in a letter to his sister he wrote: 'A new symphony, composed by a Dane named Gade, has given me more pleasure than any other work for a very long time.'

The symphony was performed at the Gewandhaus in Leipzig in March 1843; it was conducted by Mendelssohn himself and was a great success. Gade then decided to go to Leipzig to meet his idol. He was received by the members of the orchestra as a great man, became acquainted with the Schumann family and the young Joachim, listened to his own violin sonata, Opus 6, played by David, the violin virtuoso, and Mendelssohn, and himself conducted his *Symphony in C minor*. His second *Symphony in E major*, which he finished during his stay did not, however, arouse the same enthusiasm as his first. A critic writes: 'We might wish, for the benefit of Gade's second symphony, that we had not heard his first one.'

Gade could not stay long in Leipzig this time. He had received a travelling commission from the Danish state and was obliged to go on according to plan. Italy, where so many Scandinavian artists have gone to seek inspiration for their work, was the obvious goal. He was, however, soon to return to Leipzig. The board of managers of the Gewandhaus offered him the post of Director of Music, and he could not refuse to accept this honourable offer to become Mendelssohn's co-operator. In September 1844, he was back in Leipzig. His position was not an easy one, for we must not forget that the relations between Mendelssohn and Schumann were not wholly satisfactory, even though there was never open conflict between them. Mendelssohn did not entirely approve of Schumann's work as a critic, and he was perhaps unable to understand Schumann's way of mixing poetry and music. Further, Wagner, who was more than any one else a disturber of the peace in the world of music, was by this time living and working in the neighbouring town of Dresden. (In Gade's music we can trace some influence of Wagner, but he could not be described as a Wagnerian in the proper sense of the word.) There were other disturbers of the peace, too, namely the daughters of the wealthy burghers of Leipzig, who were great admirers of Gade – without attracting him. We know of one in whom this feeling for Gade was not merely enthusiastic admiration but love of unusual strength. The young Hedwig Salomon, a banker's daughter, confesses in her journal her despair on account of her unrequited love. Gade seems to have treated her only as a friend, his caution preventing his taking any steps that could tie him. There are contemporary witnesses, however, who testify that he was not without feeling for the young lady.

Among new works composed by Gade at this time there is above all the great choral composition, *Comala*, inspired, as was his *Ossian Overture*, by McPherson's poetry. There exists a direct musical link between these two compositions, for the second theme of the overture also appears in *Comala*.

Gade's stay in Leipzig was to end in sorrow. In November 1847, his friend Felix Mendelssohn died, and it was but natural that Gade took this very much to heart. A few months later the Schleswig-Holstein insurrection broke out, abetted by Germany. Gade left Leipzig with a sore heart to return to Copenhagen, where he made his home for the rest of his life, only now and then paying a short visit to Germany. In April 1852, he married Sophie Hartmann, daughter of the Danish composer, J. P. E. Hartmann.

Home again

Gade's return to Denmark wrought a marked change in his production. The works composed during his time in Leipzig are characterized by their compact elegiac sentiment, but in his later compositions it can be seen that the native Danish country music with its lighter character became a source of inspiration to him. Among the works of this period are, above all, *Holger Danskes Sange* (the songs of Holger the Dane), which have been appropriately described – by the composer Peter Heise – as 'light-blue eyed'.

Gade was soon recognized as one of Denmark's most prominent musicians. In 1850 – he was then 33 years of age – the Musical Society of Copenhagen, which institution had ten years earlier performed his *Ossian Overture*, made him their conductor. Then followed a time of hard work. The Musical Society had made great plans for reorganization and gave Gade the task of building up their new orchestra, to instruct and conduct it, and to make it qualified for any performance. Possibly it was the choice of Gade as conductor that made the Musical Society popular among musicians. Within a short time some of the most prominent musicians of Copenhagen were playing in his orchestra, many of them coming from Lumbye's orchestra. In the repertoire we find all the old classical and the new romantic symphonic works. Much of Schubert's, Schumann's, and Mendelssohn's music was now performed for the first time in Denmark, and there were also performances of Spohr's violin concertos, Bach's *Passion according to St Matthew*, Wagner's *Lohengrin* and *Tannhäuser*, works by Berlioz, and naturally many Danish compositions. It was a busy and happy time in Gade's life. On Sunday he could be found playing the organ in one of the Copenhagen churches.

Among the works that Gade created during this happy time are the *Fourth Symphony in B major* and the ballad *Elverskud.* In the symphony we recognize all the characteristics of the works of Gade's time in Leipzig, but *Elverskud* is genuinely Danish. The poem is an adaptation of an old Danish folk-song, the ballad of the knight Oluf, who escapes from Elverskud, the daughter of the King of Elves, but on arriving at his castle falls down and dies. In Gade's composition this story is told by the choir in a manner strongly reminiscent of the medieval chronicles. The poem and the music are both characterized by a quiet and objective tone.

In July 1855, Gade's young wife died suddenly in confinement. Expression of his grief is revealed in his *Sixth Symphony in G minor*, which he finished not long after this severe loss. Later on Gade married a second time. The name of his second wife was Mathilda Staeger.

Last Years

Niels Wilhelm Gade had no doubt a central position in the musical life of Denmark. There were, however, critics who thought that he was too conservative. In Brendel's *Musical History*, 1852, he is accused of being too far removed from modern life and its requirements, and it was said that he could not be expected to progress further as an artist. In academic circles, and among the students of Copenhagen, Gade's art was considered to be too international, and these Danish chauvinists and liberals preferred Hartmann to Gade. It was, therefore, a source of gratification to Gade when his music composed for the four hundredth anniversary of the University was received with great enthusiasm. Moreover, this music gave him an honorary degree at the University, and this distinction he himself regarded as the greatest honour he ever received. Otherwise the years went by in peace. In 1873 he conducted his own works in Holland; in 1876 he was summoned to England to perform one of his new works at the musical festival in Birmingham. At the musical festival in Hamburg in 1878 he met some of the friends he had made during his stay in Leipzig: Clara Schumann, Joachim, Hiller, Brahms, and Claus Groth. During these years he wrote his last two symphonies and the concert piece *Psyche*, which was his last major work; it was performed for the first time at the musical festival in Birmingham, 1882. He lived for another eight years, alert and active to the last, discharging all his duties at the Musical Society, the church, and the Conservatoire. He died on 21 December 1890, having played the organ as usual at the morning service on that day.

MICHAEL IVANOVITCH GLINKA

1804–57

W. R. ANDERSON

Musical Pre-History

We can best realize the wonder of Russia's birth of art music in the nineteenth century if we consider a few steps in the country's history, from the days of the coming among the little democratic communities of Slavs, in 862, of Rurik the Norman. By Lake Ladoga he settled, where later was the country's capital. After Kiev was established, it began to gain dominance, notably when Christianity, under Vladimir I, became the state religion. Then came the invading, destroying Mongols, in the thirteenth century. Russia for nearly two hundred years was a mere Mongol province, governed by a Khan, with Russian princes as under-lords. The struggles for freedom, under Dmitri Donskoi, provided Russian poets, novelists, and musicians with some of their most vivid pages; opera composers in due course celebrated these events. Freedom was won by Ivan III, a descendant of the original Rurik, who became Czar of All the Russias. Ivan the Terrible was one whose reign as Czar began so well, but degenerated into a tale of cruelty, mixed with religion (as so often it has been). It was his brother-in-law, Boris Godunov, who became the subject of Musorgsky's great opera. Anarchy followed his remorse-filled death. Patriotism saved Moscow from Cossacks and Poles, enemies within and without. The Romanovs came to power, and Peter the Great, in due time, became Russia's Napoleon. He toiled as a common workman abroad, learning how the rest of the world wagged. His ruthlessness built St Petersburg, into whose port the Czar himself piloted many a fine ship. It was under him that French artistic influence, in particular, became strong. This tincture in music later was important, as was that, in opera, of Italy.

It was no wonder that such a history was seized upon by many a nineteenth-century composer for an opera plot. Patriotism, the peasant love of folk-lore, and fantasy were strong excitants.

There was a little native art-music before Glinka, and the surface of the riches of folk-music had been scratched; but Glinka can truly be hailed as 'The Father of Russian Opera', a form of art that the Russians surprisingly attempted straight away: the most complex and difficult of all forms or styles. Glinka set up two of the landmarks, in *A Life for the Czar* and *Russlan and Ludmila*. His pioneer work opened the way for everything that has been wrought since, in that line, down to the operas with which composers of the U.S.S.R. now stimulate national pride. The sources of delight remain much the same: ancient history and fairy-tale fantasies.

Nearly all the members of the nineteenth-century early schools were amateurs. Most of them had another profession than music, at which they worked while educating themselves or each other. No other country can show quite the same will-to-compose by people who rarely had much background save that of the people's music. So these Russian nationalists represent perhaps the purest of the many fermenting cultures in that exciting century.

Childhood and Youth

Michael Ivanovitch Glinka was born on 20 May (old style: new style, 1 June) 1804, when Italian opera was moving towards the height of its fame. Donizetti had been born in 1797, Bellini in 1801; and from 1810 began Rossini's long series of works. In Glinka's last years (he lived only a little beyond fifty) he witnessed the dominance of Verdi's *Il Trovatore*, *Rigoletto*, and *La Traviata*.

Glinka had the advantage of a rich father, a large landowner in the Government of Smolensk, who had spent a few years in the army, but had left the service before he was thirty. He could afford to be a country gentleman. His outlook allowed Glinka to pursue his life-work with a fair amount of peace: that country life avoided rush, hustle, unseemly excitement. The Glinkas had in all ten children, of whom Michael was the second. In early years he was much in the care of a grandmother, who foolishly refused to let him develop the normal, healthy sports of childhood. His constitution was probably weakened thereby, but he had a better chance when he returned to ordinary family life.

Studious, imaginative, he did not very early show much affection for music; it was only when he was about ten that in some strange, unexplained way his imagination was seized by a musical performance;

it put him, he used to say, into a fever. He fortunately had the mean of indulging his new-found joy, for not far away there was an orchestra kept up by a brother of Michael's father, which often playe native songs and dances. From one of its members he learned th violin, and from a governess the piano.

In due course he went away to Petersburg to school (1817–22) taking private music lessons. An early teacher was the Irishman Joh Field, who wrote nocturnes which, in part, influenced Chopin's; bu Glinka's chief helper then was a German, Mayer, a pupil of Field's who wrote over nine hundred pieces, many in a very Chopinesqu style.

Glinka, prospering as a pianist, though less surely so upon the violin got a useful if limited education in opera by attendance at the theatre hearing chiefly French works. He left his school in 1822, dallied for while, not knowing what he wanted to become (he was never of th decisive, brisk executive type): travelling a little, enjoying an easy life he spent a good deal of time with his uncle's orchestra. It was profitable dallying. One is reminded of Haydn's association with a nobleman's orchestra and the opportunities it gave him of experimenting

Experimentation

His father had ideas about Michael's going into some governmen service sufficiently dignified for a gentleman, but the youth evade such a decision, preferring his rather desultory work at music, whic people of his position in life were not expected to adopt as a career. I was arranged that he should take a not very laborious post in a Ministry, one which gave him plenty of time to pursue music – and also, i a gentlemanly way, the fashionable maidens of the capital, for whos better entertainment he took lessons in dancing, and even in singing To his surprise, his once rather unruly voice developed into an instrument as expressive as his composer's imagination became. This nev interest led him to write many songs: not very strong or original ones probably much of their effect then depended on his performance o them. Few composers, by the way, have been good singers.

The coming of a new Emperor, Nicholas I, in 1825, brought political opposition and plots. The Czar's fears and repressions produce effects that developed into Nihilism and, through his general inability to the Crimean War and Russia's defeat. Glinka had the misfortune because of some of his friendships, to be suspected of political mis demeanours, but came to no harm, being quite innocent. His friend Pushkin was another similarly suspected, with no more reason.

He had no real need to work, and as the Ministry proved tedious, and his superiors tiresome, he pleaded ill-health, and resigned. There was some danger to his health, but a good deal of it was probably of nervous origin; his grandmother's early anxiety had perhaps some tendency to make him rather a hypochondriac.

He continued his somewhat dilettante pleasures, taking now a special interest in Italian music, even performing in some of Mozart's operas, and moving in literary sets. He was making occasional notes of musical ideas, some of which he worked out in his operas later. His physician in 1830 thought he ought to live abroad, so he tried German and other foreign spas and then settled in Milan with a singer friend. There, as a young man of good family, he had entry into the best houses. His musical studies were, as ever, more of an absorptive than an intensive nature; he heard the operas of the reigning masters, Bellini and Donizetti, whom he met. Mendelssohn was another acquaintance: he was gathering impressions for his 'Italian' symphony.

But Italian music, though it moved Glinka sometimes to tears, could not fill his heart with the kind of emotion that he, as a Northerner, vaguely realized was the best source of creative art. He was homesick, as well as decidedly unwell; so in the summer of 1833 he bade farewell to Italy, which had given him so much pleasure, but could never be his home.

After some helpful experience of homeopathic medicine in Vienna, he went to Berlin, and happily fell in with the one master who really was efficacious in leading him into a sounder technical world. Siegfried Dehn was this teacher, a man only five years older than Glinka: a serious, delving musician, one who first published some of Bach's neglected music, and a great many older works of importance. He was later the master of another famous Russian, Anton Rubinstein, as well as of the German writer of songs and operas, Cornelius.

Russian Opera

Dehn encouraged Glinka's new passion for Russian materials, with which he no longer dabbled. The composer realized the change in himself, doubtless intensified by his exile in Italy. So he was set on the line that he triumphantly pursued in the two operas that are his monument. He did not yet know exactly what he wanted; only that he must take a national subject that should make his countrymen, hearing it, 'feel at home'. The death of his father left him free to live where he wished. After some indecision, chiefly caused by attractions of the heart, he settled again in Petersburg, renewing and deepening his friendship with the nationalist poets and novelists, among them Pushkin and Gogol. He was always more interested in the practitioners of other arts than in those of his own – probably because he was conscious of his amateurishness.

He found one of his newer friends serviceable in providing a subject for an opera, and, fired at once, plunged into the work later to be known as *A Life for the Czar*, and sometimes by the name of the hero, Ivan Susanin, a patriot of the seventeenth century, who, as the title indicates, preserved the ruler's life by sacrificing his own. He was so eager, indeed, that the librettist (there were actually two, the first having given over the work to a Baron Rosen) tarried behind him, having to shape some of his lines to fit music already composed by the fervid Glinka.

While engaged on this labour of love, Glinka entered into another engagement, that of marriage (in 1835), an unfortunate one, to an unmusical society butterfly of seventeen.

Much of the opera was written at Glinka's family home in the country: one scene, composed in the woods, affected him so vividly that, he said, he felt frozen with fear. In rehearsing he was able to use another private orchestra, like that of his uncle. The Imperial Opera produced the work in 1836, the Czar allowing it to be dedicated to him and presenting Glinka with a ring. The title *A Life for the Czar* was then finally decided.

Its success was great. As we now hear it, the music is much what we might expect from a gifted amateur brought up chiefly on Italian opera. It made effective use of 'leading themes' and showed a fresh path to the native muse. Glinka was appointed to a newly made post, that of master of the Czar's imperial chapel: there was a fair salary, and a house. The income was insufficient for his wife's desires; indeed, they did not for long live happily together. Glinka took refuge in creative work: a new opera, written in small sections – *Russlan and Ludmila*. The subject had been treated by his friend the poet Pushkin (who had been killed in a duel in 1837).

Climax

Glinka dallied over *Russlan*; he was worried about his health and domestic happiness, a good deal of the latter being due to his own rather shady, promiscuous habits; he was easily drawn off by a charmer. Perhaps he was over-mothered, and indulged by women, as a child. In the end he and his wife separated, and he obtained a divorce in 1846.

It was 1840 before he could get up much steam on *Russlan*; at intervals he had been writing songs, an overture to a friend's tragedy of *Prince Kholmsky* and various oddments. He had fits of working at the big *Russlan* scheme, which was completed in 1842. A good deal cut, it was produced just six years after his first opera. The tale was fantastic, the plot unclear. There was not much applause, yet it was a more imaginative and original score than the other, with those oriental elements which Russians so well manipulate. It marks, in a more definite and really fresh way, many of the types of fancy and vivid point-making that were later diversified and developed in the works of Rimsky-Korsakov; and it contains, besides, quite the most genuinely Russian touches of any work up to its time. The whole-tone scale is aptly used for a magical character. This was probably its first appearance in a score.

Glinka lacked sufficient incentives to push on artistically. He travelled, spending some time in Paris and meeting Berlioz, who gave an extract from *Russlan* at one of his concerts. With the help of a rich patron, Glinka gave a concert of his works. He had a fancy to write some orchestral pieces and turned to Spain for inspiration. The gipsies and their dances delighted him, and he wrote several pieces with Spanish titles, such as the *Night in Madrid.*

In 1847 he was home again, unwell. Restless, he thought to try again in 1848 the benefit of foreign travel, but found himself refused permission – a government anxiety about the European troubles of that time being at the root of the refusal (we remember that Wagner, and many other more revolutionary folk, had to flee their country, at this time).

Only one more major piece, a Russian scene, *Kamarinskaya*, is to be chronicled. Glinka never again settled down to prolonged work, or even to the more leisurely piecing-together method that he had so often employed. He idled away his days, in part with women, travelling in a desultory fashion from time to time during his last years. Petersburg had become bitter to him, and when he left Russia for the last time he spat upon its soil: a sad finish to the prophet of nationalism.

Death of a Pioneer

It was in Berlin that he spent his last months, still having advice on composition from his old tutor Dehn. In 1857 Meyerbeer got up a concert in honour of Glinka. Leaving it, the composer caught a chill and in a fortnight was dead. The body, first buried in Berlin, was later taken to Russia and interred in a monastery at Petersburg.

High tribute has always been paid by the Russians to Glinka's pioneering, especially in his use of native dance measures and airs of a folky cast, and in his scoring, much of its happy clarity derived from the example of Mozart. He had ample tunes in his heart, and some rather mysterious fount of musicianship. In his curious amateur status he is a typical Russian composer of his day: so many of them seem to have sprung fully armed into fine artistry. A wonderful century was theirs!

CHARLES FRANÇOIS GOUNOD

1818–93

MARTIN COOPER

Early Influences and the Prix de Rome

Charles Gounod was born in Paris. His father, who died when the child was only five, was a painter gifted enough to win a second Prix de Rome and his mother a pianist, from whom he received his first musical instruction. This life with a widowed mother who was also his first guide and the former of his earliest musical taste played, I think, a considerable part in determining the complexion of Gounod's musical personality. His artistic inclinations never met any opposition at home, were indeed fostered in an atmosphere of emotional intimacy rather too exclusively feminine; so that it was only later, and so to speak at one remove from life as Gounod had come to know it, that he developed the harder, more masculine qualities, and this lack – due partly, no doubt, to temperament, but certainly not corrected by circumstances and early environment – made itself permanently felt. At the age of 18, having completed his general education, he entered the Conservatoire, where he studied counterpoint with Halévy and composition with Reicha and Lesueur, probably the finest masters any young musician of the day could have found in Europe. Halévy was a brilliant and gifted theatrical composer who himself produced at least one fine opera (*La Juive*, 1835) and trained a whole generation of French composers, including Georges Bizet. Lesueur was the solitary representative of the old Gluck tradition in France, which had borne a single fruit in Spontini and then almost disappeared, except in the works of this old eccentric with his passion for the vast, antique musical canvases of the Revolution, his interest in Greek, Roman, and Hebrew music and his inflexible principles which he succeeded in handing on to a favourite, if eccentric, pupil, Hector Berlioz. Reicha was an immensely learned contrapuntist, who had moved in Viennese musical circles, had known Beethoven personally, and had brought to France an admiration for his music, which was still virtually unknown there. The combined influence of these three men had a permanent effect on Gounod's musical ideals to the end of his life; and when in 1839 he won the Prix de Rome, it was as a fervent idealist and a determined opponent of the fashionable cult of Rossini, Donizetti, and Meyerbeer that he set out for the Villa Medici. There he found in Ingres, at that time director of the Institute, a sympathetic friend who soon responded to his charm and enthusiasm. Musically, however, the most important of his Roman experiences came from his friendship with two gifted and cultured women, Pauline Viardot and Fanny Hensel, the one a great singer and the other a fine pianist. Pauline Garcia had some of both the charm and the artistic ability of her more famous sister, La Malibran, who had inspired the whole of the literary Jeune France by her voice, her acting, and her tragically early death.

> Cœur d'ange et de lion, libre oiseau de passage,
> Espiègle enfant ce soir, sainte artiste demain,

as Alfred Musset wrote of her. Fanny Mendelssohn was a cultured German woman who introduced Gounod to the works of Bach, Beethoven, and her own brother, to the classics of German literature and especially to Goethe, laying the foundation of that fine workmanship, that thoroughness and technical competence that were to distinguish all Gounod's compositions, even the most trivial. Finally, in that other sphere which Gounod felt instinctively to be the basis and foundation of his whole life and work, the effect of three years in Rome, the heart and centre of Catholicism, was enhanced by the personal influence of the great Dominican preacher, Père Lacordaire, whose sermons were casting a spell over so many young men in Rome between 1838 and 1841. These three personalities – the two women, so utterly unlike yet both devoted to music, and the Dominican preacher – represent the three fundamental elements in Gounod's character, the three passions of his life: music, love, and, transcending both, religion.

Return to France and First Compositions

In 1842 Gounod decided to move to Vienna, where he was to begin the German portion of his Prix de Rome years. He stayed in Vienna a year, listening to a great deal of music (including the works of Beethoven) and having two masses of his own performed, no small honour for a young French composer in those days. From Vienna he moved to Berlin, where he saw the Hensels; and finally to Leipzig, where he spent happy days with Mendelssohn and was introduced to the famous Gewandhaus orchestra, probably the best in Europe during the forties of the last century. When he finally returned to France in 1843, he had been absent for four years; but he returned fundamentally unchanged, only confirmed in his musical faith and excellently equipped for the struggle that such a faith implied. His first action was to ensure a livelihood by accepting the post of organist to the fathers of the Missions Étrangères in the Rue du Bac, where he shocked many of the congregation by introducing the works of Bach and Palestrina in place of the usual theatrical vulgarities that all too often passed for church music in the forties. Meanwhile daily familiarity with the piety and heroism of the Missionary Fathers was not without its effect on Gounod. Lacordaire's preaching had fallen on fruitful ground; in 1846 Gounod decided to begin reading for the priesthood and in 1847 he entered the seminary of Saint Sulpice. He was not there long, though long enough for a publisher to announce a composition by the 'Abbé Gounod'. Either the call of the world and of music was too strong or, as he is said to have confided to a friend, he feared the emotional intimacy that he did not feel himself strong enough to prevent arising between himself and the women who might bring their secrets and their troubles to him in the confessional. Whatever the exact reason may have been, Gounod renounced the idea of the priesthood and left Saint Sulpice, though he never ceased to be a deeply religious man and a fervent Catholic.

It was only five years after he returned to Paris from abroad that Gounod appeared before the Parisian public with a full-scale composition. Those five years were spent in study and certainly the *Messe Solennelle* in G major for solos, chorus, orchestra, and organ was written, as it had its first performance in January 1851, strangely enough in London. In the same year the opera *Sapho* was produced in Paris, with Pauline Viardot in the title-role. Her name has been connected with Gounod's final decision to remain a layman, and, whatever the truth or falsehood of this may be, it was certainly she who persuaded him to turn his attention to the stage. *Sapho* was praised by Berlioz, although he found the music too fierce. '*Il faut avant tout qu'un musicien fasse de la musique*', he wrote, reversing the roles of lion and lamb. One penetrating critic discovered the real inspiration of the music, which was the music of Gluck. *Sapho* has genuinely dramatic moments, although there is already a pronounced tendency for the lyrical to outweigh the dramatic interest. The lyricism is charming and natural, with no trace of theatrical affectation. The style was already solid and masterly, Gounod having studied deeply and widely and yet learned to carry his erudition with ease and grace. The incidental music to Émile Augier's *Ulysse*, which appeared the following year, was as apt, as charming, and as little successful with the general public as *Sapho*. In despair Gounod, who had meanwhile married a daughter of one of the Conservatoire professors, Zimmermann, and had to think of financial success, turned to a more popular genre in *La Nonne Sanglante*, given at the Opéra in 1854. This was a 'Gothic' story based on Lewis's *Monk*, rather in the vein of *Robert le Diable*; but if Gounod hoped for a repetition of Meyerbeer's success he was disappointed. Although the music was praised by Berlioz and Théophile Gautier, it is inferior to *Sapho* and *Ulysse* and to the works that were to follow almost immediately. Nevertheless Gounod was making his mark, for Berlioz wrote in 1855 – 'apart from Camille Saint-Saëns, and Gounod, who has just written a very fine mass, I can see nothing but day-flies hovering over this stinking marsh we call Paris.'

Gounod's spiritual and emotional equilibrium, which must have been badly shaken by the volte-face of his abandoning the priesthood, was not wholly restored, as one might have expected it to be, by his marriage. In 1857 he had what we should probably call a nervous breakdown, so severe that loss of his reason was feared. Perhaps we should remember Wagner's impression of Gounod's character, 'a victim of his own artistic enthusiasm, in a perpetual swoon', and see in this breakdown the result of an over-sensitive nature, as conscientious as it was highly-strung, overworked, and over-excited. In any event, Gounod's recovery was swift and complete and between the years 1858–60 he wrote three of his finest works – *Le Médecin malgré lui*, *Faust*, and *Philémon et Baucis*. The Théâtre Lyrique was the least conservative of the three theatres in Paris where a young French composer could hope to have his works performed and it was there that *Faust* and *Philémon et Baucis* were given. *Le Médecin malgré lui* was a brilliant musical version of Molière's comedy, witty, quick-moving, and full of life. Gounod seems to have learned more from Mozart than from Rossini or Auber and to have divined by instinct the great comic possibilities of what passed at that time for a ferociously 'learned' style, namely counterpoint. In *Philémon et Baucis* he was handicapped by a very poor libretto; though the lyrical and descriptive music is all in Gounod's best vein, the work as a whole could only fall flat.

Faust and *Grand Opera*

The year 1859 was one of the turning points of Gounod's life. *Faust* was given at the Théâtre Lyrique on 19 March; though it was not at once a spectacular success, it soon made headway and Gounod found himself, almost without warning, in the front rank of the composers. It is hard to give an objective opinion of the music of *Faust*, but it is possible to understand a little of what the music seemed to Gounod's contemporaries if one compares it with either *Les Huguenots* or with *William Tell*, both of them indisputably great works in their way but overburned with spectacular ballets, ingenious stage-craft, brilliant and pompous orchestration, and theatricality of emotion. The charm of *Faust* lay in its naturalness, its simplicity, the sincerity and directness of its emotional appeal. Once again, the lyrical and the descriptive scenes (the Garden scene and the Kermesse, for example) are by far the strongest parts of the work and the more specifically dramatic scenes and those concerned with the supernatural or fantastic element are comparatively poor. Gounod could not compete with Meyerbeer in the arts of the theatre or in the creation of the magnificent, the spectacular. His music is never imposing: it charms when it should command attention, and the composer seems always to be searching, and too often finding, a pretext for lyrical effusions when the dramatic action demands forceful expression and a music of action. Both *La Reine de Saba*, given at the Opéra in 1862, and *Roméo et Juliette*, given five years later at the Théâtre Lyrique, suffer from this serious defect. In *Mireille* (Théâtre Lyrique, 1864) his lyrical vein found wider scope and although it was reduced from five acts to three and has since been subjected to every kind of operation, major and minor, the music remains almost wholly successful. The evocation of the Provençal landscape, the hints of folksong in the choruses and the famous *Chanson de Magali*, the musette of the shepherd-boy, and Mireille's *Heureux petit berger* show Gounod at his very best – simple, winning, genuinely naïve, and with an emotional spontaneity rare in operatic music of the sixties.

The Franco-Prussian War and England

When war with Prussia broke out in the July of 1870 Gounod was man of 52. In September he left Paris for England, not returning finally until 1874. In those four years he developed a new side of his personality and lost his position as potential leader of French music. His admiration for Mendelssohn and the attitude to music, which he had learnt from Fanny Hensel in Rome, seemed to revive in England, where he found a taste for choral and religious music – and especially that of Mendelssohn – such as was unknown in France. There was a demand for religious and semi-religious drawing-room ballads, which he was well qualified to supply, and for oratorio, to which he had already begun to turn his attention, making his first sketches for *The Redemption*, which was not finished until 1881, as far back as 1868. Religious music had been his first love, as we have seen. The *Messe Solennelle* had been written when he returned from Germany and this was followed by a *Messe à Sainte Cécile*, an *Angeli Custodes Mass*, *Messe à Jeanne d'Arc*, and another *Messe Solennelle* as well as a *Stabat Mater*, a *Te Deum*, motets, and many *pièces de circonstance*. But it was in England that he developed the religious style that endeared him to a whole generation and has ever since, at least in England, been connected with his name. The Weldon family, with whom he stayed in London – first in Park Place, Regent's Park, and then in Tavistock Square – soon introduced him to all the influential figures in English musical life and in an astonishingly short time Gounod had achieved a position in England comparable only with that which Mendelssohn had held a generation earlier. He did not forget France, and his *Gallia* (1871) was a sincere and heartfelt lamentation for the plight of his country; but when he returned to Paris he found that new forces had been mobilized in the French musical world and a musical renaissance had started in which he had no place. During the fifties and sixties he and Saint-Saëns had been pioneers, but the younger men who grouped themselves around Saint-Saëns in the Société Nationale were out of sympathy with Gounod, and his long absence, unmitigated by any notable success, had caused his name to fall out at a time when new works by French composers were appearing almost monthly and many gaining a hearing for which Gounod and Saint-Saëns would have had to fight hard, and would probably have fought in vain, before the war of 1870 and the great revival of French patriotism.

Return to Paris and Search for a New Style

Nevertheless Gounod made several more efforts to reconquer his old position and to achieve another operatic success comparable with that of *Faust.* Between 1877 and 1881 he produced *Cinq-Mars, Polyeucte,* and *Le Tribut de Zamora,* but none of the three had any success. Only in *Polyeucte* is it possible to see a genuine attempt to create a new dramatic style, a fusion between opera and oratorio in which Gounod aimed at obtaining the maximum dramatic expression with the simplest means. In his *Portraits et Souvenirs* Saint-Saëns gives a penetrating and sympathetic account of this ideal, which was a noble one, though Gounod never succeeded wholly in achieving it.

The achievement of expressiveness was always Gounod's main pre-occupation: and that is why there are so few notes in his music . . . each note *sings.* For the same reason instrumental music, *pure* music, was never his forte. . . . His great desire was to discover a beautiful colour on the orchestral palette and, in his search for this, he refused to follow the ready-made processes of the acknowledged masters but carried out his experiments directly, studying the various timbres, inventing new combinations and shades of colour to suit his brush. 'Sonority,' he once said to me, 'is still an unexplored country.'

These were always Gounod's main pre-occupations and the transition period of the seventies was really little else than a period of groping towards a new way of realizing what were fundamentally old ideals of his.

He was anxious to reduce the number of modulations to a minimum, with the idea that the composer should not make light use of such a powerful means of expression. . . . He sought to obtain the maximum effect with the minimum apparent effort, to reduce the representation of effects to mere indications and to concentrate all the interest on the expression of feeling.

If ever such an ideal was doomed to failure it was in the second half of the last century when all the musical world was dominated by the figure of Wagner. Gounod was placing himself dead against the whole current of contemporary music. He was an ageing man, whose genuine lyrical gift was inevitably approaching exhaustion and had anyhow been sadly tarnished by contact with the sentimental religiosity and facile tenderness that were the fashion of the day. In the *Redemption* (1881) and *Mors et Vita* (1884), the works in which Gounod felt that he had at last achieved the style at which he was aiming, the total effect is one of bland and tender platitude. He was all too apt, like Liszt, to mistake some portentous platitude for a new truth and, as time went on, the strain of self-consciousness, never absent from his work grew. While he was engaged on the composition of *Roméo et Juliette* he had written to a friend (and the flavour of the remark can only be got in the original French) – '*Au milieu de ce silence il me semble que j'entends me parler en dedans quelque chose de très grand, de très clair et de très enfant à la fois.*' This consciously 'childlike' simplicity is always suspect in an artist, for it almost invariably conceals an element of pomposity and insincerity that tends to grow with age, and even more with success, until it finally rots the sounder elements in the artistic nature. In fact, as Gounod grew older he came to suffer from what might be described as the same '*cher maître* complex' as afflicted Hugo and Tennyson. Not content with being just artists, these eminent Victorians must pose as prophets and, in proportion as their 'message' – the actual content of their works – became thinner, the manner in which they stated it became more and more sublime, more portentous, and more hollow-sounding. Bizet had laughed maliciously at this vein of pretentiousness in Gounod (whom he greatly admired) as far back as 1859: 'Art to him is a kind of apostolate: he used those very words to me!' and with old age the bromidic and the oracular both gained on him. '*Les enfants, ce sont les roses du jardin de la vie*' might easily have been said by Hugo but is actually one of Gounod's obiter dicta. On one occasion Bizet's widow asked his opinion of some new work they had heard together. Gounod's oracular '*C'est rhomboïdal*' called for the immediate answer it received – '*Ah! cher maître, j'allais le dire.*'

Old Age and Death

Unlike Saint-Saëns, Gounod was not embittered by the spectacle of a new generation in search of completely new ideals that he could not really understand. He had had his own share of success, world-wide with *Faust* and nation-wide in England with his later works, and could perhaps more easily afford to be generous. His judgement was not always good, as his description of Cesar Franck's symphony – 'the affirmation of incompetence pushed to dogmatic lengths' – showed; but then there is always the suspicion with Gounod that the *mot* was the thing, rather than the judgement it expressed. He begged for a sober and reasoned attitude – '*ni Wagnerophobie ni Wagneromanie*' – towards Bayreuth.

France is essentially the country of clean outlines, concision, moderation, taste: that is to say, the antithesis of excess, pretentiousness, disproportion, prolixity. A passion for the transcendental (I almost wrote 'a passion for the bogus transcendental') may put us completely on the wrong track, by which I mean that it may make us mistake size for greatness, weight for worth, obscurity for depth, vagueness for sublimity.

He himself had been a fine example of this spirit until success and a certain weakness of character had spoiled him, and in the very year of his death (1893), at the age of 75, he wrote a magnificent statement of his old faith and ideals to Charles Bordes, in whose Chanteurs de Saint Gervais he saw the embodiment of much that he himself had attempted as a young man. In the Semaine Sainte de Saint Gervais, Bordes and his choral society performed the great polyphonic classics of the sixteenth and seventeenth centuries. Gounod attended their first concerts and wrote afterwards:

It is high time that the flag of liturgical art should take the place occupied hitherto in our churches by that of profane melody and that *musical fresco* (*la fresque musicale*) should banish all the romantic lollypops and saccharine piosities which have been ruining our taste for so long. Palestrina and Bach ... are the musical Fathers of the Church: our business is to prove ourselves loyal sons of theirs and I can only thank you for helping us in that.

There spoke the young enthusiast who, nearly fifty years before, had shocked the congregations and puzzled the good fathers of the Missions Étrangères in the Rue du Bac. Gounod, with all his faults, never allowed his artistic standards to be lowered. All his life he stood for the best that he could conceive. No composer could well have differed from him in temperament more fundamentally than Debussy and yet listen to what Debussy said of him. 'Let us, without being over dogmatic . . . render him our homage. Let it be stated once again that a name lives in the memory of men for various, though not necessarily weighty, reasons. One of the best means of achieving this is to stir the emotions of the majority of one's contemporaries. Of that none will deny that Gounod made generous use.'

VICTOR ANTOINE ÉDOUARD LALO

1823–92

W. R. ANDERSON

The Provincial

Lalo is known to the great majority of music-lovers, vividly enough, as the composer of coloured Rhapsodies, rather than of his masterpiece, the opera *Le Roi d'Ys*, his only completed and published work in that kind. He was early distinctive in yet another field, that of instrumental music of the symphonic order – a style (in its more severe manifestations) little congenial to the French temperament.

Lalo belongs to the same period as Franck. Franck and he were somewhat set apart, without much backing from any considerable 'school' of composition. Berlioz had blazed a trail, but few of his temperament were found to follow it. Lalo, like Franck, was a man of the provinces. Both had little talent, and no taste for publicity. Both knew hard times, but Lalo's early life was spent in a more bohemian way than Franck's.

Lalo came of a Spanish family long settled in France: but nearly all the female side continued to be Spanish, not French. His father was a retired wounded Army officer with a fine record, who had taken a provincial government post at Lille, and there Édouard (as he was most commonly known) was born on 27 January 1823, an only son, who bore strong physical signs of his Spanish blood.

The boy was fortunate in getting excellent training as a string player from the start. His first teachers were Baumann, a cellist who in orchestras had played the Beethoven symphonies under their composer, and Müller, a violin teacher at the Conservatoire of Lille.

In the 1830s the prevailing musical enthusiasm was for opera: either the would-be grandeurs of the stunning Meyerbeer, or the Italian delights. There was no very sure background for the average student who wanted training in the classics, in chamber and symphonic music.

Lalo's first bent was for chamber music, and his studies in strings gave him a classical turn. He never played the piano, and so either heard any chamber music played, when he could, or read it from the score – one of the purest of pleasures, say its devotees; at any rate, a vitally valuable way of getting at the heart of the chamber style.

To Paris and the Bohemians

As so often we have noticed in marking the careers of composers, the student's application was approved by his father, so long as it was that of an amateur: music pursued in a gentlemanly way. The moment Lalo said he wanted to become a professional musician, trouble began. His martial father had been accustomed to discipline, and to command men. He tried to order his son's life. Édouard was as stiff as his father, and the result was that the lad set off, at sixteen, to make his own way in Paris.

It is not clear how he lived that bohemian life about which Murger and so many others have written with the gaiety and pathos of reality and romance. It is presumed that his father allowed him a trifle. At any rate, he entered the Conservatoire, where he had a short period under Habeneck, and began composition under Schulhoff and an ambitious young man, Crèvecœur, who aimed at the Prix de Rome. But his brief Conservatoire period seems to have left no impression even upon the institution's records. He had no inclination towards the type of light-operatic composition that was likely to win the Prix. He wrote a few songs, after the sentiment of the time; and in these, which he composed at intervals until middle life, we can see a little of the spirit that Fauré and others were more intensively to develop. But his chief interest was in chamber music. The works in this style that he wrote between the ages of twenty and twenty-five made no stir. Makers of concert programmes were satisfied with operatic pot-pourris and fantasias. No poorer period in French chamber music could be found. The majority of Lalo's chamber works were not published until much later. He lived by teaching and enjoyed playing the violin or viola in a string quartet and making a circle of friends, including some workers in other arts. He was one of the founders of a chamber society in the desert which, in that form of art, Paris then was. Though an excellent player, he had no ambition to shine as a soloist: his reserved, quiet nature was all against that. He was always happiest when making music with a few friends, and their choice was severely classical: the young German romantics did not largely enter into their programmes.

Marriages

At some period not clearly to be defined, Lalo married a Mme Moine, who was twenty-five years his senior. His second marriage, the only one referred to in most accounts of him, took place in 1865, to Mlle de Maligny, daughter of a general officer in the Paris command. It would seem that his happy marriage was (as with Schumann) a great impetus to new activity, after the long period in which Lalo had not found his best way in life, as far as obvious advancement went, and had indeed ceased to compose. His wife, an excellent musician with a fine contralto voice, encouraged, sustained, and inspirited her husband, who, now well over forty, began anew by attacking a fresh department of his art, that of the musical stage.

The government had instituted a series of competitions for works to be produced at the three opera theatres, the Opéra, the Opéra Comique, and the Théâtre Lyrique, the last a lively place which had been bringing out, besides the older German operas, the works of Gounod, and even of Berlioz.

First Opera and Orchestral Works

So Lalo wrote, for the competition of 1867, an opera, *Fiesque*, after Schiller's subject. It took only the third place, and he was unable to get any other theatre to produce it, though the head of the Opéra was showing some interest by 1870. That, of course, proved to be a year of disaster, and the outbreak of war prevented anything more being done, despite some friendly help from Gounod. The work had very bad luck; but parts of it were used up, after a common custom of composers, in later works, so the labour was not wholly a loss.

The activity of Saint-Saëns in helping to run the Société Nationale de Musique was noteworthy. This, in the effulgence of feeling after the Franco-German war, did much to forward native art. Lalo was another of the patriots who took part in this scheme, and some of his work was brought out under its auspices. He had found in the orchestra, and in the concerto form, new means of expression, and was indeed one of the pioneers of French instrumental composition. From 1872 the Spanish violinist Sarasate, doubtless with some special warmth of feeling for a composer of Spanish descent, made famous Lalo's *Con-*

certo in F, Op. 20, and in 1875 he was playing the *Symphonie espagnole*, the work that probably the bulk of music-lovers would name if asked to specify one piece by Lalo. A few would perhaps name, instead, the *Norwegian Rhapsody*, published in 1881. As far as gramophone records show popularity, these two seem to take up between them the average record-buyer's admiration for the composer.

His *Symphony in G minor* (1887) must be ranked among the few French works in this form that are significant; the genius of that nation has, since Berlioz, wrought most happily in other realms than the symphonic. And to be known as 'a symphonist' was little better than condemnation in the mind of the French musical public of that day. So Lalo decided that he ought to work again at opera, despite the disappointments that attended *Fiesque*.

Completion of Le Roi d'Ys

He thought of Savonarola as a subject, but after some experiments decided that the great reformer was too severe a character for operatic treatment, at least by one of Lalo's temperament. His wife was a Breton from the Vendée, and Lalo had spent some happy holidays in her native place. He was thus led to a splendid, congenial choice, that of the legend of Ys; and so we have the opera *Le Roi d'Ys*, which brought fame to the composer, and the names of whose chief characters are engraved upon the pedestal of the Lalo statue in Lille.

The story, briefly, is about a king who had long struggled with another ruler. This king had two daughters, both of whom loved one knight. Royal preference for one child brought hate into the other's heart, who, in her mad rage, betrayed the city to the enemy prince. He, obtaining from her the key to the sluices, caused the city to be flooded. At the sight of the disaster, the evil woman, in remorse, drowned herself. But the city's patron saint, rising from the waters, commanded them to fall, and all to be restored unharmed. From this opera we hear little but an air, '*Vainement, ma bien aimée*', a tenor theme which, rather oddly, was a favourite of Melba's, that she often put into her programmes.

The opera was completed in 1878, but owing to a series of not unfamiliar disappointments, including managerial vacillation, was not heard in full until ten years later, though the overture and some of the vocal music, sung by Lalo's wife, were brought forth. Meanwhile, the director of the Opéra commissioned Lalo to write a ballet. The time allowed – less than six months – was too short, and Lalo was not a quick worker. He liked the idea of essaying the form, but wished to take his time. His mind was calm; indeed, he gave the impression of being somewhat withdrawn, unenthusiastic, even cold. It was not so: merely that his social temperament was of a rather contemplative, quiet order. In company he was agreeable but reserved. His firm, neat, pleasantly decorative but modest handwriting, very clear (and thus, courteous), indicates his nature. He had no talent or interest in intrigue, a skill that the pushful have always needed, and most of the highly successful have cultivated, in every walk of life. He felt that in the ballet *Namouna* he was too narrowly confined by the necessity of, as he called it, 'writing music for legs'. Harassed by the task, and his stage taskmasters, he went down with an illness, which left him looking an old man. His good friend Gounod stepped in and orchestrated the last numbers.

The music was not very well received; part of it was even stricken with the epithet 'advanced': it was the music of 'a mere symphonist'. 'Advanced' was scarcely the word for art that really looked back in spirit to the great period of French composition whose potentate was Rameau – a period to which more than one of the later-century composers, and those of the twentieth who really earned the name 'extremist', turned an eye, and out of which many turned a tune. There was in Lalo this affinity with the classics; and perhaps the word 'symphonic' had some point, too, though as regards style, not form. Lalo was not entirely in tune with the spirit of nineteenth-century ballet; so it is not surprising that it was on the concert platform, rather than the stage, that *Namouna*, after its short career in 1882, continued to be heard.

Success

Before *Le Roi d'Ys* was finally in shape, he had produced a 'Russian' *Violin Concerto* and his *G minor Symphony*. Then, in 1888, the Opéra Comique saw the finest fruit of his skill, in that opera-legend that had been worked upon over a period of thirteen years. It had during its first two years an average of a performance a week, and it retained a permanent place in the repertory.

In writing it Lalo shrewdly realized that Wagner was the only man who had successfully dramatized opera, in the sense of so charging music with dramatic force as to produce a new synthesis. He saw that (as he wrote to a freind) so many had tried to imitate Wagner: so many, even, of French race – one by no means the most likely to enter congenially into this heavier Northern spirit. They had failed, 'some pitiably, some honourably, but all as copyists'. There had been a Parisian Wagner-furore which in part had helped to prod French composers on this dangerous path. No competitor had ever outdone or equalled Wagner, and Lalo did not intend to try.

He succeeded a good deal better than most other Frenchmen have done in making, if not the best, at least a good success, of both worlds, those of chamber (and symphonic) art and of the opera. When he wrought in the former field, he was able to find in the problems and conflicts of sound itself sufficient 'poems and dramas'; and when, as in his symphony, he recalls a theme in several places, he does it when the 'poetic or dramatic *musical* intentions' makes its recurrence seem necessary. After the quoted phrase, written to a friend, he puts in brackets: '(do not laugh!)' – obviously because he feels that at first sight there may be incongruity in denying literary influences and at the same time speaking of 'poetic musical intentions'. But with his sound sense Lalo realized more clearly than many others the differences between operatic and symphonic talent, and he had strength to steer clear of literary entanglements when writing music of the kind usually known as 'absolute'; not all the Romantics were successful in making the distinctions and keeping them clear. He was the more able to do so because of his somewhat aloof, self-reliant temperament, not easily excitable, and because of his lack of 'romantic' bias. Rather aristocratic in spirit, a selecting, meditative, fastidious artist – yet not lacking ardency – he picked his way amid many mid-century confusions and 'movements', knowing his own strength, and measuring, without much commenting upon, his limitations. There was in him (perhaps based upon his Spanish ancestry) a keen feeling for exotic interest in music, which, though we should now perhaps regard its manifestations as somewhat superficial, gives his music a glow that pleases nearly everyone. He was in no sense a chilly composer, or an 'academic' (using the word in its pejorative sense); and although normally reserved, he could lash out at fools, and heartily express his dislike of the 'perfumed music which gangrenes our French school' (as he rather mixed-metaphorically wrote). He did not disguise his opinion of some composers.

National Traits

Particularly happy is his manipulation of the various nationally-tinged rhapsodies he wrote, especially those that have his beloved violin as the solo instrument. His early training as a quartet player enabled him to get every touch and pressure of effect from strings; he had admirable orchestral taste, and his fancy (this, rather than deeply-stirred imagination) contrived structures that combine the facility and lightness of the French nature with some slight artistic wildness of the Spaniard: a wildness never fearsome or even rough, but that enjoys a fling. So we have in Lalo an unusual blend of capacities – in opera, in 'absolute' music, and in the more-or-less characteristic 'nationalist' rhapsodies that were in tune with the rising interest of his age in foreign travel and customs – influences that we find strongly colouring contemporary French literature and, in a smaller degree, European painting.

Lalo lived but few years to enjoy the success of *Le Roi d'Ys* and the popularity that came to him because of it. In 1889 appeared his *C minor Piano Concerto*; and in 1891 he was asked to write the music for a spectacular pantomime with chorus, *Nero*, to be produced at the Hippodrome. Parts of early works – *Fiesque* and other things – went into this, in which he had the help of a young composer, Leroux, who had the year before written incidental music for Sardou's *Cléopatre*. But the music of *Nero* was never published, and the manuscript was lost.

Once more he was to attempt opera, with *La Jacquerie*, but he had sketched only one act when he became ill, in the summer of 1891. His sufferings during the short remainder of his life were sharp. The opera was completed by Arthur Coquard, a versatile musician who had begun life in the law, taken a legal degree, and practised for some years, before becoming a composer (he was a pupil of Franck's), a critic, and a lecturer. *La Jacquerie* was produced at Monte Carlo and Paris in 1895; but Lalo's life had ended in a sudden heart seizure, on 23 April 1892.

His old teacher, Baumann, had told him: 'Write only what you find in yourself'; and Alfred de Musset's motto was always Lalo's standard of integrity and self-confidence: 'My glass is small; but I drink from my *own* glass.'

FRANZ LISZT

1811–86

RALPH HILL

Parents and Childhood

The Hungarian family of Liszt was probably of noble origin. Their hall-mark was quantity as well as quality. Georg Adam Liszt, born in 1755, married three times and was responsible for twenty-six children. One of his elder sons, Adam, entered the service of the famous Esterhazy family at Eisenstadt; they were the patrons of Haydn, Hummel, Cherubini, and many other musicians. In 1810 Adam was promoted land-steward on one of the Esterhazy estates at Raiding, a small town near Vienna. He took this opportunity to get married to an Austrian girl named Anna Lager. Near the end of the next year a son was born. He was christened Franz.

Franz Liszt was brought up on music, for his father was a keen amateur violinist, guitarist, and pianist. At an early age Franz was taught the rudiments of music and the elements of piano playing. He showed such precocious gifts that at nine he was considered good enough to play in public Hummel's *Piano Concerto in E flat* and to extemporize on some popular melodies. Soon afterwards Adam arranged a concert of his own at which Franz played a concerto by Ries. He was next taken to Eisenstadt to show off his prowess to Prince Esterhazy. The Prince was deeply impressed and a concert was arranged in his palace at Pressburg. It was a huge success and a fund was at once subscribed to enable Franz to undergo a proper musical training for six years. Accordingly Adam gave up his post with the Esterhazy family and decided to devote himself entirely to his son's interests. He went to see Hummel, who was Court conductor at Weimar, but the distinguished composer and pianist was not fond of prodigies and asked an impossible fee for his services. The result was that Adam returned home, packed up his belongings, and moved to Vienna, where he placed Franz under the care of Salieri for composition and of Czerny for piano. After a dozen lessons Czerny was so pleased with the boy's progress that he insisted upon teaching him for nothing.

The Beginning of a Brilliant Career

For two years Franz worked hard under Czerny, during which time he became well known in Viennese society. He played at various concerts at Vienna and Pesth. It is said Beethoven was present at one of the Vienna concerts, in 1823, and that, after Franz had played, Beethoven mounted the platform, lifted up the little pianist, and embraced him.

Adam now considered that the time was ripe for the world at large to know something of Franz, so father and son set off on an extended concert tour through Germany, on to Paris, and finally to London. While at Paris they visited Cherubini, the august principal of the Conservatoire, in the hope that Franz might be taken as his pupil. But Cherubini politely pointed out that according to the regulations foreigners could not be admitted to the Conservatoire. So the next best thing, if Franz was to have a really wide and thorough musical training, was to place him privately under Reicha, the eminent theorist and scholar, and Paer, the composer of numerous popular operas. Things went well, for Franz's new masters were excellent. Furthermore, important letters of introduction gained the young pianist admittance to the houses of leading French families, and he played at several special public concerts. 'Le petit Litz' became the fashion and he was known as the 'ninth wonder of the world'.

In the summer of 1824 Franz and his father crossed the Channel. Franz made his London début at the Argyll Rooms and immediately created a sensation. A few days later at Drury Lane he 'consented to display his inimitable powers on the New Grand Piano Forte, invented by Sébastien Érard'. The programme included a concerto by Hummel and an improvisation on a theme from *The Barber of Seville*. Society was delighted, and he was invited to appear at a command performance before George IV. Franz remained in London till the new year, devoting his spare time to the composition of an opera in one act, *Don Sancho*, which he had been commissioned in Paris to write. Having finished it, he returned to Paris to show it to Paer, who submitted it to the Académie Royale de Musique with a special recommendation. It was accepted and produced in the autumn at the Royal Opera House. A lengthy notice appeared in the London musical journal *The Harmonicon*, and although the libretto was severely handled the music was given the encouragement due to the youthful composer. In the overture, the writer says, 'many of the orchestral parts are treated with vigour and intelligence which would do honour to composers long disciplined to their art'. The opening paragraph of the notice is interesting, for it indicates the supremely high place Franz was already given as a pianist: 'The extraordinary youth, the composer of this opera, has but just entered his thirteenth year. He has been acknowledged by some of the first connoisseurs of Germany and France to merit a place among the principal pianists of Europe; nay, some have gone so far as to say that he yields the palm to Hummel only, whose immense talent as an improvisatore undoubtedly stands as yet alone and unrivalled. But the youthful Liszt is also a composer and gifted with the talent of improvisation in a high degree.'

The next two years were spent in further tours in France and England. Then in 1827 Adam died and Franz was left to make shift for himself and look after his mother. On his death-bed Adam gave voice to an ominous warning. He told Franz that he had a good brain and a kind heart, but women would control and upset his life.

Before the last war a book was published in Germany entitled *Liszt und die Frauen*. The author recorded the details of some twenty-six *affaires des cœurs*.

First Love Affair

Liszt's mother now came to Paris to look after him. He threw himself body and soul into his work, practising and teaching some ten hours a day. As with most youths of a romantic and sensitive disposition two potent influences had begun to affect his whole attitude to life – religion and love; they were to dominate Liszt's whole outlook until he died. Among his pupils was a charming girl of sixteen, Caroline de Saint-Cricq, and needless to say – for Liszt was as striking in looks as he was in intelligence – pupil and master became infatuated with each other. Caroline's invalid mother encouraged their lovemaking, but soon she died, and her husband, a Minister of the Interior, told Liszt that he had other plans for the future of his daughter. Liszt took his loss very badly and for months he remained in a state of nervous collapse. He never forgot Caroline: when he drew up his will in 1860 he left her a jewelled ring.

From childhood Liszt's favourite form of literature was the Bible, the lives of the Saints, and any other religious works he could procure. He dreamed himself 'incessantly into the world of saints', and now he begged without avail to be allowed to enter the Paris seminary. 'I hoped,' he said, 'it might be granted me to live the life of the saints and perhaps die the death of the martyrs.'

During the following two years Liszt concentrated his whole attention on perfecting his piano technique and reading with avidity theological works and romantic literature. In religion he turned to Lamennais and in politics to Saint-Simon. But 1830 was a decisive year in Liszt's life. He met Berlioz, Chopin, and Paganini and became acquainted with their music; it was entirely in sympathy with his own romantic spirit and thus opened out a new world to him. The extraordinary virtuosity of Paganini was especially inspiring. Liszt felt that, since Paganini exploited to such artistic purpose new and wonderful effects on the violin, he could apply a similar technique to the piano. In addition, the delicate poetry and subtle sonorities of Chopin, together with the brilliant and masterly orchestral achievements of Berlioz, helped to nourish the seeds of his own style as a composer.

A year or two later Liszt writes to a friend: 'Here is a whole fortnight that my mind and fingers have been working like two lost spirits – Homer, the Bible, Plato, Locke, Byron, Hugo, Lamartine, Chateaubriand, Beethoven, Bach, Hummel, Mozart, Weber, are all around me. I study them, meditate on them, devour them with fury; besides this I practise from four to five hours of exercises (thirds, sixths, octaves, shakes, repeated notes, and cadenzas). Ah! provided I don't go mad, you will find an artist in me! Yes, an artist such as you desire, and such as is required nowadays!'

The True Romantic

During the first half of the nineteenth century Paris was the great centre of all the arts. Never had so much genius concentrated on one city. Among the great names were Chopin, Liszt, Berlioz, Meyerbeer, Rossini, Cherubini, Halévy, Auber, Ferdinand Hiller, Dumas, de Musset, George Sand, Victor Hugo, Balzac, Heine, Delacroix, Corot, Gautier, and a dozen others. Into this society of romantics Liszt flung himself. He absorbed much and became a worthy disciple of the new thought. When Liszt played in public his audience were swept off their feet with ecstasy, for not only did he play divinely but he acted superbly. Someone who was present at one of these musico-emotional orgies describes in his autobiography Liszt's playing of Mendelssohn's *Lieder ohne Worte*: 'As the closing strains began I saw Liszt's countenance assume that agony of expression, mingled with radiant smiles of joy, which I never saw in any other human face except in the paintings of Our Saviour by some of the early masters. His hands rushed over the keys, the floor on which I sat shook like a wire, and the whole audience were wrapped with sound, when the hand and the frame of the artist gave way. He fainted in the arms of a friend who was turning over the pages for him, and we bore him out in a strong fit of hysterics. The effect of the scene was really dreadful. The whole room sat breathless with fear, till Hiller came forward and announced that Liszt was already restored to consciousness and was comparatively well again.'

The year 1833 was conspicuous for two events of importance: Liszt completed the first of his great transcriptions – Berlioz's *Symphonie Fantastique* – and met Countess d'Agoult, the first of the two women who dominated his life throughout. The Countess was twenty-eight years old, of high intelligence and romantic disposition; she possessed three children and a middle-aged husband with whom she had little in common. The result was that the striking young musical Spartan and the romantic young lady eloped. In her memoirs, written under the pen-name of 'Daniel Stern', she speaks impersonally of their mutual attraction: 'Strong affinities of race and temperament brought them together, but the extreme differences in their education and their station in life of necessity raised up innumerable difficulties around them. A thousand obstacles arose between them and endowed the passion that drove them towards each other with a dolorous intensity which, in more balanced days than these, love will never again know.'

They went to Geneva and there was born a daughter, Blandine. That Dame Scandal should wag her tongue vigorously was to be expected, but the waggings became exceptionally vicious and frequent, since it was one thing for a Countess to take a lover from her own stratum of society, but quite another when he happened to be a mere musician. However, the happy couple were quite indifferent to the likes and dislikes of the venerable Dame. They had their friends – George Sand, for instance, who joined them at Chamonix where they all went picnicking in the mountain valleys, discussing the while art, philosophy, religion, and the rest of the things that absorbed their interests.

A Musical Duel

On Liszt's return to Paris he found that his reputation as a pianist had been eclipsed by Thalberg, who had become the idol of musical society. Liszt gave a concert but sensed that his audience was not so responsive as before. He was piqued. Thalberg must be taught a lesson. Liszt's attitude towards his rival was not particularly admirable: he enjoyed hearing disparaging remarks about Thalberg and made no attempt to hide his own feelings. At last matters came to a head. Thalberg played at the Conservatoire before an audience of 400, while Liszt in opposition played at the Opera House before an audience of about ten times the number. Musical society took sides, and the general atmosphere was like that of an election. Finally, the two great pianists were engaged to appear together at the salon of a certain Princess. Liszt opened with his *Niobe Fantasia* and Thalberg replied with his *Moses Fantasia*. It was a battle of giants, and Liszt was unanimously proclaimed the victor. Sir Charles Hallé, who was in Paris at the time, has recorded his impressions of Liszt's virtuosity. 'Such marvels of executive skill and power,' he says, 'I could never have imagined. One of the transcendent merits of his playing was the crystal-like clearness which never failed for a moment, even in the most complicated and to anybody else impossible passages; it was as if he had photographed them in their minutest detail upon the ear of his listener.'

In 1837 Liszt and the Countess set off to Italy. At Como on 18 December their second daughter, Cosima, was born. In Milan Liszt renewed his friendship with Rossini, transcribed for piano the latter's *William Tell* Overture and the group of songs entitled *Les Soirées Musicales*, and played them in public. He also worked at a number of other transcriptions, the Paganini *Études*, and a few original compositions, some of which were later published as the second book of *Années de Pèlerinage*. While in Venice, Liszt read of the terrible destruction caused by the Danube floods in Hungary. He immediately went alone – the Countess being indisposed – to Vienna and gave ten concerts that brought in nearly £2,000. He handed over the entire sum for the relief of his compatriots. Liszt returned to Venice and within a few days continued his travels with the Countess. During a short period in Rome a son, Daniel, was born.

Liszt had a dual personality. He was a strange mixture of a great and sincere artist and a rather vulgar showman and actor: the one produced the glorious setting of the Thirteenth Psalm for baritone and orchestra, the *B minor Piano Sonata*, the *Faust* and *Dante* symphonies, and the *Fantasia and Fugue on B-A-C-H* for organ, while the other turned out a profusion of pot-boilers of which the *Hungarian Fantasia* is a fair specimen. One side of Liszt wanted a quiet life devoted to religious contemplation and to the service of music in its highest manifestations, but his other side craved for public applause and for the luxury and glitter of aristocratic drawing-rooms. He could be kind-hearted and callous, sincere and insincere, egotistical and modest by turns. In fact the man and artist were throughout an amazing contradiction.

It did not take long for the Countess to realize that her hero was by no means the paragon of artistic and moral virtue that she may have at first imagined. Liszt's visit to Vienna opened her eyes rather more widely than was comfortable. Despite the sacrifices she had made for him, and despite his fondness for her, when he returned he prattled of nothing else but his successes, particularly with the ladies, and of the aristocrats with whom he had talked and dined. The Countess tells us in her memoirs that 'he put out of sight the compositions of his own that he had sketched. But he could not so easily put them out of mind; and so, in his exasperation, drawn as he was in opposite directions, he sought, in order to escape from himself, distractions in the outer world, whence I used to see him return more and more dissatisfied, more and more out of equilibrium.'

In October 1839, the end of his liaison with the Countess was in sight. They parted at Florence: Liszt to Vienna and the Countess with the three children to Paris. In 1844 they came to an understanding and separated for good. The Countess turned to literature and some years later wrote a novel entitled *Nélida* under her pen-name 'Daniel Stern'. In reality this novel was a thinly disguised autobiography with Liszt and herself as the chief characters. All Liszt's failings are vividly and sometimes cruelly portrayed in the character of Guermann, an artist. It is said that Liszt never forgave the Countess. He did not even write to her when their two children, Daniel and Blandine, died.

The Travelling Showman

From 1840 to 1848, now at the height of his powers as a pianist, Liszt did nothing else but tour the length and breadth of Europe, revelling in a continuous orgy of hero-worship, of which the like has never before or since been seen, except perhaps for Paganini. He went to Hungary, Austria, England, Russia, Turkey, Poland, Denmark, Spain, Portugal, Germany; wherever it was, he was received with regal splendour. In Pesth two Counts and a Baron assisted by three slightly less distinguished nobles, all of them clad in gorgeous national costume, presented Liszt with a jewelled sabre; after the ceremony he was accompanied to his hotel by a military band and a torch-light procession. In keeping with the romantic spirit of the times Liszt behaved and dressed in a most extravagant manner – green gloves and a different cravat for every day in the year were two items of dress that created an impression. Those who did not pay him the respect that he considered his due were made to feel the keen edge of his tongue. He even put Czar Nicholas I in his place for daring to talk while he was playing! On one of his tours Liszt took with him the notorious adventuress, Lola Montez, who was also much sought after by Ludwig I of Bavaria.

Although Liszt aroused great attention and enthusiasm in England, he was not treated with quite the same reverence that he enjoyed elsewhere. He certainly played at Buckingham Palace to the delight of Queen Victoria, but our aristocracy saw that he kept his place. His escapades on the barbarian Continent were common knowledge and therefore English gentlemen must be careful not to have their good names besmirched. Remember the Countess and her three illegitimate children . . . and it is said there have been others! A mere pianist too!

The Princess, Weimar

Suddenly Liszt's life as a travelling showman came to an end. Three things contributed to his beginning a new life. First, he was tiring of his superficial way of living, secondly, he met the woman who was to rule him during the rest of his days, and, thirdly, he was offered the post of musical director of the Grand Ducal Court at Weimar.

In 1847 Liszt went to Kiev where he gave his last concerts. At one of them the Princess Carolyne von Sayn-Wittgenstein was present, and Liszt's wonderful playing and striking presence made a deep impression upon her. The Princess showed her pleasure by contributing handsomely to one of Liszt's charity concerts. He called on her and thanked her for her interest.

The result was to be expected.

The Princess was twenty-eight years of age. Born of Polish parents domiciled in Russia, she had inherited large estates at Kiev. At the age f seventeen she had been driven into marriage with a Russian prince y whom she had one child, a daughter. The marriage was a failure ecause Carolyne was a girl of considerable intellectual capacity. That iszt was attracted by other qualities than physical beauty is fairly cer- ain, judging from contemporary accounts of her plain and unattract- ve features. After all, she was an intelligent and wealthy princess, and iszt adored titles and intelligent appreciation. Liszt went to stay with er at one of her estates. They read Dante, and Liszt decided to com- ose a *Dante Symphony*.

Then came the Weimar period. The Princess established herself with iszt at the Villa Altenburg and hoped that a divorce could be speedily rranged. Unfortunately the Prince saw no reason why he should give p all his claims to his wife's wealth, so he clung to his legal bondage ke grim death. What with turning night into day, smoking black gars, and living in the same house as the Court musical director, the rincess was hardly considered an asset to Weimar by the good towns- olk.

One May day in 1849 Wagner, having found the Dresden police nsympathetic to his activities during the riots, presented himself at he Villa Altenburg. Liszt first met Wagner at Paris in 1840. In 1844 he eard *Rienzi* at Dresden, where he again met Wagner four years later nd had a long and intimate talk with him. Wagner stayed with Liszt : the Villa Altenburg for a week or two, but when the news came hat the police were on his track again, it was thought expedient that Vagner should retreat to Paris. Meanwhile Liszt had begun to realize he extent of Wagner's immense genius, and from now onwards he ut all his artistic influence and resources to the furtherance of Vagnerian ideals. Liszt produced *Lohengrin* at Weimar in the follow- ng year. And his support did not end there: Liszt's purse was ever pen to the demands of the impecunious Wagner.

Jeorge Eliot's Visit

During the next decade or so Weimar was turned into the centre f the 'new German school' and the Princess kept an open house, to hich came a constant stream of distinguished people – philosophers, usicians, poets, painters, and novelists, including Thackeray and eorge Eliot. George Eliot records that 'Liszt looked splendid as he onducted the Opera. The grand outline of his face and floating hair as seen to advantage, as they were thrown into the dark relief by the stage lamps. Liszt's conversation is charming. I never met a perso whose manner of telling a story was so piquant.' She went to break fast at the Villa Altenburg and among the guests were Cornelius an Raff: 'The Princess was tastefully dressed in a morning robe of som semi-transparent material, lined with orange colour, which forme the bordering and ornament of the sleeves, a black lace jacket and piquant cap on the summit of her comb, and trimmed with viole colour.' During a reading of poetry George Eliot sat next to Liszt an was carried away by 'the sweetness of his expression. Genius, bene volence, and tenderness beam from his whole countenance, and hi manners were in perfect harmony with it. Then came the thing I ha longed for – his playing. I sat near him so that I could see both hi hands and face. For the first time in my life I beheld real inspiration for the first time I heard the true tones of the piano. He played one o his compositions, one of a series of religious fantasies. There wa nothing strange or excessive about his manner. His manipulation o the instrument was quiet and easy, and his face was simply grand – th lips compressed and the head thrown backward. When the music ex pressed quiet rapture or devotion a smile flitted over his features when it was triumphant the nostrils dilated. There was nothing pett or egotistic to mar the picture.'

Liszt reorganized the Opera and conducted the Court concerts. I addition to the new works of contemporary composers, such as Wag ner, Berlioz, Schumann, Raff, and Cornelius, Liszt produced operas b Gluck, Mozart, Schubert, Donizetti, Meyerbeer, Spontini, Webe and a score of other great composers. His symphony concert pro grammes were no less wide in appeal: all the Beethoven symphonie including the practically unknown *Choral*, Mozart, Haydn, Berlio and so on. Liszt also displayed great activity as a composer. The *Trans cendental Études*, the *Hungarian Rhapsodies*, the twelve *Symphonic Poem* and the *Faust* and *Dante Symphonies* all belong to this period.

Art before Politics

Although the world of music was divided into bitterly antagonist parties fighting their battles under the banners of Mendelssohn, Schu mann, and Wagner, no one could have been more level-headed an broad-minded than Liszt. His catholicity of taste was a form of geniu He could appreciate Wagner and Berlioz on the one hand and th Russian Nationalists on the other, while at the same time waxin enthusiastic over the merits of Mendelssohn, Schumann, and Chopin. And there was no question of shallow understanding. During this period of storm and stress that lasted throughout his life Liszt remained an untiring propagandist for, and an unbiased critic of, contemporary music; he was interested in everything that he considered good of its kind, no matter to what 'party' the composer might belong. Art came before politics. A composer himself, whose innovations were generally condemned as extravagances by the conservatives and the reactionaries and merely tolerated by the followers of the greater and even more spectacular genius of Wagner, Liszt was able to thrust aside any narrow prejudices that might have arisen against those who showed so little faith and interest in his own creative efforts. Had he been entirely self-centred, like most other great creative artists, no doubt his position as a composer would have been very different.

After Liszt and the Countess d'Agoult parted, it was decided that their three children should be placed in the care of Liszt's mother. All went well until the Princess gained control of Liszt. The Princess naturally disliked her predecessor and therefore it was not long before she prevailed upon Liszt to have the children brought up by her own former governess, an elderly lady with a rather sour disposition. Thus the Princess planned to have the children taken away from any possible influence of their real mother. Even their letters were censored and they were instructed to call the Princess 'mother'. Next to the Countess she considered Wagner the most pernicious influence in Liszt's life, and she did her best to poison Liszt against him, but she accomplished little in this direction. No doubt the Princess feared Wagner would not only outshine Liszt, but that the latter would eventually become indifferent to his own creative efforts.

Liszt's affairs went smoothly for the first half a dozen years, but at short notice the Princess was ordered to return to Russia. She refused and in consequence she was sentenced to banishment. The Grand Duchess of Saxe-Weimar, sister of the Czar, declined to have anything further to do with her and the rest of Weimar Society followed suit. At the same time Liszt was finding his position none too easy. First, there were at his disposal only limited funds to carry out his artistic ideas, and, secondly, his colleague who was in charge of the Court drama pandered to the tastes of the Grand Duke and therefore pushed forward the claims of a more popular style of musical entertainment and his own department of drama. Finally in 1858 Liszt produced Cornelius's *Barber of Bagdad*, and it was hissed. It was obvious that Liszt was really the target. Liszt at once decided that Weimar was best left to its own devices and he resigned forthwith.

The Princess and the Pope

Liszt and the Princess remained at Weimar until 1861. The Villa Altenburg was shut up and the Princess went to Rome to see if the Pope would grant the dissolution of her marriage. She threw herself at his feet and eloquently presented her case. The Pope was sympathetic and after due consideration agreed to her request. At last the Princess was free to marry Liszt. It was immediately arranged that Liszt should come to Rome on the eve of his fiftieth birthday and on the following day, 22 October, they would be married at the church of San Carlo. But the Princess underestimated the power of the opposition, for at the eleventh hour, when all was ready for the ceremony, the Pope refused to allow the marriage to proceed. The Princess was in despair. Liszt certainly appears to have been upset, but in 1864, when the Prince died, no further talk of marriage was broached.

From now onwards the Princess concentrated all her energies upon religious speculation. For some time past she had been at work on a series of twenty-four huge tomes entitled *The Inner Causes of the Outer Weakness of the Church*. The more intense her spiritual and intellectual activities became, the more eccentric did she become in her mode of living. All day long and into the early hours of the morning, clad in fantastic colours, she sat cloistered in her study from which daylight and fresh air were carefully excluded. She puffed away at her black cigars continuously and the atmosphere was like that of a hot-house. Visitors, even Liszt himself, were obliged to wait in an ante-room for ten minutes in order to be 'de-ventilated' and rid of any fresh air that they might have brought in with them, before coming in contact with the Princess. 'That anyone survived,' William Wallace says, 'after a mephitic whiff of the Princess's salon must be put down to an ever-watchful Providence. Into this Paradise of Tainted Devices Liszt stepped day after day, and night after night.'

Liszt also turned to his religion. Ernest Newman in *The Man Liszt* gives a vivid picture of Liszt in his new environment. He 'tried to persuade himself that now he would give himself up heart and soul to his true vocation of solitary and saint. He settled down in a cloister that had been placed at his disposal in the church of Santa Maria del

Rosario, on the Monte Mario. There was no one in the vast place but Liszt, a Dominican priest, and a servant. The priest read mass every morning; Liszt was always present, sitting in a stall a few yards from his cell. In the latter he had a long work-table, a small library, about a dozen pictures of saints, a marble cast of Chopin's hand, and a small piano of advanced age, badly out of tune, and with a D in the bass missing. But, as usual, he was making the best of two worlds. His tribute having been paid to the spirit in the morning, in the evening he let the flesh have its fling in the kind of company it loved. Shrewd observers were conscious of something suspiciously like a pose in his way of living.' In 1865, for some reason best known to himself, Liszt took minor orders and became an Abbé. He had already set about the task of reforming the music of the Church, with the result that a series of important works issued from his pen, such as *The Legend of Saint Elizabeth* and *Christus*.

Since giving up his post at Weimar, Liszt had lost his mother and his two children Blandine and Daniel. In 1857 Cosima had married Hans von Bülow, the famous pianist and conductor and a pupil of Liszt, but seven years later she left him to live with and devote herself to Wagner. Although such an action was true to family tradition, Liszt, who looked upon von Bülow almost as a son, could not countenance it, and consequently he became estranged from Wagner. It is characteristic of him, however, that he did not withdraw his ardent support of Wagner's cause, despite the fact that he was opposing the wishes of the Princess.

Rome, Weimar, and Pesth

From 1869 to 1886 Liszt divided his time between Rome, Weimar, where he had a large circle of pupils, and Pesth, where he directed the newly formed Hungarian Conservatoire. Nearly every pianist of note of the next generation studied at some time or other under Liszt. He refused all payment, demanding only that the student should have already acquired mastery of keyboard technique. Among Liszt's pupils who lived to our day were Felix Weingartner, Frederic Lamond, Emil Sauer, and Moritz Rosenthal. Rosenthal says that Liszt was unique as a pianist: 'I remember when I first went to him as a boy – he was in Rome at the time – he used to play for me in the evening by the hour – nocturnes by Chopin, études of his own – all of a soft, dreamy nature that caused me to open my eyes in wonder at the marvellous delicacy and finish of his touch. The embellishments were like a cobweb – so fine – or like the texture of the costliest lace . . . Liszt was more wonderful than anybody I have ever known.'

Some time in 1873, Amy Fay, an American young lady, came to Weimar in the hope of studying under Liszt. On the day after her arrival she went to the theatre, where she saw Liszt in a box. Her first impressions of the great man are interesting: 'Liszt is the most interesting and striking-looking man imaginable. Tall and slight, with deep-set eyes, shaggy eye-brows, and long iron-grey hair, which he wears parted in the middle. His mouth turns up in the corners, which gives him a most crafty and Mephistophelian expression when he smiles, and his whole appearance and manner have a sort of Jesuitical elegance and ease. His hands are very narrow, with long and slender fingers that look as if they had twice as many joints as other people's! They are so flexible and supple that it makes you nervous to look at them. Anything like the polish of his manner I never saw. When he got up to leave the box, for instance, after his adieu to the ladies, he laid his hand on his heart and made his final bow – not with affectation, or in mere gallantry, but with a quiet courtliness which made you feel that no other way of bowing to a lady was right or proper. It was most characteristic. But the most extraordinary thing about Liszt is his wonderful variety of expression and play of feature. One moment his face will look dreamy, shadowy, tragic. The next he will be insinuating, amiable, ironic, sardonic; but always the same captivating grace of manner. He is a perfect study. I cannot imagine how he must look when he is playing. He is all spirit, but half the time, at least, a mocking spirit, I should say. All Weimar adores him, and people say that women still go perfectly crazy over him. When he walks out he bows to everybody just like a King!'

Crazy Women

That women still went crazy over Liszt was no matter of idle talk. He was nearly shot by one admirer, and another stripped the covering off a chair on which he had been sitting and hung it on the wall in a frame. Others would surround him while he played and pluck out his hairs with special tweezers! Perhaps the most incredible story, not to say the most revolting, is that of an elderly lady who neither smoked nor took snuff and, although fastidious over matters of personal cleanliness, exhaled a curious and obnoxious odour. It was discovered that in 1843, after a public dinner, she had obtained the stump of Liszt's cigar, which she placed in her corsage, where it remained for over twenty-five years!

In 1872 Liszt had a reconciliation with Wagner and, contrary to the wishes of the Princess, took part in the ceremony of laying the foundation-stone of the Bayreuth Theatre. In the following year the Hungarians organized a national celebration in honour of Liszt's fiftieth anniversary as a concert pianist. Three years later the Countess d'Agoult died, but Liszt appears to have been unmoved by the news. In 1876 Liszt attended the first Bayreuth Festival and in 1882 was present at the first performance of *Parsifal*, after which he spent several weeks with Wagner in Venice. He returned to Pesth and on 13 February 1883 learned of Wagner's death. His grief was heightened by the fact that Cosima requested that he should not come to the funeral. The next year he went to the Bayreuth Festival, but Cosima was too busy to see him.

Last Tour and Death

In 1886 Liszt went on his last tour. First to Paris where his *Grand Mass* was performed under Colonne, and then to London for the first time after forty-five years. Here he spent two weeks, staying at Sydenham with Mr and Mrs Littleton. Sir Alexander Mackenzie conducted the *Legend of St Elizabeth* and Liszt visited Windsor Castle where he played once again to Queen Victoria. He continued his tour on to Antwerp, Brussels, Paris, Weimar, Bayreuth, and Luxemburg. On his way back to Bayreuth to attend the Festival in July, Liszt was obliged to pass a night in the train. He caught a chill and on arriving at Bayreuth spent the day in bed. Against the doctor's orders he attended the performance of *Tristan and Isolde*, but after the death scene of Isolde he was forced to leave. Pneumonia set in and the doctor foolishly refused to allow him to have his brandy, of which he was used to drinking a bottle a day. Congestion of the lungs followed, he became delirious, and on Saturday night, 31 July, Liszt died. Two hours previously he had spoken his last word. It was 'Tristan'.

And what of the Princess? On hearing the news of Liszt's death she shut herself up completely, refusing to see or write to anyone. Towards the end of February the following year she completed the twenty-fourth volume of her *magnum opus*. Within a fortnight she was found dead in bed.

GUSTAV ALBERT LORTZING

1801–51

RALPH W. WOOD

Early Years

The Lortzings came from Thuringia. The earliest to have been traced was Hans, born in 1630, who became a hangman; and as that office was an hereditary one it stayed in the composer's family right down to his grandfather, Johann Heinrich, who, being a youngest son, caused both a right angle in the genealogical table and a pleasant change of occupation. J. Heinrich ended up as a leather-merchant in Berlin. His fifth son, J. Friedrich, became an actor, but it was an elder one, J. Gottlob, the inheritor of the leather business, who was responsible for the birth in Berlin of our Gustav Albert. His connubial partner in responsibility was Charlotte Sophie, née Seidel, (of a French emigrant family).

Those were the supreme days of Napoleonic ascendancy. Berlin, for instance, knew two years of occupation by French troops. Two natural consequences of the situation were that Germany was seething with heroic nationalistic sentiments and that insecurity, if not downright ruin, was the economic portion of very many of her people. By 1811 things were so bad for the leather-merchant and his wife that they decided to leave Berlin and to take to the stage for a living. Possibly Friedrich, the actor brother, who was prospering, had something to do with their choice of a new career, which, however, after beginning with a very successful six months' engagement at the Breslau Theatre, quickly developed into a wandering existence, often in very poor circumstances indeed. Young Albert scraped up such education as conditions permitted, sufficient at any rate to enable him when grown up to use Latin and French phrases in his letters and to produce operatic libretti on a variety of subjects with a reasonable showing of knowledge. He himself acted from the age of nine, and his main musical instruction came from one Rungenhagen, who although later well known as conductor and composer was at the time just a member of the company. The boy received a thorough musical grounding and learnt to play the piano, violin, and cello. At a very early age he had been for a time at a Singakademie. Later he by himself worked through a few theoretical volumes by Albrechtsberger and the like. Otherwise he had only the practical training, and the contact with various seasoned and knowledgeable musicians, incidental to his life in the theatre. He is said to have been a witty and fun-loving child, as well as a dutiful one.

Marriage and Family

The three, Lortzing and his parents, present for us from start to finish, in fact, a picture of ideal mutual devotion and tenderness; and when, at 21, Albert took to himself a wife (an actress, encountered in the course of his profession) she was one who fitted into the picture completely. In the early days it was common to see the names of the four Lortzings side by side on a programme; they were all appearing at the Cologne Theatre. Soon, however, their respective engagements parted Lortzing from his parents, a state of affairs to which he was never really reconciled, which on occasion he tried to alter and in the meantime tempered by always keeping up a regular correspondence with them and snatching at every chance that did offer itself for however brief a reunion. His letters to them were equally likely to be reporting the fate of some new opera of his or to be describing how he had been making little things, a doll's bed, a confectioner's shop, for his children. Unfortunately he had also to announce deaths. Of eleven children (including two pairs of twins) five died young. When separated from his kin, whatever the circumstances, he was depressed and hardly able to compose. As long as he was with them, on the other hand, he composed readily and could bear all vicissitudes.

For bearing vicissitudes he had two other resources. The first was that he was religious. Whenever in his life – and it was rather often – he was having a bad time, through death of someone dear to him, through worries about his livelihood, through frustration upon frustration of his hopes, his letters would breathe pious resignation and faith in God. His other defence was the gaiety of his heart. Fond of nice clothes, fond of wine, inexhaustibly gay – so was he when things went well. Unlike many professional humorists (comedy was always his forte, both as actor-singer and as composer-librettist), his jocoseness flowed straight out of his own temperament. Although as prone as the next man to be quickly downcast by misfortune and disappointment, he had, to reinforce the acquired consolations of religion, a natural sanguineness and elasticity. Devoid of conceit, and no more vain that was automatic in one of his calling, he carried over from his parents the sort of pride, which a friend never knows whether more to admire or deprecate, that forbade him ever to reveal to others the difficulties, particularly financial, in which he often found himself. Oddly, perhaps, with all those traits went one other, in its different way also something of a shield against adversity – his invariable strictness in the conduct of his business affairs.

Revolution and War

To the 'heroic nationalistic sentiments' of the times he was by no means a stranger. Still less was he a stranger to the times' material hazards. The Paris revolution of 1830 worried as much as it excited him, for he was afraid that the French might invade the Rhineland again, where his parents were then working. He himself was a guest-artist for a few weeks that year at the Mannheim Court-theatre, and he was a regular member, with his wife, of a company playing at Detmold, Münster, Osnabrück, Bad Pyrmont. Princelings such as financed these theatres had now to turn their expenditure rather towards the equipment of soldiery. His contract became only a six months' one. It must have been, one sees, with diverse perturbations that he would read in the newspapers about each day's events. Then there was the defeat of Poland by Russia in 1831, with a stream of refugees into Germany, enthusiasm there for a 'defeated, heroic nation', artists celebrating the mood in song and poem – and Lortzing writing *The Pole and his Child*, a one-act 'Liederspiel' that made his name for the first time really known far and wide, that happened to mark an epoch in his own creative development, and that remained in the repertoire for many years, despite such obstacles as police bans that led to its being re-titled *The Sergeant-major of the Fourth Regiment*! His *Andreas Hofer* of 1832 never reached the stage at all until 1887. ... In 1848, in Vienna, he had the anguish of losing one of his best friends, Robert Blum – writer, theatrical odd-job man, founder of the Schiller-Verein – who was imprisoned, and then shot, for left-wing political activity.

Conductor

The upheavals of 1848 also made an end of Lortzing's Vienna employment, since his theatre changed hands and name and character;

and he lost three months' salary and an impending 'benefit' into the bargain. He was a *Kapellmeister* at the time – operatic conductor. It was not until 1844 that he had ever been able to achieve the ambition of exchanging his place on the stage for one at the conductor's desk. The event, which gave him immense delight, had taken place at the Leipzig Theatre, where as a matter of fact he had been acting and singing for the previous ten years; it was a change of directors that produced his change of status. The Leipzig stage engagement had succeeded, and improved upon, the less stationary as well as less lucrative one that he had held from the time of his marriage. . . . Unfortunately Schmidt, the new Leipzig director in 1844, dismissed both Lortzing and Netzer, his other conductor, after only one year, ostensibly as a matter of retrenchment. Pokorny, a director at Vienna, got in touch with Lortzing at that point, but only installed him as *Kapellmeister* one year later still (having employed Netzer in the interim!). Lortzing had a very bad time between the two jobs and was even reduced to music-copying (one of his boyhood's occupations) to keep the wolf from the door.

Bad Times

After the 1848 disaster things were worse still. All his applications for other conducting posts were rejected or ignored. He was unable to obtain receipts due to him for his *Undine*. He had recourse to the pawnshop. In 1849 the success of his latest opera, *Rolands Knappen*, back at Leipzig (where Schmidt, gone to America, had been replaced by Wirsing) led to his receiving the offer of the conductorship there; but after much bad fortune and worse intrigue he was squeezed out. He wrote songs – songs political and songs non-political – for pittances from publishers. He even took to acting once more. He was separated from his family and unable sometimes to send them cash they urgently needed. His wife had to borrow to make ends meet. At last in 1850 he got a conducting job in Berlin – not, however, at all a good one, artistically or financially.

Operas Galore

Of course throughout his career his stage-compositions were to an extent a source of income. Performances, however, were rarely plentiful, and in any event the composer was paid neither well nor willingly. 'Pirating', moreover, went on; and in his letters at least one reference occurs to receipts withheld from him by the rascality of lawyers. Against the background of his personal life the mere chronology of his operas is interesting. Practically all his earlier pieces were mere pot-pourris of music by other men (following, be it said, a popular fashion of the day), filled out with a section from his own pen just here and there. From *The Pole and His Child* (1832) onwards he was almost always his own librettist. His first opera with music really by himself was *Die Beiden Schützen* (1836), with *Czar und Zimmermann* close on its heels. The unsuccessful *Caramor* was written for production at the annual Leipzig 'Fischerstechen' of 1839, following an opera at which Lortzing certainly put in a lot of work, but which, even if ever finished, was destroyed. In 1840 came *Hans Sachs*; and the very gay comic-opera *Casanova* was first performed on 31 December 1841 (not quite a month after the death of Lortzing's father and only a short time before the loss of an infant daughter – two very severe blows). The pleasure of being officially honoured in Leipzig by having his portrait drawn and of renewing old acquaintanceships on both sides of the footlights during a guest-performance at Pyrmont, not to speak of the better health induced by a visit to Bad Memberg for a gout cure, surrounded the completion of *Der Wildschütz* (première 31 December 1842). *Undine* was written during the not very comfortable spell of conducting under Schmidt. The heart-breaking griefs and anxieties following the loss of the Leipzig conductorship accompanied the creation of the homely and comic *Der Waffenschmied* (produced by Pokorny in Vienna, 1846, and before long the most popular of all Lortzing's works). The comic-opera *Zum Grossadmiral* was written in Vienna, but the ill-treatment of *Undine* in that city by the critics led Lortzing to contrive its première at Leipzig (13 December 1847). In May 1848, he began the libretto of *Regina*, a serious opera reflecting current political events, but the work, though soon finished, was never performed in his lifetime. The score of *Rolands Knappen*, the comedy that he also produced during those blackest months of his career, was completed in March 1849. *Cagliostro*, a comic-opera that he sketched in 1850, was never finished, but the première of *Die Opernprobe* (one-act comic opera) took place at Frankfurt-am-Main, on 20 January 1851. Away in Berlin the composer, who was complaining of being depressed and not feeling well, died of a stroke the very next morning.

JACOB LUDWIG FELIX MENDELSSOHN-BARTHOLDY

1805–47

MAX PIRANI

Descent

The life of Felix Mendelssohn-Bartholdy, examined in the light of his ancestry, presents an interesting example of a development that proceeded not by reversion to type, but by means of a contrasting evolution.

He was born in Hamburg, of Jewish parents with Jewish traditions rooted in Jewish culture, but, though one can find in his spiritual internationalism, his restlessness, his 'Wanderlust', and in the fluidity and adaptability of his genius, the residuum of his Jewish ancestry that has enriched European music with a glow of Oriental colour, yet nowhere in his work can be discovered even a trace of either the Synagogue or the traditional lamentations which such an origin would suggest.

Indeed, his artistic heritage was the purely Teutonic and Christian music of his adored Bach and of Handel, his intellectual upbringing was based on German and international literature, and his life was spent in an almost exclusively non-Jewish social milieu.

It was Felix's grandfather who accomplished the emergence from the Ghetto, a feat of considerable difficulty, requiring strength of character combined with unusual intellectual capacity, but Moses Mendelssohn's qualities went beyond these limits, for he became a master of German philosophy and his research paved the way to much original work in metaphysics and aesthetics.

His sons were brought up in an enlightened atmosphere; so much did Moses' religious breadth of view permeate his family that a break with the Jewish faith resulted. His second son, Abraham, and his two daughters became converts to Christianity, but before Abraham took this step his children, among them Felix, had been baptized.

Abraham had married Lea Salomon, a Jewess of Berlin, and it was on the advice and example of Lea's brother that the conversion was decided. The name of Bartholdy, then adopted, was due to the same influence, for it had been that of the former owner of Salomon's garden!

Youth

When Felix was three years old his family escaped to Berlin, for life in Hamburg had become complicated by the French occupation. Abraham was a banker and, foreign domination proving as detrimental to his business as it was distasteful to his feelings, Berlin offered better prospects and a freer life.

Lea was a highly cultured woman and an excellent musician, and Felix and his sister Fanny had every encouragement to develop their abilities. Musical education began with five-minute lessons and Felix's progress was not forced; before long it was he who set the pace, leaving his mother and his sister to admire his precocity.

At the age of seven he was taken to Paris where he was taught the piano by Madame Bigot and for the first time was influenced from outside the family circle.

On the return to Berlin, his education, musical and otherwise, began in earnest. He studied piano with Ludwig Berger, musical theory with Zelter (who was Goethe's musical oracle), and languages with Heyse (the father of Paul Heyse the novelist); he also learned to draw and to play the violin.

At the age of nine he played in public for the first time and 'was much applauded'. At the age of twelve he began to compose systematically and prolifically, and from this time onwards his future career as a musician was accepted as a matter of course.

His environment was conducive to an easy and harmonious development of his talents. The Mendelssohn household was in the habit of having frequent musical evenings, at which the four children, Felix, Fanny, Rebecka, the younger sister, and Paul, performed. Felix's compositions were often included in the programmes and he had invaluable opportunities of playing and conducting before an audience. Abraham's position as a successful business man and Lea's artistic gifts had been instrumental in creating a salon that many Berlin notabilities attended regularly and that attracted most visiting musicians.

Among the latter was Weber, who came to Berlin in 1821. He cast the same spell upon Felix as he did later upon Wagner and the enthusiasm he aroused remained with Felix throughout his life. Another contact of the same year was with Goethe, when Zelter took Felix to

Weimar and introduced him to the poet. The boy's mentality can be gauged by this letter written to his parents describing the visit:

November 6th, 1821.

After church I went to the Elephant Hotel where I made a sketch of Lucas Cranach's house. Two hours later Professor Zelter came, calling out: 'Goethe has come, the old gentleman has come!' We instantly hurried downstairs and went to Goethe's house. He is very kind but I do not think any of his portraits are like him. . . .

After that I walked in the garden with him and Professor Zelter. He does not look like a man of seventy-three, rather of fifty. . . .

Every morning I get a kiss from the author of *Faust* and *Werther*, and every afternoon two kisses from the father and friend Goethe. Think of that! In the afternoon I play to Goethe for about two hours, partly Bach fugues and partly improvisations.

Another journey that left lasting impressions was a family tour of Switzerland in 1822 and for the first time Felix's composition reacted to the influence of national idiom, to be developed later in such works as the *Scotch* and *Italian Symphonies*; not that the pieces founded on Swiss tunes dating from this period have any great artistic significance, but they betray a readiness to assimilate external ideas that proved to be of great importance in Felix's development as a composer.

A similar influence was the outcome of a visit to the Baltic in 1824 when Felix first saw the sea, but this time the period of gestation was longer, and it is in the overture *Meeresstille*, composed four years later, that these impressions were translated into sound.

Moscheles was a visitor to Berlin in the same year and spent much time with the Mendelssohns. He gave Felix piano lessons, though by this time the boy had become, in Moscheles' own words, a mature artist and had attained more than local celebrity.

In Paris in 1825 he appeared both as pianist and composer. He seems to have made a better impression on the French musicians than they made on him, for in his letters he complains of ignorance, of charlatanism, and of irreverence in the performance of great music.

Abraham's business was flourishing, and in 1825 he bought a new house, the family home of the future. His resources, pecuniary and social, were always at the disposal of Felix, who was spared many of those struggles so often associated with artistic achievement. Abraham in his paternal pride said wittily, 'Formerly I was the son of my father, now I am the father of my son'; an instance of commerce bowing to the arts in the true Jewish tradition. The racial heritage was also reflected in family attachments, especially in that of Felix and Fanny, a relationship intensified by similarity of taste and temperament.

Shakespeare and Bach

In 1826 Felix and Fanny read some of Shakespeare's plays and the immediate result was the composition of the *Overture to A Midsummer Night's Dream*. This, written for piano duet before it was orchestrated, demonstrated the principle of placing design before colour, a principle followed by Felix constantly both in his own method of composition and in the theories he propounded in his later teaching days.

His only noteworthy achievement in opera dates from this same period. *Die Hochzeit des Camacho* had been written a year earlier, but in the negotiations for its performance in 1827 Felix met with the first serious obstructions of his career: he overcame them finally, though Spontini, then Director of the Berlin Opera, put every obstacle in the way both of the rehearsals and of the performances. The work was adversely criticized in the Press and by the public, and, partly for this reason and also because he never again found a libretto to his liking, it was his last effort in the operatic form.

This creative activity did not retard his general cultural development and his matriculation at Berlin University followed studies in literature and classical philology. His recreations included gymnastics, swimming, dancing, billiards, and chess; and neither now, nor when his professional career grew more arduous, did he allow such diversions to be excluded from his life.

Felix, from early youth, had been a fanatical lover of Bach's music, an inheritance from Lea. Her remark when Fanny was a baby, four years before Felix was born, that 'the child has Bach fugue fingers', indicated the tastes that were to be inculcated in her children. Bach's works were little known in Germany at this time and Felix, in his determination to share his own joys with the world, prepared a revival of the *St Matthew Passion*. The preparations began with the organization of a small choir for private rehearsal and culminated in a public performance on 11 March 1829, the first since the death of Bach. There was great opposition to the project (even Zelter at first lacked confidence in the practicability of a performance), but Felix, together with a few fellow enthusiasts, including Devrient, a well-known singer, actor, and *littérateur*, succeeded in carrying out the plan. So uch public interest was aroused that the work was repeated on Bach's irthday, 21 March.

This successful outcome of Felix's altruistic efforts had far-reaching esults: it was the beginning of the movement that led to the formation of the Bach Gesellschaft; it inaugurated, by the creation of interest mongst a public to whom the composer had been literally unknown, e Bach cult of our own day; and it caused Felix to allude to his ncestry. 'It was an actor and a Jew,' he said to Devrient, 'who estored this great Christian work to the people.'

ravel

Felix's musical career up to the age of twenty had been meteoric but rofitless, and it was now decided that he should prepare to live by is profession. Berlin had become uncomfortable, for his fellow nusicians were antagonistic, partly because of his youthful egotism nd partly on account of his racial origin, which no amount of holy vater could conceal. His black hair with its natural wave emphasized e Jewish features, and Thackeray in describing him ('His face is the nost beautiful I ever saw, like what I imagine our Saviour's to have een') was not making Italian Primitives the basis of his comparison.

So foreign travel was ordained to combine a professional career with bservation and experience of the world at large. There was even a iggestion that Felix's permanent home might be found outside his wn country, and in the search for a possible future field of activity he isited London in 1829. This, the first of ten visits that he paid to ngland, proved a momentous experiment. He appeared as composer, onductor, and pianist with equal success in each role. His charming nanner was a great asset and he danced, dined, and was fêted to such n extent that his father wrote admonishing him not to forsake music or Society. He renewed acquaintance with Moscheles and made many iendships that were to stand him in good stead in later life.

At the end of the London musical season he went to Scotland, where atural beauties gave him inspiration for the *Fingal's Cave Overture*; e thematic material of the *Scotch Symphony* can also be traced to this eriod. On the return to London in September, an accident – he fell om a carriage – kept him in bed for two months and prevented his tendance at Fanny's wedding: she married Wilhelm Hensel, the ainter, in October.

Felix reached Berlin to find that a Chair of Music had been founded

at Berlin University with himself as the proposed occupant, but h
was not ready to embrace a pedagogic career and declined the honou
in favour of continuing his journeyings.

Through Weimar, Munich, and Vienna (where he writes in disgus
of the prevalent musical taste) he went to Italy, arriving in Rome i
November 1830. The following winter was devoted mainly to th
assimilation of impressions, musical and artistic, and his numerous an
detailed letters give a vivid picture of his experiences. He was en
thusiastic about the singing of the Papal Choir in Palestrina and Allegri
but the ritual music of the Catholic Church, especially the chantin
of the Psalms, was too much for a Lutheran upbringing superimpose
on a Jewish mentality, and he neither understood nor liked it.

His travels next took him through Switzerland, where he walke
over mountain passes, sketched, wrote lengthy descriptive letters an
played the organ at remote churches. By way of Munich and Düssel
dorf (a visit that was to have an important sequel) he found his way t
Paris, where the most noteworthy meetings were with Chopin an
Liszt.

He had by this time decided to settle in Germany, but befor
returning home he once more visited England. This time his organ
playing, particularly a performance at St Paul's Cathedral, attracte
great attention. He may be said to have brought to this country a nev
technique, especially in the treatment of the pedals, which was t
become the basis of English organ-playing.

He returned to Berlin in July 1832, and at the instance of Devrien
applied for the post of Director of the Singakademie, vacant on accoun
of Zelter's death. Perhaps Felix's refusal of the University professor
ship two years earlier had repercussions during the election tha
followed his application, or perhaps the earlier prejudices were sti
strong; in any event the candidature was a failure and he lost by a wid
margin of votes. Berlin was not yet his, but he ignored defeat and gav
several concerts during the ensuing winter, introducing to Berlin
besides new works of his own, Beethoven's *Pianoforte Concerto in G.*

Düsseldorf

The year 1833 marked a turning-point in Felix's life: hitherto he ha
been a musical free-lance, but now he was offered a definite appoint
ment. This followed on his conductorship of the Lower Rhin
Festival. The offer was a contract for a period of three years, durin

which he was to direct the Opera, the theatre, and all other public musical establishments of Düsseldorf.

But Düsseldorf was too conservative to hold him: the new broom swept too clean. Felix began by dismissing the Director of Church Music and performed Palestrina Masses instead of the customary insipidities. Then he attacked the Opera to such purpose that at the first performance under his directorship there was a riot in the audience. A lack of business instinct was partly responsible for his troubles, and he over-estimated both the Düsseldorfers' capacity for artistic appreciation and the prices they were prepared to pay for their seats.

After a few difficult months he asked to be released from the main part of his duties, retaining only the position of Honorary Intendant. However, he remained resident in Düsseldorf for more than a year longer, composing a great deal and conducting there and elsewhere, but the preliminary arrangements for the opening of a new theatre led to so much discord and such mental distress on Felix's part that, on being invited to become conductor of the Leipzig Gewandhaus Concerts, he made haste to accept, and moved to Leipzig in October 1835.

Leipzig

Felix afterwards wrote, 'When I first came to Leipzig, I thought I was in Paradise', and indeed Purgatory seemed to have been left behind, for his new appointment was highly congenial. Ferdinand David was his *Konzertmeister* (this brilliant violinist was born in Hamburg, in the same house as Felix) and they worked together in amity and in complete sympathy: the *Violin Concerto* was a later outcome of this friendship. The business management of the concerts was not Felix's duty and he could again devote his energies exclusively to music.

One of the first visitors was Chopin, to whom Felix introduced Clara Wieck: she and Schumann had made Felix's acquaintance soon after his arrival in Leipzig. Moscheles came immediately afterwards and he, Clara and Felix played Bach's *Triple Concerto in D Minor* at one of the first concerts of the new regime.

On Moscheles's departure, Felix paid a flying visit with him to Berlin and for the last time saw Abraham, who died suddenly just after the return to Leipzig. This was the first break in the family circle and it affected Felix very deeply. He went so far as to write 'a new life must now begin for me, or all must be at an end – the old life is severed.' But the immediate result was to stimulate his work on the oratorio *St Paul*, begun in Düsseldorf and in which Abraham had taken great interest. Together with his enthusiasm for the Leipzig concerts, this occupation prevented his loss from becoming an obsession.

Notable performances of Beethoven's *Choral Symphony* and Mozart's *D minor Pianoforte Concerto* were among the events of the first Gewandhaus season, Felix appearing as both conductor and pianist. His reputation as the latter had not diminished and contemporary criticism gives him a high place as a virtuoso.

The first performance of *St Paul* had been arranged to take place in Frankfurt, but the illness of Schelbe, the Director of the Frankfurt Cäcilien-Verein, necessitated its transference to the Lower Rhine Festival at Düsseldorf. However, Felix was destined to visit Frankfurt without delay, and the opportunity came when he was asked to take over Schelbe's duties on the termination of the Leipzig season.

In Frankfurt he fell in love, and this new experience had a devastating effect: he wrote, 'I can neither compose, nor write letters, nor play the piano!' The cause of this emotional upheaval was Mademoiselle Cécile Jeanrenaud, the daughter of a clergyman of the French Reformed Church, who, fortunately for *Elijah* and other unwritten works, reciprocated his feelings. Their marriage took place in March 1837, after a winter almost devoid of composition, though a strenuous season in Leipzig could not be avoided.

On his marriage, Felix finally cast aside all hereditary inhibitions: he was now a Christian gentleman and Berlin and London were to recognize him as such. Leipzig University had already conferred upon him the honorary degree of Ph.D., and his importance as a leading figure in musical life was continually increasing.

The Birmingham Festival brought him to England again in the autumn of 1837. He conducted *St Paul*, played his new *Pianoforte Concerto* (in D minor) and gave an organ recital. His propaganda for Bach continued in frequent performances of the great organ works, and he is reported to have aroused intense enthusiasm by his unconventional and grandiose interpretations.

Through Frankfurt, where he had left Cécile, he returned to Leipzig. The Gewandhaus concerts were resumed, and Felix introduced new features into the programmes. Historical and international grouping of composers was intended to acquaint his audience with the development of music, while new works, including many of his own, were frequently performed.

His first son was born on 7 February 1838, and was christened Carl Wolfgang Paul: each of his five children was to be provided with three names, perhaps on account of his own richness in this respect. Cécile had a serious illness after the confinement, and for Felix this was the first of several periods of anxiety caused by family ill-health.

After a visit to Berlin, which had as its object the introduction of Cécile to Lea and Fanny, Felix began to sketch the preliminaries for *Elijah*. He had decided on this after flirting with the idea of an oratorio on the subject of *St Peter*, but the Old Testament prophet proved the stronger attraction. The composition was to occupy Felix for nearly eight years.

In 1840 Liszt played in Leipzig and created a bad impression by charging exorbitant prices. Felix arranged a musical soirée for him at the Gewandhaus, in order to pacify both the virtuoso and his public, providing thereby an instance of the friendly attitude he held towards his colleagues.

New Projects

Felix's popularity with the Saxon Government encouraged him to propose the establishment of a Conservatorium of Music in Leipzig. The funds were to be provided by a legacy which had been bequeathed to the town, and Felix considered that an opportune moment had arrived to strike in the cause of Art. From 1840 to 1843 negotiations were in progress: Felix had lost the impatience of the Düsseldorf days and was prepared to work steadily towards the fulfilment of his desires. He also initiated a scheme to erect a monument to Bach in front of the Thomas-Schule, and he gave concerts and recitals in order to raise the necessary funds.

The *Lobgesang*, composed as a *pièce d'occasion*, was the reason for his next English visit (the sixth), for the work was to be performed at the 1840 Birmingham Festival and Felix was invited to conduct it: this time he was in England only a few days. The *Lobgesang* was given twice in Leipzig during the following season, and its favourable reception, including expressions of enthusiasm from the King of Saxony, raised hopes for the prospects of the Conservatorium.

But trouble was brewing for Felix, and ambitions for Leipzig were to remain in the background for some time yet. His brother Paul came to visit him with a proposal, confirmed officially later, that he, Felix, should take charge of the Music Department of an Academy of Arts, to be founded in Berlin at the instance of Wilhelm IV, the new King of Prussia.

Felix foresaw difficulties, and in any event a change from the contented, productive life in Leipzig was not attractive, but the nature of the invitation, which gradually assumed the shape of a Royal Command, left the reluctant subject without choice, and after a busy winter in Leipzig, which concluded with a performance of Bach's *Passion* in St Thomas's Church, he removed to the family house in Berlin in May 1841.

His fears were well founded: ignorance and intrigue hampered his activities. As *Kapellmeister* to the King of Prussia he had theoretically a free hand, but he found himself involved in a series of conferences that produced no results. He wrote in October, after five months of abortive effort, 'If you allude to the project for establishing a Music Conservatorium here (in Berlin), then I regret to be obliged to say that I know no more about it than everyone else. . . . Years may pass, nothing may ever come of it.'

This discouragement was intensified by dissensions in the orchestra under his charge and by the coldness of the public. At the King's request, he wrote music to the *Antigone* of Sophocles and, as usual, found in composition an escape from mundane vexations. The completion of the *Scotch Symphony* was an excuse for him to leave Berlin for its first Leipzig performance in March 1842, and again for its first London performance at a Philharmonic concert in June. This time Cécile accompanied him across the Channel and was a witness of his popularity in England.

Felix received two Commands to Buckingham Palace, and he recounts with some naïveté his reception by Queen Victoria and the Prince Consort, the account beginning, 'Yesterday evening I was sent for by the Queen, who was almost (!) alone with Prince Albert.' He played the piano to the royal couple, heard the Prince Consort play the organ and heard the Queen sing. The only blot on this golden page was provided by the royal parrot, which drowned the music with its screams, so that Felix had to carry it out of the room, cage and all.

Felix delayed his return to Berlin as long as possible, touring Switzerland in the summer, visiting Frankfurt in September, and stopping at Leipzig to conduct the first Gewandhaus concert of the season. In Berlin he found the organization of the Academy as far from completion as ever and, losing patience, he tendered his resignation. This was accepted in part, but he yielded to the King of Prussia's persuasion that his appointment should merely be modified. He was now to be 'General Music Director', certain compositions were demanded from him, he had special responsibilities concerning church music, but, for the present, he was not obliged to reside in Berlin.

He at once moved to his beloved Leipzig, but was hardly settled there when Lea died, an event which caused him great grief, particularly as his leaving Berlin had affected her severely. But once again he found relief in his work, which was soon resumed with the old vigour.

The Conservatorium

The King of Saxony had at last agreed to Felix's plans for the Leipzig Conservatorium, and in April 1843 it was opened in the Gewandhaus buildings. The staff of professors included himself, Schumann, and David. Felix supervised the whole of the teaching and also gave individual piano lessons. His instruction was confined to the interpretative aspect; he left technical routine to be dealt with by assistants, a method hardly consistent with modern ideas!

The King of Prussia was asking for the compositions he had commissioned, and the first of these to be finished was the *Incidental Music to A Midsummer Night's Dream*. The first performance was given in Berlin in October and, in view of the increasing pressure of work arising from the King's demands, Felix decided that he must again move his household. Since his mother's death, the family house was his property and in November he was once more installed there.

Arrangements had been made for Ferdinand Hiller to conduct the Leipzig concerts, for Felix was overworking and overworried: the Berlin annoyances, the constant journeys and the ever-present thoughts of *Elijah* were proving a strain on his strength, but he could not rest and accepted an offer from the Philharmonic Society of London to conduct six concerts in the summer of 1844.

The Conservatorium was in the meantime feeling its way without the services of its Director, but it had been judiciously organized, and Felix, knowing that there was no fear of its extinction, was content to leave it until his energies could again be devoted freely to professional duties.

After a short stay in Frankfurt, he made one more attempt to solve the Berlin problems, but without success, and again he resigned all those duties that required him to reside in the capital. This time the King of Prussia acquiesced, and in December 1844, Felix took the only course consistent with his physical condition, going back to Frankfurt for a long holiday.

It was not until the following September that he was fit to resume active work, though he had been composing consistently throughout the year. The attractions of the Conservatorium and the Gewandhaus Orchestra proved too strong to be disregarded indefinitely and he returned to Leipzig as soon as his health would permit.

During the winter of 1845–6 Felix worked at high pressure. He taught pianoforte and composition at the Conservatorium, conducted the Gewandhaus concerts, and concentrated intensely on *Elijah*. One act of importance to Leipzig was the invitation he sent to Moscheles to become pianoforte professor at the Conservatorium: it was accepted, and Moscheles proved invaluable to the institution when Felix was forced finally to cease work.

The Climax of Elijah

Whether or not *Elijah* can be ranked as highly as the productions of Felix's youth, it nevertheless marks the culmination of his career as a composer. Throughout the past eight years of triumphs and discouragements the oratorio had been constantly in his mind: he spared no pains to make it, from both the technical and the musical aspects, as perfect a work as he was capable of conceiving. He gave his whole heart to its composition and taxed his strength to a degree that was evident only when the work was completed. He had the satisfaction of witnessing its success, but even this meant added effort, and his last two visits to England at a time when he should have been conserving his energies hastened the final breakdown.

He made other journeys before these: in May and June 1846, three weeks were spent travelling in the Rhineland, and he conducted successively at Aix, Düsseldorf, Liège, and Cologne. He had success everywhere, but returned to Leipzig tired, faced with the task of completing *Elijah* in time for the Birmingham Festival.

After rehearsals in London, Felix conducted the first performance of

Elijah in Birmingham Town Hall on 26 August. It met with overwhelming enthusiasm, and Felix himself wrote equally enthusiastically of its performance and of the audience's reception. The journey home fatigued him greatly, but he immediately began the final revision of the oratorio of which almost every movement was altered before publication.

He was overtaxing himself constantly: a demand from the King of Prussia for a setting of the German Liturgy set him to further composition and this work, together with some others, was written during a short creative burst. Moscheles had arrived and had taken over the direction of the Conservatorium: Niels Gade had relieved him of the main part of his conductor's duties; but Felix insisted on taking charge of some of the Gewandhaus concerts and on instituting examinations of students in his capacity of Conservatorium Director.

He even began work on another oratorio, to be called *Christus*, and by the time he left Leipzig in April 1847, for the London performance of *Elijah*, his appearance reflected his exhausted state. He spent a busy month in England, conducting *Elijah* four times in London and once each in Manchester and Birmingham, conducting and playing at a Philharmonic concert, giving pianoforte and organ recitals, and again visiting Buckingham Palace.

He returned to Frankfurt in September, weary and ill, and two days after his arrival heard of Fanny's death. This had a disastrous effect: it was a blow from which he never recovered. Switzerland welcomed him again in early summer, but he could not work and spent his time drawing and painting. In September he returned home to Leipzig and found commissions waiting for him, but he refused them all: a *String Quartet* and a few fragments were all that was written in these last months.

A visit to Berlin was too vivid a reminder of Fanny and further reduced his condition. Fits of depression were followed by a serious attack of shivering and head pains on 9 October: after a temporary recovery he relapsed, and from a third attack on 3 November he never recovered consciousness. He died on 4 November.

Mendelssohn's epitaph could hardly be better expressed than in the words of Dr H. C. Colles, who writes in *Grove's Dictionary*, 'he was the composer whose versatile abilities dominated the musical taste of Germany during his life, and of England for a generation or more after his death.'

JAKOB LIEBMANN MEYERBEER

1791–1864

DYNELEY HUSSEY

Origins

One of the remarkable features in the history of French music is the recurrent infusion of foreign blood, which has given it new vigour whenever native genius has seemed to have exhausted itself. Even ballet, the characteristic product of France, was created in the first instance by an Italian, Baldassare di Belgiojoso (or Balthasar de Beaujoyeulx as he called himself in France), whose *Balet comique de la reine* was produced before the court of Henri III in 1581. It was again an Italian, Lulli, who founded French opera, in whose development ballet played so important a part. Later, in the middle of the eighteenth century, came the German, Gluck, with his ideas of dramatic propriety, which appealed to the French sense of logic and provided a classical opera in their own language for an audience sated by the conventions of Italian companies. He was followed after the Revolution by three more Italians – Cherubini, whom Beethoven esteemed above all his contemporaries, Spontini, and Rossini, whose *William Tell* is the archetype of the true Parisian 'grand' opera. Last of all (unless we are to include Stravinsky) came Jakob Meyerbeer, a Jew from Berlin.

When he arrived to take up a more or less permanent residence in Paris in 1830, Meyerbeer was in his fortieth year and possessed of a considerable reputation won in the theatres of Italy with a number of operas whose very names are now forgotten save by historians of music. This strikingly handsome man with his fine features, about whose wide forehead with its deep-set black eyes the dark hair curled luxuriantly, had an air of seriousness and nobility, touched with melancholy. During the past two years he had suffered much personal anguish through the successive loss of two children of his recent marriage and of his father, to whom he was devoted.

That father was Jakob Herz Beer, a native of Frankfurt-am-Main, who had acquired wealth as a banker in Berlin. He was a man of wide literary and scientific interests and his house was frequented by the distinguished men of the time. His wife, Amalie Wulf, was a woman of rare intellectual gifts and noble character, of whom Heine declared that 'she could not lie down in peace unless she had done some generous deed.' It was from her father, Meyer Liebmann Wulf, who left his eldest grandson an income of more than 250,000 francs for life, that the composer acquired the first part of his adopted surname. There were three younger sons of the marriage, of whom Heinrich, born in 1794, alone achieved no particular distinction. Wilhelm, born in 1797, besides succeeding to his father's business, became an amateur astronomer of some repute, while the youngest, Michael, made a name as a poet, among his compositions being a drama, *Struensee*, for which his brother wrote an overture and incidental music in 1846.

Early Years

Young Jakob Beer early showed an exceptional bent towards music. There are stories of his playing on the pianoforte at the age of four tunes he had heard on the barrel-organs in the streets; and, as a boy of nine, he gave a public performance of Mozart's *Concerto in D minor*. With wealthy parents sympathetic to his musical leanings, the boy had good teachers. The first was Franz Lauska, a pupil of Clementi, whose interest he aroused in the promising young pianist, so that the great man himself came to stay with the Beers in 1801 and gave young Jakob, now ten years old, a course of lessons. This was an especial favour, granted, perhaps, to wealth as well as to exceptional talent; for Clementi had by this time given up taking pupils in the ordinary way.

The boy had also begun to try his hand at composition, and in this same year of 1801 he composed a cantata in honour of his father's birthday. So, although it was as a pianist that he was at first expected to make his name, a teacher of composition now had to be found. He studied first with Karl Friedrich Zelter, Director of the Singakademie, a friend of Goethe, some of whose poems he set to music. Zelter seems to have been less sympathetic to the young Meyerbeer than he was later in life to Mendelssohn, and his pupil soon exchanged him for Bernard Anselm Weber, director of the National Opera in Berlin. Weber, who was a pupil of the famous Abbé Vogler, was an ardent admirer of Gluck's operas, which he introduced to the Berlin Opera and, presumably, also to the notice of his young pupil.

Whilst studying with Weber, Meyerbeer sent one of his exercises, a fugue, to Vogler at Darmstadt. After an interval of many weeks he received, instead of the expected commendation, a treatise upon fugue a merciless analysis of his own effort, and a fugue composed upon the same theme by the Abbé. The industrious apprentice was not chilled by this cold douche of theory. He diligently set to work upon a fugue in eight parts, which he despatched to Darmstadt. This time he received the reply: 'Come to me and I will receive you as a son.'

So at the age of eighteen Meyerbeer became a member of Vogler's household, where he found, among others, Johann Gänsbacher, later *Kapellmeister* of the Cathedral at Vienna and already an accomplished composer of church music. Shortly after his arrival, Carl Maria von Weber, the future composer of *Der Freischütz*, rejoined Vogler's class. The youth from Berlin found himself in stimulating company, whose host was the most distinguished musical theorist of his day and a man of quite extraordinary character. The young men, besides writing their exercises under Vogler's supervision and practising on the organ, indulged in literary composition. Meyerbeer was one of the founders of the *Harmonischer Verein* or Musical Club, whose object was to further the appreciation of art through criticism written by experts. They wrote under pseudonyms, and Weber, who signed himself Melos, proved the most accomplished of these self-appointed critics. He was to become one of Meyerbeer's foremost 'appreciators'.

First Compositions

Meyerbeer was soon composing on his own account and in 1810 some settings of religious poems by Klopstock were performed in Berlin, as well as an operetta, which failed to attract the public. His first important work, however, was an oratorio, *God and Nature*, performed in Berlin in May 1811. Of this Weber wrote that, though it smelt too much of the lamp, the harmonious beauty of the ideas, and the ardent spirit with which they were expressed, were altogether remarkable. Various cantatas and a *Sinfonia Concertante* for violin, pianoforte, and orchestra followed in 1813, Meyerbeer playing the pianforte part in the latter work.

The most important event of 1813 was the production of *Alimelek* (*Die Beiden Kalifen*), a comic opera with an Arabian Nights' theme, at Stuttgart under Weber's direction. For, although its repetition in Vienna with a different cast was not a success, it brought the composer to the Austrian capital, where contacts with Hummel and Salieri had an important influence upon his future career. A contact with Beethoven was less fruitful; Meyerbeer played one of the big drums in the performance of *Wellingtons Sieg*, but Beethoven seems to have seen through the pretensions of the young pianist and composer.

Hummel's playing was a revelation of a technical virtuosity beyond his ken, and Meyerbeer withdrew from the world for ten months in order to remodel his pianoforte technique. He emerged from this retirement with a virtuosity that might have made his fame and fortune as a pianist, even in the age of Liszt and Chopin. One who heard him in later life speaks of his 'austere performance, very rhythmical and impressive in the manner of Weber.' This same Weber regretted his friend's attraction towards a pianist's career in one who had 'so many things to say – the creations of his own brain'. But his preoccupation with the pianoforte, which produced also a number of showy compositions for the instrument, did not last long. Meyerbeer was hankering after theatrical success. He took counsel with Salieri, who was still occupying the position of Court-composer to the Emperor, which he held in Mozart's day. And Salieri gave him the sound, if perhaps from an Italian obvious, advice – to seek experience and his fortunes south of the Alps. The discipline of Latin precision of statement is certainly the most useful corrective to the nebulous ideas of Germanic romanticism.

In Italy

With the same ardour with which he had applied himself to studying pianoforte technique anew, Meyerbeer now set his mind upon revising his ideas concerning opera. In deference to his father's wishes, however, he went first to Paris, where he spent the year of 1815 and witnessed the final collapse of the new order and the temporary restoration of the old. During his sojourn he wrote two French comic operas, which were found among his papers. They were not produced and may be regarded as exercises. Meyerbeer was a wealthy young man and he could afford to bide his time before attempting the most difficult conquest of all – the artistic conquest of Paris.

'Italy was enjoying the delights of a sweet ecstasy. The people had, so it seemed, found at last their long hoped-for paradise; all that was needed to complete their bliss was the music of Rossini. I was caught, like the rest . . . in this fine web of sound. I was bewitched in a magic garden, which I had no wish to enter, but which I could not avoid.

All my thoughts, all my faculties became Italian; when I had lived there a year, I thought of myself as a native. ... That so complete a transformation of my inner life must have a radical effect upon the style of my music will be readily understood. I did not want, as is commonly supposed, to imitate Rossini or to write in the Italian manner, but I had to compose in the style which I adopted under the compulsion of my state of mind.' – So forty years later Meyerbeer looked back upon his sojourn in Italy. We may suspect a note of special pleading in his explanation of his adoption of the Rossinian manner; but we need not doubt the verity of his enchantment. He was not the first young artist of the Romantic age to be captivated by renascent Italy. At this very time a young author from Grenoble was ranging the peninsula in passionate admiration of its art and its women, acquiring the material that he was to incorporate, under the somewhat ludicrous pen-name of Bombet, in a Life of Rossini, and, under the immortal one of Stendhal, in *La Chartreuse de Parme*.

Rossini was a potent ingredient in the Italian brew that these young men from abroad found so intoxicating, and this potency was distilled especially in operas now long forgotten – serious operas, not the comedies like *The Barber of Seville*. At this moment *Tancredi*, the epitome of them all, was going its triumphant rounds, while city after city echoed to the strains of 'Di tanti palpiti'. Well might Meyerbeer succumb to the universal fashion, when he heard the new work in Venice, most bewitching city of all. Always suggestible and inclined to eclecticism by nature, he refashioned his music upon the Italian model. As one of his biographers remarks, 'He had no style of his own to abandon, but he abandoned Vogler's without regret.' To signalize this change of style, he Italianized his forename to Giacomo and dropped the hyphen he had used hitherto in his surname. With his chameleonlike adaptability he produced within three years a perfect Italian opera, called *Romilda e Costanza*, which was given in Padua in 1818. To achieve success with an Italian audience, who could only with difficulty be persuaded to listen to any music not composed by Rossini, was no mean feat. Meyerbeer proceeded to repeat his success, in Venice with *Emma di Resburgo* (who crossed the Alps and appeared in Vienna as *Emma von Leicester*) and finally in 1820 at the Scala in Milan, the summit of every Italian composer's ambition, with *Margherita d'Angiù*, which was also given at Munich and shortly afterwards in France, Belgium, and England.

Carl Weber, torn between affection for Meyerbeer and dismay at his friend's desertion of German ideals, enquired, more in sorrow than in anger, how a German artist, gifted with such *enormous* creative powers, could sink to the level of an imitator in order to win the applause of the mob. To save Meyerbeer for Germany he set himself to restore the prestige of his Arabian Nights Singspiel, *Alimelek*, which the Viennese had scorned. Even when, in 1820, as Director of the Opera in Dresden, he found himself compelled to give performances of that popular success, *Emma* now *von Rosburg*, he also revived *Alimelek*, and pointedly invited the public, and incidentally their composer, to 'look on this picture and on that' – the one bearing the stamp of genuine German art, the other a product of a dilettantism ready to try its hand at anything.

Back to Germany

When Meyerbeer returned to Germany in 1821, Weber hoped that he would renounce his infatuation with Italy and become his 'old self' again. But success was tempting and the sound of applause grateful in his ear. So an invitation from the Scala brought him back to Milan with a new opera in the spring of 1822, and thence to Rome, where he was preparing another, when he fell ill and was compelled to return to Germany for a cure at Spa. The following winter was spent at home in Berlin, where he occupied himself with the composition of a German opera, *Das Brandenburger Thor*, which, for some reason or other, was never produced. It would seem that Weber's influence and the waning of his first enthusiasm for Italy, coupled possibly with his ill-health, combined to produce a crisis in Meyerbeer's artistic career at this point. Or it may be that, all along, he saw his ultimate mark, and that his Italian venture was only a part of a deliberate plan for his technical education and, in particular, for the acquisition of that knowledge of the human voice, and how to write for it, which as Salieri had advised him, could only be found in Italy.

Whatever the cause, Meyerbeer's next opera, *Il Crociato in Egitto* (*The Crusader in Egypt*), composed in Berlin and produced at Venice in December 1824, shows a remarkable change in the composer's style. It foreshadows, in a somewhat crude and uncertain way, those later works, by which his name is remembered, where his mastery of Italian vocal style is grafted upon his more solid native genius. It would probably not be inaccurate to suggest that *Il Crociato* was written with one eye on Paris. A year before he had written to Levasseur, the bass who had sung in *Margherita d'Angiù* in Milan and was to be the creator of the bass rôles in his Parisian operas:

> I am delighted at what you tell me of the good opinion which the Director of the Opéra has of my feeble talents. You enquire whether I would like to work for the French stage. I assure you that I should consider it a greater glory to have the honour of composing for the French Opéra than for all the theatres in Italy, in which, moreover, I have given my works. Where else than in Paris should I find the immense resources which the Opéra affords to an artist who wishes to write really dramatic music? . . . You may ask why, in view of these considerations, I have not so far tried to write for Paris. It is because I am told here that the Opéra is hedged about with difficulties and one must normally wait years and years before getting a hearing. That gives me pause. I confess that, perhaps, I have been spoilt on this score in Italy, where they have up to now sought me out. . . .

Il Crociato is a synthesis of various styles, manipulated with Meyerbeer's astonishing capacity for absorbing and co-ordinating other men's ideas, which did in the end produce a style that may be called his own. The new manner was triumphantly successful not only in Italy, but in countries as far afield as Russia and Brazil. The opera was staged in London and in Paris at the Théâtre des Italiens, where Rossini was in command. The theatre was really too small for an opera on this grand scale, and it was necessary to make a number of cuts and alterations. Rossini's helping hand on this occasion won him Meyerbeer's gratitude and affection, to which he never ceased to give effusive expression even though Rossini in later years hardly concealed his dislike of Meyerbeer's mature operas.* Allowance must, perhaps, be made, in judging Meyerbeer's attitude towards Rossini, for his patent desire to keep in the good graces of the influential doyen of Italian opera, whose power was all the greater in his retirement and whose wit was, indeed, a weapon to be feared.

Meyerbeer's movements between 1824 and 1830 are not exactly known. There is no clear evidence of his having accepted Rossini's invitation to assist at the final rehearsals of *Il Crociato*. It is probable that he spent the greater part of these years in Berlin, where in 1827 he married his cousin Mina Mosson. The deaths of his father in 1825 and

* The 'Jews' Sabbath' remark is apparently apocryphal, though it seems to accord with Rossini's opinion.

of his own two children, which have already been mentioned, affected him deeply and account for his withdrawal from public notice. To these losses were added the deaths of his old master, Lauska, and his friend, Carl Weber, in 1826. But he was not idle. During these years he amassed a collection of French operas from Lulli onwards and set himself to study them with all the thoroughness he had applied to Hummel's pianoforte technique and Italian vocal methods. Nor did he confine himself to music; his researches included French history and art and the character of the people. If the celebrated definition holds good, Meyerbeer certainly took sufficient pains to earn the title of genius.

Paris Success

The results of these studies were brought to light in 1831, when Meyerbeer astonished the musical world and made the fortune of the Paris Opéra with *Robert le Diable*. A romantic book by Scribe, in which were combined history and legend, heroics and allegory; the novel scenic designs of Ciceri, who substituted for the conventional antique settings with their 'apparatus of cupids, bows and quivers', a broadly designed décor that relied upon mass effects rather than on minutely accented details; and finally the brilliant instrumentation of Meyerbeer's music, its vigorous declamation, and its showy Italianate melody that could on occasion attain an expressive power unparalleled even in Rossini's *William Tell*; all these ingredients combined to make *Robert le Diable* one of the outstanding landmarks in operatic history. Meyerbeer had created a new genre, which was to dominate the countries that drew their artistic inspiration from France during the rest of the century and had a great influence upon operatic developments in his native Germany. Like most original inventors, Meyerbeer was surpassed by those who later put to their own uses the new ideas he had created with so much assiduity and technical skill – in particular, men of greater natural genius, Richard Wagner and Giuseppe Verdi.

The lavish production of *Robert le Diable* was made possible only by a special State subvention to the Opéra, whose director, Dr Véron, even then would not agree to the hire of the organ required in the last act. For this the composer paid out of his own pocket. 'No-one will ever know,' wrote an eye-witness of his labours, 'what the rehearsals cost Meyerbeer in loss of sleep, in fright and loss of confidence, and even in despair. He had an eye for everything – poem, music, scenery, costumes, singing and the dances.' Ballet, it will be remembered, had an important part in French opera; and one of the astonishing things in this astonishing work was the ballet of nuns rising from their graves in the cloister garth, led by Mlle Taglioni herself as *l'abbesse damnée* – a rôle for which I refrain from giving the English equivalent.

In contrast to the opera-composers of the preceding generation, who turned out as many as two or three operas a year, Meyerbeer's subsequent works came at long intervals. Five years elapsed before *Les Huguenots* was produced in 1836. An immense historical drama in five acts, embodying not only the antagonisms of powerful rulers but also the religious strife of the people at the time of the Reformation, could not be set to music in the new and elaborate orchestral manner at the speed with which Donizetti could string together a number of pretty arias with tonic-and-dominant accompaniment, that would serve indifferently for Anne Boleyn or Lucrezia Borgia or Lucy, the Bride of Lammermoor. The new book was again by Scribe, that ingenious theatrical craftsman, whose invention knew no limit save in the reasonable development of effect from cause.

The composition of *Les Huguenots* was further protracted owing to the ill-health of Meyerbeer's wife, whom he took to Italy for a cure. He had entered into a contract with the Opéra to compose a new work for the theatre immediately after the success of *Robert* and was subject to a forfeit of 30,000 francs if the opera was not finished by the due date. With incredible meanness, Dr Véron, who had personally made an enormous profit out of *Robert*, insisted on his pound of flesh, which Meyerbeer paid without a word, and took his wife and his half-finished score to Milan. He was discussing with Scribe the possibility of producing the new work at the Opéra Comique, when Véron was superseded by Duponchel, who had been helpful and friendly during the production of *Robert*. Despite the care lavished on the staging of the new opera, which was even vaster and more elaborate than *Robert*, despite, too, the sensational display in the ballet of Queen Marguerite's ladies bathing in the Cher, the public, who expected a repetition of that resounding success, was at first disappointed, and it was some time before *Les Huguenots* achieved the popularity that was to endure well into the present century.

Meyerbeer next projected an opera, again with a libretto by Scribe, which was eventually to become *L'Africaine*, but in the course of working on it, he made so many demands on Scribe for alterations –

even the inclusion of Vasco da Gama as the hero of the work was an afterthought – that the librettist withdrew his book. Meyerbeer, thereupon, turned his attention to another subject, John of Leyden, who became the hero of *Le Prophète* produced in 1843. This contains some of the small amount of music from Meyerbeer's pen familiar to modern English audiences. For four numbers of its Skating Ballet – performed originally on the roller-skates newly devised by an ingenious inventor who was engaged to give the dancers at the Opéra lessons in their use – are included in the ballet, *Les Patineurs*, which is one of the most popular pieces in the repertory of the Sadler's Wells Ballet.

Return to Berlin

In the meantime Meyerbeer had been summoned home by his sovereign to take up the post of General-Musikdirektor in succession to Spontini. This appointment necessitated his presence in Berlin for a part of the year, and Meyerbeer at first took his duties very seriously. He composed marches and dance-music, cantatas and occasional pieces, of which the most important was *Ein Feldlager in Schlesien* (*A Camp in Silesia*), written for the re-opening of the Grosstheater after its destruction by fire. With Jenny Lind in the cast and Frederick the Great complete with flute among the dramatis personae, this piece survived its occasion and brought its composer a handsome profit.

For a time he also took to conducting opera, revived the works of Gluck and *The Magic Flute*, and mounted with especial care the operas of his dead friend, Weber. He secured the production of Wagner's *The Flying Dutchman*, which had been rejected by Munich, and proposed that the composer should direct the performances. Owing to various delays, however, Wagner's opera was not given until 1845, two years after its production in Dresden.

Wagner's conduct towards Meyerbeer is one of the less creditable chapters in his discreditable career as a man. For even while he was writing to Meyerbeer in sycophantic language that marks him for a toady, he was publishing anonymous and pseudonymous articles attacking Meyerbeer's music in the most scurrilous terms he could lay his pen to. Later, when Meyerbeer was dead, he further blackened Meyerbeer's name by pretending that he had secretly done all he could to prevent Wagner's works getting a hearing – an unfounded accusation, which has too long coloured the accepted view of Meyerbeer. It was enough for Wagner and his friends that Meyerbeer was rich, successful, and a Jew.

Meyerbeer found the strain of conducting too much for him and soon surrendered this duty to a less sensitive assistant, except on special occasions. He was occupied also at this time with the composition of the overture and incidental music for his brother Michael's drama, *Struensee*, produced in 1846. The overture is Meyerbeer's most important and successful orchestral composition and might well be given an occasional place in our concert-programmes instead of one of the little group of more hackneyed overtures.

Opéra Comique

Returning once more to Paris, Meyerbeer, never content to rest on his laurels, set out to conquer in a new field, to beat the Parisians on their own particular ground – the Opéra Comique – where in 1854 *L'Étoile du Nord* was produced. It was a very 'grand' opéra-comique, incorporating a certain amount of music from *Ein Feldlager in Schlesien*. Verdi, who was at the first performance, declared that he understood little or nothing of it, but 'the good public thought it divine!' He also quoted an article by Dumas, who wrote:

> What a pity Rossini did not produce his operas in 1854! But then Rossini had not the German wit to set a success simmering six months in advance on the stoves of the newspapers and so prepare for an explosion of intelligent appreciation on the night.

Meyerbeer was, indeed, an adept in the art of 'advance publicity' and was fortunate enough to be able to afford it. Verdi's simple, upright soul was shocked at the lavish presents distributed by Meyerbeer and his wife in the right quarters before the production of a new opera. Meyerbeer's sensitiveness to criticism had developed to a degree that can only be called pathological. He spared no pains to convince an adverse critic of his error, and he certainly did all he could to smooth the way for a good opinion of his work. Nor did he spare himself in other ways. Each opera was subjected to endless rehearsals and revisions; scenes were added and subtracted until the total published score was so unwieldy that producers are compelled to make selections in order to reduce the opera to a reasonable length. *Les Huguenots* has especially suffered from this superfluity and consequent reduction.

L'Étoile du Nord was followed in 1859 by a second opéra-comique, *Le Pardon de Ploërmel*, better known as *Dinorah*, which is of lighter calibre. Meyerbeer then resumed the burden of *L'Africaine*, which was to occupy him for the rest of his life. He did, indeed, compose some music for Berlin during his visits there and represented his country at the International Exhibition of 1862 in London, for which he wrote an Overture. But *L'Africaine* was his chief concern. He had first taken up the subject over twenty years before, and now, more than ever, he refashioned its libretto (to the increasing exasperation of M. Scribe), re-wrote its music, added new numbers, and vainly sought the ideal cast for its interpretation. By the end of 1863 his task was completed, the singers were engaged, and the opera was put into rehearsal. As usual, Meyerbeer continued to polish and retouch his score, protracting the rehearsals into the spring of 1864. Then on 23 April a new character entered the drama. Meyerbeer fell ill – his health had for long been poor – and on 2 May he suddenly died in the presence of his two daughters and his nephew, Jules Beer, author of a funeral march in memory of his uncle, which evoked from Rossini the question: 'Would it not have been better if you had died and your uncle had composed the march?'

Mme Meyerbeer and her eldest son hurried from Berlin, but arrived in time only to accompany the dead composer home on his last journey, which began with a solemn procession through the streets of Paris. *L'Africaine*, or as much of the huge mass of music Meyerbeer had composed as could be performed in rather more than six hours, was at last produced in 1865. It was witnessed by a young composer from Nelson Street, Edinburgh, who was much impressed by the seamanlike handling of the huge ship on the stage, but also remarked upon the injustice of the neglect into which Meyerbeer's operas have since fallen. Indeed, as R. A. Streatfeild rightly says, 'Meyerbeer was extravagantly praised in his lifetime; he is now as bitterly decried. The truth, as usual, lies somewhere between these extremes.' He had plenty of intelligence and a real understanding of the theatre. He took, as we have seen, infinite pains to perfect his work, but his labours were directed rather towards attaining the greatest effect than towards an ideal artistic creation. His music suffers from this lack of real integrity as well as from the mass of detail that his scores accumulated under his persevering revisions. But he will always have an important place in musical history, and it may fairly be said that his true monument is the sumptuous building erected in 1875 by Charles Garnier to house the Académie de Musique et de Danse – the Paris Opéra, whose opening programme included 'the benediction of the swords' from *Les Huguenots*.

CARL OTTO EHRENFRIED NICOLAI

1810–49

JOHN S. WEISSMANN

With the name Nicolai music-lovers as a rule associate *The Merry Wives of Windsor*, his comic opera based on Shakespeare; and then their thoughts turn to Verdi and Vaughan-Williams, both of whom set the same story. But Nicolai, besides being a good composer, has something far more important to his credit – if musical culture is considered more important in its consequences than single works of individual composers. I refer to his founding of the Philharmonic Concerts in Vienna; this, judging by the subsequent results and influence, was a momentous feat. Who was then this director of music, this composer?

Childhood, Youth

Carl Otto Ehrenfried Nicolai was born in Königsberg, on 9 June 1810. His father, Carl Nicolai, studied law, but being of unstable character soon abandoned that career for the more care-free existence of teacher of music and elocution. Pursuing his profession at various places, ultimately he was engaged at an institute in Warsaw. Here he met and subsequently married the head-mistress, who was to be Otto's mother.

They set up in Königsberg, but home-life was not for Nicolai senior. He was frequently absent giving music-lessons in the neighbouring towns, and when he was amongst his family his quarrelsomeness and egoism did not create an ideal atmosphere. His wife finally divorced him, and little Otto stayed with his uncle during his father's absence.

The musical gifts of the boy were discovered soon enough by his father: he decided that his son was to be a prodigy. However, the methods of musical training employed by him were anything but agreeable. Severe punishments, hard blows were usual occurrences; it would not be surprising had Otto developed a dislike for music. It is related that Otto, who was given to day-dreams, was indulging in his habitual reverie at the keyboard, only to be discovered fallen asleep by his father. The punishment was abnormally severe: he shut his son into a dark chamber in the loft, where the poor boy was discovered half-frozen next morning. Unable to withstand the sufferings, Otto took to flight without money, food, or other necessities. He reached in a pitiful condition the place where his mother lived, but she, not being particularly well-off, could not accept the additional responsibility a son would entail. Consequently, after a short stay, Otto again set out on foot and got as far as Stargard, where he was introduced to Adler, a wealthy assessor.

This well-to-do official was known as a philanthropist and a musical amateur among the local celebrities. He listened with sympathy and incredulous surprise to Otto's request to help him organize a concert for his benefit and so to obtain the necessary funds for his travel to Berlin. Asked to prove his capabilities, young Nicolai picked up a copy of music – which happened to be a Hummel concerto – and played it at first sight with astonishing dexterity.

The assessor took a liking to the talented young boy, introduced him to his friends, and thus enabled him to perform in private and in public. After about a year's stay in Stargard, it became clear that to receive regular and adequate training in music he would have to go to Berlin and try his luck there. His old friend Adler procured him letters of introduction to the foremost musicians then in Berlin, and Otto mounted the mail-coach, full of great expectations, on an autumn day of 1827.

Berlin

At the time of Nicolai's arrival, musical life in Berlin was dominated by the two 'official' institutions, not so much by their positions as by the personalities of their leaders. Spontini ruled at the Opera and Zelter at the Singakademie.

The former, a composer of grand-operas (now defunct) and one of the outstanding conductors of his time, is fully characterized in musical history books. Zelter, on the other hand, less well known, is an interesting figure. His 'real' profession was architecture; expressing it less decorously, he was a builder. Music was his great passion and he studied with C. F. Chr. Fasch, the founder of the Singakademie (an institution resembling the Royal Choral Society). When Fasch died, Zelter took over the administration of the institute; shortly afterwards he was appointed to the Royal Institute of Church Music with a regular salary. From that time onwards he abandoned his craft and lived for music only. He had a thorough knowledge of the 'old style', was a famous teacher, and had a wide circle of acquaintances among contemporary artists and musicians. His reputation rests on his settings of Goethe and Schiller, both of whom were his friends. Zelter, a robust, bluff person with a heart of gold behind a rugged exterior – already in the last years of his life – took a liking to Nicolai: not only the personal charm but the great talent that Zelter discovered in him made the old man friendlily disposed.

Zelter took the young man under his patronage: he not only gave him lessons himself, but saw to it that his spasmodic general education should be duly completed. At the Gymnasium zur grauen Kloster Otto found systematic training in singing and theory; Zelter also got a royal stipendium to enable Nicolai to pursue his studies at the Institute of Church Music where, under Bernhard Klein and Ludwig Berger, he received a thorough schooling in the 'olden style of writing', i.e., the style of classical vocal polyphony. He made great strides in his studies, his voice developed, and in 1831 he became a member of the Sing-akademie. In the previous year he composed a *Gloria* and an *Agnus Dei* dedicated to the Institute and planned another work for the Church, a *Te Deum*, which he finished in 1832.

Zelter also introduced him to the society of his friends and colleagues, which in fact meant the leading musicians and other notables of the day. Nicolai benefited a great deal from having a free entrance into his master's house. He frequented the 'salon' of the Mendelssohns, parents of the composer, and the house of Schleiermacher, one of the greatest theologians of his time.

The handsome young man was popular with everyone. He was of a sensitive nature and tried to hide – unconsciously – this characteristic of his under vivacity and a rather sharp tongue. He and Mendelssohn, both being pupils of Zelter, had many occasions for arguments on musical questions.

During all these social and other diversions Nicolai was mindful of his work: a number of songs were finished and even these first fruits of composition found venturesome publishers. The bulk of his compositions of this time were church music. Two major instrumental works were also produced, a *Symphony in D*, and a *Christmas Overture*.

His *Te Deum* was performed in 1833; unfortunately his two beloved teachers could not attend the performance. Zelter died in 1832 and Bernhard Klein followed him a few months later.

The effect of this double loss on Nicolai's affectionate disposition was very depressing. A visit to his father, who was at Posen (Poznan) at the time, afforded him the necessary distraction, and on his return he began to realize his plans with a youthful vigour characteristic of him. He composed some vocal pieces for the church, organized a series of lectures on thorough-bass and harmony, and little by little gained a reputation as a serious-minded church musician.

This reputation attracted the attention of Carl von Bunsen, the Prussian ambassador to the Holy See, whom he met at Schleiermacher's and who subsequently engaged him as organist to the embassy chapel at Rome. Bunsen himself was a theologian who strove to reform certain matters, especially in connexion with divine service; he hoped to employ Nicolai to advise him on musical subjects.

He set out for Italy in December 1833; his first station on the way was Leipsic, where he had the pleasure of having his *Christmas Overture* performed. A week later we find him in Munich. He crossed the Brenner on 30 December 1833, and found himself in Italy on New Year's Day. In Verona he visited the Teatro Filarmonico where he heard Donizetti's *Anna Bolena*. His first contact with the typical Italian operatic life drew a self-assured criticism; his German sense of discipline revolted against the spectacle of chattering, drinking, and so on in the opera house during the performance. He is full of contempt for the general musical practice in Italy: not even church music escapes his severe censure.

Staying for a short while in Padua and in Venice, and visiting Bologna, Florence, and Leghorn, he ultimately arrived in Rome on 28 January 1834.

Rome

At first his official duties as organist were not exacting, nor was his salary on the lavish side, yet, by widening his circle of acquaintances, most of whom became his pupils, he was doing well. Bunsen introduced him into Roman society, and his genial nature, his handsome appearance, and his extraordinary dexterity at musical performances – playing or singing – soon made him a favourite there. He, in his turn, lost his head and heart soon and often; he particularly admired the beauty of the English ladies. Through society he became one of the best-known music teachers in the city. Now we find him taking lessons in the severe Palestrina style with the great exponent of that art, the regens chori of the Sistine Chapel, Baini.

Rome, with its buildings, its sculptures, its art-treasures, and its spiritual associations of 2,000 years, overwhelmed his intellect: he wrote page after page of enthusiastic praise of it to his father, and his critical attitude towards things Italian gave place to an admiration of Latin genius. He frequented operatic performances; indeed shortly after his arrival he saw Bellini's *Norma* and the music impressed him. Meanwhile he was also immersed in the strict style and listened with rapture to the choir of the Sistine Chapel, composed vocal pieces for the church, and made transcriptions for the book of chorales of Bunsen.

His gradual change is important, especially in connexion with his music: it finds expression in that exuberance of melodic invention, in those eminently singable phrases conspicuous in his subsequent works.

In April he heard the new opera of Bellini, *Montecchi e Capuletti*, and this and other performances, operatic life in general, stimulated him to write a memorandum on operatic matters which he submitted to the Prussian Court.

Gradually, then, a conversion began to take place in his artistic outlook. He rarely misses opportunities to listen to opera; and in another letter to the Prussian Intendant in Berlin he makes overtures: 'he would be glad,' he says, 'to be able to write something for the Royal stage.'

On his holidays in 1835 he made a trip to Naples, where he listened to performances at San Carlo and other opera houses, but was not impressed by their standards. The important event of his journey – and also perhaps of his career – was his meeting with Donizetti.

Having returned to Rome after a prolonged leave, he continued his duties as organist, though with less enthusiasm. His teaching connexions widened and he gave many lessons, chiefly to English residents there, who frequently invited him to London. But he had different plans. He managed his affairs with considerable skill and sent copies of his compositions to many publishers (some also to London); he also mentions in a letter to his father his wish to relinquish his post as from 1836.

He had designs in connexion with the Singakademie, he even

envisaged founding a State Conservatory of Music in Berlin, in which he had Bunsen's complete support.

Yet his relations with his employer were cooling off; when Bunsen was appointed to the Ambassadorship to England, he welcomed the chance to regain his freedom.

His compositions – besides a number of masses, motets, psalms, and other ecclesiastical works – included another *Symphony in D major* written for a competition in Vienna (which he failed to win), and a *Funeral March* in memory of Bellini, who died at that time. This work was performed between the two acts of *Sonnambula* produced in memory of its author. He left Rome in July 1836.

Travels in Italy

At first he decided to visit his mother in Warsaw. On his way there, however, he made a halt at Macerata, where he met the hospitable Watts family, known to him from his days in Rome. The Watts persuaded him to stay with them, and he enjoyed the distraction provided by the surroundings. The approaching epidemic, however, drove him to Bologna. He had various plans in mind: he applied for membership at the Accademia Filarmonica and, last but not least, tried to get a commission to write an opera. A chance soon presented itself, although not in altogether happy circumstances. News reached him of the death of Mme Malibran and he was invited to write a cantata in memory of the great singer. The work was finished in eight days and was constructed on novel lines. Tableaux alternated with music-numbers, but, owing to bad management, the performance was not entirely a success. Another memorable event of his improvised visit to Bologna was his becoming acquainted with Rossini, who was very friendly to the young composer and gave him, besides some practical hints, letters of introduction to the manager of the opera in Milan.

On his way there he had a disagreeable experience: he was held up in Piacenza by the Austrian police, suspecting him to be a dangerous republican. He arrived in Milan in December 1836, with the avowed purpose of writing an opera and thereby attaining reputation and success. The letters of introduction, as also the news of his Malibran cantata, went far towards securing a good reception with the manager of the Scala, who was also director of the Italian opera in Vienna. Yet it seemed that opera writing could not be undertaken for some time. Amongst the numerous concerts he gave in Milan, there was one 'benefit' at which an opera of his, or a portion of it, was performed. It took place in April 1837, at the Scala Theatre and the work was entitled *La Figlia Abbandonata.*

His prolonged stay in the city resulted – if not in the writing of the planned opera – in an important engagement: Merelli, the manager, offered him a conductorship in Vienna, carrying with it a handsome salary. Nicolai accepted the offer and we find him as conductor at the Court Opera House at the Kärntnerthor in June 1837.

Vienna

His début in the imperial city was well, if not enthusiastically, received. *Montecchi e Capuletti* was given; between the two acts Nicolai conducted one of his own overtures. In March 1838, his *Christmas Overture* was performed at the Gesellschaftsconcerte. The young musician soon made his way in Viennese circles; he informs his father of several soirées at which Clara Wieck (Robert Schumann's wife) played his piano compositions and the prima donna of the opera sang his songs.

He had begun his opera entitled *Rosmonda* and hoped to produce it at the theatre under his direction. His colleagues, on the other hand, Conradin Kreutzer and one Reiling, could not get on well with Nicolai; they succeeded in putting him out of favour with the management, and soon Nicolai realized that his opera would not be performed there, if Kreutzer could help it, and further that his engagement, terminating at the end of June 1838, would not be renewed.

Italy Again

From 1838 to April 1841, Nicolai went from one place in Italy to another in the hope of an engagement and above all in the hope of an occasion to write an opera. Thus he visited Venice, Verona, Turin, Milan, and Rome and succeeded in getting contracts to write one opera each for Turin and Trieste.

Meanwhile he had to struggle for a living: he was not in great demand as music-teacher, life was expensive even at that time, and soon he found himself in Rome with no money in his pocket. That happened on 21 October 1838 – according to a note in his diary. But friends, among them a Pole, Count Wielhorsky, helped him out of the tight corner, and he was again frequenting society. He records his meeting with Liszt, of whom he had no high opinion at that time, took part in the carnival and then set to work in earnest. In September he finished his *Rosmonda*, already begun in Vienna. It was first performed, under the title *Enrico Secondo*, in Trieste on 26 November 1839.

The performance was not altogether a success. Nicolai showed great promise as an operatic composer, but *Rosmonda*, after all, was his first stage-work, influenced principally by the star of Italian opera composers, Donizetti. It is nevertheless remarkable that Caroline Ungher, the great soprano, deemed it not unworthy to sing the title-role of this first work.

Shortly afterwards his second stage-work, *Il Templario*, based on a story by Walter Scott, was first performed at the Teatro Regia in Turin on 11 February 1840. This work brought at last success which even surpassed Nicolai's sanguine expectations. The opera was staged subsequently in Genoa and at the Scala in Milan. At the height of his success he fell in love, as so often before, the lady in question being an attractive opera-singer. Nicolai was seriously considering marrying her, yet the two artistic temperaments could not harmonize sufficiently to make a happy matrimonial life. Meanwhile, passing through all the excitements engendered by this sentiment, he was working on his new opera, destined for the Carlo Felice Theatre in Genoa, *Gildippe e Odoardo*, based on Tasso's *Gerusalemme Liberata;* it was first performed on 26 December 1840. The success was not so overwhelming as that of *Il Templario*. Nicolai, embittered by the cool reception, refused an offer of a text that brought success to another composer, the libretto of *Nabucco*, which was composed by Verdi. The latter, in exchange for *Nabucco*, ceded to Nicolai the libretto of *Il Proscritto*. The deal confirmed Verdi's sense of theatre: *Nabucco* was Verdi's first great success, whereas Nicolai's *Proscritto* failed lamentably at the Scala on 13 March 1841.

Vienna

Nicolai, who believed that he had written his best music in this score, felt more than offended: he was disgusted. An offer, by his old friend Merelli, to stage *Il Templario* in Vienna was therefore welcome. In ten days' time he arrived in Vienna again. His engagement was for the post of first conductor at the Court Opera House, replacing Kreutzer. *Il Templario* had a resounding success, thanks to careful preparation and meticulous performance. During the holidays he realized an old plan of his: he visited his mother in Warsaw.

Proserpina, which he began in Milan, was abandoned, and in 1842 Nicolai announced a prize competition for librettos. This brought him more than thirty plots; none of them pleased him. As his contract obliged him to write at least one opera, he hastily rearranged his *Il Proscritto*. Kapper, a Viennese writer, helped him with the libretto, and the work, which cost him a great amount of time and vexation, was performed under the title *Die Heimkehr des Verbannten* on 3 February 1844, at the Court Opera House (Kärntnerthor).

His directorship heralded a new era in the theatre. He produced *Don Giovanni*, *Fidelio*, and operas of his beloved Donizetti in quick succession, everyone of them rehearsed and presented with the same precision, care, and scrupulousness.

The Philharmonic Concerts were revived – or rather inaugurated – on Easter Day 1842, and his methods resulted in a perfection that was unheard-of even in musical Vienna. His guiding idea was to present the compositions of the classical masters, such as Beethoven and Mozart, in the most accomplished performance attainable. The novelty of having several rehearsals, the innovation of organizing an orchestra of professional musicians, resulted in performances that immediately commanded the attention of the public. One of the first acts of Nicolai in his capacity of Director of the Philharmonic Concerts (the title presumably in deference to the English institution) was the performance of the *Ninth Symphony* by Beethoven in its entirety. The success was so great that the performance had to be repeated in the same season (1843).

Another – salutary – innovation in connexion with the concerts was the ban on instrumental virtuosi. Singers were admitted as necessary for the performance of the Ninth or works with vocal parts; therefore the soloist's performance of some arias could not be refused.

The Philharmonic Concert given at the end of the Viennese concert season has since then become a tradition. It was faithfully observed until the outbreak of war in 1939: these 'Nicolai-Konzerte' were benefit performances for the players.

During the Vienna period Nicolai wrote a great number of songs, several church music pieces (among them an eight-part *Paternoster*), a symphony, and a sonata for the piano. His principal work, however, is his opera *The Merry Wives of Windsor*.

Since his arrival in Vienna Nicolai had been searching for a suitable libretto. At last his imagination caught fire from Shakespeare's comedy. He sent detailed plans of the first few scenes to his librettist, Hofmeister. The latter was promised twenty louis d'or for every act. Circumstances, however, compelled him to transfer the task to another writer. Hofmeister, living in Cassel, could only deliver with considerable delay. Mosenthal had the advantage of living in Vienna.

Nicolai, then, was in a position to announce in September 1846, that his opera was about to be finished. However, the director of the Court Opera made difficulties, pointing out that the work was contracted for the previous year; the other conductors at the theatre also jumped at the occasion to get rid of their rival. Nicolai, in a temper, took offence, decided that he could not work in these circumstances, tendered his resignation to take effect in 1847, and even interrupted his work on the opera.

Last Years in Berlin

On 23 May 1847, Nicolai left Vienna. First he took a holiday in order to cure his rheumatism, which, beginning to afflict him already in 1845 with a severe attack of headache, grew steadily worse. The excitements about his work, the responsibilities, aggravated his condition. He again visited watering-places in the Austrian Tyrol and Hungary; he felt better afterwards, but unfortunately the cure was not complete.

Negotiations about his Berlin appointment had been begun years ago. He received several invitations to Berlin, but always preferred to keep his Vienna contract, whereby he was Director of Music at the Court Opera and conductor of the Philharmonic Concerts. The events in connexion with his *Merry Wives* however caused him at last to accept the invitation of his king, and accordingly he was appointed Musical Director of the Cathedral Choir (Domchor) and first conductor at the Royal Opera House. His début there took place on 12 March 1848, when he directed Spontini's *Vestale*.

His *Merry Wives* was approaching completion and a number of other works were also undertaken. On 11 December 1847, he finished the overture and a few days later this, other parts of the opera, and a patriotic hymn, *The Voice of Prussia*, were performed. By royal command the opera was to be performed as soon as finished, but the events of 1848 postponed it, and the first performance could only take place on 9 March 1849, under Nicolai's personal direction. The opera, originally with spoken dialogues, was performed with recitatives added by Henry Proch, in Vienna.

Nicolai conducted only four performances in Berlin: he died of a sudden stroke, at the summit of his career, on 11 May 1849.

Of his works, many were published, but a great number, including church music, two operas, the *Christmas Overture*, a symphony, a string quartet, songs, and works for the piano, remained in MS. His music is characterized by two influences: on the one hand they manifest a highly accomplished technique, the roots of which lay in church-music, that is, the strict style of the great polyphonists (especially Italians); on the other a fresh, flexible, soaring melodic invention comparable only to Mozart's. His brilliant orchestration, full of surprising and novel ideas, is remarkable.

Nicolai began his career of composer as an ecclesiastical musician and his reputation in this respect might be inferred from his appointment in Rome. Bearing this in mind, it is the more surprising to find him turning to composition of 'Italian' operas. Passing over the psychological reasons – which would deserve a special study – one guesses at purely economic factors that contributed to his change of heart. Yet the strict style and free melodic invention came to a perfect fusion in his masterpiece, *The Merry Wives of Windsor*.

JACQUES OFFENBACH

1819–80

STANLEY BAYLISS

Mystery of a Name

England, one suspects, is often regarded as if it were the only country whose music has been dominated by foreign visitors; but France, too, has not been without such influences. The names of Lulli, Gluck, Cherubini, and Meyerbeer at once spring to mind. And the subject of this biography, a German-born Jew, is said to typify the France of the Second Empire.

There has been some mystery about his real name. Popular tradition held it to be Levy, while Riemann's *Musiklexikon* gives it as Ebserscht. Kracauer, in his *Offenbach and the Paris of his Time*, has Eberst. Percy Scholes, however, in *The Oxford Companion to Music*, plumps for Wiener, quoting as authority a letter from Offenbach's grand-daughter to the Editor of the *Radio Times* (29 January 1932).

Why Offenbach?

Jacques or Jakob Offenbach was born at Cologne on 20 June 1819. In an autobiographical fragment he placed his birth two years later in 1821 and so added further confusion to the mystery surrounding him. It will be seen, therefore, that he did not adopt the name Offenbach because he was born at Offenbach-am-Main. The change was made by his father, who left that town when he was twenty and settled in Deutz, a suburb of Cologne, where his colleagues referred to him as 'Der Offenbacher'. He was a wandering musician, earning his living as cantor in various synagogues and as a fiddler at taverns and dance halls. He married Marianne Rindskopf, daughter of a money-changer and lottery-office keeper. And one of Offenbach's ancestors had published a collection of Hebrew chants.

His father taught him to play the violin at a very early age. Jacques himself said that when he was seven years old he didn't play badly, but that even then he dreamed more of composition than all the scales and exercises in the world.

Three years later, his father brought home a violoncello, and Offenbach at once wanted to give up the violin and take to the cello, a wish that was not granted him, ostensibly on account of his poor health. But of course the usual romantic story follows. He studies in secret and one day surprises every one by being able to take part in a string quartet, the cellist of which had not put in an appearance.

To Paris

To further their musical education, the father took Jacques and his elder brother Jules, a talented violinist, to Paris. This was in November, 1833. His one desire was to get Jacques admitted to the Conservatoire, and, with letters of recommendation, he called upon Cherubini, director of that institution. Cherubini, then aged seventy-three, was a stickler for the rules; and the rules laid it down that no one of foreign birth could be a student at the Conservatoire. Offenbach's father, however, was a good bargainer and ready talker and at length succeeded in persuading Cherubini to hear his boy play. That was sufficient. Before he had finished playing, Cherubini said: 'I will go to the Minister, and you shall be admitted, my boy, I give you my word.' Having succeeded in getting what he wanted, and after making arrangements for lodgings and the welfare of his sons, Isaac Offenbach returned to Cologne.

Jacques was in the class of Vaslin, and later he became a member of the orchestra of the Opéra Comique, where, with the complicity of the colleague (Seligmann) who shared the desk with him, he indulged in practical jokes, which brought penalties that reduced his monthly salary of eighty-three francs almost to nothing.

He left the Conservatoire in 1838 and, having made the acquaintance of Fromental Halévy, had lessons in composition from the composer of *La Juive*. Halévy had a high opinion of Offenbach's talent. He wrote to his father: 'I see your sons very often . . . the younger, more particularly, appears to me destined for real success in the realm of composition, and I shall esteem myself happy to be able to co-operate in encouraging and seconding him in his studies and work.'

Although Offenbach wrote many songs, fantasies, and dance pieces, success did not come quickly to him. Among his output were waltz suites for Jullien, the celebrated or notorious conductor, famous for his quadrilles and London 'Proms'.

Jacques was three years in the orchestra of the Opéra Comique and apparently was very unhappy there. His experiences of the irritations caused at rehearsals by inconsiderate composers made him resolve that he would treat the artists who performed his own music as decently and as gently as possible.

Sacred Music in a Wanton Waltz

One of his waltzes was entitled *Rebecca*, and knowingly or unknowingly he had introduced into it tunes or echoes of tunes used in Jewish sacred ritual. *Le Ménestrel* therefore administered a snub: 'Was it absolutely necessary to burlesque melodies sanctified by religious observance in a wanton waltz? Not in the least. But nowadays it is necessary at all costs to be original.' But the conductor Jullien had indulged in a similar practice the year before. Kracaeur says that, after all, Offenbach's father did not scruple to sing tunes from *Der Freischütz* in the synagogue; but that anticipation of General Booth's resolve that the devil shouldn't have all the good tunes is not quite the same thing, surely.

When he left the orchestra of the Opéra Comique, Offenbach, it seems, also broke off his connexion with Jullien. He tried his hand as a composer of vaudevilles, with no great success. A cardinal influence upon him now was Friedrich von Flotow, composer of *Martha*, who advised him to frequent the salons, the idea being to become well-known and talked-about by putting in appearances among the fashionables, then to stage a public concert and rely upon one's acquaintances to buy a large number of tickets.

Début at a Soirée

Flotow took Offenbach to the next soirée of the Comtesse de Vaux. He was nineteen years of age, but once his instrument was between his knees and he began to play, he lost all nervousness and awkwardness. 'My friend,' wrote Flotow, 'was a great success.' Following that up, Offenbach gave his first public concert at the end of January 1839. But he was puzzled. Should he become a performer (and that meant what we would call a freak or eccentric performer, imitating all manner of things, and making his instrument sound like anything except a cello)? Or should he court popularity with waltzes and ballads? And then there was the theatre.

An opportunity came with a commission to write some pieces for a vaudeville, *Pascal et Chambord*, at the Palais Royal. According to Offenbach, this was at the instigation of Anicet Bourgeois, one of the authors. The first night was 2 March 1839. It was a failure. Grassot, the comedian, proved to have no voice, and as a result Offenbach had to cancel half the finale he had written.

Soon afterwards, Jacques and Jules visited their home at Cologne. On seeing him, his mother said: 'But I don't know you! Are you my child?' and fainted. The next year both were to return so that they might see her before she died.

Marriage

Among the salons frequented by Offenbach was that of Mme Mitchell, a Spaniard who had married as her second husband John Mitchell, an Englishman, bookseller, concert agent, and lessee of the French theatre in London.

The salon that Offenbach happened to attend was in honour of a Carlist general, and on his entrance many remarked his resemblance to E. T. A. Hoffman. Here he was introduced to Herminie, Mme Mitchell's daughter by her first husband. They fell in love, and Offenbach asked her hand in marriage. Mme Mitchell made two conditions. The first was that he should score a success in England, the arrangements for the tour being easily arranged by John Mitchell. Offenbach went to England and scored the requisite success. There is extant a letter in which he playfully writes of his being summoned to Windsor and playing before the Queen, the Prince Consort, the Tsar of Russia, and the King of Bavaria. Strange how light-opera writers have a following of crowned heads!

The second condition was that he should become a Catholic, and this he did. On his conversion, the Comtesse de Vaux, to whose salon Flotow had taken him, acted as his godmother. Jacques Offenbach and Herminie D'Alcain were married on 14 August 1844.

Germany Once More

When revolution came in 1848 and prevented the production of a piece of his at the Théâtre Lyrique, Offenbach left Paris and, with his wife and child, returned to his native Cologne. But in Germany, too, there were revolutionary troubles. Here Offenbach composed *A Song of the German Boys* and *The German Fatherland* and reverted to signing himself Jakob.

However, after the production of a German version of his *L'Alcôve* at Cologne in January 1849, Offenbach returned to Paris. On 2 December 1851, came Louis Napoleon's coup d'état, with its consequent effects upon writers, artists, and musicians. It has been argued that the restrictive measures of the régime made people all the readier to welcome and enjoy Offenbach's light-heartedness.

At first there were bad times for Offenbach; and his father died in April 1850. Arsène Houssaye offered him the position of musical director at the Comédie Française. Here he obtained many reforms for the betterment of the music at the national theatre, took the opportunity of playing his own compositions as frequently as possible, and was at loggerheads with the actors and actresses, who felt, presumably, that the musical side was intruding far too much. Being sharers in the profits of the theatre, they objected to stalls being sacrificed to make room for Offenbach's enlarged orchestra.

Alfred de Musset asked him to write music for Fortunio's love song in *Le Chandelier*. The actor of the part was to be Delaunay; having heard his speaking voice, Offenbach thought that naturally he must be a tenor and accordingly wrote the song for that voice, only to find that Delaunay was a deep bass.

His ambition was to have a work accepted by the Opéra Comique, but, in spite of performances of small pieces at small theatres, he still had to rely on concerts for his theatre music to be heard. His dance music was favourably noticed by Prince Jerome. Nevertheless, on 9 May 1854, Offenbach was writing to his sister: 'the golden future of which I dreamed is not approaching.' He contemplated emigrating to America and did musical criticism for Houssaye's paper *L'Artiste*.

A Theatre of His Own

'I remained,' Offenbach wrote, 'at the Théâtre Française for five years. It was then that the idea came to me of starting a musical theatre myself, because of the continued impossibility of getting my work produced by anybody else. I said to myself that the Opéra Comique was no longer the home of comic opera, and that the idea of really gay, cheerful, witty music – in short, the idea of music with life in it – was gradually being forgotten. The composers who wrote for the Opéra Comique wrote little "grand operas". I felt sure that there was something that could be done by the young musicians who, like myself, were being kept waiting in idleness outside the portals of the lyrical theatre.'

Hervé (Florimond Ronger), however, got in first, and gay music was heard at his theatre, the Folies Nouvelles, at which none the less, under the prevailing theatrical licensing laws, he could produce only one-acters, and even those had to have only two characters. Offenbach called upon Hervé, flattered him, and his *Oyayaie ou la Reine des Îles* was accepted.

A World Exhibition was to take place in Paris in 1855, and near its site Offenbach found a very small theatre originally owned and run by a conjuror. By pulling strings that he held as a result of his stay at the Comédie Française – the 'strings' included Prince Jerome and the Comte de Morny, Napoleon III's half-brother – he secured the theatre. His licence was for 'pantomimes and short musical sketches with three characters'.

He would call the theatre the Bouffes-Parisiens and fixed 5 July as the opening day. He therefore had twenty days to make financial arrangements, recruit singers, commission authors, write the music, and rehearse it. Some of the authors let him down, and consequently he called in Ludovic Halévy, a civil servant. He and Henri Meilhac were to be the main collaborators with Offenbach. Halévy was nephew to the composer of *La Juive*.

The opening programme consisted of a prologue, a pantomime on Rossinian themes, a country idyll entitled *Une Nuit Blanche*, and a musical farce, *Les Deux Aveugles*. These two blind men became all the rage, ran for four hundred performances, and won a command performance at the Tuileries during the Crimean Peace Congress.

Berthelier, the singer who had made a success of *Les Deux Aveugles*, was instrumental in introducing to Offenbach an actress who was to figure in many of his hits. This was Hortense Schneider, who made her début at the Bouffes, 31 August, in *Le Violoneux* (based upon a Breton legend). It is remarkable that Offenbach, Halévy, and Hortense Schneider all had German forebears.

Having to seek winter quarters for his Bouffes, Offenbach found them at the Théâtres des Jeunes. He opened this on 29 December 1855, with *Ba-Ta-Clan*, a *chinoiserie musicale* with words by Halévy. It was a great success and gave its name to a celebrated *café-concert*.

In the *Revue et Gazette Musicale de Paris* Offenbach published an article outlining the 'principles' on which he ran the Bouffes-Parisiens.

'The Bouffes-Parisiens will try to revive the primitive and true species. It was in the musical sketches repeated in the old comic operas, in the farce that the theatre of Cimarosa produced, and in the first Italian masters that it scored its success. Not only do we want to follow that example, but we want to tap this inexhaustible source of old French gaiety. We have no other ambition than to create at once, and if you will reflect for a moment, that is no small ambition. In an opera which lasts scarcely three-quarters of an hour, it is necessary to have ideas and "ready-money" melody. Note again, that with this small orchestra – with which, nevertheless, Mozart and Cimarosa were satisfied – it is very difficult to conceal faults and inexperience that an orchestra of eighty musicians may hide. . . .'

Besides writing the article, Offenbach also organized a competition. Among the judges were Auber, Fromental Halévy, Ambroise Thomas, Gounod, and Scribe. After a weeding-out process, six surviving candidates were given a libretto to set to music by Ludovic Halévy entitled *Le Docteur Miracle*. This was quite different from the Doctor Miracle of the *Tales of Hoffmann*. Here the plot turned upon an indigestible omelette! The prize-winners were two composers destined for fame: Charles Lecocq (composer of *La Fille de Madame Angot*) and Georges Bizet (of whom nothing more need be said). Both prize-winning works were produced and both were complete failures.

Soon after this competition, Offenbach wrote *Mesdames de la Halle*, the first work in which he was able to use a chorus and any number of characters.

Relatively he was still without a big success, although this was not far distant, but before he wrote and produced *Orphée aux Enfers*, Offenbach staged an arrangement of Mozart's *Impresario* and Rossini's *Bruschino*. Rossini called him 'the Mozart of the Champs Élysées'.

Production of Orphée aux Enfers

The great day came at last and *Orphée aux Enfers* was produced on 21 October 1858. Most operatic treatments of the Orpheus legend had been serious affairs, but in 1793, at the Théâtre de la Cité, Offenbach had been anticipated by *Le Petit Orphée* (music by Deshayes), which was a kind of parody of Gluck's masterpiece. In that, Orpheus played the flageolet; Offenbach made a violinist of him! After an uncertain start, *Orphée aux Enfers* ran for 228 performances and at the end of April 1860, was given a gala performance at the Italian Opera in the presence of Napoleon III. There were, of course, critics who did not like the classic myths mocked or maltreated; a German critic, in 1863, called it 'brothel music', his verbal style rather anticipating the violent racial diatribes of the Nazis who banned Offenbach's music entirely from his native Germany. The original version was in two acts and four scenes, but in 1874 it was extended to four acts and twelve scenes.

Offenbach was to write at least a hundred scores by the time he died. Among those that preceded his posthumous *Tales of Hoffman*, notable were *La Belle Hélène*, *La Vie Parisienne*, *La Grande-Duchesse de Gérolstein* (apparently seen by all the crowned heads of Europe except the Emperor of Austria!), *Madame Favart*, and *La Fille du Tambour-major.* A Christmas broadcast by the BBC some years ago showed that *Robinson Crusoe*, now but little known, contained some of his best music.

As we have seen, Offenbach had always wanted a work of his to be produced at the Opéra Comique. At last he was to have his wish. *Barkouf* (book by Scribe and Boisseaux) was produced there in December 1861, and had only seven performances.

French Citizenship

Offenbach became a naturalized Frenchman in January 1860, in which process he was helped by the Comte de Morny, Napoleon III's half-brother and part-author under the pseudonym of Saint-Remy, of '*M. Choufleuri restera chez lui le . . .*' The outbreak of war between France and Germany, ten years later, nevertheless placed Offenbach in an awkward position. Was he not a German by birth and a Frenchman by election? He therefore went to Italy, his letters from there protesting his fidelity to France and speaking of the Germans as '*des horribles gens, des horribles sauvages*' led by '*Guillaume Krupp et son horrible Bismarck*'. It would seem that he remained in Italy throughout the war, for Brancour quotes a letter from his wife, dated 10 March 1871, in which she says her husband will be returning to their summer residence, Étretat, in a fortnight, and that the war had seriously undermined his health.

The Third Republic was not as kind as the Second Empire to Offenbach, although he collaborated with yet another big theatrical figure, Victorien Sardou, in *Le Roi Carotte*, the subject taken from Hoffman's tale, *L'Histoire Héroïque du Célèbre Ministre Klein-Zach, Surnommé Cinabre.*

His health undermined, his finances shaken by the turn of the tide and his management of the Gaïté, Offenbach continued to work extremely hard, having a work-table fixed up in the cab that took him from theatre to theatre.

His collaborators Meilhac and Halévy turned aside to write a successful non-musical play, *Frou Frou.*

He sought to recuperate himself in America. After his return to France, one or two minor works were produced; in December 1878, came *Madame Favart*, one of the most delightful of his scores, but only a *succès d'estime*. The following year he wrote *La Marocaine* which also was unsuccessful, although it has an attractive local colour.

With his hundreth score, *La Fille du Tambour-major*, Offenbach regained something of his former glory. It reached its hundredth performance on 7 March 1880, and the one hundred and first was given in honour of the garrison of Paris. He had written this work while in bed racked with gout. The story was not unlike that of Donizetti's *La Fille du Régiment*, but a *tambour-major* was always a popular subject with French authors.

Offenbach now had a presentiment that his end was near. He would try to write a work that would be the crown of his artistic career, a work that would hold the stage when his lighter and frivolous works had become dated and existed only in the repertoires of military bands and light orchestras.

The Tales of Hoffmann

He therefore worked intensely and feverishly at *The Tales of Hoffmann.* His librettist was Jules Barbier. For some reason Meilhac and Halévy had refused to write him a book for the 1878 Exhibition, but it is not necessarily the subject of Hoffmann that they turned down. The opera was based upon a play by Barbier and Michel Carré, *Les Contes Fantastiques d'Hoffmann*, which had been performed at the Odéon in 1851. The critics then had said it would make a good opéra-comique, and Offenbach, it would seem, had also then discussed the matter with Barbier. There had been pour-parlers for its production at the Théâtre Lyrique in 1877. The libretto had been written and given to Hector Salomon, the chorus-master at the Opéra. It is said that Salomon had almost finished the composition of his score when he unselfishly withdrew in favour of Offenbach.

In spite of his anxiety to finish *Hoffmann* and his foreboding of death, Offenbach also worked at *La Belle Lurette* which, after his death, was completed by Leo Délibes. Of *Hoffmann*, however, Offenbach managed to finish the score except for the orchestration and he was able to hear fragments of it at a rehearsal in the Salle Favart. Several numbers were performed at a musical evening given by him at his home on 18 May 1879. Carvalho, director of the Opéra Comique, and Jauner director of the Ringtheater, Vienna, were present and competed for the honour of first staging *Hoffmann*. Offenbach accorded it to Carvalho.

On 3 October 1880, while he was writing and surrounded by friends and relations, he suddenly fainted. 'I believe,' he said, 'that this night will be the end.' A priest was called, and Offenbach died at three o'clock in the morning of 5 October.

The funeral service was held at the Madeleine on 7 October, and the procession on its way to Montmartre passed by the theatres with which Offenbach had been identified, the Bouffes, the Opéra Comique, and the Variétés. Hortense Schneider, to whom Offenbach owed so much and from whom he had had to suffer a good deal of 'artistic temperament', came to Paris from her retirement in the country to attend the funeral.

Victorien Sardou could not speak because of his emotion. August Maquet praised Offenbach's indefatigable courage, and Victorin Joncières spoke of the sure and devoted friend, full of spirit, the man of irreproachable honour.

Some one remarked to Léonce, a great comedian in the operettas: 'M. Offenbach died quietly, without noticing it.' And Leonce replied: 'Ah, he will be very astonished when he does!'

The Tales of Hoffmann, orchestrated by Ernest Guiraud, was performed at the Opéra Comique on 10 February 1881. Things did not go altogether as Offenbach would have wished, because the third act was suppressed. According to Kracauer, the third act in the original version was that which is now played second, the Giulietta episode. To cut this meant cutting the Barcarolle and, to bring this in, the Antonia story was produced as though it were taking place in Venice and not Munich!

Offenbach's lasting fame thus dates from 1881, for while, in spite of the efforts of Sir Alan Herbert with *La Vie Parisienne* and *La Belle Hélène*, the successes of his lifetime scarcely weather transportation, the posthumous *Tales*, as I can testify from personal experience, are equally effective in their original French and in English and Flemish translations.

NICCOLÒ PAGANINI

1782–1840

FRANCIS TOYE

Early Miracles

No musician, perhaps no man, has ever lived about whom there gathered such a cluster of fantastic legends as about Paganini. To his contemporaries he remained always a Hofmannesque, saturnine figure. His matchless skill in playing the violin had been acquired during imprisonment for the killing of his wife or his mistress, nobody was quite sure which; in return for the mastery of his instrument he had, like a second Faust, sold his soul to the devil who might sometimes be seen guiding his hand during a concert and on at least one occasion driving him away afterwards; and so on. Paganini himself, who knew the box-office value of these legends and the extent to which they increased the already extraordinary effect of his already sufficiently weird personality upon his audiences, seems deliberately to have encouraged, when he was not laughing at, them. He had his reward, however, for there is little doubt that they were largely responsible for the incredibly savage treatment of his body after death.

Even divested of its Satanic trappings Paganini's career was remarkable enough. Born on 27 October 1782, at Genoa, the son of a packer in the port, he came near to being buried alive at the age of four in a catalepsy following some infantile ailment. His devout and always loving mother, to whom he never failed throughout his life to give that passionate devotion characteristic of so many Italians, proclaimed at the time of his birth that a Heavenly Messenger had promised that he should be the greatest violinist the world had ever seen. The less devout may prefer to describe him as having been born with an unparalleled genius for playing the violin (if that is any more explicable), because by the age of five he performed so well that his father, the least mystical of men, insisted on his spending all his time practising; and by the age of eleven, practically self-taught, he made such a stir at his first public concert that a group of Genoese clubbed together to send him to Parma where he could study the violin with Rolla, perhaps the best-known teacher of the day, and composition with Paer. For Paganini had started composing almost as soon as he had started playing the violin; to be exact, at the age of eight. What Paer taught him we do not know; we do know however that Rolla said that there was nothing he could teach him. Even Kreutzer, when he heard him, could hardly believe his ears – Paganini was then fourteen or at the most fifteen.

Spurred on by his father, who was bent on extracting the maximum possible profit from his son's virtuosity, young Paganini gave a series of widely successful concerts throughout Tuscany, of which the financial results were such as to enable him henceforward to live independently of the Genoese establishment, though he never, at any time, failed to contribute to its upkeep. His first essays in independence can hardly be described as edifying; he indulged in dissipation and gambling so recklessly that he came, on the one hand, near to ruining permanently his already precarious health and, on the other, to having to sell his treasured violin to pay his debts. He was saved by something akin to a miracle.

In 1801, a lady of the Tuscan nobility carried him off to her castle in the country, where he remained for three years learning something about agriculture and leading a healthy country life. Even now we do not know the lady's identity. Paganini always referred to her as 'Dida'. She played the guitar and, to please her, Paganini learned that instrument also, very soon achieving a mastery of it almost, if not quite, as complete as of the violin. Moreover he took advantage of his leisure and gradually improving health to perfect the new violin technique he was continually inventing: the plucking on the strings, the extension of the range of harmonics and of double-stoppings, and so on. The world has reason to be grateful to 'Dida', whoever she may have been.

Travels and Colleagues

Whether she sent him away or he left her of his own accord we do not know, but we hear of him next at Lucca where he had gone in 1805 after a year at Genoa. Here he attracted the attention of Elisa Bacciocchi, Napoleon's extremely aggressive and difficult sister, who had made her husband Prince of Lucca. She made Paganini, on the other hand, conductor of the Opera, gave him a resplendent uniform and charged him with the official organization of her music generally.

His salary was not large but his opportunities for love-affairs, almost as important in his eyes, were many. One of these is said to be enshrined in the well-known duet, *Scène Amoureuse*, for the G and E strings only; and incidentally it is from this time that dates one of the characteristics of Paganini's playing that most impressed his contemporaries: his astonishing mastery of the G string, on which, including harmonics, he is said to have achieved a compass of three octaves. When, later, Elisa was made Grand-duchess of Tuscany by her august brother she bade Paganini accompany her to Florence; which he did, but not for long. He was bent on a wandering life and independence. While still at Lucca, he had begun making regular tours. Indeed it was on one of these, at Turin, that he nearly succumbed to the intestinal trouble that was to afflict him all his life.

We know surprisingly little about Paganini's Italian tours, three main ones in all and ranging over the years from 1810 to 1825. Milan, where he gave nearly forty concerts in five years, became his favourite centre, and it was there, in 1813, that he was first definitely hailed as the greatest violinist in the world, accounts of his prowess being despatched by newspaper correspondents to the various capitals of Europe. Equally significant perhaps, it was in Milan that he was able especially to indulge in his passion for hearing chamber music, in particular Beethoven's, and sometimes taking part in it himself. Here, too, he had the celebrated contest with the French violinist, Lafont, whose tone he generously admitted to be stronger than his own, perhaps because nobody else would admit any comparison at all between the two players. But then Paganini was always something more than fair to his fellow-virtuosi, witness Lipinsky, the Polish violinist, with whom he appeared in a double concerto at Piacenza, and, even more remarkably, Spohr, whom he described as 'the finest singer on his instrument'. The very real and lasting friendship between Paganini and Spohr does credit to both men in that they were utterly dissimilar alike in personality and taste.

Rossini, Ill-health, Domesticity

His most important friendship, however, was with Rossini, whom he first met at Bologna in 1814. The two men got on famously always; it was for Rossini that he consented to conduct the first performance of *Matilda di Shabran* in 1821 in Rome, where, incidentally, the two dressed up as beggars during Carnival and electrified the city by their exploits. More important still, there is no doubt that Paganini was much influenced by Rossini's music, for he was particularly fond of writing variations on themes from his operas.

Towards the end of this period Paganini's health, never robust, took a turn for the worse; and in 1823 he was brought very low by a persistent cough and gastritis, not to mention the opium he began to take by way of alleviation. In the end an American doctor cured him, at any rate temporarily, but the whole year saw him out of action either at Genoa or Como. Paganini's infallible prescription for trouble or disease was a new love-affair, on this occasion, for the first and only time in his life, with permanent results. In 1824 he contracted a liaison with a singer, Antonia Bianchi, so intimate and serious that he took her to Genoa where his mother received her with remarkable indulgence. Paganini seems really to have believed, not merely said as always, that he had at last found the ideal companion. Antonia accompanied him on his tours and sang at all his concerts. Finally, in 1825, at Naples, she discovered that she was with child. Paganini, radiantly happy at the prospect of becoming a father, removed her and himself to Palermo, where in July a son was born, Achilles Cyrus Alexander (Achillino for short!), on whom for the rest of his days Paganini lavished a devotion and a care as admirable as unexpected. He gave much thought to his education, he took him everywhere, and when, still a tiny boy, Achillino broke his leg, Paganini himself nursed him, remaining immobile for hours lest the setting be prejudiced. Antonia unfortunately did not come up to expectations; she turned out to be a jealous scold of the first water who, whether Paganini gave her cause or not, make his life a positive burden. He stood it for three years, finally pensioning her off with the condition that he should keep the sole rights in the boy.

Vienna, Prague and Germany

In 1828, for the first time, Paganini left Italy as the result of a pressing invitation to play in Vienna, where he created a furore surpassing even anything that he had experienced in his own country. The Emperor named him his 'Imperial and Royal Virtuoso'; his personality and his appearance inspired operas, plays, poems, and medals. Not improbably the six months he spent in the Austrian capital were the most brilliant and the most successful of his entire life. In Prague, on the other hand, for some reason that has never been wholly explained, his reception was comparatively cool; moreover he was there stricken again by illness, this time in the form of an affection of the larynx, which, many years later, becoming tuberculous, was destined to be the immediate cause of his death.

In 1829 he embarked on the conquest of Germany, beginning with a triumphant three months in Berlin, where he was ardently championed by Spontini as well as Meyerbeer, whose friendship dated from Italian days. There followed a prolonged succession of tours to the various Germany cities, large and small: Leipzig, Frankfurt, Munich, Hanover, Hamburg, and so on. Everywhere it was the same story: he came, he saw, he conquered, whatever the preliminary prejudice against him. The Court of Westphalia made him a Baron; he may have paid, he certainly intrigued, for the title long wanted for Achillino's sake at least as much as for his own. A lady, whom he much fancied, fell violently in love with him and, had she not already possessed a husband, he would certainly have married her if only because he thought she would make an ideal mother for Achillino. So altogether Germany and Austria did something more than their duty by him, and even Paganini himself, notoriously alive to the importance of money, was constrained to admit that they had proved so profitable that he need never play the violin again.

France and England

In March 1831, he gave his first concert in Paris, where he stayed a couple of months and wrote his *Concerto in D* to please and flatter the Parisian public. Despite the now familiar triumphs alike with the public and professional musicians, he does not seem to have been altogether happy there. Wherever he went the familiar legends about his Satanic attributes and dark, unavowable crimes were, and always had been, current. Whereas, however, the Germans and Austrians had treated these more or less as part of his romantic paraphernalia, the more precise French gave them a definitely malicious twist, which moved him to angry protest.

In May of the same year, giving concerts at Boulogne and Calais on the way, he went to London. Here again there were the usual triumphs, the usual tours, the usual social successes – all the conventional attributes in excelsis of the virtuoso's life then and now. Those familiar with the details of the visits of Rossini and other distinguished musicians to England, at or about this time, will not need to be told how low was the state of music there. The outstanding impression of England carried away by Paganini must have been one of a rather unpleasant nationalism manifested over and over again in indignation that he and his impresario should charge so highly for the concerts and that so much good English money should be taken away by a mere foreigner. It looks as if the English were becoming tired, as well as aware, of being the milch-cows of musical Europe.

Finale: Assessment

Paganini's first visit to England lasted ten months, but he returned in 1832 and 1833, as well as to France, Holland, and Belgium. Nothing need be said about these final tours of his except to chronicle the fact that he met and made friends with Berlioz, from whom he commissioned *Harold in Italy* to display his skill as a player on the viola. Though he eventually declined the work owing to the solo parts not being important or showy enough, he always remained on excellent terms with Berlioz and allowed himself towards the end of his life to be used as a stalking-horse when a rich benefactor wished to ease the difficulties of that erratic genius (so akin as regards romantic hyperbole to Paganini himself) by the gift of a large sum of money. At the end of 1834 he returned, in wretched health, to Italy. His beloved mother had died two years before, and Genoa had nothing to offer him except a Gold Medal struck in his honour. The Duchess of Parma made him a Knight of St George; the Roman Society of St Cecilia elected him an honorary member. He had given a charity concert at Piacenza, another, probably his last, at Turin, and he had bought an estate near Parma where he might spend his declining years in peace and comparative affluence. Fate, however, willed otherwise.

In 1837 Paganini had allowed his name to be associated with a new Casino in Paris, where the profits were mainly to be derived from gambling and Paganini concerts. The authorities refused to sanction the former, and his ill-health effectually prevented the latter, so that the enterprise failed miserably. Fleeced by the speculators and persecuted by the law, Paganini had to spend many miserable months in Paris, ill and almost voiceless owing to his larynx trouble; indeed, as one of his biographers pungently remarks, he very nearly ended his career in the prison where it was falsely reputed to have begun. Ultimately, the poorer by 60,000 francs, he escaped, in February 1839, to Marseilles, moving in the winter to Nice, at that time still an Italian possession, where, on 27 May 1840, he died. Since he had not received final Absolution from the Church the clerical authorities, doubtless not uninfluenced by the fantastic legends attached to his name, refused to allow his burial in consecrated ground. Achillino, now the Baron Achille Paganini, who, one is glad to know, had tended his father lovingly to the very end, waged a long and expensive war for five years to remove the ban. Even then Paganini's body found no abiding place, till, after being buried in one church-yard, dug up, and buried again in another, what remained of it was finally transferred in 1926 to the Camposanto at Genoa, where, unless it has in the meantime been bombed or shelled, it permanently rests.

The importance of Paganini in the history of European music is not perhaps sufficiently recognized in this country. His influence on the technique of violin playing, apart from any controversy as to its direct or indirect nature, was incalculable, to be compared only with that of Domenico Scarlatti on the harpsichord and Clementi, Chopin, or Liszt on the pianoforte. Directly or indirectly, the whole modern school of violin technique could never have existed without him. As a player, moreover, Paganini must surely be judged the greatest violinist who ever lived; it is often forgotten that his playing moved his audiences just as much as it astonished them. As with the great *castrati*, his technical virtuosity was allied with, not divorced from, an irresistible emotional appeal. This is the explanation of the great influence he exercised on Liszt and other contemporary musicians. As a composer he is not of course in the first rank, but the best of his compositions can in no wise be regarded as mere virtuoso music. So much is clear when we listen to Menuhin playing one of the Concertos, and with the twenty-four *Capriccios* for violin alone, written in Genoa while he was still a lad, the case is even stronger. Who is prepared to dismiss a set of pieces of which one has served as a theme for variations not only by Brahms but also by Rachmaninoff, of which several others were transcribed for the pianoforte by Schumann and Liszt, whose *Campanella*, incidentally, is based on a movement from one of the concertos? Emphatically Paganini remains among the great musical figures of the Romantic Movement.

GIOACCHINO ANTONIO ROSSINI

1792–1868

FRANCIS TOYE

Boyhood and Youth

Rossini, the son of the municipal trumpeter of Pesaro (an officer who corresponds approximately to our own town crier), showed signs of musical genius in very early years. At the age of fourteen he played with something more than competence on the viola and the horn, while his efficiency on the cembalo was such that he was often employed at various local theatres to accompany the recitatives and to train the chorus. He was even better known, perhaps, as a boy-singer, and, more important still, though in all probability few people realized the fact, he had written a considerable amount of music; a song for soprano and some duets for horn intended for him and his father, who, in addition to municipal trumpeting, played that instrument in the local theatre. He had even composed a collection of isolated operatic numbers that were good enough, with some slight revision, to be successfully produced half a dozen years later in Rome as the opera *Demetrio e Polibio.*

All this would have been remarkable enough in any boy of fourteen, but it was doubly so in young Rossini, whose musical instruction up to that time had been of the most rudimentary description. His aptitude for singing he probably owed in the first instance to his mother, originally a seamstress, who knew little about music but who seems to have been a natural singer of talent. He did not get any kind of serious teaching on the cembalo or in composition until he was twelve years old, as the masters provided for him before that date were, to put it mildly, unsatisfactory. Probably the most significant musical influence in his boyhood was exercised by a priest, Don Malerbi, who, in addition to coaching him in singing, first instilled into young Gioacchino that enthusiasm for Mozart and Haydn which was to remain with him throughout his life.

Moreover, the circumstances of his boyhood were scarcely con-

ducive to study of any kind. His father, commonly known as 'Vivezza', owing to his gay and impulsive disposition, was a fiery republican continually getting into trouble with the authorities for his advanced opinions. This eventually led to the loss of his modest municipal appointment, and he and his wife earned a precarious living by seeking employment in various small theatres in and around Bologna. In their absence Gioacchino was left at Pesaro in the charge of his aunt and grandmother. Nominally he was supposed to be receiving some kind of education in reading, writing, and arithmetic, and even in the elements of music, but in practice he seems to have done little except get into mischief. An uncommonly high-spirited boy, he had a vitality that manifested itself in a naughtiness probably unique in the annals of great masters of music. Various methods were tried to curb it, including apprenticeship to a blacksmith, but till his tenth or eleventh year nothing had any effect.

By the time, however, that his parents settled definitely in Bologna (1804) he was more or less a reformed character, and two years later, when his voice broke, he studied not only the cello but also counterpoint at the Liceo Musicale with something very like diligence. His teacher, Mattei, a pupil of the illustrious Padre Martini, was a pedant who believed fanatically in the virtues of strict counterpoint, and Gioacchino always said he had learnt more from the scores of Haydn and Mozart than from all Mattei's teaching. In return Mattei nicknamed him 'Il Tedeschino', or the Little German. Nevertheless the authorities were sufficiently satisfied with his academic progress to entrust him with the writing of a cantata on the occasion of the annual prize-giving in 1808, when he himself received a medal for counterpoint. Moreover, before or about this time he wrote much music of value: five agreeable string quartets, some orchestral variations and two overtures, of which the second was subsequently attached to his first opera.

He finally left the Liceo in 1810, not, as is usually said, because Mattei told him that he now knew enough to write operas, if not church music, but because it became increasingly necessary for him to provide for his father and mother. Besides, in the autumn he received a letter from Venice asking whether he would go there and write a one-act opera. His answer was to go at once; it was his first real chance.

The First Operas

Fortunately for Rossini his first opera, *La Cambiale di Matrimonio*, was a success, though the singers thought that he attached too much importance to the orchestra. It led to his being commissioned to write several one-act operas of the same kind, of which one, *Il Signor Bruschino*, has acquired fame as exemplifying Rossini's love of a practical joke. Thinking, it is said, that the manager had purposely palmed off on him a bad libretto owing to his youth and inexperience, he is reported deliberately to have played every kind of trick with the score, writing impossible passages for the singers, and so on. In fact the story is not true, as anyone who reads the score of the charming little opera will immediately see for himself.

Almost immediately afterwards, Rossini produced the work destined to establish him as a composer of real importance. This was *Tancredi*, a serious full-dress opera this time, based on Volatire's romantic tragedy. *Opera seria*, as the Italians called it, was a highly conventionalized form, and *Tancredi*, though we should probably find it stilted nowadays, was welcomed as exceptionally fresh and original. It contains in fact almost the only tender love music that Rossini ever wrote, and the Venetians adored it. One of the tunes, the famous 'Di tanti palpiti', became so popular that the whole of Venice is said to have sung snatches of it from morning till night. Once, in the Law Courts, the public had to be ordered to stop humming it.

In the same year, 1813, only two and a half months later, Rossini was fortunate enough to win a success, if possible even more pronounced. This time it was a comic opera, *L'Italiana in Algeri*, which positively took Venice by storm. Never, people said, had there been such sparkling, exciting music. Their enthusiasm was not unjustified, for, despite a rather silly libretto, *L'Italiana* still seems as fresh as ever. True, there is no trace of sentiment in it, but the high spirits and sense of fun are irresistible.

The success of two such strongly contrasted operas as *Tancredi* and *L'Italiana* gave Rossini undisputed musical primacy in that part of Italy. The public, accustomed to the facility indispensable to an Italian opera composer at the time, may not have been so astonished as we are at the production of two such diverse masterpieces in less than six months. But the originality of them must have appeared even more clear. Besides, Rossini was at least as popular as a person as he was as a composer. He was twenty-one; he was good-looking and witty. All the ladies fell in love with him, and his various love affairs were discussed almost as much as his operas. By common consent he had become the most famous and popular figure in Venice.

Rome and The Barber of Seville

Three years had sufficed to turn Rossini from a promising student into one of the most famous of contemporary Italian composers. Milan now wanted him, and he produced two operas there, neither of which was conspicuously successful. Nor was the *opera seria* with which he again tempted fortune in Venice at the end of 1814. The escape of Napoleon from Elba immediately threw Italy into a ferment, reviving the old political troubles with which he had been only too familiar in his childhood and which cannot have helped matters. It must have been with a sense of relief that he accepted a contract in the spring of 1815 to go to Naples.

Here, too, all was not plain sailing by any means. The Neapolitans considered Rossini a foreigner, and they despised foreigners because they thought that only Neapolitans had any real knowledge of music. Further, the impresario of the opera, one Barbaia, was renowned for his ruthless and autocratic methods, and especial regard had to be paid to the idiosyncrasies and whims of Isabella Colbran, who was his prima donna and also his mistress. Rossini was fortunate enough to win the confidence of this powerful couple almost at once, so that when, towards the end of the year, he produced his first opera for Colbran he was able to have his own way in two very important matters of detail. Hitherto the recitatives in opera had been accompanied on the cembalo. In this opera, *Elisabetta*, Rossini provided an orchestral accompaniment. More important still, he wrote down for the first time *all* the notes to be sung by the singers. Experience had taught him that the improvisations in which the singers of the time used to indulge might be good or might be bad, but that in either event they were liable to alter the character of the music. So, taking advantage of Barbaia's prestige and Colbran's popularity, he launched as an innovation what has since become an accepted practice.

One of the terms of Rossini's contract was that he should be allowed on certain occasions to leave Naples. He took advantage of this in November to go to Rome, where he wrote for the Argentina Theatre the work by which he is mainly remembered today: the mmortal *Barber of Seville.* He had not gone to Rome with this articular opera in view; the choice of Beaumarchais' play as a subject vas almost the result of an accident. It is impossible here to tell the vhole interesting story of the birth of this astonishing masterpiece or o give more than the barest outlines of its chequered infancy. Those vho are interested will find a full description in the fourth chapter of ny book on Rossini.

Apparently Rossini wrote the music in less than a fortnight. True, e made use of a few ideas from previous operas and appropriated odily the 'storm music' from another. People sometimes imagine hat he did not write a new overture because the overture now ssociated with *The Barber of Seville* had already done service on two ther occasions. This, however, is not the case. *The Barber* originally ad an overture of its own which has since been lost. In short, the time ccupied in the composition of this opera is one of the standard niracles of music; it hardly seems possible that the notes could be vritten down in two weeks, much less thought of. The feat becomes ll the more remarkable in view of the quality of the music. *The Barber* has remained for more than a hundred years one of the most opular comic operas in the world, perhaps the most popular. The nusicians, headed by Beethoven and Wagner, have admired it no less han the general public. Not only is the music, with its sparkle, its ustle, its satirical humour, delightful in itself, but it provides just the ight interpretation of Beaumarchais' play, with the mocking ersonality of Figaro dominating the whole.

Yet on its first production on 20 February 1816, *The Barber* was ractically hissed off the stage by an audience that seems to have gone o the theatre determined to ruin it. The management was excessively npopular to begin with; the partisans of Paisiello (who had successully set the same subject to music) were bent on finding fault; there was series of those untoward accidents too often associated with first ights. Rossini was so discouraged that he slipped out of the theatre nd went home, where the prima donna, Giorgi Righetti, going round o offer consolation later in the evening, found him apparently asleep. t was almost certainly a pretence, for Rossini was the most nervous nd sensitive of men and always did his best to hide his real feelings. But he soon had his revenge. The second performance of *The Barber* vas as successful as the first had been disastrous. From that day it has ever looked back.

Work in Italy

During the next five and a half years Rossini's life is little but chronicle of various operas, the majority of which need not even b specified. His headquarters remained at Naples, where he contrived, a usual, to enjoy himself, consuming large quantites of macaroni an oysters, drinking the agreeable wines of the country, and embarkin upon a serious love affair with Isabella Colbran. But he was not idle far from it. For during the period in question he wrote no less tha sixteen operas, mainly for Naples but also for Rome, Milan and othe cities.

The first of these that need be mentioned was *Otello*, a setting c Shakespeare's play, or rather of a travesty of Shakespeare's play, whic in its day was regarded as one of the great operas of the world. An indeed there is some beautiful music in it, notably in the last act, bu we are never likely to hear it again. A year later (1817) came *L Cenerentola*, produced in Rome with, in the first instance, results a unfortunate as those of *The Barber*. This very mundane version of th story of Cinderella is not dead by any means, as those who have hear recent performances in London, Paris, or Florence will know fo themselves. It is a delicious score, one of the most workmanlike eve penned by the composer, full of fresh musical ideas and of particularl felicitous ensembles.

Mosè (1818) and *Maometto II* (1820) need not detain us, the les because they only exist now in the revised versions subsequently mad by the composer for Paris. But *Mosè* was in its day one of Rossini' most popular works and the famous 'Prayer', so familiar to out great grandparents, took Europe, and even England, by storm; while sever of the impressionable young ladies of Naples are said to have been s moved by it that they were afflicted with nervous prostration! Be tween the two came *La Donna del Lago* (1819), which is none othe than our old friend 'The Lady of the Lake', an opera that is of intere as foreshadowing certain characteristics of *William Tell*. But perhap the most important of all these operas in a sense was *La Gazza Lad* or *The Thieving Magpie*, which Rossini went to Milan to produce i 1817. *La Gazza Ladra* is not quite a comic opera and not quite a *opera seria*. It may be considered the first ancestor of the school c Realistic Opera which subsequently found so much favour in Italy There is some splendid music in it, especially the overture, whic begins with the then unheard-of-innovation of a drum roll. Indee ıost of Rossini's overtures possess an excellence that their gradual re-ıtroduction at our orchestral concerts is again beginning to make vident to modern ears.

In 1822 Rossini's Neapolitan career came to an end with the opera *Zelmira*. Barbaia, who had gone to Vienna to restore the fortunes of ıe Kärnthnerthor Theatre, wished Rossini to join him there with his ıtest opera. What might have been the complication of Rossini's ıarriage to Isabella Colbran during this very year does not seem to ave been a complication at all. On the contrary, everything worked ut most satisfactorily, and towards the end of March, Rossini, accom-anied by his wife and several members of the Neapolitan company, eft Italy for Vienna. It was the first time he had visited a foreign ɔuntry.

At Home and Abroad

Rossini's music had already acquired a European reputation, but 'iennese musical circles were sharply divided as to its merits. If a good ıany of the German musicians, headed by Weber, were hostile, society nd the public were almost unanimous in their enthusiasm, which was ı fact often pushed to extreme lengths. This exaggeration may well ave explained Weber's hostility, for which, as a matter of fact, he ıbsequently apologized to Rossini. But Schubert always liked his ıusic and was far more influenced by it than is usually realized. eethoven himself, though he cared little for the *opera seria*, recog-ized Rossini's genius as a composer of comic operas. 'Give us plenty f *Barbers*,' he said when Rossini, filled with admiration for the *Eroica ymphony*, went to see him and pay his respects. The meeting must ssuredly be reckoned one of the most dramatic in the history of ıusic. On the one hand the prematurely aged, deaf Beethoven living ı lonely squalor; on the other Rossini, young, urbane, witty, the vourite of everybody in Vienna. Rossini himself was so moved by that he tried to inaugurate a subscription to provide Beethoven with ıore comfortable quarters, but the Viennese, who had very definite pinions about Beethoven, refused to support him, and the project ll through.

Rossini's four months in Vienna were a succession of festivities and iumphs, so that he was probably glad enough to pass the summer uietly at his wife's villa just outside Bologna. He did not produce any ew work of importance till the following year, when the famous opera *Semiramide* was performed in Venice at the beginning of February 1823. The defects in *Semiramide*, which are numerous, seem more obvious to us nowadays than its merits, but at the time it was considered the greatest opera of the day and has been described as being to Rossini very much what Austerlitz was to Napoleon. For in this very year no less than twenty-three of his operas were being performed in different countries – and he was only thirty-two!

At that time England stood in much the same relationship to the world of music as the United States does now. It was the country where musicians went primarily to make money. So it is hardly surprising that such a popular figure as Rossini had now become should have been invited to London, where he arrived early in December. The ostensible object of his visit was to write an opera for the King's Theatre, but for one reason or another the opera never materialized. He was wholly successful, however, about money; by singing at parties, accompanying Isabella at the piano and so on he made some 175,000 francs, an enormous sum for those days. London Society welcomed him with open arms during his few months' stay, and he even enjoyed the privilege of singing duets with George IV.

Paris and William Tell

On his way to London, Rossini had stopped in Paris, where he now returned in August 1824. Paris was at that time the centre of European culture and, though on personal, nationalistic, and even musical grounds some French musicians were hostile to Rossini, the Court and the Government were extremely desirous to have the most brilliant composer of the day in residence there. They established him in general command of the Théâtre Italien, devoted, as its name indicates, to the production of Italian operas, and later, when this contract came to an end, they invented for him the extraordinary post of Composer to His Majesty and Inspector General of Singing at a yearly salary of 20,000 francs.

Except for an insignificant trifle, Rossini never wrote, probably never intended to write, an Italian opera for Paris. His goal was the Opéra itself, where performances had to be in French. With this in view he took considerable trouble to study not only the French language but the idiosyncrasies of French taste and French singing. The first results of this were apparent in *Le Siège de Corinthe* (1826) and *Moïse* (1827), revised and considerably elaborated versions of

Maometto II and *Mosè* respectively. *Moïse* in particular has some splendid music, notably in the choruses, but the principal interest of these operas to us is historical, in that they were the forerunners of the school of Grand Opera subsequently identified with the Opéra in general and Meyerbeer in particular. Then, in 1828, he produced *Le Comte Ory*, a work of lighter calibre, which contains some of the most elegant and delightful music he ever wrote. This too is of great historical importance, in that it influenced and helped to form the characteristics of the whole school of French Comic Opera.

But the climax of Rossini's Paris career, perhaps of his whole career, was the opera *William Tell* (1829). *William Tell*, which is, of course, based on Schiller's play of the same name, is unique among Rossini's operas for the conscious trouble he took in writing it. For originality, for carefulness of workmanship, for elaboration of scoring, it stands in a class apart. Verdi, Wagner, and Meyerbeer were all influenced by it. Even to-day the overture, which is in reality a symphonic poem in miniature, remains an acknowledged masterpiece.

Yet *William Tell* never enjoyed the popular success deserved by the qualities of the music. Partly the poor quality of the libretto was to blame; partly the excessive length. On the other hand, to call it a failure, as is sometimes done, is absurd. Headed by Berlioz, the musicians of the world lavished their praises upon it; it secured for the composer the Legion of Honour and a Serenade from the distinguished conductor, Habeneck, and the Conservatoire Orchestra; it achieved five hundred performances in Paris alone during the composer's lifetime.

Still, there can be little doubt that Rossini, accustomed to the applause of the multitude, was disappointed at the result. The Opéra Directorate subsequently turned their main attention to Meyerbeer and contented themselves with giving *William Tell* in a mutilated form, sometimes indeed only one act. It was on such an occasion as this that the Director, chancing to meet Rossini in the street and thinking to please him, said that the Second Act was being given on that very night. To which Rossini, who was as caustic as he was witty, merely replied, 'What! the whole of it?'

The Latter Years

As the whole world knows, Rossini never wrote another opera after *William Tell* – one of the most extraordinary phenomena in the history of art. He was only thirty-seven years old, at the very apex of his fame. The problem of 'the Great Renunciation', as it has been called, has provided material for much speculation and I myself have fully discussed it elsewhere. Speaking generally it may be said that it was in part the result of accident, in part of circumstances, and in part of deliberate volition.

When Rossini left Paris for a long rest, he had every expectation of writing another opera in accordance with the terms of his contract. But in 1830 there came the Revolution in Paris which overthrew the Government and incidentally destroyed the contract. Gradually, moreover, his health began to give way. The dissipation of his early years coupled with the intense strain of his working life – he had written more than thirty operas in twelve years! – had enfeebled his nerves to an extent that eventually became pathological. For instance, his first journey in a train prostrated him for days, and the news of the death of someone he cared for, of his adored mother especially, affected him like a serious illness. Furthermore, he undoubtedly felt that his day was done, that people were far more interested in music like that of Meyerbeer's, which he disliked, while remaining on friendly terms with the composer himself. He was out of sympathy with the revolutionary spirit of the times; he disapproved of the new orientation of the Italian theatre, and above all he bitterly deplored the gradual decline in the standard of singing. Rossini was not exactly lazy but he needed a stimulus to exertion, and the stimulus was lacking. He had made enough money to live on; he had no children. Why bother? Perhaps in reality he acted wisely. Heine thought so and considered his retirement a sign of genius as distinct from mere talent.

He did, in fact, write two other major works, one, the well-known *Stabat Mater* some ten years later, and the other, the *Petite Messe Solennelle*, at the very end of his life. Neither of these works is written in a style considered appropriate nowadays to ecclesiastical music, but the *Stabat Mater* has some beautiful numbers, and the *Mass*, though less well known, is in its way a masterpiece. Rossini called it 'the last mortal sin of my old age' and commended it and himself to his Maker in what is assuredly one of the most curious dedications ever penned.

The facts of Rossini's life during the thirty-nine years after *William Tell* are of little interest. He went to Italy and made journeys to several European countries, but he still kept Paris more or less as his head quarters. Perhaps the most important event was his separation from Isabella, who had become tiresome and very extravagant, and his increasing intimacy with a reformed demi-mondaine called Olympe Pélissier, whom he subsequently married a year after Isabella's death in 1845. She proved to be the most devoted and self-sacrificing of wives and without her devotion it is more than probable that Rossini would have ended his days in a madhouse.

By the time he returned to settle down in Bologna in 1836 the condition of his nerves had grown definitely worse. He was still able, however, to enjoy life, and during the winter of 1837, which he spent in Milan, his musical parties were the talk of the city. Later he devoted much time and trouble to the reorganization of the Liceo Musicale at Bologna; he even wrote a little music, completing in fact, the *Stabat Mater*, of which he had written the first six numbers whilst on a journey to Spain nine years previously.

Gradually, however, his health became worse, and a demonstration against him in 1848 on account of his supposed lukewarmness in the cause of Italian independence came as a climax to his trouble. He fled incontinently to Florence, where, during the next seven years, he lived a life of almost complete retirement, exceedingly miserable, in an acute state of neurasthenia, hardly able to taste or assimilate his food and tortured by sleeplessness. In despair Olympe determined at last to remove him to Paris, trusting that the change of environment and doctors might prove beneficial. Her judgement proved right, for after a year or two's drastic treatment Rossini, if not completely cured, was able once more to find some pleasure in life. He was once again one of the idols of Paris, the father, real or putative, of all the best witticisms; every celebrity who visited the capital made a point of coming to see him. Among these was Wagner, with whom he had a particularly interesting discussion on the past, the present, and the future of music. Despite their extreme divergence of views the two men never ceased subsequently to entertain a genuine respect for one another.

For many years Rossini had written no music of any description, but in 1857 he began writing those amusing trifles from some of which Respighi fashioned the ballet known as *La Boutique Fantasque*. In the first instance they were mainly designed for the famous Saturday evening parties which he gave at his flat in the Rue de la Chaussée d'Antin. Every singer of repute who visited Paris wished to be asked to sing at these, and the fashionables of the city vied with one another to secure invitations. Rossini's Saturday evenings became, indeed almost as famous as his operas.

During the summer months he retired to a villa he had built fo himself at Passy, where he died after a comparatively short illness o 13 November 1868, attended to the last by the devoted Olympe. H was buried in the first instance in Père Lachaise, but nineteen year later, at the request of the Italian Government, his remains wer removed to the Church of Santa Croce at Florence, the Westminste Abbey of Italy.

He was worthy of the honour, for, though he had never been any thing of a hero either in life or art, he was a great musician, mor richly endowed by nature, perhaps, than any except the very greates No one has ever known better how to embody in music the joy o living. Even to-day, nearly a hundred years since his retirement fron professional life, his exuberant vitality and genial laughter surprise an delight us. Essentially a lover of the good things of this world, h never rose to supreme emotional or spiritual heights, but the worl has reason to be grateful for the tonic qualities of his sparkling an often highly sensitive music.

FRANZ PETER SCHUBERT

1797–1828

WILLIAM GLOCK

Early Years

Franz Schubert was born in Lichtenthal, a suburb of Vienna. Both his father and his mother had come to Vienna from Austrian Silesia. The family records can be traced back to the sixteenth century. Karl Schubert, Franz's grandfather, was a farmer and local magistrate at Neudorft, near Alstadt (there were thirty-five Neudorfs thereabouts) and in 1780 had erected, on the height above his house, a statue of Christ on the Mount of Olives, which excited great admiration. He had thirteen children, of whom nine died young, and Franz Theodor, the composer's father, was to repeat that experience almost exactly with his first marriage. The people of the district were serious and hard-working, and from them Vienna recruited many of her best officials, teachers, and intellectuals. Franz Theodor, who came to Vienna as assistant teacher to his brother, became quickly distinguished for his industry, moral character, stamina, and piety. Elizabeth Vietz, whom he married in 1783, came from a mountain town called Zuckmantel, which had experienced several wars and had been burned to the ground six times during two hundred years. Economic progress was impossible, and when the father, Franz Johann, impoverished by the Seven Years' War, took desperate steps that led to his ruin, the sons and daughters were forced to earn their living abroad and left, one and all, for Vienna.

Life must have been very hard, even for parents accustomed to denial and adversity. Franz Theodor applied continually for a better post than that at the parish school '*zu den heiligen vierzehn Nothelfern*', but government intrigue, and his extraordinary success in a school that had previously fallen into extreme disrepute, postponed the fulfilment of his hopes for many years. The attendance at the Lichtenthal school had, from no pupils at all, reached 174 and was later to increase to 300. At this time schoolmasters at the parish schools in Vienna received no salary. They could have free lodging in the school and were entitled to one florin school-money per month from each pupil. It is unlikely that schoolmaster Schubert ever earned more than £35 a year during Franz's childhood.

Little is known of Franz's early years but that he was of a cheerful, companionable nature and quickly afforded proof of his extraordinary gifts. Of his earliest three teachers in music – his father, Ignaz, the eldest brother (then about twenty), and Michael Holzer, the parish organist – only the first could contain his astonishment. He was determined that all his sons should follow his own profession. Ignaz, who taught Franz the pianoforte, tells of his surprise when his young brother declared, after a few months, that he would no longer need his instruction. Michael Holzer, a good-natured man of about thirty-five, a notable drinker and a fairly accomplished musician, said that whenever he wished to teach Franz anything he found that it was known already. He therefore looked on and was filled with pride and astonishment.

Many geniuses have had more stubborn instruction. But few have lived their youth in such an atmosphere of music as pervaded Vienna at this time and still fewer have had the opportunity to gain such practical experience through continual performances in choir and orchestra as Franz Schubert was now to have.

The possibility of Franz's becoming a choirboy in the Chapel Royal must have appealed tremendously to his father, for it meant also a free education at the Imperial Konvikt, which was the most important boarding-school in Vienna. When, therefore, a vacancy for one boy soprano was announced, Franz, now nearing his twelfth year, was entered for the examination. The beautiful quality of his voice and his expressive manner of singing had already won him fame in Lichtenthal; in addition, his cleverness and advanced knowledge of music enabled him to surpass easily all the other candidates, who had been making fun of his 'miller's suit'.

The Konvikt

There were places for eighteen choirboys in the Konvikt, of whom ten belonged to the Chapel Royal and eight to the Court Church. As there was a teaching staff of over twenty, the choristers must have formed only a small percentage of the students. Their existence imposed the cultivation of music as a subject and certainly lent an added impulse to its practice, but the Konvikt did not exist only for choir-boys. Other subjects were considered of more importance than music.

Though it is unjust, therefore, to criticize the Konvikt for neglecting the musical education of a young genius, it yet remains a striking fact that Schubert did not begin the study of counterpoint until he was over fifteen. An exercise sheet of this time has been preserved, on which four *canti fermi* are written in a shaking hand, that of Salieri; the counterpoint above, in contrasting boldness, shows Franz to have been as yet unskilled in the art. Salieri had been deeply impressed by *Hagars Klage*, a huge composition for voice and pianoforte by Schubert, who, as a consequence, and on account of his blameless reputation, was allowed to go from school alone to take lessons from the famous Italian.

His music master within the Konvikt was Wenzel Ruzicka, whose energy and enthusiasm the school governors were never tired of praising. From him Franz probably learned a good deal: economy of notes, how to write for the voice, and to achieve beauty of sound even when striving for the sharpest characterization. That Ruzicka was a Moravian was doubtless not without importance as well.

Orchestral practices at the Konvikt had been inaugurated by the Director, Dr Innocenz Lang, who was keenly interested in music. The orchestra numbered twenty-nine players; there were sixteen strings, eight wood-wind, two horns, two trumpets, and percussion. On beautiful summer evenings walkers returning from the Basteien would listen at the opened windows; there were such crowds that the street was impassable, and a mechanic named Hanacek, who lived opposite, brought out every chair in his house for the ladies to sit upon. Franz at first stood behind the leaders of the second violins. The keenness and certainty of his playing at once attracted attention and won for him the truest and most sensible of all his friends, Josef von Spaun. Franz presently became leader of the orchestra and often conducted when Ruzicka was absent.

Every evening after supper two overtures and a symphony were performed. The music ranged from Haydn, Mozart, and Beethoven to Krommer and Kozeluch, whose works are now forgotten. Schubert used warmly to defend the rather antiquated style of Kozeluch against that of Krommer, whose cheerful and vigorous compositions had won great popularity. His favourite overtures were those to *Figaro* and *The Magic Flute*; of the symphonies the two that made the deepest impression on him were the G minor of Mozart and the D major of Beethoven.

The orchestral practices were a continual source of enjoyment, but other circumstances conspired to make life at the Konvikt rigorous. The teachers were strict, unsympathetic Piarist monks, there was no womanly supervision or care whatever, and the food was scanty. Franz's earliest known letter, addressed at the beginning of his last year at the Konvikt to his brother Ferdinand, affords touching proof of this. 'You know,' he says, 'from experience how sometimes one wants to eat a roll and a few apples, and all the more when after a modest dinner one can only look forward to a wretched supper eight-and-a-half hours later.' The Bible is then quoted in support of charity, and Franz's irresistible description of himself as 'your loving, poor, hopeful, once again poor, and to be remembered brother' leaves one convinced that the last months were eased by a few kreutzers from brother Ferdinand.

The Gymnasium reports do not confirm the often repeated view that Franz was without talent or interest in less absorbing pursuits than music. Not until his final year do the reports contain any disagreeable details. But upon being offered the Meerfeld Scholarship (the highest honour a choirboy could win) provided that he remedied a '2' for mathematics during his vacation, Franz resolved to leave the Konvikt. The decision expressed more than a distaste for mathematics. Clearly, it was not only his spare time that had become dedicated to music. Josef von Spaun had been generously providing him with manuscript paper, in the utmost secrecy for fear schoolmaster Schubert should come to hear of it. Franz Theodor did, however, make the discovery, and when Schubert was fourteen forbade him the house.

The Dream

This obstinate, unimaginative course must have affected the young composer deeply. After a year Elisabeth Schubert died, and father and son were reconciled at her death-bed. Many years later, after another quarrel and a final reconciliation, Franz wrote the allegory known as 'My Dream'.

'I was one of many brothers and sisters. We had a good father and mother. I felt a deep love for them all. One day my father took us to a feast. My brothers became very merry there. But I was sad. My father thereupon came up to me and ordered me to taste the delicious foods. But I could not, and at that my father in anger banished me from his sight. I turned on my heel and, with a heart filled with infinite love for those who scorned it, wandered into a far country. For years I was torn between the greatest sorrow and the greatest love.'

Then followed his mother's death. 'From this time onwards I stayed at home again. Then one day my father led me once more into his pleasure-garden. He asked me if it pleased me. But the garden was altogether hateful to me and I dared not reply. Then he asked me a second time, excitedly, whether I liked the garden. Trembling I told him 'No'. At that my father struck me and I fled. For the second time I turned away and, with a heart filled with infinite love for those who scorned it, wandered again into a far country. Through long, long years I sang my songs. But when I wished to sing of love it turned to sorrow, and when I wanted to sing of sorrow it was transformed for me into love.' . . . After a passage of great beauty and vision, the dream concludes: 'My father I saw too, loving and reconciled. He folded me in his arms and wept. And I still more.'

Of Franz's profound suffering there can be no doubt. His decision to leave home and school-teaching, to win freedom though it meant living in crushing poverty, was not taken lightly. But to this we must return later.

Schubert and Salieri

It is tempting to discover in the subjects of Schubert's first vocal compositions at the Konvikt some reaction to his banishment. But possibly such titles as *The Parricide* and *The Corpse Fantasia* represent nothing but boyish tastes. Schubert's model in these tremendous ballads of twelve and seventeen movements was Zumsteeg, and through him he was attracted to Schiller, whose predilection for the horrible had once been noticed by Goethe. Zumsteeg had been a great friend of Schiller, had set tremendous stretches of his poetry enthusiastically to music, and was much admired by Haydn for his 'imagination and fine sense of form'. Schubert imitated, but not slavishly; he must have gained a great deal from such exercise and above all from the style and character of the music, which was thoroughly German. Soon his energy and invention began to surpass that of his model. It was Salieri who, as has been related, was so impressed by *Hagar's Lament*, another ballad of the same year modelled on Zumsteeg, that Schubert was allowed to go alone from the Konvikt to study with him. The Italian thereafter devoted his energies to turning Schubert against such things.

That Salieri advised him to set the poems of Metastasio to music rather than those of Goethe and Schiller is of little importance. Salieri also found fault with *Figaro*, and said that the closing scene of the first act of *Titus* was dramatically quite wrong; but this did not convince even an average talent like Josef Hüttenbrenner, who was a fellow pupil with Schubert. The natural antipathy of Salieri to German poetry was supported by a colossal ignorance of the language, which he excused by saying that he had lived in Germany only half a century; his criticism of Mozart was founded on jealousy. Yet both Schubert and Beethoven before him were attracted to this man. And that Schubert was proud of being his pupil may be seen, for instance, in the inscription of a work of 1815 – '*X Variations pour le Fortepiano composés par François Schubert, Écolier de Salieri, premier Maître de la chapelle impériale et royale de Vienne. . . .*' Two operas of this year also bear the remark, 'pupil of Salieri'.

Metastasio used to let Salieri, when they were alone, declaim sometimes whole scenes of operas; Salieri says how useful this was, and Metastasio thought it absolutely necessary for all song writers. Both believed that 'well spoken is half sung'. Schubert undoubtedly learned good Italian diction from Salieri and a certain skill in *opera buffa*. He developed a style, already noticeable in the second subject of the overture to his first opera, *Des Teufels Lustschloss*, which has an individuality apart from the rest of his music.

But development and characterization, and the ability to recognize when a libretto was undramatic, Salieri could not teach. And Schubert had not the ornamental brilliancy and theatrical dash that enabled Rossini to triumph temporarily with libretti almost as poor as Schubert's own. The story of Schubert's operatic ventures, of his repeated attempts to improve his fortunes at the worst possible time, is perhaps the most depressing of all. The greatest harm Salieri did was to initiate this history of tragic waste, of fine music buried beneath impossible libretti and of failures that darkened Schubert's days with bitter disappointment.

Before leaving the Konvikt, at the end of October 1813, Schubert had finished his *First Symphony*, in D. It was dedicated to Innocenz Lang. The second subject of the first movement is very much as Mozart would have rendered the theme in the last movement of the *Eroica*. Schubert had to wait until his *Fifth Symphony*, in B flat, to escape stiffness 'like a delightful child overawed into perfect behaviour not by fear or priggishness but by sheer delight in giving pleasure.' But already the instrumentation is individual, especially in the andante. Earlier in the year, he had composed a cantata for his father's name-day festival, which must have surprised even himself, for the inscription at the end is 'For my father's name-day!!!'

He now entered the St Anna Training College. His momentary submission to his father's design for living may be explained as arising from a wish to avoid the seven years' conscription to which every man between the ages of 16 and 45 was liable. In 1814 he became teacher of the lowest class at his father's elementary school in the Säulengasse. The history of the next three years is simple and astonishing almost above any other in the whole of art.

Wonderful Years

Schubert finished *Des Teufels Lustschloss* in May 1814. His first *Mass*, in F, was performed at the Lichtenthal church in October and was such a success that his father presented him with a five-octave piano and Salieri boasted of him as his pupil. Unable to afford a copyist, Schubert wrote out all the parts himself, of which the string ones alone filled eighty-six pages. It was now, while waiting for a second and more important performance ten days later at the Imperial Church of St Augustine, that Schubert composed *Gretchen am Spinnrade*. Goethe, in discussing knowledge that is innate with the poet, says he could, in *Faust*, know by anticipation how to describe the hero's gloomy weariness of life and the emotions of love in the heart of Gretchen; and only this, that the inner world is native to the genius, can explain the miracle achieved by a youth of seventeen. The marvellous accompaniment, the perfect modulations, and absolute dramatic fitness of every detail of the song have excited the wonder of all musicians. With *Gretchen*, as has often been said, German song was created.

A month previously, Schubert had composed the first movement of the *B flat Quartet* in the unbelievably short time of four and a half hours. This was the prelude to a year of unparalleled creative activity, during which Schubert composed six operas, two Masses, two symphonies, three sonatas, and 144 songs. To describe such productiveness as the result of industry would be nonsensical. There is no documentary evidence of his other activities during the year 1815. Schubert's life had become music. It is with astonishment that we remember his six hours' daily instruction of small children in the rudiments of reading, writing, and arithmetic, at a yearly salary of 32s.

There is excellent music in the operas. The overture to *Der Vierjährige Posten*, still frequently played, is delicious; the lightnings in *Fernando*, the snakes in *Die Freunde von Salamanka*, and Olivia's 'creeping alone through the rooms' are depicted with almost Handelian power and realism. In the last-named opera occurs also the melody that Schubert used nine years later for the variations in the octet.

Splendid as much of this music is, the songs, in which Schubert already frequently reaches perfection, are a far greater achievement. Among his thirty settings of Goethe in 1815 are several – *Heidenröslein*, *Meeresstille*, *Wanderers Nachtlied*, *Rastlose Liebe*, and *Erlkönig* – universally known and celebrated. The story of Schubert 'whelming' the *Erlkönig* on to paper is a familiar one. He hurried off to the Konvikt with two friends, Spaun and Mayrhofer, who had called on him and found him in a state of tense excitement; and there Ruzicka played through the song, putting in the vocal line on the piano, and, when exception was taken to the minor ninths on the words 'Mein Vater!', defended the music, saying how inevitably it suited the text, how beautiful it was (not ugly as they said) and how happily resolved. The poem of *Rastlose Liebe* so excited Schubert that he was for a time in a kind of ecstasy, until he freed himself from its effect by expressing it in musical form. In a single day, that of the anniversary of *Gretchen am Spinnrade*, he composed eight songs.

1815 marked a climax. Such an unceasing urge to create had never before been known. Yet in the following year Schubert wrote 110 songs (of which *Der Wanderer* is the most famous), two *Symphonies* – the fourth and fifth, in C minor and B flat – a *Mass*, an opera-fragment and the three *Sonatinas for Pianoforte and Violin*. The record is still astonishing. Not until 1817 does his productiveness approach common standards. There are no dramatic works, no symphonies, no church music; only one chamber work, three overtures, two of them in the Italian style and reflecting the momentary rage for Rossini, forty-seven songs, and seven *Pianoforte Sonatas*. The centre of interest and experiment has changed. Schubert had recently met one or two very talented pianists, among them J. von Gahy, who became a fine interpreter of his music and with whom Franz was especially fond of playing pianoforte duets. Some of his friends possessed the most modern instruments, and Schubert was inspired by their fresh possibilities;

he also won a close acquaintance with contemporary pianoforte music. There was thus every incentive for this first grand essay in a medium that Schubert was to enrich with so many noble and magnificent works.

The Significance of the Sonatas

That sixty-five pianoforte sonatas were being published every year around 1800 and in 1850 only three might be said to epitomize musical history in the first half of the nineteenth century. Schubert was the last great composer of pianoforte sonatas.

His unshakable earnestness is nowhere more clearly seen than in his determination to solve the most serious and difficult artistic problems, while his contemporaries in Vienna were busy writing short lyrical pieces with new attractive titles. He felt an overpowering responsibility. His incessant striving to balance matter and form satisfactorily was presided over by the perfect examples of the previous generation. The figure of Beethoven, above all, inspired him and to an equal extent weighed him down throughout his years of mature creation. Goethe maintained that he 'rid' himself of Shakespeare by writing *Goetz von Berlichingen* and *Egmont*; but the only musician whose greatness is comparable with that of Shakespeare was too immanent, both in time and place, for Schubert not to have remained fundamentally affected.

The opinion that Schubert's instrumental music is weak in form has acquired an almost legendary force. It rests partly upon a too rigid conception. His finest movements have continuity and inevitableness; they are not protracted to any greater length than the magnificent themes demand. If his music has not the tension of Beethoven's, it is partly because contrasts to him were not dramatic, but simply existed. He was led therefore to fill his movements with a richness of content and was dramatic not in conflict, but in the development of a single idea to its highest pitch.

The Turning-Point

The kindness of Joseph von Spaun in providing Schubert for many years with manuscript paper has already been related. He was untiring in his support and encouragement of the young composer. When

Schubert was nineteen, Spaun wrote a delightful letter to Goethe, asking him to accept the dedication of eight small volumes of Schubert's songs, whose publication would be a 'beginning to his musical career'. Schubert's songs and numerous other compositions have, he says, already 'won the applause of strict judges of music as well as of music-lovers, of men as well as of women'; it is stressed that Goethe's magnificent poems are responsible not only for the existence of many of the songs, but also to an important extent for the composer's development as a song-writer; and finally, that the pianist who plays the songs to Goethe 'must not be wanting in skill and expression'. There came no answer. Goethe was doubtless overwhelmed with letters of this sort; his favourite composer was Zelter, who, when given a poem, first tried to conjure up a living picture of the situation, then read it aloud till he knew it by heart, and upon reciting it again found the melody came of its own accord. Goethe, at his age, could not be expected to reconcile himself to such music as *Erlkönig*, which both in its substance and in the manner of its inception bore so strange a contrast to Zelter's gentleness and subordination.

In the same month as Spaun's letter, April 1816, Schubert applied for a musical post at Laibach, but without success. He had, it is certain, fallen very much in love with a girl named Therese Grob, who had a beautiful soprano voice and had two years previously sung the solo part of the *Mass in F*. She was not beautiful. 'But she was good,' Franz is supposed to have said, 'good to the heart. For three years I hoped to marry her, but could find no situation, which caused us great sorrow.'

Still more do these first attempts to win recognition and to obtain a settled job express a determination to follow the career of music, an intense and by now irresistible desire to escape from a household in which there reigned a perpetual atmosphere of schoolmastery and the most rigid paternal opposition to such a career.

Franz may have been persuaded to some extent by his new friends, Mayrhofer and Franz von Schober. It is also possible that he felt himself no longer in the same position in the second family, for his father had married again eleven months after the death of Elizabeth. There had been an addition of two daughters, now aged two and three respectively; and Ignaz, the eldest child, was forty-one when Anton, the nineteenth and last testimony to Franz Theodor's procreative energy, was born in 1826. It is hardly surprising that the latter kept a family register of such occurrences.

We may, in the cold language of the conscription papers of 1818, catch a glimpse of the Schubert sons. Ignaz, schoolmaster, is 'hunch-backed'; Ferdinand and Carl are both married, the former a school-master, Carl a landscape painter and tall of stature. Franz is described as *schwach*, which was the military term for 'thin'. His height is just under five feet two inches. He certainly increased in bulk afterwards, though Spaun says he was solidly built and by no means a 'lump of fat' and that his very youthful friend Moritz von Schwind already sur-passed him in circumference.

A change was encouraged by habits which became an integral part of Schubert's existence. We have reached the turning-point in his career, signalized by the first pianoforte sonatas and an end to prolific song-writing.

The three sonata periods, culminating in 1817, 1825, and 1828, re-present a division that may, without vital modifications, be observed in Schubert's output as a whole. There was a new outburst in 1822, with *Alfonso und Estrella*, the *Mass in A flat*, the *Wanderer Fantasia*, and the *Unfinished Symphony*, and in 1824 began the last intense period of composition, culminating in 1828 when Schubert produced master-piece after masterpiece at a dramatically forced tempo.

After 1817, the succession of musical events is, for a while, no longer an almost completely satisfying tale in itself. Five comparatively fallow years followed upon freedom.

Schubert and Vienna

Eduard von Bauernfeld, in a letter to a prospective biographer of Schubert, thirty years after the composer's death, declares that the only possibility lies in a kind of poetical description. Even to-day, when innumerable documents have been collected about his uneventful life, the same attitude persists. Failure to recognize Schubert's stature as a composer has been inflamed by the fanciful develop-ment of certain themes, all of them tending to an unserious view of his personality. He was, of all the great composers associated with Vienna, the only Viennese. His boyhood was spent in an atmosphere affected by the nobility of four of the greatest musicians the world has known; in a city, also, filled with popular music of all kinds. Vienna was, as Professor Dent has pointed out, the meeting place of musicians from Italy, Hungary, Poland, and Bohemia – all of them countries where there is a 'widespread primitive gift for singing and playing instruments'.

In Schubert's works there is a perfect fusion of popular and serious music; we may discover in the *C Major Symphony* the characteristics of *Bratl* music and of the calls of lavender-women, in a simple Ländler the boldness and force of the third movement in the *D minor Quartet.*

There were other influences besides those of Gluck, Mozart, Haydn, and Beethoven on the one hand, of marches and street songs on the other. In 1816–17 the operas of Rossini took Vienna by storm. *L'Inganno Felice*, *Tancredi*, *L'Italiana in Algeri*, and later *Elisabetta* and *Otello*, enjoyed a fabulous success. Of the last, Schubert wrote in 1819 to his friend Anselm Hüttenbrenner – 'One cannot deny him (Rossini) extraordinary genius. The instrumentation is sometimes most original, the voice-parts also, apart from the usual Italian gallopades and several reminiscences from *Tancredi*.' A critic writing in 1824 about some recently published Schubert songs finds also in *Wehmut* reminiscences of *Tancredi* – the 'famous bass from the first finale, B♭ D F – B♭ E♭ G♭ – B♭ D♭ F♭ G♭ – B♯ D♯ F♯, and so on, four or five times' – a progression he then suggests to pianoforte tuners as a test of cleanness.

It is difficult to estimate the influence of Rossini on Schubert, for music has not yet become, in such matters, a dependable prey to analysis. The *C major Symphony* has been described as a conflict between Rossini and Beethoven, the change from minor to major at the beginning of the *A minor Quartet* as typically Rossinian. But the side-by-sideness of suffering and ecstasy exists deep down in Schubert. The change of mode in the *A minor Quartet* is not facile; the emotional effect is not in that, but in the ecstatic soaring upwards of the original theme. It is comparable with the miraculous changes in *Auf dem Flusse*, in *Der Wegweiser*, and in *Trockne Blumen*. They are made suddenly, without sophistication as in Chopin, for instance, and nothing in music is more deeply affecting.

The Italian influence may be seen unmistakably in certain works, in the marches (where the change of mode is facile, like Rossini's) and in the *Sixth Symphony* or in the finale of the *G major Quartet*. It is confined rather to procedures recommended by their temporary fascination for Viennese audiences.

It is important to realize that Franz Theodor's stubbornness was dictated not only by his conception of music as a precarious means of existence, but also by his fear of the atmosphere into which his son, as a free artist, would be drawn. Franz's boyhood was lived under the shadow of invasions more portentous than that of Rossini. Dr Reeve, an Englishman who was in Vienna during the first campaign of 'War and Peace', has left a vivid picture of the conditions there. Politics were not discussed. No circulating libraries were allowed, no reading-rooms or clubs. There was the most rigid censorship of books and newspapers.

English papers, Dr Reeve complains, stopped many days at the Post Office to pass through this formality. The people were kept in ignorance. Amusement had become their only object. Shops closed early so that their owners might return to the suburbs in time to prepare themselves for the opera. 'The Viennese,' says Dr Reeve, 'are never at home and alone.' There might be some occasional fantastic sign of war in the bodies of French soldiers floating down the Danube and said to have been drowned by the Russians; then, suddenly, Napoleon enters the city, subjecting it to untold hardship. The censorship was powerless against enlightenment of this kind. But professors who were so bold as to interest their pupils in Kant were dismissed. The Viennese did not, like the Fabians, have to 'stretch their foreheads like concertinas' in order to understand one another's small talk. Conversation at table, the English visitor tells us, was of lovers and diseases. The only adventures that were restricted were those of the mind.

It is difficult to exaggerate the significance of this. Schubert's quickness to absorb the past and present of Viennese music, or to reflect the momentary triumph of a foreigner, finds only an apparent parallel in his reaction to Viennese life. The Schuberts came of a stock most antipathetic to the looseness and gaiety of Vienna, and Franz's attitude to life remained deeply earnest. But, though music was unhampered by the censorship, Schubert became intimately acquainted with men who were sharply affected by the narrowness of the State and whose whole behaviour was expressive of violent protest. He himself wrote music for a libretto that had been already banned. 'Light head, light heart!' he wrote in his diary while still a schoolmaster; 'too light a head usually conceals too heavy a heart.' His youth was touched, midway, by tragedy. The fabric of his thought and feeling was darkened by an overwhelming despair, which found upon occasion an accompaniment of more than usually excessive lightheartedness. Schubert's life cannot be interpreted as a comfortable acceptance of Bohemianism and foolhardiness, but rather as a tragedy of exhaustion in conflict with the unlucky times and with the prevailing reckless conception of living.

The Circle

From his earliest days, friendship had been almost as necessary to Schubert as music itself. That he had a remarkable gift for making friends is certain.

'I need hardly tell you that with my natural frankness I get along very well with all these people,' he writes from Zseliz, after a lively description of everyone there, from the coachmen to the countess.

In those inexplicable years of miraculous creativeness and of constraint as a schoolmaster, Schubert began to gather round him a circle of young men who were attracted by the magic of his personality and held together by it, though they were of the utmost diversity of character and aim.

In the hours spent with his friends Schubert found some compensation for the hard circumstances of his life, as well as some relaxation from work, in which he must have used himself up with fierce intensity. He was not happy in every kind of society. 'Schubert is much praised,' wrote Carl Beethoven, 'but is said to hide himself.' An explanation of this may be discovered in a passage from Franz von Schober's Memoirs: 'As much as Schubert liked to join the companionable circle of his friends and acquaintances, which he always enlivened with cheerfulness, wit and a healthy judgement, so much did he dislike appearing in formal society, in which he earned for himself through his retiring and unobtrusive behaviour the quite undeserved opinion that his personality, apart from music, was altogether insignificant. If, unhappily, there chanced the opportunity to spend in an intimate circle an evening already promised to some such formal society, or if a lovely summer evening tempted him into the open air, Schubert was easily led to break his word, a thing that was often reckoned heavily against him, though it was the only kind of disloyalty of which he was capable.'

Schober, the most intimate of Schubert's friends (of which a delicate proof may be seen in his styling himself Schobert), was a brilliant, cultured and worldly-wise young man, resembling a little, perhaps, Handel's friend Mattheson. Bauernfeld, who first met him in 1825, comments in his diary on Schober's adventurous life and how he had just been for a time an actor (in Breslau) *à la* Wilhelm Meister. 'He is liked by women in spite of his rather crooked legs. . . . Moritz (Schwind) looks upon him as a god. I find him fairly human, but interesting.' Schwind, whose correspondence with Schober is couched habitually in extravagant terms of affection and admiration, was not alone in his hero-worship. Schober was certainly a most persuasive talker.

In Bauernfeld's 'Parody on the Schubert Circle', which was read on New Year's Eve, 1825, Schober, as Pantalon, decides that the innermost nature of life is in rest. He despises position and occupation; work, even the most intellectual, is unworthy of him. He will, in future, lie on his bed, his flower-bed, and, imitating the plants, keep before him only the eternal substance of man and women and in doing so lead life back to its pure, original condition. This philosophy is greeted by Harlequin (Schwind) as 'magnificent, godlike, superhuman'. Schober had bought the Lithographical Institute, founded by Count von Palffy, and came into contact with Schwind through a few small orders, one of them possibly in connexion with six lithographs by Schwind to illustrate *Robinson Crusoe.* Schwind had been brought up in the Oriental Greek colony of Vienna. He was brilliantly gifted and entered the university at the age of fourteen. He sketched promiscuously, on books and walls and in illustration of letters, at an early age, but did not decide on painting as a career until about the time he met Schubert. His art was affected fundamentally by Schubert's music, in which he could find a depth of feeling and clarity of expression absent from contemporary painting. Many of his works perpetuate the Schubertians in a delightful manner. He had red cheeks (a family trait), deep-set dark-blue eyes, and a queer way of entering a room, always one foot and one side first, as if he were proving the ground.

If Schwind was the most distinguished painter, Bauernfeld and Mayrhofer were the circle's most distinguished men of letters. Bauernfeld was a schoolfellow of Schwind. He met Schubert in 1825. Schwind made him read some of his poems to Schubert, the two then played pianoforte duets and all three afterwards repaired to the Gasthaus, where the friendship was firmly cemented. Bauernfeld, like Mayrhofer and many other poets at that time, was a government official. He became a favourite among Viennese dramatists. He was associated with Schlegel and Tieck in the famous 1826 edition of Shakespeare's plays, translating the *Two Gentlemen of Verona, The Comedy of*

Errors, *Troilus and Cressida*, *Henry VIII*, and *Antony and Cleopatra*, and others in collaboration with Mayrhofer. His temper was robust, he wrote, in a single year, nine plays and lived to the age of ninety. All this is in great contrast to Mayrhofer, who was a hypochondriac, a romantically unhappy product of the time. There were others. Spaun has been mentioned; Stadler, Holzapfel, Senn – old friends from the Konvikt days – even the renowned Grillparzer upon occasion, all used to join Bauernfeld, Schober, and Mayrhofer in reading their poems to the circle. There was a 'reading society', often mentioned with enthusiasm in Schubert's letters. Franz von Hartmann records over twenty meetings in the earlier part of 1828. Schober always read, apparently; the works of Tieck and Kleist predominate; once it is poems by Schober, also Heine's *Reise-ideen* (in which Hartmann finds 'much wit but a false tendency') and Goethe's *Pandora* and *Faust*, which Schober read 'gloriously'. Kupelwieser, who taught Schwind for a while, drew. Above all, Schubert played his pianoforte works or accompanied his songs. Wonderful evenings they must have been, in which Schubert scattered without stint the riches of his divinely musical mind. The Schubertiads, for such they were called, were commemorated often in verse and drawing; by Mayrhofer's *Geheimnis*, for instance, which Schubert himself set to music, though with a different feeling certainly from Handel's when he set Cardinal Pamphilij's *Hendel non può mia musa*, and by Schwind's drawing, in which Death and the Powers of Darkness kneel behind Schubert, admitting their impotence. Schubertiads and literary meetings were sometimes preceded, and almost invariably followed, by entertainments of a more comfortable and less inspiring kind. On only one occasion after the above-mentioned readings of Kleist, Tieck, and Goethe does the diarist not repair to some Gasthaus. He is home at 9.45. Often it is the early hours of the morning before the friends leave Bogner's Café, or the Schnecke or the Rebhuhn, and Schwind runs through the streets, imitating the flight of a bird, or there has been a heavy fall of snow, and a fight begins, Spaun and Franz Hartmann against Fritz Hartmann, Schober, and Schwind, Spaun defending himself magnificently with outspread umbrella, while Schubert takes no part.

Towards Recognition

Though the circle enfolded many of the most talented artists in Vienna, they were, nearly all, too young, too poor, and too much without influence to be able to crown with any material results their enthusiasm for Schubert and their conviction of his genius. It was Schober who, after some difficulty, managed to persuade Michael Vogl to meet the young composer and hear some of his songs. Vogl was one of the most famous singers of the time; Schubert, when Spaun used to take him to the opera already as a pupil at the Konvikt, had worshipped him from afar, above all in Gluck's *Iphigenia in Tauris*. The story of the meeting is familiar, of Vogl's telling Schubert there was stuff in him, but that he was too little of an actor and not enough of a charlatan. Schober says in his Memoirs: 'A partnership between the two artists, which grew more and more close, until death broke it, followed upon their first coming together. Vogl opened to his friend with well-meant advice the rich treasure of his experience, cared in a fatherly way for the satisfaction of his needs, for which his income from compositions was at that time insufficient, and prepared the way to fame through his magnificent interpretation of the songs.' Vogl took Schubert with him on visits to the Salzkammergut and Upper Austria. They were fêted everywhere. Schubert writes to his brother Ferdinand: 'The way Vogl sings and I accompany him, so that we seem to be fused for a moment into a single being, is something entirely new and unknown to these people.' In addition to Vogl's propaganda, help, and encouragement, one or two critics, Baron von Schlechta, for instance, were writing conscientious, appreciative, and intelligent articles on Schubert's music, and the young composer was being introduced to influential families, the Fröhlichs and the Sonnleithners and many others.

'The Friends of Music'

Leopold von Sonnleithner had played an active part when, in 1812, the 'Society of Friends of Music' was founded. There were then over four hundred members, who belonged nearly all to the upper bourgeoisie; thirty years previously such a society would have been unthinkable. The 'concerts of the nobility' had ceased in 1808. Schubert as a boy had taken part in chamber music at home with his father and brothers, somewhat in the manner of the Bach family. There were countless circles of this kind in Vienna. The Schuberts themselves were always moving from house to house in order to accommodate an ever-increasing number of players, and the need for a concentration of forces was strongly felt. Within the 'Friends of Music' a series of concerts called '*Private Abendunterhaltungen*' were presently begun; their object was to 'enliven members with music and decent conversation'. On 25 January 1821, Gymnich, a talented amateur, sang Schubert's *Erlkönig*, and thereafter Schubert's name appeared frequently on the programmes. One Herr von Jenger was commissioned by the society to write a biography of Schubert, though after the appointed three months the manuscript was still 'owing'. In 1826 Schubert was given 100 gulden; he had just dedicated his *Sixth Symphony*, in C, to the society, but it was not performed until a month after his death; the great *C major Symphony* had to wait until 1850 to be given in its entirety at a society concert, though in 1839 two movements were played, separated by a Donizetti aria. Schubert's music, apart from his songs, was hardly recognized. It must be remembered that there were only seven years between the publication – by private subscription – of Schubert's first works and his death; by which time about 180 songs had been printed, nearly all of them magnificent, though there appeared soon afterwards many that Schubert himself might have made no attempt to publish; in addition, many valses, marches, and four-handed works, but only three pianoforte sonatas and one string quartet (in A minor) and no symphonies or dramatic works whatever. Some of his greatest works were not published until after 1850. The existence of the 'Society of Friends of Music' was significant of deep changes in Vienna, and the situation was aggravated for Schubert by his dislike of high society, his inability to reconcile 'town-bred politeness and human sincerity'. His hardship was founded on this, that he was without patronage – the exception will appear shortly – and could not possibly live on the income brought in by his compositions. With the exception of two opus numbers, all Schubert's works up to the time of his death were published by Viennese firms; and these, headed by Diabelli, offered him terms – even when they themselves approached him – that were inhuman. Schubert had also no instinct for his own advantage. He sold Diabelli the rights of eighteen volumes of songs for 800 florins; he wrote to Goethe in 1825 and sent him songs which a non-musician was not likely to appreciate; he dedicated to Beethoven nothing more representative of his genius than the *E minor Variations*, op. 10 – though this may have been because it was the only serious instrumental work he could get published at that time (1822).

Schubert was always anxious to obtain a definite and continuous job, in order to insure himself against a desperate poverty. He went in 1818 to Zseliz in Hungary, as music teacher to Count Esterhâzy's children. There he lived with the servants, wrote some vigorous and interesting letters, received two gulden per lesson, and, if not then, on his second visit in 1824, became enamoured of the count's younger daughter, Caroline.

Illness and Death

That so little is definitely known about Schubert's romances has frequently inspired novelists and playwrights to adventurous and picturesque theories. Even the best of Schubertian plays, by Carl Costa, has for its central theme a clearly unhistorical feminine rivalry for the hand of the composer. The prevailing uncertainty on these matters is due probably less to any clever concealment on Schubert's part than to his lack of recognition during his lifetime.

His letters were not jealously saved; of his diary, only extracts from eleven days remain; the others were sold by an antiquarian, leaf by leaf, as curiosities. Beethoven's last doctor left a convincing account of the musician's final illness; but in Schubert's case there is scarcely any evidence of treatment.

That his youth was touched by tragedy we have said, tragedy that plunged him from time to time in immeasurable grief. In 1824 he writes to Kupelwieser: 'Picture to yourself someone whose health is permanently injured . . .; picture to yourself, I say, someone whose most brilliant hopes have come to nothing, someone to whom love and friendship are at most a source of bitterness, someone whose inspiration . . . for all that is beautiful threatens to fail, and then ask yourself if this is not a wretched and unhappy being.' His illness, the responsibility for which has often been ascribed to Schober, marks properly a division in his life. He was a patient at the Vienna General Hospital at the beginning of 1823, where, in intense physical pain, he composed *Die Schöne Müllerin*. It is not absolutely certain that Schubert had contracted venereal disease. Bauernfeld's remark that 'Schubert is half-ill; he needs young peacocks, like Benvenuto Cellini' need signify very little, as a reference to the passage in the Memoirs will show. The suggestive facts are not this, or Schubert's having for a time to wear a wig, but the length of the illness, in which loss of hair was only an incident, its intermittent nature, and possibly the failure of his friends to mention it by name. Early in 1824 Schubert is found fasting for a fortnight – though fasting, it seems, was a treatment prescribed for any chronic illness; a little later he begins a new course of diet and baths; in April, his left arm is hurting and he cannot play the piano at all. Then, for a year and a half, he is apparently well; but there comes another attack in the form of frequent and terrible headaches. He was exhausting himself, moreover, in a last dramatic outburst of composition. Spaun says that 'no one who ever saw him at his morning's work, glowing and his eyes aflame, even with a changed speech . . . will ever forget it. . . . I hold it beyond question that the excitement in which he composed his finest songs, the *Winterreise* in particular, brought about his untimely death.'

In October 1828, Schubert went to live with his brother Ferdinand in the rural suburb of Neue Wieden; on the last day of the month he was having supper at a tavern when suddenly he started up after a mouthful of fish and said he had been poisoned. On 12 November he wrote to Schober: 'I am ill. I have had nothing to eat or drink for eleven days, and can only stagger, exhausted, between chair and bed. . . . If I eat any food at all, I cannot keep it down. Come to my rescue in this desperate condition with something to read.' He has read four novels by Fenimore Cooper and asks for another, should Schober have one.

The length and progress of the illness correspond with that of a virulent attack of abdominal typhoid, which, owing to unhygienic conditions, was a very common disease at that time in Vienna. It had no connexion with the illness whose course we followed previously.* Schubert fell into a delirium. He thought he was being buried alive. Ferdinand tried to persuade him that he was in his own room and lying on his own bed. 'No, it is not true,' was the answer, 'Beethoven is not lying here.' In the afternoon of 19 November, Franz Schubert died.

'The last master of Song has passed away,' wrote Grillparzer in his funeral oration for Beethoven.

As Anschütz read the words on that famous occasion, Schubert stood at his elbow. After the ceremony, Schubert and some friends drank to him who should most quickly follow Beethoven. On the anniversary of this momentous day there was given a public concert of Schubert's works, from which he gained £32. It was the first and the last.

* See detailed article by Dr Schweisheimer in the *Zeitschrift für Musikwissenshaft* (Leipzig).

A bundle of his manuscripts, among which must have been some of the greatest music the world has known, was valued at 8s. 6d.

Evaluation

A man who may be dismissed with anecdotes, a composer without intellect or even consistency of ideal and experiment, whose creations were unconscious and hardly understood by himself; such has been the common conception of Schubert.

That it was so in the very beginning may be seen from a letter of Anton Ottenwald, written just after he had made Schubert's acquaintance at Linz in 1825, in which he tries to reconcile Schubert's discourse 'on art and poetry . . . and on the relation of the ideal to life' with all he had heard of his way of composing. Ottenwald expresses his increasing astonishment at each fresh proof of a profound mentality.

The musicians in Schubert's circle were tragically blind to his greatness. Max Friedländer relates how Franz Lachner, a well-known contemporary and friend of Schubert, said to him as an old man: 'It's a pity Schubert did not learn as much as I did; otherwise, with his extraordinary talent, he would *also* have become a master'; while Randhartinger, who was at school with Schubert, declared himself 'sorry that his friend remained until the last a bit of a dilettante'. These ideas have persisted. Busoni called Schubert a talented dilettante; others have contented themselves with a description of his music as 'adipose tissue'.

Yet this is the Schubert we have observed, at the age of fourteen, modelling himself energetically on Zumsteeg's ballads; perfecting his mastery in two hundred songs before *Erlkönig*, his opus 1; who copied out the full score of the minuet in the *Jupiter Symphony* and acquired practical experience and the widest knowledge of Viennese classical music as a choirboy and violinist for five years at the Imperial Konvikt. It is the Schubert who composed two symphonies, one of such infinite poetry, poignancy, and colour, and so perfectly expressed, that it has won deeper affection than any other work of its kind; the other so tremendous in idea, of such power and exhilaration, that only the greatest Beethoven may be played directly after and not lose significance for the excited imagination. It is the Schubert of the *String Quartets* in A minor, D minor, and G, and of the unapproachable *Quintet in C*; of the seventeen pianoforte sonatas and of nearly four hundred pages of pianoforte duets, among them such wonderful works as the *Fantasie in F minor*, the *Grand Duo in C*, and *Lebensstürme*. In all these branches of composition Schubert created works that have not since been surpassed. In another, that of song, he is unequalled among all the composers.

'To make an epoch in the world,' says Goethe, 'two conditions are notoriously necessary – a good head and a great inheritance.' Schubert had a magnificent inheritance, the dawn of German lyrical poetry and its timely perfection in Goethe, which circumstance (granted his peculiar gifts) determined the flavour and magnitude of his achievement as certainly as did the French Revolution that of Napoleon and the darkness of the Popes that of Luther. Schubert had a finer appreciation of poetry than his predecessors. His general culture was not in such stark contrast to his musicianship as has often been supposed.

He responded unfailingly to great poetry, but was also quick to seize upon some picturesque detail or situation in a poem of secondary significance, should it provide a fine musical possibility. Already at the age of seventeen Schubert's vision had a marvellous quality, which enabled him to reach the universal through the particular. A conception of 'the endless and incommensurable' was not necessary to him. His invention in the songs is absolutely inexhaustible. Not only has he a unique power of evoking in the very first bars of a song the poetic atmosphere of his subject, there is also unending resource in the balance and colour of modulations, in enlarging or condensing phrases and compensating this through variations in melody or rhythm, until everything is of the greatest liveliness and plasticity.

When we turn to the man, it is to be astounded at the physical feat represented by the enormous amount of music he composed in seventeen years. His letters from Zseliz and on his journeys with Vogl reveal not only poetical appreciation of the scenery but a lively gift of characterization, a robust way of thinking, and observation of minute details. Schubert the child of Vienna, the disappointed lover, and down-trodden musician is too comfortable a conception. His modesty and simplicity have led to under-estimation of his character.

We have seen his attitude to Rossini; how different was that of Berlioz, who on meeting a Rossini enthusiast 'eyed him with a Shylockian scowl' and growled between his teeth, 'Miscreant! would that I might impale thee on a red-hot iron.'

Schubert's was a simple, outwardly uneventful life, without hatreds or intrigues, without dramatic triumphs or defeats, without fame or fortune or momentous journeys. Inwardly, the scene is of untold warmth and richness. Life and music share most, perhaps, that dual quality whose effect Dvořák, with just emphasis, likened to that of 'gathering clouds, with constant glimpses of sunshine breaking through them.'

ROBERT ALEXANDER SCHUMANN

1810–56

A. E. F. DICKINSON

The Romantic Temper

Many creative artists are uncommunicative outside their art. Of Handel and Bach, who tell us so much about themselves in their music, there is not much else to learn except the particulars of their changing environment. Perhaps it was inevitable that the *élan vital* should be lacking from other channels of self-expression, such as letter-writing or what we may call musical agitation. The romantic movement changed this relation of art and life. The workaday craftsman yielded to the self-exploring and self-conscious artist. Beethoven's drawing-room successes did not blind him to the essential unresponsiveness of his patrons, on which subject he wrote and acted characteristically. But for him this constant embitterment at an unheeding world was too accidental to detract from his artistic integrity.

Sensitive from the first, Robert Schumann soon proved an out-and-out romanticist, increasingly conscious of a musical mission to a philistine world and interested alike in every rapture of self-development and every pain of social frustration. As a composer he began by writing lyrical ballads, followed by symphonies and music-dramas more lyrical than architectonic. Literary leanings, a lack of Beethoven's more concentrated creative urge, and a certain didactic strain bent his activity also to a long bout of musical journalism. This continuous thought about music and musical opinion naturally overflowed into many characteristic letters. Schumann's music thus provides the supreme and abiding landmark in a sentimental journey of musical endeavour, of which he himself has significantly supplied the supporting details.

Schumann had, however, an essentially retiring disposition. He was shy both about his music and in it, and in society his long silences, not only (like Beethoven) before strangers but before friends, were a continuous hindrance to his effective influence. We receive a constant impression of an escape from the world into the inarticulate unresolved moodiness of an eccentric personality. It is thus often necessary to guess at the real psychological factors behind the conventional gestures of expression, alike in the 'life' and in the music.

The Three Periods

Schumann's life may be divided into three main periods. His first twenty years were spent chiefly at his home at Zwickau and ended with two years at the university. Then came the important fourteen years at Leipzig. Schumann was now the avowed musician, and his common round of interest centred about his own creative activity, the *New Music Journal* and Clara Wieck, whom he married in 1840. Finally there were six years at Dresden, four years as conductor at Düsseldorf, and two in an asylum at Endenich.

Schumann's musical progress begins with the production of most of his piano music (1830–40) and of most of his songs (1840). The next four years show a stage of orderly instrumental expansion. The remaining period presents music of every kind. The years 1830, 1840, and 1844 thus appear as the turning points of both his life and his art. In 1830 he began at last his desired career. In 1840 he attained to married happiness and a new release of creative spirit. By 1844 he had reached a developed maturity, from which he might conceivably have climbed to supreme heights, had not antagonistic surroundings and increasing mental derangement combined to distract him from his proper musical growth and ultimately to arrest it altogether.

Early Life

It is tempting to guess at Robert's chances of heredity. His father August, a clergyman's son, was sent away to school, but was soon destined for the grocery business. The early influence of an uncle led him towards poetry and philosophy, and after settling down as a married grocer he fled into the book business, in which he had already snatched considerable experience. By the end of his sadly overworked and dyspeptic life he had written much and published a pocket World's Classics series and his own translations of Scott and Byron. He combined a capacity for hard work with considerable speculative enterprise and cultured tastes with a notable desire to spread the literary gospel. Robert was less fortunate in his mother, a sentimental woman with passionate outbursts of visionary fervour, which impressed

Robert unduly. She opposed his hankering for such a precarious career as music, but she made up for it by gratifying almost every other wish. His letters to her indicate her gloomy, introspective outlook. Robert was the fifth child. None of the children reached fifty, and Emilie, the fourth, died in her twentieth year, a nervous wreck. It was not a very healthy family.

Robert was sent to school at six and at ten passed on to the Lyceum of about 200 boys, where he spent eight years. He did reasonably well in class, aided no doubt by fatherly encouragement, and being at a day-school he was spared the early nervous strain that would have overtaken him. He showed gift as a pianist at school 'evenings'. He founded a school literary society and conceived a liking for Homer, Sophocles, Tacitus, and the then popular Jean Paul, whose highly strung emotionalism became a permanent influence. Meanwhile a limited but energetic town musician named Kuntzsch taught him music. His early performances included piano-duet arrangements of Haydn, Mozart, and Beethoven symphonies (happy beginnings), ingenious extemporisations in illustration of local personalities and the direction of a small band of eight. Schumann also heard much classical chamber music (then a rare experience) at the house of a keen amateur, Carus, whose nephew's wife, Agnes, became one of the composer's many musical intimates. Choral concerts at Zwickau appear to have been rare, but there was plenty of well organized orchestral and band music, and the operas included *Don Giovanni* and *Der Freischütz*.

Schumann was fortunate enough to be taken at the age of nine to hear the great pianist Moscheles at Carlsbad. Clearly young Robert's music occupied the serious attention of his father, in spite of the mother's opposition. August must have remembered acutely his own early cultural ambitions. But he died in 1826, leaving the mother free to thwart at her will; two years later Robert was sent to Leipzig university to study law. He was now beginning to show the ready self-indulgences of a spoilt youth, including a rather lordly taste for pretty girls, champagne and a generally higher standard of comfort than his allowance permitted. He expected his mother to pay up.

At the University

On leaving school, Schumann meditated in this strain:

Now the inner man must come forth and show what he is: thrust out into existence, flung into the world's night, without guide, teacher and father – here I stand, and yet the whole world never appeared to me in a lovelier light than now as I confront it and, rejoicing and free, smile at its storms. (Translation by Niecks.)

Like many other testimonials this is distinguished partly by what it does *not* contain – for example, a resolution to settle down and study law. The next two years proved how ineffective Schumann could be without his father at hand as guide, friend, and in the best sense father. He started by going off with a newly found kindred spirit and Jean Paul lover, Gisbert Rosen, a law student who was quitting Leipzig for Heidelberg. He enjoyed in this way a congenial tour of Bayreuth, Nuremberg, Augsburg and Munich. At Augsburg he stayed with a Dr von Kurrer, through whom he met Heine at Munich. Schumann also developed a passion for Clara von Kurrer which was sufficiently romantic not to cause any friction with her fiancé or any lasting regrets afterwards. His affection for Rosen was deeper and may have strengthened a previous hankering for Heidelberg.

Meanwhile there was jurisprudence at Leipzig. In compensation, Schumann practised chamber-music with Agnes Carus and at the Wiecks'. Wieck was his piano teacher, a man of fierce and advanced ideals, as Schumann's biographer Niecks shows. Wieck held decided views about piano teaching and his own capacity to teach, but he was systematic rather than pedantic, and his empirical principles sprang from musical impulses and considerable teaching experience and were suitably modified for individual pupils. He welcomed virtuosity when it appeared – Clara, aged nine, was already showing it – but he also believed that the piano must sing. Schumann was a disputatious and forgetful pupil, but he must have absorbed much sound principle and practical knowledge. In addition Wiedebein, a minor composer, gave him some useful advice on song-writing. The Gewandhaus orchestral concerts impressed Schumann and account, perhaps, for the contrasts that permeate his piano music. These musical recreations were his chief outlet, not undergraduate life, which disappointed him by its rude heartiness. As it was, he was already complaining of constantly needing to be cheered up. Not for him the glow of knowledge mastered.

In 1829 Schumann migrated to Heidelberg. He now enjoyed a richer social career, with Rosen and others as the permanent figures in a continually changing circle; and in Professor Thibaut he found both a vivacious lecturer and a sympathetic musician of the cheerfully

limited type. He also heard Paganini twice at Frankfurt, an event that i
recorded in some piano arrangements. Another thrill was Pasta's singing at the Scala, Milan, visited during a tour of Switzerland an
Northern Italy. But Schumann's reports of the slovenliness both o
Italian performances and of Heidelberg pianists suggest a critica
standard; and his much applauded virtuosity at a Heidelberg concer
must have been a challenging record of his increasing musica
accomplishment.

After another year of intellectual dallying his musical impulses too
the offensive. Legal ambitions were easily crushed. After some twent
years' struggle 'between poetry and prose' (as he put it), what romanticist could doubt which was the aggressor? So he wrote to his mother
emphasizing the call of genius, his determination to work hard, an
the awfulness of the alternative; finally he invoked Wieck for confirmation. Wieck's sublime confidence in his own teaching powers lef
him in no doubt about Schumann's potential virtuosity under hi
guidance, but he naturally questioned Schumann's will to make goo
and proposed a six months' trial. Schumann was ready to accept anything, so long as it was to be music there and then. But this struggl
left him limp. After a month's dawdling at Heidelberg, he went on
pleasure trip *en route* for Leipzig. His first letter home frankly confesses his intellectual apathy. How very reassuring for Frau Schumann
Yet there is no greater testimony to Schumann's natural musica
genius than this gauging within himself of depths as yet unplumbed
As a composer he had written some of *Papillons* and the *Abeg
Variations*, all pieces of brilliant individuality (as Grillparzer noted in
Vienna paper), but scarcely a foretaste of later developments. Thu
signally does a categorical 'Know thyself!' attend every nascen
individuality.

Music at Last – Exit the Virtuoso

Schumann at first lodged with Wieck, who had now married again
and here, surely, there was every inducement to settle down. But h
wanted to be everything at once – pianist, conductor, and composer fo
a start. The reckless and secret adoption of a finger-adjuster of his ow
devising (after chafing at the slow progress of the first two years) rule
out once and for all the possibilities of piano virtuosity. Despite over
year of varied treatment of a dislocated third finger, Schumann had i
1833 to face the fact that he could never be a concert-pianist, neve

even the best player of his own piano works. Apart from the dissipation of talent that was certain to prevail in such a wayward nature, the career of a concert-pianist needed sterner stuff than Schumann was made of. We may cheerfully consider the disappointments he was saved as well as the creative happiness to which he instinctively and successfully turned. His pain at not being able to interpret his music himself was greatly to be alleviated by having a fine substitute in his own wife. There remains the possible disadvantage to his piano style that a lack of continued virtuoso-experience entailed. But only, after 1840 do the piano works show a less masterful, more prosaic manner.

The Leipzig Years

For composition Schumann had placed himself under Dorn, who was thorough. This did not last long, but Schumann learnt the uses of fugue and the general value of reflection and method. He also studied lovingly Bach's *Preludes and Fugues* (Book I). It is interesting to read the romanticist's just tribute. 'Bach was a man; with him nothing is half done.' Yet he admired Jean Paul as fervently! The products of Schumann's own work-shop were now beginning to accumulate. The piano music will be considered later. A *Symphony in G minor* received public performance but was never finished.

During this fairly full creative period (1830–40) various events of personal importance occurred and also the growth of a fresh undertaking, the editing of a new music periodical. In 1833 Schumann was ill, and the deaths at the end of the year of his favourite brother Julius and sister-in-law Rosalie aggravated his melancholic condition. He begged his mother not to refer to these bereavements! One wonders why Agnes Carus or some other suitable person could not induce Robert to pull himself together. But probably he was in too neurotic a condition to be cured except, perhaps, by an expert mental healer. (He had got thoroughly 'worked up' over the cholera panic in 1832, and the family anxiety about his excessive beer and cigars suggests that in his moods of depression he could not resist these indulgences.) It is not surprising that in this unstable state he turned for consolation to a buxom, well-connected young girl called Ernestine von Fricken, a resident pupil of Wieck. A year before, he had likened Clara to a distant altar-piece, but she was only fourteen and was away in Dresden. The separation, however, proved almost as intolerable to him as to her. The discovery of Ernestine's illegitimacy decided him to break off the unhappy engagement. Clara's star was now in the ascendant. Ernestine's identity has been preserved in *Carnaval* in the motto-theme of A-s-c-h, her native town, and in *Estrella*, a piquant portrait; and her father gave Schumann the theme for the *Études Symphoniques*. On the whole Niecks shows good ground for summarizing this as an episode of errors, in which serious neurosis played a significant part. It is a little odd, then, that during these morbid years the new paper came to birth and a flourishing youth under Schumann's editorship. It may be said in his defence that he was not the first person or the last to be such an ardent social reformer that he had no time to shoulder family burdens; also, that the effort of founding and maintaining a new paper, however thrilling, left him in a dependent, impressionable state of mind in which to encounter Ernestine's physical vitality and promise of riches.

The New Music Journal

The idea of a serious music journal, for the purpose of combating the general mediocrity of the German musical atmosphere, arose in 1833. After continual meetings of the group thus called into existence, plans were complete. Schumann had of course had publishing experience in his youth. At first there was a board of director-editors. Wieck appears to have been the presiding and protecting spirit, Schumann the anonymous editor-in-chief, and the other principals were Knorr, a teacher, and Schunke, a gifted pianist whose initiation is romantically described in the *Journal*. In the background was, among others, Henriette Voigt, a charming personality to whose sensitive perceptions and musical household the *Journal* also pays happy tribute. In 1835, after nine months of twice-weekly publication, Schumann's editorship was openly declared. He carried on till 1844, defying all expectation. Ten years later he published a large selection of his own contributions, which includes the famous 'Hats off, gentlemen – a genius!' article (*Allgemeine Zeitung*, 1831) on Chopin's early *Variations*. In 1838 he went to Vienna with every intention of establishing the *Journal* there, but he found the atmosphere too reactionary. The *Carnival Jest* records this visit. Quarterly musical supplements began in 1838.

These ten years of disinterested musical propaganda – Schumann very rarely mentions his own works – are a remarkable chapter in musical history. Previously music criticism had either been fiercely analytical or fatuously eulogistic. The new *Journal*, while containing few of the theoretical essays promised in the prospectus, discussed new or forgotten musical developments with a composer's acuteness of ear, unwarped by a composer's prejudices, and with a dramatic vividness and a poetic touch that recall the dialogues of Plato. Never before or since has there been such a persistent attempt to greet personally the new generation and yet sift the good from the pleasing, finished work from laboured, art from virtuosity, genius from talent. The genius of German music has always been built up on a wide foundation of earnest experiment, and 1834–44 was, like our own time, a period of not easily scanned transition. Thus, at a time when originality was almost a crime, Schumann gave the steady support of his critical interest to newcomers; he secured many 'local correspondents'. Always wholehearted in his favours, his perpetual panegyrics on Mendelssohn seem forced, but against these and other likeable adorations must be set the clairvoyant discoveries (from very early works) of Chopin and Brahms and the just recognition of the sheer magic of Berlioz and Wagner and the charming clarity of Bennett. As convincing fundamental hypotheses stand Schumann's rhapsodic but profound appreciations of the inexhaustible poet, Bach, of the Promethean Beethoven, and of the 'everlasting youth' of Schubert, of whose *C major Symphony* he proved the discoverer in every sense of the word. And his principal hate, Meyerbeer, was a perfectly reasonable one. Nor was our critic unmindful of performers: he gave virtuosity its due meed, and he recognized the importance of a 'preparatory school of public performance and concert routine', such as the Euterpe Society at Leipzig provided. He also pleaded for a complete publication of Bach's works.

Apart from this steady construction of tested and working critical assumptions for the benefit of an ignorant and wayward public, the *Journal* introduces us to Schumann's 'romantic' bias for a concretely emotional interpretation and his derived interest in harmonic shades of meaning. But while he encourages general culture, he despises cheap literary comparisons and insists on the widest possible aural training, such as can distinguish the trite melody of fashion from the deeper melodiousness of folk-song and the established masters. Many an odd sentence could profitably be learned and marked by performers, critics, and audiences of to-day. And no editor was politer to his contributors.

This conscious movement to ring out the false was dramatized by

Schumann to himself as a league of spiritual personalities against the philistine confederacy of mediocrity and circus virtuosity. Somewhat in the same spirit, and after the manner of the Walt and Vult of Jean Paul's 'Flegeljahre', the editor often openly regards *himself* as a league of two complementary personalities, Florestan the ecstatic and Eusebius the sensitive, who also appear in odd superscriptions over some of the piano music. This division of the mind's response to art and life is useful when opinion has not grown to integral judgement (a distinction that the common dogmatism of to-day frequently obscures). It is also to be kept in mind in dealing with the elusive integrity of many pieces of Schumann's music. The first *Piano Sonata* is frankly 'by Florestan and Eusebius', a quaint but accurate statement.

Mendelssohn and His Circle

This regular work kept Schumann going in many ways, being a realistic antidote to introspection as well as a basis of middle-class existence, and in 1835 a new stimulus arose in the arrival of Mendelssohn, fresh from triumphs at Düsseldorf, to conduct the Gewandhaus concerts. The relations of Schumann to Mendelssohn are somewhat obscure: after being friendly they became strained, anyhow on Mendelssohn's side. It is easy to see the attractions for Schumann of Mendelssohn's musical masterfulness as composer or conductor – a conductor who did something more than lead was a rare phenomenon at the time – and of his quick perceptions, wide culture, and surface cordiality. It is less easy to understand how Schumann's adoration ignored Mendelssohn's smugness and 'push'. On the other side, while Mendelssohn's views on Schumann's amateurishness and journalistic tendencies are known to have been decidedly tart (in spite of all the admiration in and out of the *Journal*), a letter from Mendelssohn to Klingemann in 1847, which refers to malicious gossip attributed to Schumann, remains unexplained; and the omission of all reference to Schumann in the published Mendelssohn letters does nothing to remove the impression of a singular lack of generous impulses. There is no evidence of jealousy or party feeling on either side.

Another arrival, though a fleeting one, was Chopin. Wieck was elated, for here was Clara's opportunity. She played, besides two Chopin études, Schumann's first sonata. A month later she played the sonata to Moscheles. In the following year Ferdinand David arrived as leader of the orchestra and resident soloist. Schumann saw much of this fine musician later at the Leipzig conservatorium: they must have had much in common. Another newcomer in 1836 was Bennett, with whom Schumann enjoyed the most cordial relations, while retaining critical reservations about the size of his creative genius. Bennett on his side was not more than politely impressed with Schumann's own music (up to that date), but he did much for it in England later, in happy recompense for the early interest taken in his own music by the *New Music Journal*. Frontiers were of no consequence here.

Clara Wieck

Early in 1836 Schumann's mother died. He did not attend the funeral. The deepening intimacy between Clara and himself was now patent to all, and there began the four years' painful struggle with her father, which in certain aspects of paternal obstinacy and egotism resembles the romance of Elizabeth Barrett and Robert Browning. On realizing the changed situation, Wieck packed Clara off to Dresden. It is easy to understand his thoughts. Clara was now approaching the crisis of her career. What could upset things more than to allow her to tie herself up with this impecunious and intemperate young student? That Clara could at the moment entertain other ideas of happiness than successful virtuosity scarcely occurred to him, for this crowning vicarious triumph had been his goal for years. When the now devoted couple continued to defy him, he brought Clara back to Leipzig, forbade her to see Robert, threatened him, and constructed round him a network of disapproval, slander and malice. A 'friend', Carl Banck, furthered the cause of mutual mistrust.

A year later Clara played in public the first sonata, which Robert had dedicated and sent to her a year before. Music was the only sign of love she could show him. He was at the concert, of course, and through a friend who was present they got into touch and on the next day became engaged. He wrote to Wieck to ask for his consent. Wieck became as offensive as ever and later was slandering Clara as well as Robert. (He grew more beside himself as time went on.) Meanwhile they had decided to get his consent by law. The question of Robert's temperance became the main issue in the proceedings, but at last Wieck had to abandon his case. In September, 1840, the pair were united. (I have outlined the story as pieced together by Litzmann in his *Clara Schumann*.) Just before this, Schumann received news of the honorary doctorate conferred on him by the University of Jena, for which he had 'worked hard'. In this year, too, Liszt flashed into his acquaintance. 'Liszt's world is not mine', he wrote.

Piano Music

We may now turn to the large body of piano music that Schumann had produced in the last ten years. Some of it is widely familiar to modern concert-audiences and needs no comment, but, as Schumann himself observed even of his most popular and animated piece, *Carnaval*,* his many subtleties of mood do not lend themselves to public presentation; and he was particularly fond of writing suites of delicately contrasted pieces. He is therefore chiefly for the private performer and listener and, like Bach, demands the intimacy of 'music on the hearth'. There is much worth exploring, and so would be the sketch-books now at remote Zwickau, if they were published. The *Fantasia* (1836) and *Humoreske* (1839) are the biggest creations, without possessing the calibre or cumulative power of a Beethoven sonata, and the earlier *Sonata No. 1* and *Études Symphoniques* are not far behind. The miniatures should not be neglected: *Papillons*, the *Intermezzi*, the *Davidsbündlertänze* and the later *Bunte Blätter* and *Albumblätter*.

A deeper note, reflecting the passionate struggle of 1836–40, underlies the *Fantasiestücke*, *Kinderscenen*, *Kreisleriana* (a romantic greeting both to Clara and to Hoffmann), *Novelletten*, and *Nachtstücke*. Many of the individual numbers of these sets are highly developed entities. From the simplest (such as the beautiful epilogue to the *Kinderscenen*) to the most elaborate or fanciful, they present something so genuine and sensitive that their friendly reception into musical circles is assured. Well might Schumann feel more than a journalist.

Songs

Up to now Schumann had, in spite of Schubert's signal example, a prejudice against song-writing. In 1840 songs began to come and it ended in being a song year. The dictum 'What Schubert was to Goethe, Schumann was to Heine' must be challenged. Schumann's songs do not attract, like Schubert's, by their abundant musical flow from their poetic source, but rather by their fitness to given poetry, as in the exquisite restraint of *Ich hab' im Traum geweinet*. Their appeal

* On this see Browning, *Fifine at the Fair*, xc–xcii.

thus centres round a particular taste for the German romantics. Within these limits the songs include many fine and distinctive examples. Two sets, the *Dichterliebe* and *Frauenliebe und Leben*, contain complementary expressions of Schumann's glowing romantic sympathies, but one must not forget the more isolated ecstasies of *Frühlingsnacht* and *Mondnacht*, and the dramatic power of ballads like *Belzatsar*, *Der Schatzgräber*, and the popular *The Two Grenadiers*. It will be noted that, like the orchestra in Wagner, the piano offers usually the chief comment and always 'the last, the parting word'.

Robert and Clara

Meanwhile the man and the woman, the creative composer-journalist and the modest executant, were settling down. Fortunately Clara was of the admiring kind and was prepared to stop practising if it interfered with Robert's composing, although she realized that they could ill afford to wait on opportunity. (Daughters were born in 1841 and 1843.) Something of the ins and outs of this problem and of other close relations is recorded in the diary, which they kept for three years, each writing nominally in alternate weeks. We can there observe their pilgrimages through the '48' and Beethoven symphonies, played from score, as well as the shared raptures over new works and worries over the demands of the 'beastly' paper, regular and not too lucrative. Clara had long kept a diary. But she needed her own art too.

In 1843 the Leipzig conservatorium was founded by Mendelssohn after much negotiation, and Schumann obtained a post on the staff for piano and composition. This engagement was interrupted by a Russian concert tour with Clara in 1844, followed by a break-down in health and departure to Dresden, but the loss of so absent-minded and ineffective a teacher as Schumann cannot have been widely felt.

First Orchestral Works and Chamber-music

During these last four years Schumann was expanding rapidly as a composer. He advanced into orchestral, chamber, and dramatic-choral music, and his powers noticeably matured in the process. In 1841 came two symphonies, separated by a symphony without slow movement, whose complex title *Overture, Scherzo, and Finale* has perhaps concealed its subtle coherence. The latter was followed by a fantasia which we now know as the opening of the *Piano Concerto*. Another symphony was sketched but went no further. The first *Symphony in*

B flat, originally conceived as a 'Spring' symphony (with titles to each movement), echoes Beethoven's lyrical B flat masterpiece. The work is loosely constructed. Schumann's themes often begin well but do not lead to anything in particular, so that they make a fussy show of individuality or are too quickly forgotten in a new subject. But with a sympathetic conductor, capable of integrating the straggling episodes and uncouth orchestration as well as of realizing the ecstatic intention of the general conception, the symphony can make a striking public appearance, second only to Beethoven and Schubert in its period. Its cheerful tunefulness and generally original impulse triumphed over its awkwardness at the first performance and secured its composer a wide interest that he had not enjoyed before. The ensuing *Symphony in D minor* (now No. 4, owing to a late revision) is more deeply conceived. It has striking moments, such as the spacious opening, the forecast of the finale theme in the first movement, the main theme and violin arabesques of the romance, and the transition from the scherzo to the finale. The use, too, of themes and other gestures for connecting the movements was a notable change from the set style of the classical period. It prepared the way for Franck. The lack of a spontaneous expansion, inherent in the themes, remains. In the one-movement fantasia the piano is always at hand as announcer and illuminating commentator, so that despite orchestral jejuneness ('Chamber-music!' is one verdict) the development is well and truly planned. This movement is thus at once the pianist's joy, the public's favourite Schumannianum and the critical Schumannite's consolation.

In 1842 Schumann's initiative produced three *String Quartets*, a *Piano Quintet*, a *Piano Quartet*, and three pieces for piano trio. The quartets, like the symphonies, show a lack of string experience or perhaps of sheer aural observation, such as he displayed so much as a teacher; there is too much cross-string writing, in unhappy imitation of pianistic arpeggios. These works carry Schumann's distinction without adding much to it and cannot be ranked with the Brahms and Franck quartets as in the authentic line of succession. They often meander and are weak structurally. The quintet, on the other hand, is a masterpiece of music and of piano-string writing.

Oratorio

Next year, after an attack of nervous exhaustion that had obliged him to stop work, Schumann wrote the *Variations* for two pianos, two cello, and horn, later to become the smoother set for pianos only, and the cantata *Paradise and the Peri*, which is an oratorio in general structure, but not in vocal texture. In spite of the composer's timidity at rehearsal – a quality that was to prove so fatal later – the work was well received and repeated with increased enthusiasm in a week. The plastic, sensuous metre and marked terseness of 'Lalla Rookh', from which the libretto was translated and adapted, makes good material for an elaborate setting, and the fanciful idealism appealed to Schumann. The oratorio, like all oratorios, is too long, and its shallow sentimentality (especially the glorification of a 'righteous war') and frequent invitations to exuberant bathos are all too readily accepted by the composer; and his vein of pious choral reflection suffers from Mendelssohn's facile graciousness of manner. These disbeliefs suspended, there are many striking touches, and the lyrical tone of the whole is remarkably well sustained.

Departure to Dresden – Further Expansion

In 1844, after the Russian concert tour, Schumann decided to place the *New Music Journal* in other hands. In August his health broke down and he went eventually to Dresden, where after a neurotic crisis he improved and later decided to settle. Here an exclusive, opinionated society had little time for newcomers, but in Dresden he enjoyed the sparser musical routine. Meanwhile a fresh phase of romantic idealism had gripped him in *Faust*. This effort, and certain tricks that his ear or brain now began to play him, left him in a helpless, morbid state for most of 1845. The main distractions were the artistic figures whom Ferdinand Hiller gathered round him, including the painter Bendemann, best of friends, and that clever, 'mad', loquacious Richard Wagner, who had sent his score of *Tannhäuser*. It is not difficult to see why the reserved and disinterested Schumann did not incline to the flamboyant and egotistical Wagner or to the unabashed earthiness of his musical appeal, far-reaching as it might be. A further stimulus to energetic life was a new interest in counterpoint, which issued in the playful academicism of the canonical studies and more pleasing sketches for pedal piano and in the sextet of *Organ Fugues* on the theme B-A-C-H, the romanticist's *Art of Fugue*. Finally, the orchestral fantasia expanded into the *Piano Concerto*, the breezy finale of which is Schumann's *L'allegro*. In the following year appeared another vigorous work, the *C major Symphony* (No. 2), the moodiness of which reflected, as he explained later, his struggle with carnal apathy. The work is different from its predecessors without being an advance on them.

The year 1847, which began with the hazards of concert touring in Vienna and elsewhere, was a time of unusually varied creative activity and included two good *Piano Trios*, many choral pieces, and a start at an opera, *Genoveva*, which was completed in 1848. A Schumann opera on a sensational story was something of a misfit, and the composer's efforts to tone down the libretto did not help. Schumann had little of the dramatic virtuosity that animates a successful opera or of that command of generating motif which illuminates the lightest Mozart and the heaviest Wagner: his was a lyrical frame of musical ideas. Golo, that Iago-like figure, is more like Werther at times! Yet *Genoveva* contains some splendid music, and as one of the early experiments in romantic German opera, as opposed to the 'canary music' of Italy, presents many subtleties of characterization.

Another undramatic work of 1848 was the music for Byron's *Manfred*, which is best judged as a musical illustration for the original, rather than as incidental stage music. We can then appreciate without any feelings of inappropriateness the first three and last numbers of Part II and above all the fine overture, whose thick scoring is no hindrance to its revelation of the sombre Manfred – Schumann.

Earlier in this 'the most fruitful year of my life' Schumann took on Hiller's male choir (for a year) and founded a choral union of his own, with Clara as accompanist. The latter society, though dogged by Schumann's inarticulateness and lack of command, was a thoroughly progressive, sociable, and spirited affair, as Niecks was able to learn from a member. Bach, Handel, Palestrina, Mendelssohn, and Schumann were the chief composers. This regular choral experience and his previous dramatic experiments enabled Schumann to complete *Scenes from Faust*. Part III was performed on the same day at Weimar, Leipzig, and Dresden, at the celebration of the Goethe centenary in 1849; the whole work was first given in 1862. Beginning with the final Transfiguration scene (1844) Schumann warmed to Goethe's greater inspiration, but in different stages and degrees. The ominous Part II is the most interesting of the later additions, the overture being tired work. Part II is Schumann's greatest choral effort. Its subject and mystical treatment suggest a comparison with Brahms's *Requiem* and Elgar's *Dream of Gerontius*. After these masterpieces of sheer music and intensely personal emotion, the gospel of the Ever-womanly sounds self-conscious, diffuse, and chorally academic or awkward. In its own wayward and fanciful style the work is highly original and sometimes great.

Schumann was no political agitator, and the Dresden revolution of 1849 drove him to find a securer bower of the muses in a little village near Dresden. Here he continued his silent existence in a lively household. There were now five children, 'the wife, as of old, always striving onwards.' Clara must certainly have had her share of striving. Fortunately she was encouraged by the fresh creativeness that the Dresden move seemed to have facilitated. For the family Robert had written the *Album for the Young*, which is still proving one of the best of its kind. He wrote during this period (1848–50) the charming duets *Bilder aus Osten*; notable choral works, *Requiem for Mignon, Nachtlied*, and the breezy *New Year's Song*; attractive sets for vocal ensembles; the lyrical *Cello Concerto* and a most eloquent movement for piano and orchestra (op. 92); and solos for oboe, clarinet, and cello, all pleasantly typical.

The Appointment at Düsseldorf

During this time Schumann was agitating for a conductorship, and in 1850 he obtained one at Düsseldorf through the recommendation of Hiller, the out-going conductor. After another concert-tour and the production of *Genoveva* at Leipzig, the Schumanns moved. The new opportunities were considerable and make one marvel at the German municipal tradition in music. There was a regular and trained choir and orchestra, well capable of performing new works, whether Schumann's own or the talent of the young that he had always sponsored and to which he now devoted an entire concert, an honour without precedent. Behind this organization was the enthusiasm that Mendelssohn, Rietz, and Hiller had built up in turn by their energy and perseverance; it greeted the Schumanns with varied serenades on their arrival. The leader of the orchestra and a frequent visitor to the house was Wasielewski, afterwards to become Schumann's biographer. There was also a capable musician named Tausch, who acted as deputy-conductor from time to time.

The first season appeared to the Schumanns to have been a success, but there is much indirect evidence to the contrary. Schumann was far too absent-minded a conductor to gain the confidence of an orchestra, much less of a choir, and at rehearsals he was incredibly uncommunicative, uncommanding, and unobservant. The musical or social irregularities that simply escaped his notice (not just his control) are the subject of many amusing tales; also, he could not bear to be contradicted. He was, of course, unaware of his shortcomings and took cold offence at the want of respect that became open in the choir in the second season; he regarded it as mere philistinism. In 1852 he was again seriously ill. Tausch deputized capably, and the desire for his permanent substitution became vocal; in 1853 he was put in charge of the choral practices. The discontent at Schumann's conducting continued, and the holding of the Lower Rhine festival at Düsseldorf did not help his supporters. A new eccentricity was that he imagined all tempi to be too fast. After much anxious discussion in the autumn, the committee tactfully suggested that for the sake of his health Schumann should give up for a time the conducting of all but his own works, Tausch being willing to act as general substitute. Schumann's characteristic reply was to absent himself from the next rehearsal, and from that moment he ceased practically to be conductor. In his thorough account, Niecks has shown that the committee acted most carefully and sympathetically in the whole matter, and that Tausch was very unfairly regarded by the Schumanns as an intriguer.

Brahms and the End

At the height of this unpleasantness, Schumann was visited by a young composer with an introduction from Joachim, Johannes Brahms. Schumann at once saw, even in the immature work he had brought, the genius for which he had been looking, to crown the romantic aspirations of the period with classical dignity and orderliness. He wrote and told Joachim that this was 'he that should come' and in the *New Music Journal* uttered his belief in the 'deep song-melody' of the new composer. Later in 1853 the Schumanns had a successful tour in Holland, and on his return Robert collected his critical writings for publication. Then came disintegration, attempted suicide by drowning and two years in a private asylum, where the patient was visited by Brahms, Joachim, and von Wasielewski among others. The known details of this collapse may be interesting to the student of morbid psychology, but are scarcely in place here. The main fact appears to have been that an increasing failure to adapt himself to his environment, and the resulting submission to all the melancholy of imagined frustration, combined with physical causes to unseat what will-power he had left.

At Düsseldorf, Schumann wrote the *Rhenish Symphony* (No. 3 in E flat), and the *Violin Concerto*, mistakenly revived in 1938; *The Pilgrimage of the Rose* and other choral ballads; an indifferent *Mass* and *Requiem*, a Teutonic oratorio on Luther having failed to crystallize; the attractive Weber-like *Braut von Messina* overture and three overtures into which pomp and circumstance enter as tritely as in *Finlandia*, and after which the gloomy *innigkeit* of the two violin sonatas is a relief; the forcible *Fantasiestücke* (op. 111) and well-knit fughettas for piano; and finally the thoughtful *Morning Songs*, which brought the composer back to his starting-point, piano lyrics.

The Man and His Art

A sense of frustration haunted Schumann's existence, and accounts, perhaps, for the absent, introverted look that Niecks remembered and the portrait in *Grove's Dictionary* confirms. In society he was always going off in a huff; as conductor and teacher he was incapable of 'tackling' anybody; his critical work scarcely routed the philistines; even as a composer he could only feel himself a fore-runner, apart from the fact that in reputation he was chiefly Clara Schumann's musical husband. His romantic spirit remains: like Rousseau, '*Si je ne vaux pas mieux, je suis autre.*' It is refreshing to turn to the enthusiastic and inquisitive pages of the *New Music Journal*, to the lyrical fervour of the symphonies and to the unpretentious sincerity of a fanciful but consistent musical idealism. In any account of the wider growth of musical appreciation in the last hundred years an Englishman is proud to mention Parry and Holst, but in their eloquent and may-sided plea for a deeper reverence for the uses of music these pioneers were anticipated, first and foremost, by the life-work of Robert Schumann, whose devotion to the musical cause was the chief part of his religion.

BEDŘICH SMETANA

1824–84

COLIN MASON

Birth of Czech Music

Frantisek Smetana is the man who by virtue of his son's glory ranks proudly in the pages of history as the grandfather of Czech music. Like his compatriot, another fortuitously famous Frantisek, the fathe of Antonin Dvořák, he was a tradesman. They were men of simila character, both amateur musicians of the homely sort that had abounded in Bohemia for generations, both proud of their sons' talents, bu both considering music a pleasant diversion for tradesmen. And just a father Dvořák was determined that his son should follow him as a butcher, so, nearly twenty years earlier, was father Smetana determined that his son should follow him as a brewer. Not surprisingly then, the pattern of Smetana's youth is little different from that o Dvořák's.

According to most biographers, Bedřich, better known in Englanc as Frederick, Smetana was Frantisek's eighth child, but his first son and was borne by his third wife. Frantisek's more than normal elatior was no doubt due to the fact that he saw in his son someone to carry the name of Smetana further into the history of brewery, but he likec music well enough to put his son to study it with a local musician. Sc Bedřich became a competent violinist at the age of four and showec himself a prodigy of almost Mozartian infant and juvenile talent, if ir fact he did not go one better than his predecessor. The popular legenc tells that Mozart's desire as a child to play second violin in a quarte remained ungratified, whereas Bedřich is supposed at the age of five to have played first violin in a quartet performed on his father's name-day. On 4 October 1830, for a similar occasion in honour of the Emperor, he played a piano solo at a public concert; but even these amazing feats could not persuade Frantisek to consider his son as anything but a prospective brewer.

In 1831 the family moved from Litomysl to Jindrichuv-Hradec fo the father to take up another job. Here the boy's general and musical education continued, first at school, later at the Gymnasium, but always in the completely Austrian rut into which the oppressors had forced all Czech activities, when they allowed activity at all. He sang in the choir at church, where the organist looked after his musical tuition until 1838. Then he was sent to Jihlava and Nemecky-Brod for a short time. Finally he went in 1839 to enter the Gymnasium at the much dreamed of Prague, at that time almost an Austrian city, where the embers of Czech nationalism hardly glowed under the weight of Austrian domination.

Prague

For young Smetana Prague was primarily a city of music, and his musical activities occupied far more of his time and energy than his other studies. He took piano lessons from Batka, formed a quartet with his friends Butula, Kostka, and Vlcek, for whom he wrote a string quartet and various polkas, studied as much contemporary music as possible, frequented concerts, but did not work satisfactorily at the Gymnasium. As a consequence, he was removed by his father to the care of a cousin, a teacher at Plzen, but with little result. There he composed, acquired a reputation as a local virtuoso playing Liszt, Thalberg, and Heller, gave lessons, improvised dances for social gatherings, and dreamed wildly of becoming a Lisztian Mozart. All this served to convince his tolerant cousin that the boy was cut out to be a professional musician and nothing else, so he attempted to dissuade Frantisek from making him a brewer. Frantisek raised few objections, but offered no help; he was not too well off at the time and provided Bedřich with twenty florins to launch himself in Prague as a pianist and composer. Thus in 1843, like Dvořák sixteen years later, the nineteen-year-old Smetana arrived in the capital with no money, no reputation, little experience, but much talent and resource.

At Prague he tried to make a living as a piano virtuoso. His future mother-in-law, Katherine Kollar, whom he had met with her family some years before and come to know very well, recommended him to Josef Proksch, who gave him his first methodical instruction in composition for nothing more than the promise of payment when Smetana could afford it. A further recommendation from Kittl, an influential musician in Prague, brought him a fairly agreeable job as music master to the households of Count Thun at an equally agreeable salary of three hundred florins per year, plus board and lodging. The job provided bread and butter, even if little scope for any exhibition of patriotism, and if Smetana was not in quite the position he would have wished, he was at least comparatively contented there for several years. He was able to remain under Proksch, who regarded him as an exemplary pupil, and he continued his contact with the Kollar family, whose daughter Katherine, like him, was now teaching music in noble households.

In 1848, Smetana, by his own or perhaps by the Count's decision, left the Thun family (to be replaced, rather ironically, by Katherine) for a freer life in Prague. Freedom however meant poverty, for no position was to be found. Smetana had some idea of starting a music school; to raise funds he gave a concert tour without success. So with a judicious mixture of boldness, humility, and pathos, he wrote to Liszt the sad tale of his career, dedicating his Opus 1 to the master and requesting a loan of 400 florins to start the school. For security he still had no more to offer than he had to Proksch for his lessons on credit four years earlier, but Liszt did not disappoint him. Though in his reply no mention was made of money, a short time afterwards the school came into being at Prague and soon began to flourish, so well in fact that on 27 August 1849, Smetana was able to marry Katherine Kollar.

Composition

Well as the school went, Smetana was determined not to be a mere pianist and teacher all his life. During these years he had achieved little in the way of composition, but his patriotic and musical character had been forming. Apart from Beethoven, modern music was his chief interest; Schumann, Chopin, Liszt, and Berlioz he devoured, particularly after the visits of the last two to Prague. He was overwhelmed by *The Fantastic Symphony*. Liszt's virtuosity inspired him to emulate him at the piano. Among the revolutionaries his sympathies lay above all with Chopin for his nationalism; what the mazurka and the polonaise were to Chopin, the polka and the furiant were to Smetana. Like the Russian Nationalists he saw Chopin as the original leader of them all; his attachment to him lasted all his life.

Under these influences he had written many nationalistic piano works, some of considerable merit, but all still practically unknown outside Czechoslovakia. By 1848 his national feeling had reached the greatest heights, where it was indeed to remain for the rest of his life. This nationalism extended beyond purely musical fields of course. Smetana had made the acquaintance of Karel Havlicek, a leading political agitator, and this had sharpened his political awareness. But he felt that he could best help the cause by composing and propagating national music, so he devoted himself thereafter to nationalist composition that should if possible be universal too.

Despite these feelings and hopes, despite the at least intellectually revolutionary atmosphere of Prague, in the five years after his marriage Smetana was almost suffocated there, without real scope or opportunity for expressing in music what he had now come to regard as its chief purpose. The Austrians, scenting revolution, kept an even stronger hold on Czechoslovakia than in Smetana's student days. He continued tamely with his school and organizing concerts; in 1850, on the recommendation of Proksch, he was even made court-musician to the recently abdicated Austrian Emperor, Ferdinand I, who had retired to Prague. Such was the life of the Czech nationalists in those days. At last, to complete his despondency, his five-year-old daughter died in 1855, after already showing brilliant musical talent. The emotional stress arising from this tragic incident led Smetana to write one of his few 'abstract' works, the fine *Trio in G minor*, which aroused much admiration in Liszt.

So to Sweden

Eventually, unable to tolerate the conditions of Prague any longer, Smetana accepted an offer of a post at Gothenburg in Sweden, for which he had been recommended by the pianist A. D. Dreyschock. On 11 October 1856, he left Prague to take up his new job. Gothenburg offered much more scope for his activities as organizer, for, though he found it a conservative city, it took fairly readily to the modern music he offered with the old, besides providing him for the first time with a respectable salary. He became a well-known and liked public figure in Gothenburg, highly respected for his talents and conscientiousness. Life was for once fairly easy and he began to devote himself to the composition of more important works. In 1857 he was able to visit Liszt at Weimar, where he was considerably influenced by the interest in modern comic opera, particularly Cornelius's *Barber of Bagdad*, which was to have its première in 1858. In that year too he fetched his wife to live with him in Gothenburg and on returning settled there to work for several years.

His life was temporarily disrupted in 1859 by the death of Katherine, who had been finding the climate too harsh and died on her way back to Prague. Certain chroniclers have been rather disturbed by his quick recovery from this blow, for on 10 July 1860, not much more than a year later, he was married again, to another Bohemian girl, at Obristvi. This second wife, Barbara Ferdinandi, also found Gothenburg uncongenial, but had no intention of returning alone like her predecessor, still less of remaining to die, so, in May 1861, the Smetanas left Gothenburg to return to Prague.

Back to Prague

Their immediate reward, in spite of that fact that in the city now the Austrian oppression had been slightly relaxed and the revolutionary spirit slightly revived, was poverty. In the 1861-2 season Smetana was obliged to give a concert tour through Germany and Holland in order to meet expenses. By the time of his return, Czech cultural activities were slowly growing and Smetana devoted himself wholeheartedly to their furtherance. He conducted and organized choral, orchestral, and chamber concerts for the numerous newly founded societies, took part himself in founding the national Umelecka Beseda (Society of Arts), composed nationalist works for his choral society, and in the press lashed Italian opera with all the sharpness of a very caustic tongue. Such an occupation would normally be as futile as abusing Hollywood absurdities, but Smetana, a practical man, supplemented his scathing criticism with the offer of a new kind of opera. From public subscription the Bohemian Diet had succeeded in raising enough money to erect a Provisional Theatre until it became possible to build a truly worthy National Theatre. For it, Smetana proposed to write a series of national operas, beginning as early as 1862 upon *The Brandenburgers in Bohemia*, a Czech historical opera, which he completed the next year.

The Operas

The Brandenburgers, compared with Smetana's subsequent operas, is a poor thing, both in libretto and music, but at the time it was something entirely new. As a consequence, because it gave expression to the rising national feeling, when it was first produced under Smetana's direction in January 1866, it was an overwhelming success. Smetana, who was already in popular favour for his musical activities instantly became a national hero. With the production he entered on the happiest period of his life. He was determined to provide the National Theatre with a series of essentially Czech operas of different kinds. Already in 1866 he had another ready, which he had been composing while waiting for the production of *The Brandenburgers*. The new opera was the one that has since proved his most popular and the only well-known one outside his own country, *The Bartered Bride*. The librettist was the same as for the first opera, but he had made a better job of the second. *The Bartered Bride*, as it was originally presented in the Provisional Theatre in 1866, was considerably different from the one we know now, but it served to consolidate Smetana's success with the musical public of Prague. In fact it served too well, for he was expected to continue to turn out jolly operas of the same kind for evermore.

The reception of his first two operas naturally gratified Smetana, though he was later rather contemptuous of it. He was now the leading composer of Czechoslovakia, conductor of the Opera, in the public eye something of a national hero. His own inward satisfaction, too, at seeing his ambition to advance the national cause through music beginning to be realized, must have been very great. Inspired by his success, he immediately began his third opera and completed it in a very short time. From the happiness and comedy of *The Bartered Bride*, he had turned to the tragic legend of *Dalibor*, the story of the fight of the Czech people, and particularly their leader, against imperial oppression, a subject near to the heart of the people of Smetana's day. But topical as the subject was, despite all its particular aptness for the time, the opera failed at its first performance on 16 May 1868. Even the occasion, that of the laying of the foundation stone of the National Theatre, could not excite the listeners into any sort of enthusiasm: and their rather negative reception of it was warm beside that of the critics, who fell on the work with one accord. Smetana was discouraged by the generally cold reception among the ordinary public and positively infuriated by the charge of Wagnerism hurled at his head by critics pretending to have the interests of the National Opera at heart, when they really wanted nothing but an excuse to abuse Wagner and Smetana.

The composer's disappointment however did not tempt him to try another *Bartered Bride* to restore himself to popular and critical favour. He continued with his preconceived plan of creating a varied operatic repertoire for the National Theatre. But his next opera was not to be a work for absorption into the repertoire: it was to be reserved for the greatest patriotic occasions only and waited so long for such a one for its first performance that Smetana never heard it. Perhaps his least nationalistic work, it is yet his most national, based on the historical Czech legend of 'Libuse', regarded then as one of the country's most glorious national inheritances. Owing to the long delay in the production Smetana was never able to enjoy the success of his music, which held a worthy place in general Czech esteem beside the original poem.

When Smetana finished *Libuse* at the end of 1872 he had completed the first stage of his creation of a varied national opera by giving besides the somewhat experimental historical *Brandenburgers in Bohemia*, a rustic comedy, a historical tragedy, and this 'festival picture' which he would not call either opera or music-drama. All four works, though very different from one another, were completely national not only in effect but in inspiration. Only now that he had achieved this did Smetana begin to think of doing something else on the lines of *The Bartered Bride*, and for the first time he decided to go abroad, in fact to France, for his inspiration, taking as a subject the play by Malleville, *The Two Widows*. Even this, however, he translated into Czech, transplanted to a Czech setting, and imbued with an essentially Czech spirit. So ardent was his nationalism that all else had to give way to it. Everything he touched interested him now only as a potential medium for the expression of some part of his national thought or for the awakening and sustenance of Czech culture. He was even unsympathetic to other contemporary national workers after his own heart, such as the rising Russian group who were trying to create a Russian national music and particularly an opera.

This may be seen from a letter sent home by Borodin during a trip abroad, in which he mentions that at one time during these years Smetana violently opposed a suggested production in Prague of an opera by one or other of the Russian 'Five'. This slight narrowness on Smetana's part however does not lack justification in view of the hard battle he was having for Czech music, especially since he devoted himself absolutely to the national cause, perhaps at the expense of quick and wide personal recognition abroad. He was, in fact, so immersed in his work that since 1866, after the production of *The Bartered Bride*, he had lived quietly and uneventfully and there is thus little for the biographer to record in the chronicle of his life during these years except the progress in the composition or production of this or that opera. They were undoubtedly Smetana's happiest years, despite the failure of *Dalibor* and the rather less than remarkable success of *The Two Widows* (produced March 1874). He was able by his official position at the opera (one of the few official positions that are also congenial) to continue composing, if not very quickly, at least without the worry of financial difficulty. And in his own country, in spite of much jealousy and vicious criticism, he was widely honoured both as a composer and as a nationalist.

Disablement

The end to the period of contentment came shortly after the production of *The Two Widows*, when Smetana began to notice symptoms of some defect in his hearing. First he found that he heard tones differently in each ear and was later worried by a continual noise like that of a waterfall in his head. Naturally it soon became impossible for him to conduct or give piano lessons. In the autumn of 1874 came another blow to add to the terrible torment of his coming deafness, which was already worse than ordinary deafness, for by not destroying all sensitivity to sound it converted everything to maddening, unintelligible noise. When Smetana wrote in desperation to the directors of the National Theatre asking to be relieved of his duties for a while, though they were not unsympathetic, word of his malady went round among his most vicious critics. Their immediate response was to make this an opportunity of publicly discrediting him, by charging him with laziness and hypochondria, charges so fantastically untrue that one can hardly believe them possible. In the past eight years Smetana had written four operas and the tone poem *Vysehrad*, simultaneously carrying on extensive duties as director and conductor of the opera in addition to a good deal of teaching work. Granted he had not been prolific, but he had obviously worked consistently and steadily throughout the entire period.

Shortly after this attack, on the night of 19–20 October, Smetana suddenly became totally deaf, according to his own account as a result of the paralysis of the acoustic nerve, though the effects of the paralysis were unfortunately by no means purely aural. Smetana was forced by this circumstance to resign permanently all his duties at the opera and elsewhere in Prague. After a year of great financial expense vainly occupied in trying to find a cure, Smetana accepted his fate and retired to live with his daughter at Jabkenice.

Still a Composer

For some years he was still able to work well. Being relieved of his official duties he could concentrate entirely on composition, so, though he composed more slowly, he managed by devoting all his time to the one occupation to complete operas at the same rate as before. Moreover he also found time for more non-operatic compositions; his deafness had inevitably brought with it some change of character. Seeing that he could no longer live for the present and the future, as he had always done before, he was forced nostalgically to relive his past life and re-enjoy the beauties of his country; consequently from the expression in music of patriotic feeling and ideals he passed to the expression of personal ones. Just as men who have reached the normally uneventful later stages of life write their autobiographies, so Smetana, for whom at fifty life was virtually over, wrote his in music, which he had always regarded as primarily a vehicle for the expression of literary ideas.

Thus we find Smetana during the first two years of his deafness composing not only one of his loveliest operas, *The Kiss* (a village love story like *The Bartered Bride*, less comic though equally popular in Czechoslovakia), but also the first four tone poems of the cycle *My Country*, and the first *String Quartet*, in E minor, in which he depicts the course of his life up to the time of composition, 1876. The first movement is a portrayal of his early romantic period, the second of his young happy dancing days, the third an expression of his love for his wife and the fourth of his joy in being able to create national compositions, until the tragedy of his deafness.

Though this work met with a cold reception when submitted to the Prague Society of Chamber Music, Smetana was somewhat compensated by the success of *The Kiss*. He had not been able to supervise the production himself and had entrusted it to Adolf Cech, who produced it with brilliant and lasting success in November 1876. The quartet too, though it made no headway in Czechoslovakia, was not long in drawing attention abroad.

All this however was of little use to the composer, whose condition was growing slowly but steadily worse. Not only his hearing, but his memory and in fact his power of thought were showing signs, at first very slight, of being affected. Any work involved greater mental effort and exhaustion now, so progress became even slower. Nevertheless by the end of 1878 Smetana had completed yet another successful opera, *The Secret*, a romantic tale again of village life, love, jealousies, and intrigues. In this year too he wrote *Tabor*, the fifth poem of *My Country*, and in 1879 the sixth and last, *Blanik*, as well as a fine set of Czech dances for piano solo.

Final Triumphs and Last Struggles

In 1880 two temporary gleams of pleasantness came out to illumine Smetana's life, the first when Liszt wrote to say that the 'splendid first quartet had delighted them all' at Weimar, the second when his *Libuse* won the competition for an opera to open the new National Theatre. The next year it was performed with great success by Adolf Cech. But Smetana was little able to appreciate the occasion, for not only was he afflicted by deafness, but in this year the additional cerebral complications of his disease became more manifest and his powers of composition began to decline more and more rapidly, until eventually work became almost an impossibility. To work at all needed tremendous concentration, owing to his bad memory, yet so to concentrate involved a risk of straining his nerves to such an extent as to put him in danger of losing his reason altogether. We can only marvel at Smetana's productions, which continued to appear in spite of all this. In spring, 1881, he began yet another comic opera, *The Devil's Wall*, the libretto of which is as ridiculous and extravagant as anything in all opera. In little more than a year he finished it, though he notes on the score that the work was completed with terrible difficulty. When it was done, he thought highly of it and was very proud of his achievement in managing to make a satisfactory job of it in spite of the labour and anguish it cost him. Yet when it was first produced in autumn, 1882, the hostile critics did little but abuse him for the senility of the composition.

Perhaps feeling that his creative life was now nearly at an end, after the opera Smetana turned again to his autobiography in chamber music, and in a second string quartet resumed the story of his life after the onset of deafness. Even the composer himself was unhappy about the effectiveness of this quartet, thinking that executants and listeners might find it incoherent. Nothing could deter him from composing, but he was at last beginning to feel that he was losing his grasp of music. Towards the end of 1882 he had a more serious loss of memory than any before and even temporarily lost the power of speech. But he picked up again and in 1883 finished the quartet. It has never rivalled the first in popularity with musicians or the general public, although Arnold Schönberg is reported to have said that it was a great revelation to him. Much of the pathos of Smetana's last ten years is expressed both intentionally and unintentionally in this quartet. But that of the remaining year was beyond the powers of musical suggestion. Still undefeated by his weakness, in 1883 Smetana completed an orchestral prelude *The Carnival in Prague* and began another opera *Viola*, to a libretto adapted from *Twelfth Night*. For several months he worked at it unceasingly, as far as his brain would allow, until the strain became too much for him. In January 1884, perhaps because he had worked so hard, his power of mental concentration became too small for him to compose at all and, after the first act had been completed, he was forced not only to leave the opera, but to forgo all further composition. Such were the terrible circumstances that finally reduced one of the most industrious of composers to silence.

Thereafter, the mental decline was steep, but fortunately Smetana was spared much more of life in this state. Shortly after his sixtieth birthday, celebrated in Prague by a concert, his closest friend Srb persuaded him to enter an asylum, and there he died on 12 May 1884.

LUDWIG SPOHR

1784–1859

LESLIE ORREY

Birth and Childhood

Ludwig (or – to give him the Gallicized form of his Christian name that he preferred – Louis) Spohr was born at Brunswick, the eldest of a family of six. His father, a doctor by profession, was also a man of some musical attainment and played the flute; his mother both played the piano and sang. Young Ludwig thus grew up in a musical atmosphere and indeed seems to have played a part in the family musical evenings at a very tender age. This at first took the form of childish duets sung with his mother; but a small violin, bought for him at a fair by his father, fired his imagination while he was still only about five or six, and on this he made such rapid progress that, according to his own account, he was soon able to take part with his parents in easy trios for piano, flute, and violin.

In about 1791 chance brought a French emigrant, Dufour, to Seesen, whither the family had moved in 1786. Although only an amateur violinist, he was sufficiently skilled to give young Ludwig some serious lessons and was so impressed with his progress that he persuaded the family to let him study for the musical profession, instead of for medicine as his father had originally intended. To this end he was sent to Brunswick, to study first of all with Kunisch and later with Maucourt, the best violinist in the Brunswick orchestra. His counterpoint lessons with Hartung were cut short by the teacher's ill health and Spohr was practically self-taught at composition.

By this time he was fourteen years old, and his younger brothers were making such a call on the family exchequer that funds for his further instruction were no longer forthcoming. Accordingly, father Spohr took the extraordinary step of sending his eldest son, alone, to Hamburg, with some letters of introduction to friends there, to begin his professional career as a solo artist! The rebuff he received there may well be imagined. The first person he presented his letters to, Professor

Busching, convinced him of the rashness of such an undertaking. Concerts, then as now, were impossible without money or without the draw of a well-known name. Besides, it was midsummer and all the wealthy were out of town. So poor Ludwig, completely deflated, took the only sensible course and (quite literally) directed his footsteps towards Seesen again.

First Travels

But Spohr, whatever else he lacked, was never wanting in self-assurance. Determined that Germany should have the opportunity of appraising his qualities as a virtuoso, he conceived the bold idea of addressing a petition himself to the Duke of Brunswick and waylaid that noble gentleman one morning in the Palace park. His effrontery had its reward, and shortly afterwards, on 2 August 1799, he obtained at the early age of fifteen his first professional appointment.

From this moment, in the time-honoured phrase, he never looked back. The Duke, himself a violinist, appreciated Spohr's gifts, but realized that he was still only half-trained; so in 1802, after an unsuccessful approach to Viotti and Ferdinand Eck, it was finally arranged that Spohr should study with the latter's young brother, Franz Eck. Eck was just embarking on a tour to Russia, and Spohr accompanied him. He kept a fairly full diary of this journey, which took him to St Petersburg, where he met Clementi and Field, via Hamburg, Danzig, Königsberg, and other towns. He also wrote his first *Violin Concerto*, Op. 1, and some violin *Duets*, Op. 3.

Returned to Brunswick, he was appointed first violin of the ducal orchestra. The next year was spent in hard work at his fiddle, modelling his playing on that of Rode, whom he heard in Brunswick in 1803, and in composition (*Concerto* in D minor, Op. 2, and another in A major, which was never published). In the autumn of 1804 he set out on his first important concert tour, visiting Leipzig, Dresden, and Berlin and meeting with considerable success wherever he went. At Leipzig he got entangled with a young singer, Rosa Alberghi, who took his flirtation rather more seriously than he intended. In Berlin he met such distinguished players as Bernard Romberg and Dussek, also Meyerbeer, then a boy of 13. An interesting commentary on the taste of the time is afforded by his story of the quartet parties there, when Romberg, a cellist, expressed his surprise that Spohr could waste his time on such stuff as the Beethoven quartets!

Gotha and Marriage

His next advancement was not long in coming. In June 1805, he was offered the post of Director of the Ducal Orchestra at Gotha, and, the terms being acceptable to the young musician, he began his duties there in October, at a salary of nearly 500 thalers. His stay at Gotha was important in more ways than one, for it was there that he first met a young pianist and harpist, Dorette Scheidler. (She had also some considerable skill on the violin, but Spohr, with a violent prejudice against women violinists, advised her to give up the practice of that instrument, 'so unbecoming to females'!). The two were at once attracted to each other and it was not long before Spohr, who had written various compositions for harp and violin, which they had played together, had, in his own sentimental words, proposed 'that they should play together for life.' She swooned into his arms in the most gratifying way, and they were married the following year (2 February 1806).

The spate of compositions continued unabated: concertos, quartets, the *Concertante for Two Violins* (Op. 48), and first attempt at an opera, *Die Prüfung*, which, however, got no further than rehearsal. In October, 1807, the two Spohrs set out on their first joint tour. It is unnecessary, and would be tedious, to follow him through all these concert travels, which occur with great frequency throughout his life, though it must be realized that they bulk very large in his history. He was just as much a travelling virtuoso as a composer; moreover these tours brought him contacts with all the important musicians and musical centres of Europe and often materially affected his future. This particular tour, for example, took him to Stuttgart, where his meeting with Weber was to have important repercussions later; on a tour in 1812 he so impressed Count Palffy, the proprietor of the theatre An der Wien in Vienna that he was immediately offered a three years' contract as leader and director of the orchestra at that theatre, at a salary three times his present one. Such an offer was too much for Spohr's business instincts, and, as the other conditions of the appointment sounded satisfactory in the extreme, he could not refuse it.

Operas

A big factor influencing his acceptance was the chance it seemed to give him to prove his worth as a composer of opera. Writing for the stage was one of the few matters over which Spohr ever betrayed the slightest hesitancy or lack of self confidence. *Die Prüfung* he took no further than rehearsal; his second opera, *Alruna*, had been favourably received on its production at Weimar, in 1808, but Spohr subseqently felt dissatisfied with it and allowed only the overture to be printed. The next, *Die Zweikampf mit der Geliebten*, was produced at Hamburg only after the greatest of difficulties and with a certain amount of re-writing. It seemed as if his diffidence was justified, and, if it would be wrong to say he had no talent for dramatic composition, it certainly came with less facility than other forms of composition. It must be remembered, too, that his only formal instruction in the theory of music and in composition had been the few desultory lessons with Hartung in the early Brunswick days.

His fourth opera, *Faust*, though destined in the end to be one of his best and most popular works, was not without its setbacks. It was written at high speed, between May and September 1813, in the full confidence that it would be staged in Vienna. But an unfortunate difference with Count Palffy prevented this, and it was not until 1818 that Spohr had an opportunity of mounting the work at Frankfurt (Weber had in the meantime conducted two productions of it during his brilliant period at Prague.)

Zelmire und Azor, his fifth opera, produced at Frankfurt in April 1819, is by his own confession indebted to Rossini, of all people. Spohr's difference with Count Palffy had led, in 1815, to his resignation; after a stay at Carolath, in Silesia, Spohr with his wife and family (two children, both girls; his only son had died when but three months old; a third daughter was born in 1818) had gone on a protracted tour through Switzerland and Italy, combining music with sightseeing, meeting many interesting people including Paganini and hearing for the first time the music of Rossini. This produced a violent revulsion of feeling, only slightly modified by subsequent hearing of his operas; it is amusing, therefore, to find Spohr admitting that 'little as I was an admirer of Rossini's music, yet the applause that *Tancredi* had met with in Frankfurt was not wholly without influence on the style of my new opera.'

London, Dresden, Cassel

In 1820 Spohr paid his first visit to England, a country that was to make him very welcome on several subsequent occasions. This visit was notable for two things. First, the Philharmonic Society, at whose invitation he came, relaxed their rule that had previously banned all concertos but those of Beethoven and Mozart; and secondly, it marked the occasion of the introduction of the conductor's baton to London. The direction of the orchestra had up till then been a dual function, shared between the first violin and the gentleman at the piano, a relic of the days of the continuo and the figured bass. With a large orchestra like that of the Royal Philharmonic Society the lack of precision resulting from such divided rule may well be imagined. Spohr succeeded in getting his own way in this matter despite the opposition of some of the more conservative of the Directors of the Society; partly owing to this, and partly to his temerity in stopping the orchestra at rehearsal to 'remark in a polite but earnest fashion' on some of the shortcomings of the playing, the performances under his direction were of an excellence that London till then had but rarely experienced.

Returned to his native Germany Spohr next went with his family to Dresden, where Weber was busy with the rehearsals of *Freischütz*. The success of this, which he confesses to be quite unable to understand, turned his thoughts once more in the direction of opera. He had been led, quite by chance, to a romance, *La Veuve de Malabar*, which, it is interesting to recall, had previously provided a libretto for Mozart. He had already sketched some of this before coming to Dresden and now turned to it in earnest. The result was *Jessonda*, the most successful of all his operas with the possible exception of *Faust*. It was given a splendid performance, under Spohr's direction, at Cassel on 28 July 1823; since then it has had many revivals, especially in Germany, and in fact survived until well into the twentieth century.

The story of Spohr's appointment to Cassel is well known. Towards the end of 1821 Weber called on him with the news that he had just been offered the post of *Hofkapellmeister* to the Elector of Hesse-Cassel. Weber, however, was quite satisfied with his position at Dresden (what, one wonders, would his fortune have been if he had accepted?); would Spohr consider it, if he wrote back to the Elector suggesting his name? Spohr most decidedly would, and in a very short space of time the great violinist found himself secure for the remainder of his life in a well paid job, with the prospect of pleasant and interesting work in interesting surroundings, with six to eight weeks' leave of absence each year and absolute artistic control of all the opera in his hands.

Programme Music: Some Experiments

The works he wrote during his long stay at Cassel are among his finest. They include three programme symphonies – No. 4, *Die Weihe der Töne* (1833); No. 6, the 'historical' symphony (the four movements of which are: the age of Bach and Handel; Haydn and Mozart; Beethoven; the present day – i.e., 1839); and No. 9 and last, entitled *The Seasons* (1849). Other works of a more or less experimental nature were the four *Double Quartets*; the *Quartet Concerto*, Op. 131, harking back to the idea of the concerto grosso; and the *Symphony* for two orchestras, Op. 121, in which he reverts to an old practice of J. C. Bach, Mozart, and Haydn, but couples it with a programme. His eighth violin concerto, the *Gesangsscene*, Op. 47, is much earlier and was written during his Italian tour (1816).

These departures from the normal run of symphonic writing are interesting and rather surprising. Spohr was a curious blend of deep-seated conservatism and enquiring radicalism, with the former predominating. Although, as we have seen, he played the (early) Beethoven quartets, there is no evidence that he had any real insight into Beethoven's mind; he saw these essentially communal works from the narrow and individualistic view-point of the first violin. He was unsympathetic to the later Beethoven; in the whole of his *Autobiography* there is no reference to the greatest of all violin concertos; he confesses to no relish for the *Ninth Symphony*, and finds the last movement 'monstrous and tasteless'. Yet he was very early in the field in support of Wagner, whom he considered 'the most gifted of all our dramatic composers of the present time', and produced *The Flying Dutchman* in 1843, only a few months after its first performance in Dresden. It is true that he did not receive the later Wagner so enthusiastically and found things in *Tannhäuser* 'ugly and excruciating to the ear'. His own compositions betray the same duality, the conflict between his forward-thinking mind and his musical temperament, which was not sufficiently imaginative to vitalize the new forms his brain conceived.

The Oratorios

So far Spohr had gained success in all the styles of composition he had attempted, save oratorio, though, as we have seen, opera gave him considerable trouble. His one attempt at oratorio, *Das Jüngste Gericht* had been a failure; now Rochlitz, the editor of the Leipzig *Allgemeine*

Musik Zeitung, sent him a poem entitled *Die letzten Dinge*, and Spohr et to work enthusiastically; by November 1825, he had the first part eady. A performance of this, with piano accompaniment, was well eceived, and Spohr felt encouraged to push on with all speed, to have t ready by the following Good Friday, and, in the Lutheran Church t Cassel on 25 March 1826, was given the first complete performance f a work that was to receive perhaps the most overwhelming opularity of all his compositions. And indeed *The Last Judgement*, to give its English title, has maintained its place in the repertory of choral ocieties almost to this day.

In 1839 Spohr paid his second visit to this country to direct a new ratorio, *Calvary*, at the Norwich Triennial Festival. The enormous opularity his works had obtained over here ensured him a brilliant eception, and, despite some bad manners on the part of a section of he Norwich clergy who took exception to the theme of the new ratorio, he enjoyed as warm and enthusiastic a welcome as it has ver been the lot of a musician to receive. It was a real sorrow to him hat he was not able to secure permission to attend the next Festival, n 1842, when another oratorio, *The Fall of Babylon*, specially written or Norwich, was given an almost equally enthusiastic performance nder Professor Taylor.

Altogether Spohr made six journeys to England and each time was eceived with even more than the usual measure of adulation the English proffer to foreign musicians, distinguished and otherwise. As sample of both the homage paid to him and the Gargantuan musical ppetite of the London of a century ago we may quote a concert, given n his honour in 1843, when no less than seven of his chamber works vere given. The performance was timed to begin at 2 p.m., with an nterval for *déjeuner* at 5. Thus refreshed, artists and audience returned o the attack at 7 p.m., and the company 'listened until late in the vening!'

Spohr's colossal energy and tireless activity continued almost un- bated until within a short time of his death. It was a sad moment in is life when, in November 1857, he was pensioned off, after thirty- ive years' service at Cassel; he still felt capable of his duties and was nuch hurt by this enforced retirement. Shortly afterwards the break- ng of an arm put an end to his violin playing and, though he con- inued to compose, he wrote nothing more of importance. He passed way peacefully, at Cassel, on 22 October 1859.

Retrospect

It is a sad reflection on the error of contemporary judgements that Spohr, in his lifetime regarded as at least the peer of Beethoven, should now be remembered only by a line in a comic opera. Yet the last generation has seen the total eclipse of the whole of his vast output. Ten operas, nine symphonies, thirty-four quartets, four double quartets, eight quintets, four oratorios – so the list goes on, an astonishing record for a man who combined the duties of a composer with those of a concert director and travelling virtuoso.

Such neglect is perhaps not completely justified, but it cannot be denied that there are serious flaws in his work. During his lifetime his works gained enormously from his own personal popularity and prestige, for as a violinist he was of the first order and as a conductor also first rate. But, sincere and worthy artist though he was, he lacked that depth of feeling requisite for the finest creative artists. There are many passages in his *Autobiography* that indicate only too clearly his lack of self-criticism, his egotism, his want of understanding of the deepest emotions. The account of the death of his first wife (in 1834) is a case in point. There is much superficial emotion; he is in such despair that he cannot undertake the arrangements for the funeral, but has to leave these to his son-in-law while he goes away to recover; but it is impossible to drive completely from one's mind the suspicion that the dominant emotion was one of irritation that his work had been interrupted. And a sentence from his *Life*, just after his second marriage in 1836, is very significant. (The proposal, by the way, was by letter; the whole thing reads somewhat like a business proposition.) The ceremony over, he writes, 'I now lived again in my former and accustomed domestic manner and felt unspeakably happy with my wife!' It is just this lack of the finer feelings, this running away from all the great emotional crises of life, that prevented his work from reaching the highest levels and stood in the way of his finding really satisfying musical treatment of such immense themes as the Last Judgement and Calvary.

WILLIAM STERNDALE BENNETT

1816–75

W. R. ANDERSON

Musical Antecedents

William Sterndale Bennet was one of the great gentlemen of music: caught in a poor period, when we were enslaved by our delight in Mendelssohn, he was a willing slave to professional duty, cheerfully making the best of the academic world while exercising, in nooks and corners of time, his graceful talent as a composer.

To see him sympathetically, we may consider what happened to English music from the period around 1600, when we took up the torch of madrigal and church music from Italy and made it burn with new brilliance, to the time of Bennett. The record shows ups and downs, with more descents than rises. Two centuries before Bennett's day our madrigalian era was a climax of inventive genius and adaptive skill. On the whole our highest qualities have been shown rather in developing than in initiating musical styles, devices, and forms. After the declensions of the Commonwealth, we had the sadly short life of Purcell – under forty years. He, caught in a worse period than even Bennett's, had infinitely higher powers.

We too readily bowed before foreign art. The influence of men like Purcell was weakened by Charles II's bringing over French musicians and the general enfeebling trends of Court power, ever hampering to art. With Purcell's death, near the end of the seventeenth century, died our brightest hope. In the eighteenth, Handel bestrode our narrow world like a Colossus, coming in the glow of his Italian experience to tempt fortune here: to enjoy high success and endure bitter failure. Our own aims, hopes, and nature were exploited (in the good sense) by Arne. Composers such as Croft, Greene, and Boyce wrote sterling church music; around the turn of the eighteenth and nineteenth centuries there were Battishill, Crotch, and the Wesleys (of the great family famous both in the pulpit and at the organ). The ballad operas flourished a while longer: no country ever did a small thing better, ever since the famous *Beggar's Opera* of 1728. Dibdin's sea music, the operettas of Shield and Storace and the works of the freely-borrowing Henry Bishop took us into Victorian days.

We should not omit a thankful word for the glee, an English invention: and we remember that the Irishman Field, a great traveller abroad, influenced Chopin's nocturne style and was one of the teachers of Glinka; but our influence upon foreign music was as a drop compared to the oceanic force of the conquering Germans, Italian opera-writers, and, later, such Frenchmen as Gounod. Bach was almost unknown to us. Handel's influence was weakened only when Mendelssohn so sweetly led our straying fancy to fresh woods and pastures new. Our own men, Balfe, Wallace, with Benedict, a foreigner, satisfied our every desire with operas like *The Bohemian Girl*, *Maritana*, *The Lily of Killarney*, built upon obvious models, chiefly Italian (Bellini, Donizetti, Rossini), German (Weber), and French (Auber and others).

Early Years

It was into this English world, then, that William Sterndale Bennett was born at Sheffield on 13 April 1816, only a few years after Wagner Liszt, Chopin, Schumann, and Mendelssohn. He was the son of the organist at the Parish Church and came of a Derbyshire family. His grandfather was a lay clerk at Cambridge, where, in the next century the grandson was to become Professor of Music. His mother, too, had a connexion with that place, her father being curator of Cambridge's Botanical Gardens.

The child lost both parents, within a year of each other, soon after he was three and was adopted by his grandfather. One of the two friends after whom he was named also looked after him until he was old enough to go to Cambridge, at eight, as a chorister of King's College. There he met the Principal of the Royal Academy of Music (which had been founded in 1822), who, impressed by the lad's ability advised that he be given a chance at the new institution. So, at ten Sterndale Bennett became a free student in the halls he was later to rule, at Tenterden Street.

He learned to play the violin under Oury and Spagnoletti, the latter a distinguished orchestral leader. Bennett took most keenly to the piano and was praised for 'neatness and lucidity' in Beethoven qualities inherent in his nature, it would seem.

His training as a chorister was not forgotten: at one of the Academy's opera performances he appeared as Cherubino in Mozart's *Marriage of Figaro*; and he sang at St Paul's on occasion. Other teachers were Charles Lucas and W. H. Holmes, for harmony; and later Dr Crotch, one of our masters of church music, developed Bennett's skill in composition, as did Cipriani Potter, who also led him into the higher reaches of pianoforte study.

Early Compositions

A concerto by Bennett was produced in 1833 at an Academy concert. Mendelssohn, in England for a third visit (his *Italian Symphony* was on that occasion a delightful novelty) happened to be present. He found great promise in the youth and invited him to Germany, 'not as pupil, but as friend'. There must have been something very winning in Bennett's charm. So began a fine friendship and the strongest influence in the young composer's life. If he had only been able to find the individual strength to transcend 'influences', he might have paralleled the fame of his new friend. He aroused high hopes in many German musicians. Schumann, in the magazine that he founded, wrote of him in 1837 as 'a very delightful individuality . . . a gentle, quiet spirit, that labours on high . . . like an observer of the stars. . . .' 'The old prejudice against English music' had, Schumann went on, begun to waver, through the names of Field, Onslow, Potter, Bishop, and others, and Bennett was yet another who would powerfully help to abolish that prejudice. He did not fail to note the resemblance of Bennett's music to Mendelssohn's and aptly, though kindly, compared the former's art to that of one 'who lingers beside a balmy lake, on which the beams of the moon are trembling' and Mendelssohn's to 'the broad, deep, slumbering surf of the sea'. Bennett's piano pieces, *The Lake*, *The Mill-stream*, and *The Fountain* he described as, 'for truth to nature, colour, poetic conception, musical Claude Lorraines'.

Schumann dedicated his *Études Symphoniques* to Bennett, and inserted into the finale a passage from an opera about Ivanhoe – one in which Ivanhoe sings the praises of England's knights: an obvious compliment to the young Englishman (though Schumann could not foresee that Bennett would one day be created a knight).

From Bennett's diary in Germany we find that he considered the general level of performance not high, but the majority of performers better respected than in England. Probably he gained a little in freedom and warmth from his intercourse with the enthusiastic Romantics but he was slow in becoming intimate with his chief idol, Mendelssohn

The Teacher

Before the time of this trip, Bennett had composed several sym- phonies and piano concertos while still at the Academy. Afterwards his life was that of a busy professional man: organist (for a year) teacher, and finally Principal of his musical alma mater. His sense o duty tended to stifle his opportunities as a composer. Teaching tool up an astonishing amount of time. We learn that in the first half of th year 1848 he gave piano lessons for an average of nearly thirty-sever hours a week, besides appearing at fifteen concerts and taking classe at Queen's College. For some of the teaching he made extensiv railway journeys, often having to catch a train at 6 a.m. In his late years of teaching he used a tiny carriage, in which he continued t work, and even to eat: but earlier, he tramped or bus'd about London

In 1843 he applied for the post of Professor of Music at Edinburgh University, but found that he could not give up all other work an live there, as was desired. He was then in the thick of that endles round of teaching that he felt necessary. It was in this year that h founded the Bach Society – fired by Mendelssohn's admiration for th then neglected composer, who was almost forgotten, even i Germany.

He married in 1844 the daughter of a Commander in the Navy; sh had been a student at the Academy a little before Bennett, and thi clever, tactful woman was a great support and joy to him for eightee years. He undertook marriage on the £300 a year he was then earning Not for another six years did he touch £800.

1851 found Bennett taking on additional, honorary, toil as one o the musical jurors of the Great Exhibition in Hyde Park.

He was associated with the Philharmonic Society for many years having first been invited to play a concerto when only nineteen an still a student. He became in due course a Director. At one time his to sensitive nature was bruised by an upset, not in itself very significan such as has happened many a time where two conductors are con cerned, both of whom happen also to be composers. After it Bennet gave up much of his public playing and in some ways withdrew into his shell, busying himself with teaching.

He was offered the post of conductor of the famous Gewandhau

Concerts at Leipzig, but refused, perhaps because of the weight of work at home or of that gentleness which made him diffident about rebuking players. He would not stamp, shout, or rap on the desk, in the forcible manner that was then often necessary to control an orchestra. He was so modest that he would consult the leader as to tempi – treating him as an equal.

At a Leeds Festival, related Dr Spark, a chorus bass remarked 'He don't lead us much; but wait till we sing "He led them through the deep", in *Israel*, and we'll lead him!' So they did – almost to disaster.

From this first Leeds Festival comes a classic story. In *The Messiah* he asked that the full band should not come into 'Lift up your heads' until 'He is the King of Glory'. Dr Spark tells how an old Halifax Handelian, who played the double bass, determined on a supreme effort. He said to his cellist son, 'Did'st hear that, Jim? Reych us t' rosin'; rubbing vigorously, and beaming, he cried, 'Nah look out, Jim. I'll show him *who* is t' King o' Glory!' And, adds Spark, 'the vigorous rasping of that double bass and cello was absolutely unparalleled in the history of bowing and scraping.'

Cambridge and the R.A.M.

In 1856 Bennett was appointed Professor of Music at Cambridge and in the same year resumed his Philharmonic connexion, after the little quarrel of 1848. He held this conducting post for a decade, until the Royal Academy of Music called him to be its Principal in 1866. The Philharmonic bestowed upon him its gold medal, a token struck in 1871 to commemmorate the association of Beethoven with the Society. It bears the master's effigy.

His course as Principal of the Academy was not of the easiest. It was in a poor state, and, not long before he was installed, some of those who should have guided its fortunes were inclined to abandon the enterprise. Bennett fought them, stuck to the task, and brought the Academy forward into happier times.

He had never more than a small monetary reward for all his devoted work; but his merit was recognized by a knighthood – though only four years before he died.

For various festivals Bennett wrote cantatas, such as *The May Queen* (for Leeds), a pastoral still sung by the milder-aspiring choral societies. His piano works of the larger order have vanished from the repertory; the delicate sketches are still enjoyed. His pianoforte style was that of

Clementi: he sometimes, though rarely, attained that Chopinesque floriation which is essential growth, not just external decoration. It is a little curious that his last published work (its opus number is only 46), a piano piece entitled *The Maid of Orleans*, showed a spirit partly new, in that its themes are labelled, in the manner of Liszt.

Bennett was (as Stanford described him in the early seventies) 'a small figure of a man, whose dignity of bearing made him look half as tall again as his stature warranted; with a well-proportioned and squarely built head, lovely and sympathetic eyes, and an expression of unmistakable kindliness and charm. . . .' His was the temperament of the upright English gentleman, with that reserve which has so often prevented our shining in the more flowery paths of composition or interpretation. He enjoyed cricket at Lord's. A sterling character, who cared little for personal gain, he ever placed duty before profit or prestige, in that spirit which H. G. Wells happily defined when he wrote: 'The first distinctive element in . . . the educated *persona* is the conception of self-abnegation, of devotion. The individual belongs, he has made himself over, to an order consecrated to ends transcending any personal consideration. This is the essence of priesthood, of professionalism, and of all artistic and literary pretensions. . . . The element of devotion in this priestly-learned tradition is absolutely essential to the processes of civilization.'

THE STRAUSS FAMILY OF VIENNA

JOHANN I (Father of the Waltz) 1804–49

His sons:

JOHANN II (The Waltz King) 1825–99

JOSEF 1827–70

EDUARD 1835–1916

ROBERT ELKIN

The Waltz

In the last twenty years of the eighteenth century a new kind of dance took root in Bohemia, Austria, and Bavaria and spread rapidly over the continent of Europe – the waltz. As to its origin, the experts are not in agreement. Perhaps it sprang from various sources; but the most probable of these are pretty certainly the old peasant dances such as the Ländler or Drehtanz, which Schubert put to such charming uses. Be this as it may, it is not surprising that the pleasure-loving folk of Vienna were among the first to take the new dance to their hearts and that the tunes pervading the early boyhood of Johann Strauss the First were in waltz tempo.

Johann I's Boyhood

Johann I was the son of an inn-keeper in the Viennese suburb, Leopoldstadt. Before the infant was a year old, his father was drowned in the Danube and his mother married another inn-keeper called Golder. At a very early age, Johann was presented by his stepfather with a cheap Bavarian fiddle, on which he taught himself to pick out all the tunes that came to his ears – especially those in 3/4 time. One day he shocked his stepfather by announcing that he wished to be a musician; but the inn-keeper would hear of nothing so vulgar and apprenticed him to a bookbinder. Bookbinding, however, was so little to his liking that after a short period of great misery he tucked his fiddle under his arm and ran away, without any clear idea of where he was going or how he was to keep himself. He had not been away many hours before he was discovered, asleep on the slopes of the Kahlenberg, by a friend, who promptly took him home to his parents.

The escapade, however, bore excellent fruit, for this friend now persuaded Johann's parents to let him be taught the violin and the viola and even, in due course, to join a restaurant band conducted by a gifted though disreputable musician named Pamer, first at an inn called 'The Golden Pear' and later at the fashionable Sperlsaal (popularly known as 'the Sperl'). When he was fifteen, Johann joined forces with a friend, four years his senior, called Josef Lanner; and the pair, together with two other youths, formed a quartet, which went around playing at all the smaller inns of the district. It was a happy, carefree period in Johann's life. The young players made music, earned money, spent it as soon as earned, indulged almost daily in practical jokes of every kind and took no thought for the future. The quartet prospered so well that after a while Lanner augmented it into an orchestra of twelve, with Johann as first violin and 'leader'; with the result that the two friends were henceforward to be seen at the larger and more fashionable inns and rose several degrees in the social scale. At this point Lanner began to feel that the waltz tunes in his repertoire were feeble, banal, four-square, primitive affairs; and, though he had never been taught composition or orchestration, he set to work to try and write something better. In this endeavour he was so successful that he soon found it easy to sell his waltzes to such famous publishers as Diabelli and Haslinger. Meanwhile the orchestra was in such great demand that Lanner decided to divide it into two sections, retaining the management of one himself and placing Johann in control of the other. This arrangement, unhappily, stimulated rival ambitions; the friendship became strained; and after a peculiarly violent quarrel the two decided to go their separate ways.

Waltz-mania in Vienna

In the year before his parting from Lanner, Johann had married a handsome young woman called Anna Streim; when, at the age of twenty-one, he became a father, he had to give up his thriftless habits and work hard to provide for his family. He began composing his own waltzes, and found – like Lanner – that there was an immediate market for them. He was acute enough to see that the tyranny of 3/4 time needed to be broken down by elasticity in the phrase-lengths, piquant orchestration, syncopation, and other devices. What Weber had done in his *Invitation to the Waltz*, he too would do. He took lessons in composition and orchestration and was not above borrowing thematic material from Beethoven and Meyerbeer. In a few years' time Johann had so far consolidated his position that he employed two hundred players, distributed among several bands, and had secured a six-year contract as musical director at the 'Sperl', the scene of his early apprenticeship under Pamer. Vienna was now waltz-mad. Chopin, coming there in 1830 with a view to giving some recitals, observed ruefully that 'the Viennese have turned their back on anything serious; Lanner and Strauss and their waltzes have put everything else in the shade'; Wagner, a couple of years later, found '*Zampa*-mania in the Josefstadt and Strauss-ecstasy everywhere; the waltz is a narcotic more potent than alcohol'.

Johann I Captures Berlin and Paris

By 1834, Vienna had become too small for Strauss, and in November of that year he took his orchestra to Berlin, where he had the formidable task of breaking down the Prussian's inborn aversion to anything emanating from Austria; but when the handsome young man, with his pale face, coal-black hair, burning eyes, and gypsy temperament, played his waltzes at the Konigstädter Theatre, all opposition melted away and he received an overwhelming ovation. In the next year or two he visited many other cities, not only in Germany but also in Holland and Belgium; and in 1837 he took an orchestra of twenty-eight players to Paris, then under the spell of Meyerbeer. In Paris, Strauss had to face the competition of the great Musard, playing quadrilles with an orchestra of nearly a hundred at his own hall in the Rue Vivienne, and of Dufresne, serving a more solid menu at the Salle St Honoré; he was therefore exceptionally nervous at his first concert, especially when he saw such celebrities as Auber, Cherubini, and Berlioz in the audience. But he need not have worried; the very novelty, both of the music and its execution, carried the day and he was again triumphant. A few weeks later, he played before King Louis Philippe, who received him with the utmost cordiality and rewarded him with a gift of 2,000 francs and a diamond pin. At this point, Musard deemed it prudent to enter into a partnership with Strauss for a series of thirty concerts, the Viennese playing one half of the programme and the Parisians the other. Berlioz, who had a keen ear for orchestral playing, thought very highly of Strauss's little band, especially the violins and wood-wind, and he laid special stress on its superiority to other bands in the vital matter of rhythm.

London, and a Breakdown in Health

In the autumn of 1837 Strauss embarked on a long tour, embracing the principal cities of France, Belgium, England, Scotland, and Ireland. In April 1838, he and his orchestra arrived in London, which was then *en fête* for the coming coronation of Queen Victoria and in the mood to spend money lavishly on virtuoso musicians. He played at Buckingham Palace, at the first State Ball to be given since the Queen's accession; at the Russian Embassy; at Almack's, Willis's Rooms, and many other fashionable resorts; and in the course of four months he gave no fewer than seventy-two London concerts, some of them in conjunction with the famous pianist-composer, Ignaz Moscheles, and the eleven-year-old 'prodigy' violinist, Teresa Milanollo. With difficulty dissuaded from visiting America after the coronation, he returned to France, where his players showed a tendency to revolt against overwork and a too long absence from home. During a second visit to England, in the autumn of 1838, Strauss was taken ill, decided that he could not recover in the English climate, crossed hurriedly to Calais, and collapsed while conducting a farewell concert there. He was taken to Paris, and thence home to Vienna, in a state of alarming weakness. He lay in bed for many weeks and then took a foolish risk by getting up to conduct at a ball at the Russian Legation. Half-way through the evening he collapsed again, and this time the doctors took a grave view of his condition and told his wife that it would probably be years before he could appear in public again. He was not made any happier by discovering that his eldest son Johann, for whom he planned a respectable business career, had been secretly receiving violin lessons from a member of the Strauss orchestra and appeared to have every intention of following in his father's footsteps.

Father and Son

In spite of the doctor's gloomy predictions, Strauss recovered from his illness in a few months and resumed his public appearances. At this point he became infatuated with a charming but quite uneducated young women called Emilie Trampusch; he set up house with her, and she bore him five children, the first of whom he had the effrontery to christen Johann. Deserted by her husband, Anna Strauss now determined that her own Johann should be properly trained as a musician and should in time avenge his father's insults by beating him on his own ground. By the time he was nineteen, Johann II was ready to face the world. He obtained from the magistrates a licence to provide an orchestra for entertainment in public places; in October 1844, he made his first appearance in the garden of Dommayer's famous restaurant. Supporters of his father among the audience raised a furious protest; but when he played a set of his own waltzes, ingratiatingly entitled *Die Gunstwerber* (Wooers of Favour), the opposition began to subside. The more he played of his own waltzes, polkas, and quadrilles, the greater the enthusiasm grew; and by the end of the programme it was clear that, both as fiddler and composer, the son was at least the equal of his father. At one o'clock in the morning, the crowds at Dommayer's refused to go home; then the young Johann did a very charming and touching thing. After gesturing for silence, he led his orchestra in his father's most popular waltz, *Loreley-Rheinklänge*. The audience was deeply moved; and finally his father's supporters, now completely won over to the young man, carried him shoulder-high from the platform.

Last Days of Johann I

Meanwhile Johann I had been appointed bandmaster of the First Bürger-Regiment (the Viennese civil militia) and his old friend Lanner of the Second. On the death of Lanner, the vacant position was given to Johann II; thus Vienna could enjoy the odd spectacle of two Johann Strausses conducting rival bands in rival uniforms. It was in his capacity of bandmaster that Johann I composed the famous *Radetzky March* to celebrate the victory gained over insurgent Italian armies by the Austrian General Radetzky in the German revolution of 1848. Since the General belonged to the Hapsburg faction and not to the Viennese Republican Party, Johann I was regarded as a 'reactionary' and began to receive abusive and threatening letters. Disturbed by this form of persecution, he left Vienna and took his orchestra on tour, meeting everywhere with a good deal of hostility. Finally, in the spring of 1849 he visited London, was received at Court and gave a highly successful benefit concert under royal patronage. But even in England the threatening letters from Republican partisans pursued him, and he was far from happy. In July he was back again in Vienna, where he found that politics were not such a disturbing factor as he had feared. An immense audience was present at his first concert, and his spirits began to revive. In September he caught scarlet fever from one of his own and Emilie's children, complicated by a cerebral inflammation, and in a few days he was dead. Emilie promptly packed everything up in a hurry and took herself and her children away; and when Josef (Anna's second son) came to the apartment he found his father's body lying almost uncovered on the floor.

Thousands of people attended the funeral procession of Johann I two days after his death; the members of his orchestra bore the coffin, and the leader, Amon, carried the dead master's violin, with its strings broken, on a black cushion. The funeral service was held in the Cathedral; a few days later a memorial service was held, at which Mozart's *Requiem* was sung and Johann II conducted the Strauss orchestra.

Johann II and Josef

Johann II now took over his father's orchestra, amalgamated it with his own, and devoted himself to carrying on his father's activities. Everywhere, and all the year round, the Strauss orchestra played. Like his father before him, Johann II was appointed director of the Court Balls and was expected to be present at all important functions; when he was not playing he was composing, for melodies 'gushed out', as he himself expressed it, 'like fresh water'. He was, in fact, a more talented composer, if a less inspired player, than his father; he conceived a great admiration for the music of Wagner, and indeed it was he who gave the first performance in Vienna of excerpts from *Lohengrin* and *Tannhäuser*.

It was not long before overwork brought its inevitable result; when he was only twenty-eight, he collapsed one morning in a faint, was found to be seriously ill, and was ordered to take a long rest. Who was now to direct the Strauss orchestra? His younger brother Josef must come to the rescue. Josef was an architect by profession; though he had enjoyed playing pianoforte duets with his brother in their boyhood, he was not a musician and had little desire to be one. The suggestion that he should give up the work that really interested him and direct the family enterprises, even for a limited period, was at first coldly received; in the end he let himself be persuaded and set to work with methodical assiduity to fit himself for the task. He worked hard at the violin and at theory; realizing that a conductor was also expected to compose, he managed to produce a waltz, which he diffidently entitled *The First and Last*. He had neither the striking good looks nor the magnetic personality of his father or his brother, but his very shyness and earnestness won the sympathy of the good-hearted Viennese public; by the time that Johann II returned from his convalescence it began to appear that once again there were to be two Strausses simultaneously in the field. The *First and Last* waltz had been so well received that Josef had been persuaded to produce another, to which he had given the whimsical title *The First after the Last*; then an astonishing thing happened: Josef, who had made a great fuss over producing one waltz, suddenly developed an amazing fecundity and produced over two hundred compositions in the course of about seventeen years.

Three Brothers

In 1854, while Johann II was on holiday at Gastein, he was approached by a railway director from Russia and offered a munificent salary if he would accept the position of conductor during the summer seasons at the Petropaulovsky Park near St Petersburg. Johann accepted the offer and became a person of some eminence in Russia during those summers, the Czar being a frequent and enthusiastic patron of his concerts. While Johann was thus engaged in Russia, Josef remained in charge of the Strauss orchestra in Vienna; the work was heavy, and in 1859 Johann I's third son, Eduard, was called in to assist. Eduard, at that time a young man of twenty-four with ambitions to enter the diplomatic service, was the most industrious, patient, conscientious, and even-tempered of the three brothers. (It was due to him that in 1870, when Josef died, the orchestra was not disbanded but was maintained, under his leadership, for another thirty years.) Eduard made his début at a great festival held at the Diana dance-hall in February 1859; for this occasion the orchestra was divided into three sections, each of them conducted by one of the three brothers, until the final gallop, which was played by the complete orchestra. The typical 'Strauss waltz' had meanwhile undergone further changes under Johann II, who saw that the best way of development lay along the lines of more extended introductions and codas, more contrasted themes and longer-breathed phrases.

The Blue Danube

In 1860 Johann II made the acquaintance of a gracious and talented lady, Jetty Treffz, who had at one time been a celebrated opera singer but had now retired and was living with Baron Moritz Tedesco whom she had been unable to marry because he was a Jew and she a Catholic. Johann fell violently in love with her, and after a while thei mutual affection grew to such a pitch that the lady made a frank confession to the Baron and asked for her freedom. With great magnanimity, the Baron not only gave his consent but made a generou settlement on her, and she was married to Johann in the St Stefan Cathedral in 1862. He was now a comparatively rich man, and Jetty persuaded him to take things a little easier. Josef and Eduard were to take over the bulk of the work, and Johann was only to conduct or occasions of special importance. Composition, however, was anothe matter. In 1867 Johann Herbeck, conductor of the famous Vienn Men's Choral Association, expressed himself as dissatisfied with th meagre male-voice repertoire then available and asked Johann t compose a choral waltz. Inspired by a poem by Karl Beck, in whicl the words 'the Danube, the beautiful blue Danube' came at the en of each stanza, Johann produced the music of his famous *Blue Danub Waltz*, and the Choral Association's lyric writer, one Josef Weyl wrote some singularly bad words to fit it. Its first performance, at th Dianasaal on 13 February 1867, was not a great success, and nobody could have guessed that within six months its sale would be runnin into seven figures. Later in the same year Johann II made a triumphan appearance in Paris, in connexion with the World Exhibition; late still, he visited London at the invitation of the Prince of Wale (afterwards Edward VII), gave six concerts at Covent Garden, an commemorated his visit by composing a waltz and a quadrille base on English tunes. In the next few years there followed *Geschichten au dem Wienerwald*, *Wein Weib und Gesang*, *Neu-Wien*, *Tausend und Ein Nacht*, and many more waltzes well-known the world over.

Death of Josef

Meanwhile, as Johann II's life became easier, Josef's became mor strenuous. He enjoyed neither the robust physique nor the philosophi equanimity so necessary for a busy conductor and was therefore poorl equipped to deal with the numerous contretemps so apt to arise in th tricky business of concert-giving. In the course of one of a series c concerts that he conducted in Warsaw, in the summer of 1870, misunderstanding among the players caused a breakdown in pe formance. Josef was panic-stricken, collapsed in a faint, fell off the platform on to the floor of the hall and was taken home with a bleeding nose and a wound in the head. The doctors diagnosed concussion of the brain, and his condition was so grave that his wife was hurriedly sent for from Vienna. After some weeks he was brought home, in the hope that Viennese doctors might save his life, but a few days later he died. He was only forty-three. Though less popular, perhaps, than either of his brothers, he was deeply mourned, for his contemplative nature and the distinctive quality of his music had found many admirers. Polkas were his special forte, and it is not generally realized that the delightful *Pizzicato Polka*, usually ascribed to Johann II, was in fact the joint production of Johann II and Josef.

Johann II Turns to the Theatre

It was at about this time that Jetty Strauss persuaded her husband, not without great difficulty, to emulate the successes of such composers as Offenbach and Suppé and to try his hand at an operetta. His first essay in this medium, *Die Lustigen Weiber von Wien*, was never produced, because the leading lady demanded by him was not available. He wrote another, *Indigo und die vierzig Räuber*, which succeeded in spite of a poor libretto; and a third, *Karneval in Rom*, with which he was not very satisfied. At last Richard Genée and Karl Haffner provided him with the libretto of *Fledermaus*, and he knew that this was what he had been waiting for. He threw himself into the task with furious energy, and in just over six weeks the music was finished. *Fledermaus* was produced at the Theater an der Wien in April 1874; it completely missed fire. The people of Vienna, still suffering from the effects of a disastrous financial crash in the previous year, were not in the mood for high spirits, and the operetta ran for only sixteen performances. In Berlin, however, it was better appreciated, and its success there (one hundred consecutive performances) caused the Viennese to revise their opinions when it was again presented in their city later in the same year. From then onwards its success everywhere was assured. Bruno Walter has described it in these terms: 'Beauty without heaviness, levity without vulgarity, gaiety without frivolity, and a strange mixture of exuberant musical richness (somewhat resembling Schubert) and popular simplicity.'

America and Italy

In 1876 Johann II visited Boston to take part in the celebration of the centenary of America's independence, and the good people of that city treated him to such an exhibition of hero-worship and adulation that his modest soul was profoundly shocked. He was no less shocked by what he considered to be the inartistic consequences of attempting to make music on an inflated scale. In a hall specially built for the occasion and holding a hundred thousand people, he found himself required to conduct a chorus of twenty thousand singers, with an orchestra to match, and needing the services of a hundred assistant conductors. The result, he reported afterwards, was 'an unholy row'. After this mammoth affair he conducted at several more concerts and balls, both in Boston and New York, before embarking thankfully on his return journey. He had not taken kindly to musical mass-production.

Next, Johann II took his orchestra on a tour of Italy. He made the discovery that Italy was his spiritual home, and the many operettas he composed from this time onward displayed a marked Italianate strain.

In 1877 Jetty Strauss died and Johann II married a young singer called Angelica Diettrich, thirty-three years his junior. The marriage was dismally unsuccessful, and Angelica left him five years later. At the age of fifty-eight, he married again – this time a charming widow, Adèle Deutsch, who restored his youth and made him extremely happy.

Zigeunerbaron, *and After*

The next event of importance in Johann II's career was the production, in October 1885, of the operetta *Zigeunerbaron* (The Gipsy Baron), inspired by a visit to Buda-Pesth. It created a furore, had a first run of over eighty consecutive performances in Vienna and quickly spread all over the civilized world. Three years later he wrote the *Kaiserwalzer* (Imperial Waltz) in honour of the Emperor Franz Josef, who had been forty years on the throne. It is regarded by connoisseurs as the most beautiful of all his waltzes.

In his latter years Johann II became very friendly with Brahms, who played the Strauss waltzes with great enthusiasm. Gustav Mahler adored him; Wagner, on his sixty-third birthday, asked an amateur orchestra to relieve his weariness with a programme of Straus waltzes; Liszt and Rubinstein both realized the possibilities of the waltzes as pianoforte solos.

In May 1899, Johann II contracted double pneumonia. He died in the following month and was buried near Schubert and Brahms.

The End of a Dynasty

At the time of Johann II's death his brother Eduard had been conductor of the Strauss orchestra for nearly thirty years, Johann having left it in his hands when he began writing operettas. Eduard took the orchestra all over the world, his programmes including, besides the Strauss compositions, a good deal of classical or semi-classical material, much of it specially arranged by his father, his brother Josef, or himself. The orchestra was engaged for the Inventions Exhibition in South Kensington, in 1885, when its daily concerts were a great attraction; and in 1890 Eduard took it on an extended tour in America – where he found that people were no longer inclined to dance in three-pulse measure, having been seduced by the 2/4 rhythms of John Philip Sousa. A little later Eduard lost the very considerable fortune he had amassed, owing to speculations by his wife and his two sons. Much litigation ensued and he became greatly embittered. In 1900 he made a second American tour and won back much of his lost capital; but on the return journey his players staged a mutiny against him because of his tyrannical methods, and when he arrived home he immediately and finally disbanded the orchestra his father had founded seventy-eight years before. He retired altogether from public life and lived on his memories. In 1907, in an extremity of bitterness, he employed a stove manufacturer to burn every sheet of the Strauss manuscripts – an operation that took no less than five hours to complete. He lingered on until 1916 – a year in which the tango and two-step were supreme and the waltz, as a measure for dancing, was in eclipse.

CHARLES LOUIS AMBROISE THOMAS

1811–96

MARTIN COOPER

Since the rehabilitation of Charles Gounod in the years immediately following the First World War, historians and critics of music have had to look elsewhere for a name to sum up all the iniquities of academicism, false sentiment, and meretricious stagecraft, which constituted in their eyes the 'Meyerbeer succession' in France. Meyerbeer himself found a defender in Bernard Van Dieren, Gounod was adopted by 'les Six', and Ravel had kind words for Saint-Saëns whose crimes were in any event not primarily operatic. No one, that I know, has ever found a kind word for Ambroise Thomas, who sixty years after his death has come to symbolize everything contemptible in musical composition. Many of his casual detractors have not heard a note of *Mignon* except the Gavotte and know nothing of *Hamlet*; but mud, once thrown, sticks, and it is convenient to have a name that can be used as a symbol of all one dislikes without having to go into boring details. It is not my intention to attempt a spectacular rescue of Thomas's reputation as a composer. His musical character was neither vigorous nor profound, he was neither strikingly original nor brilliantly gifted in any one direction; but neither, I believe, was he the contemptible 'reactionary' or the weak sentimentalist of legend. He was in many ways the typical conservatoire-director. That he was also a gifted composer of very much the second rank should not irrevocably damn him in the eys of a generation the directors of whose conservatoires are not outstandingly more gifted men and whose operatic composers would think themselves indeed fortunate if they could hope to write a *Hamlet*, let alone a *Mignon*, comparable with those of Thomas.

Ambroise Thomas was born at Metz, on the outskirts of France, that is to say, and he was therefore one of those 'peripheral' French composers – like Grétry, Hérold, Franck, and Ravel – who are none the less French for having a natural affinity with the artistic world of a neighbouring country. His father was a music-teacher and the boy was put to music at the age of 4. At the age of 17 he was sent to the Paris Conservatoire and became a pupil of Zimmermann (Gounod's future father-in-law) and Lesueur, the master of Berlioz and Gounod. In 1829 he won the first prize for pianoforte and in 1832 the Prix de Rome, Lesueur's seventh pupil to take the prize. His sensitive and emotional nature and his coming seventh in the scale of Lesueur's successes earned him the nickname of the '*note sensible*' (an untranslateable pun on the French term for the seventh degree of the scale). In Rome Thomas busied himself with chamber music and wrote a quintet, a quartet, and a trio. This last work, his *Trio*, Op. 3, earned a very fair and something like a final judgement which might be applied to all his music, from Schumann.

It is not heavy, not light, not classic, not romantic, not deep, not sickly, but always euphonious and in some places rich in fine melodies.

But it would have needed a most remarkable and unusual character to continue with chamber music in the 1830s, and the taste of the day and Thomas's own gifts and inclination made it inevitable that he should turn his attention to the opera. In fact his first work for the stage, the comic opera *La Double Échelle*, was given in Paris only five years after he had won the Prix de Rome, in 1837, and in the next twenty-three years (up to 1860, that is to say) Thomas wrote no less than seventeen opéras comiques, operas and ballets. A list of their names gives an insight into the taste of the period: 1838 *Le Perruquier de la Régence*; 1839 *La Gipsy* (ballet), and *Le Panier Fleuri*; 1840 *Carline*; 1841 *Le Comte de Carmagnole* (opera); 1842 *Le Guerrillero* (opera); 1843 *Angélique et Médor* and *Mina*; 1846 *Betty* (ballet); 1849 *Le Caïd*; 1850 *Songe d'une Nuit d'Été*; 1851 *Raymond ou le Secret de la Reine*; 1853 *La Tonelli*; 1855 *Le Cœur de Célimène*; 1857 *Psyché* and *Le Carnaval de Venise*; 1860 *Le Roman d'Elvire*.

This was, of course, the life of the ordinary eighteenth-century composer and as unlike that of the typical Romantic as could well be. Thomas had learned a trade and his business was to practise that trade to the best of his ability. It probably never occurred to him to question the artistic value of the genre in which he worked. The musical and dramatic idiom of the *opéra comique* as perfected by Auber he regarded as a datum, the material in which he worked. His business was to supply what the public wanted in as good a form as he knew how and, not being strikingly original by nature, the music he wrote was workmanlike and served its purpose excellently. It has not survived the disappearance of the genre from public favour any more than have the vast numbers of opera serias by Italian composers of the eighteenth century or the oratorios produced by conscientious English organists throughout the nineteenth. Not even Handel's music will make us accept the conventions of Italian *opera seria* and that of the young Thomas will certainly not resurrect the French *opéra comique* of a hundred years ago. The best, and probably one of the most typical, was *Le Caïd*, an extravagant Oriental comedy describing the adventures of a French adventurer in Egypt, with a comic sergeant-major and a soubrette heroine and a great deal of burlesque local colour. The music is frankly Italianate and the work owed part of its success to the fact that the first night coincided with a particularly brilliant performance of Rossini's *L'Italiana in Algeri* of which both music and plot of *Le Caïd* might almost be an intentional parody.

With the *Songe d'une Nuit d'Été* Thomas had a slightly different problem. *Le Caïd* and its predecessors had sprung from a world in which the humour and the choice of situations were still dictated by a taste formed by eighteenth-century standards and only half acknowledging the full Romantic flood that was engulfing all other art-forms from the thirties onwards. The midsummer night's dream, which depicted Queen Elizabeth falling in love with Shakespeare when visiting a noisy Bohemian party incognito, her constituting herself as his 'muse' and only just escaping from his violently amorous advances, was fully in the Romantic taste. The libretto is even more extravagantly silly than it sounds, but Thomas found in it an opportunity to express a certain delicate and almost timid Romantic feeling, a power of description, and a real though restricted sense of colour for which there had been no openings in his earlier works. In *Psyché* (1857) his librettists, Michel Carré and Jules Barbier, had presented the same kind of dramatization of a myth as they had produced six years earlier for Gounod in their *Sapho*. The throwing of a discreetly Romantic light over the landscape of ancient Greece suited Thomas as it had suited Gounod, and though *Psyché* has nothing like the dramatic power or the lyrical intensity of *Sapho*, the qualities of orchestral colour and musical workmanship employed for descriptive purposes are once again to the fore, as they had been in the *Songe d'une Nuit d'Été*.

Meanwhile success was coming to Ambroise Thomas in the form of official recognition. In 1852 he succeeded to Spontini's place in the Académie des Beaux Arts and in 1856 he was appointed Professor of Composition at the Conservatoire. Among his pupils were Théodore Dubois, a future director of the Conservatoire; Bourgault-Ducoudray, the scholar and folk-song expert, whose classes had such a strong influence on the next generation of Conservatoire pupils; and Massenet, in whom one side of Thomas's character found the perfect expression that he never quite achieved in his own music. For Lesueur's '*note sensible*' had not belied his nickname as he grew older. He had had thoughts of becoming a priest, and a discreet admirer could say of him, as of Gounod, at the end of his life that '*Saint Paul et les femmes se sont partagé son cœur avec la musique*'. But a native modesty or a weakness of dramatic fibre, or both, prevented Thomas from ever achieving in his music the whole-hearted sensuousness and the uninhibited dramatic representation of that eternal and unrelieved femininity that was Massenet's contribution to the operatic repertory. It is not easy to obtain a very clear idea of Thomas as a teacher from the '*enseignement doux parfois, et vigoureux aussi, où semblait se mêler le miel de Virgile aux saveurs plus âpres du Dante*'. Was Massenet describing a real experience in deliberately beautiful language or simply delivering himself of pious phrases by the side of his old master's grave?

The longest interval in the list of his works up to date separates the *Roman d'Elvire*, the failure of 1860, from *Mignon*, Thomas's masterpiece, which was produced on 17 November 1866. He himself was not conscious of having so excelled all his previous efforts, but in fact *Mignon* stands head and shoulders above everything he had written hitherto. He was 55 when it appeared, successful but not in the same rank as Gounod nor with anything like the wide reputation of Saint-Saëns. Was it the success of *Faust* in 1859 that, consciously or not, inspired him to achieve a new height? Partly, I think; for the music of *Mignon* has an undoubted affinity with Gounod, which is much less marked in the *Songe d'une Nuit d'Été* and *Psyché*. The novelty of *Faust* is difficult for the twentieth century to understand, but all Gounod's contemporaries were aware of it. Although the music contains plenty of Meyerbeerian fingerprints, *Faust* really marks the first successful break-away from the Meyerbeerian domination of the French operatic world. Gounod's natural lyricism, the simplicity and unaffectedness of the best of his melodies and the genuine sentiment that inspired them were something new in 1860. Ever since Meyerbeer's *Robert le*

Diable (1831) the spectacular element and what can only be described as 'stagey' effectiveness had dominated grand opera in France. Gounod in *Faust* and Thomas in *Mignon* made a real revolution, though they retained many Merybeerian features in the cut of their melodies and a tendency to stop the gaps of musical inspiration with effective noise. Both turned to Goethe for a libretto and Michel Carré and Jules Barbier as librettists. It was Goethe treated '*à la française – avec un mélange de grâce aimable and de logique un peu bourgeoise*,' as one critic aptly expressed it. But whereas Gounod's music was pre-eminently lyrical and emotional, *Mignon* contained rather a '*musique soignée, élégante, moins inspirée que délicatement ouvragée, moins originale par le pensée que variée par le tour et la recherche ingénieuse des sonorités, plus symphonique assurément que dramatique, un peu madrigalesque mais en tout cas pleine d'interêt*,' as the same critic described it. (It is interesting to see how the negatives of Schumann's early criticism have never fully developed into unhesitating affirmatives, as though it were always easier to say what Thomas's music was not than to define its positive qualities.) One thing is clear – although Thomas learned much from Gounod and in many ways resembled him, there is no question of mere imitation: Thomas's talent was perhaps a small thing, but it was essentially his own.

In *Hamlet*, which appeared two years later (1868), he attempted a theme with which he was eminently unsuited to cope. There can be no question of making an opera of Shakespeare's play: that was clear to everyone, fortunately including the librettists (again Carré and Barbier). The libretto does in fact tell a perfectly intelligible and interesting story and Thomas's music, which seems rather obviously theatrical to modern taste, is eminently suited to the libretto. Since *Mignon* there had been a strange interchange of musical civilities in Paris, which was not without its effect on Thomas's music. Verdi, invited to write a work for the Opera, had in 1867 produced his *Don Carlos* there: and in planning his score for the Parisian public, he had borrowed not a little of the manner of Meyerbeer, the genius loci as he imagined. In actual fact, *Faust* had, as we have seen, inaugurated something like a new era in French operatic history, so that Verdi had unconsciously slightly miscalculated his effect. Thomas, on the other hand, was very struck by Verdi's music and in *Hamlet* the influence of Meyerbeer is really no longer direct but makes itself felt in a foreign, Italianate form undoubtedly traceable to Verdi. The opera was a great success. Marmontel described it as a '*suprême exemple d'éclectisme, reliant les fougeux élans mélodiques des maîtres italiens à la science de l'école allemande, fortifiée elle-même par l'expression vraie du drame, qualité toute française.*' In actual fact Thomas was never more than a mediocre melodist and the most successful scenes are not the lyrical but the dramatic. The famous ghost scene and Hamlet's scene with his mother have real dramatic power and beauty, provided that a modern audience can be persuaded to accept the musical and dramatic idiom and not to expect something that Thomas never intended to give – namely either the rich metaphysical overtones of Shakespeare or a stark realistic tragedy in the Mussorgsky manner. Thomas's *Hamlet* is the story of a Second Empire palace revolution, as legitimate an interpretation of the facts as our own Elizabeth version, but quite different. The part of Hamlet, originally written for a tenor, was re-written for the baritone Fauré and the great Ophelia was Galli-Marié, though she did not take the part in the first performance. The score is interesting for what is, I think, the operatic début of the saxophone.

The successes of *Mignon* and *Hamlet* won Thomas the Directorship of the Conservatoire on the death of Auber (1869), though the appointment was not made until 1871, after the war and the commune. For all his 60 years Thomas, as a Lorrainer, insisted on doing all he could to help the national cause in the war and the annexation of his native province to Germany was a bitter blow to him. During the last twenty-five years of his life his main interest lay in the Conservatoire, into whose constitution he introduced several important reforms. He instituted lectures on the general history of music and appointed Bourgault-Ducoudray, in whose classes many of the innovations he so suspected were first hatched. An orchestral class and compulsory vocal classes for sight-reading were begun and in general he did his best to raise the standard of tuition in all branches and to increase the professors' salaries and the general budget of the whole institution. His only work of note after *Hamlet* was *Françoise de Rimini* (1882), but his vein of invention was exhausted and the work had only a *succès d'estime*. It was in these last years of his life that he won a name for uncomprehending and bigoted conservatism, exactly as the old Cherubini had done half a century earlier. The violence of his refusal to admit Fauré to a professorship testifies to the sureness of musical instinct that smelt innovation where less sensitive musicians could see only drawing-room grace and insipidity: but it is also, I think, to be explained by the bitterness of a disappointed man. Lesueur's '*note sensible*' had become 'Monsieur de Sombre-Accueil' in his old age. Thomas's two notable successes had come at the end of an era in French music and with the growth of the Société Nationale, and the sudden flowering of a younger generation of musicians in the years immediately after the Franco-Prussian War, he was left stranded, the representative of an older musical world, *vieux jeu* within a few years of his triumphs. Gounod and Saint-Saëns, with many more strings to their bows, could make places for themselves in the new world, even if they were no longer leaders. Thomas was too small a man and he took refuge in conscientious administration and the safeguarding, as he saw it, of the eternal values of the art that, give him his due, he understood thoroughly in his limited way. After all, it is the business of Conservatoires to conserve, just as it is the business of rebels and innovators to rebel and innovate; and music would be in a poor way if either failed in their duty. Thomas was right to disapprove of Debussy's early audacities: too many conservatoire-pupils rebel against strict discipline and merely become slovenly hack-writers without any distinction. Debussy was right to rebel; but only time and experience could prove his justification and the 'blood of the martyrs is the seed of the church' in the Conservatoire as everywhere else. Massenet's loyal tribute to his old master, rather too beautiful and a little unprecise, is nevertheless a fitting epitaph to Thomas's long life spent entirely in the service of music. '*A le voir passer si simple et si calme dans la vie, enfermé dans son rêve d'art, qui de nous, habitués à le sentir toujours à nos côtés, pétri de bonté et d'indulgence, s'était aperçu qu'il fallait tant lever la tête pour le bien regarder en face?*'

GIUSEPPE VERDI

1813–1901

FRANCIS TOYE

Early Days

Perhaps the most important thing to remember about Giuseppe Verdi is that he was born a peasant and, in many respects, remained a peasant at heart until the day of his death. His father was in fact an inn-keeper, but differed in no way from the other peasants of the tiny hamlet of Le Roncole near Busseto, a small town in the plain of Parma. This plain, wind-swept, muddy, and often fog-bound in the winter, sun-baked and dusty in the summer, has nothing of the idyllic about it; the hardness of life there during boyhood may explain the roughness and the stubbornness as well as the practicality and the integrity of Verdi's character.

Young Verdi, though not in the least remarkable for precociousness like Rossini or Mozart, showed signs of musical sensitiveness at an early age. The playing of the organ in church and the performance of an old wandering violinist, outside his father's inn, exercised an irresistible fascination on him. A broken-down spinet, bought for him by his father, was such an important part of the secret life of his boyhood that he kept it all his life; it was perhaps the only real friend of his childhood. By the time he was ten years old his aptitude for music had become so evident that his father, to his eternal credit, decided to send him to Busseto. The little boy had already learnt enough from the local organist himself to play the organ in the church, but further instruction, alike in music and letters, was indispensable.

By a stroke of good fortune there lived in Busseto a friend of his father's, Antonio Berezzi, a grocer, who was one of the most active spirits in the local Philharmonic Society. Barezzi, struck by the boy's seriousness and application – he still once or twice a week trudged six miles to Le Roncole and back in order to keep his yearly salary of 100 lire as village organist – offered him employment in his business. This meant that he was brought into close contact with all the activities of the Philharmonic Society and enjoyed the use of his employer's piano. Meanwhile his musical studies were continued with one Provesi, the director of the society and organist of the local cathedral, and it was about this time (1828) that Verdi wrote his first compositions, which may still be seen in the archives at Busseto: orchestral pieces for the Philharmonic Society, church music, and a few piano duets for himself and Margherita, Barezzi's attractive daughter. Thus early Verdi acquired the habit of writing music to fulfil practical requirements that continued during the whole of his active career.

It must not be imagined that these compositions possess much value, though they were considered remarkable enough at the time to win him a certain local fame and popularity. More important still, they convinced Barezzi and Provesi that it was imperative for him to be sent to Milan to pursue his studies further. Thanks to a local charitable trust, and the private generosity of Barezzi himself, sufficient money was provided for the purpose; and at the end of May 1832, Giuseppe Verdi went to Milan.

Tragedy and Triumph

One of the first things that Verdi did in Milan was to apply for admission to the Conservatoire. It was refused him. The fact has often been cited as one of the classical instances of academic ineptitude, but not altogether with justice. His compositions were in all probability more remarkable for their mere existence than for any outstanding merit; his method of playing the piano must have been distinctly provincial; his personal appearance awkward and unattractive. Besides he was eighteen, while fourteen was the maximum age of the usual candidate. To admit him at all the examiners would have had to waive the rules; they decided not to do so. Events have proved that they made a bad mistake, but it is unfair to blame them excessively.

Young Verdi, though much discouraged, was not beaten. Advised to go to a private teacher called Lavigna, he pursued his studies with such assiduity that that fortunately competent musician had every reason to be satisfied with his progress. By a lucky accident, moreover, he attracted attention to himself by his skill in accompanying a choral society of ladies and gentlemen who were rehearsing Haydn's *Creation*, so that he eventually directed one of their concerts and wrote a wedding cantata for the president of the society.

Suddenly news reached him that his old master, Provesi, was dead and that his friends in Busseto expected him to return to carry on his functions. The ecclesiastical authorities, however, who seem to have been at war with Barezzi and the Philharmonic Society, refused to accept him as organist, so that he had to content himself with the directorship of the society, his meagre salary being augmented by various perquisites. For three years he remained at Busseto, during which time he married Barezzi's daughter, Margherita, and worked at the music to an opera libretto given him by the conductor of the amateur choral society in Milan.

In February 1839, his engagements at Busseto terminated. Verdi, with his eighteen-year-old wife and their two little children, Icilio and Virginia, moved to Milan, where he had hopes of getting his opera produced. Though his friend the conductor had severed connexion with the theatre, he was eventually able to place it with the impresario of La Scala, and here, on 17 November 1839, *Oberto, Conte di San Bonifacio*, the first Verdi opera, was given to the world. It achieved what we should now describe as a *succès d'estime*, but the success was genuine enough to induce the impresario, Merelli, to entrust him with a second opera for the following year.

In the meantime tragedy descended on Verdi. His young and adored wife, Margherita, died. The two children she had borne him, Virginia and Icilio, had also died during the two preceding years, so that now, whilst working on the opera that, to complete the irony of the situation, was comic, Verdi had lost everything that was most dear to him in the world. In the circumstances it is scarcely surprising that the opera, when eventually produced, proved an utter failure. Indeed it is probably true to say that this sequence of tragic events left an indelible impression on Verdi's character.

His first reaction was to fly from music in any form, and, had it not been for the tact and kindness of Merelli, he might never have written another opera. But Merelli, who believed in Verdi, literally thrust upon him a libretto on the subject of Nebuchadnezzar. At first Verdi refused to have anything to do with it, but he eventually read it and, as he read, found the music spring to his mind. Thus was born the opera *Nabucco*, destined, when it was produced at La Scala on 9 March 1842, to lay the foundation stone of Verdi's fame and fortune. No question of the success not being genuine on this occasion! *Nabucco* enjoyed a veritable triumph and made Verdi the fashion, ties, hats, and sauces being named after him. Even today we can sense the quality of the music. Of all the early operas of Verdi, *Nabucco* is the one that still remains the most alive.

Some Early Operas

Just a little less than a year later, Verdi's second opera, *I Lombardi* (1843), was produced at La Scala. The work is interesting, not only because it provided the first instance of those disputes with the Austrian censorship that were so frequent in Verdi's career, but because, even more than with *Nabucco*, the Italian public identified themselves with the patriotic aspirations uttered on the stage. The idea of independence was fermenting strongly in Italy just at the time, and undoubtedly two of the reasons for Verdi's early success were his close association with the movement and the new strength and fervour of his music, which in this respect differed entirely from that of his great predecessors, Donizetti, Bellini, and Rossini.

These attributes of Verdi became even more marked in *Ernani*, an opera produced in Venice in 1844. This is scarcely surprising, for not only was the subject itself suspect to those in authority, but Victor Hugo, the author of the play from which the libretto was taken, was the very embodiment of romantic liberalism. *Ernani* was the occasion of many patriotic demonstrations in the theatre, the hero becoming identified with any proscribed patriot and the words of one of the choruses being changed into a tribute to Pius IX, who was regarded at the time as the most probable saviour and unifier of Italy.

Apart from any question of patriotism, *Ernani* deserved its success, for there are some magnificent pages in it, notably in the last two acts. Its outstanding characteristic may be defined, perhaps, as an almost brutal sincerity of emotion, and, as the subject demands, there is a greater human interest in it than in any of its predecessors. Its fame soon spread beyond Italy. It may be said to have done for Verdi in Europe what *Nabucco* and *I Lombardi* had done in Italy. Incidentally, it was the occasion of first bringing him into association with Piave, the resident poet and stage-manager of the Fenice Theatre, who was destined to provide the libretti for so many of his best-known operas.

During the next two years Verdi wrote four operas: *I Due Foscari* (1844), *Giovanna d'Arco* (1845), *Alzira* (1845), and *Attila* (1846). The last is certainly the best of them, for here again we have a taste of the strength and sincerity that were Verdi's most valuable attributes as an opera composer. But the opera immediately succeeding it was on a different plane altogether. This was *Macbeth*, produced in Florence in 1847. It reflects a more cultured attitude, the product perhaps of the new friendships recently made by the composer. It also provides the first instance of that passion for Shakespeare which Verdi kept during the whole of his life. Most important of all, it shows the composer as attempting something new, something that may not unreasonably be called Music Drama. For this reason Verdi experienced considerable trouble with his singers, to whom, in any event, the concept of a serious opera without a love interest was utterly strange. Verdi was inflexible, as always, in his demands, and in the end the opera achieved a great success, the new orchestral effects and the power of the declamatory writing arousing especial praise.

The value that Verdi himself attached to *Macbeth* is shown by the dedication of it to Barezzi and by the fact that some twenty years later he found the score attractive enough to subject it to a complete revision. In this revised form *Macbeth* has been successfully revived in recent years.

In the summer of 1847 Verdi was invited to London by Lumley, the impresario of Her Majesty's Theatre, to write an opera for Jenny Lind. A couple of his operas had already been heard in England where Chorley of the *Athenaeum* and Davison of *The Times* disliked them almost as much as they were later to dislike the music of Richard Wagner, both denying him any gift for melody whatsoever! Nevertheless, the opera in question, *I Masnadieri*, was a fair success, though it would be idle to pretend that it is an opera of any particular distinction. Biographers have written that Verdi much disliked London. This is inaccurate except as to the climate. He was much impressed by the city itself, writing to a friend in Italy that 'if only London had the climate of Naples there would be no need to sigh for paradise'.

At any rate he seems to have preferred London to Paris, where he went after the production of *I Masnadieri*. The object of his visit was the production at the Opéra of a French version of *I Lombardi*, which eventually materialized as *Jérusalem*. Probably the most interesting aspects of Verdi's Paris stay were personal. First he paid visits to poor dying Donizetti; secondly, he frequented the society of a lady called Giuseppina Strepponi, who, on her retirement from the operatic stage, had settled there as a singing teacher. She had already made friends with Verdi in the early days at Milan, but from now onwards she was destined to play in his life a role of ever-increasing importance.

A Trilogy of Favourites

The year 1848, heavy with revolutionary troubles in many Euro-pean countries, witnessed the first abortive attempt to achieve Italian independence. As an ardent patriot Verdi was inevitably very much concerned, contributing to the common cause a patriotic opera called *La Battaglia di Legnano*, which in fact possessed musical as well as patriotic merits. From the musical point of view, however, it cannot be compared in interest with his next opera, *Luisa Miller* (1849), founded on Schiller's *Kabale und Liebe*, which must be regarded as one of the milestones in his career. Hitherto Verdi had dealt exclusively with broad emotions on the heroic scale; the woes of Luisa are tender and intimate, the forerunners of the more familiar woes of the immortal *La Traviata*.

We come to what may be called the trilogy of Verdi's most popular operas in 1851, when, after an exceptionally arduous contest with the Censorship, *Rigoletto* was produced in Venice. The tragi-comedy of this contest is related in full in my book on Verdi. It must suffice here baldly to state that the Censorship objected to almost everything in Victor Hugo's *Le Roi s'Amuse*, from which Piave had adapted the libretto; the King, the Hunchback, even the sack containing Gilda's body! When, however, the difficulties were finally adjusted and *Rigoletto* was produced, it immediately achieved the greatest success from a purely musical point of view that Verdi had yet experienced. What is more, the success was deserved. Even Piave could not spoil Victor Hugo's fine story, whereof the dramatic qualities were so much enhanced by the music that Victor Hugo himself, who started with violent prejudice against the opera, became one of its warmest admirers. We can still sense the extraordinary quality of this music in which orchestra and voice alike combine to heighten the poignancy of the situations. The famous quartet in the last act remains to this day one of the acknowledged operatic masterpieces of the world, so truly does every character express itself in the music; even a popular tune like *La Donna è Mobile* serves a dramatic purpose when heard in its proper place in the opera. There is something sombre and rugged in the simplicity of *Rigoletto* that entitles it to be called truly great, and it always remained one of Verdi's especial favourites.

The second of the trilogy, *Il Trovatore*, made its appearance in Rome in 1853. Verdi had written it even more rapidly than *Rigoletto*, in fact in four weeks, but the reader must be warned that Verdi gave his operas a great deal of preliminary thought before he began to write the music down. Its success rivalled that of *Rigoletto*, and it still remains probably the most popular of Verdi's operas. When sung as it should be sung (which rarely happens nowadays), the quality of the music, though more democratic than that of *Rigoletto*, is very striking. These magnificent tunes possess a vitality and a sincerity that compel our allegiance, though it may be admitted that the orchestration is in no way remarkable. Verdi, who had been deeply affected by the recent death of his mother, obviously translated much of his emotion into the portrayal of the relations betwen Azucena and her son, and the story is not in reality nearly so absurd as is usually supposed.* *Il Trovatore* may be summed up as essentially an expression in music of the hot-blooded romantic drama of chivalry.

La Traviata, the third opera of the trilogy, produced in Venice in 1853, was, unlike its predecessors, a complete failure at first. The singers were mainly responsible; they sang badly to begin with, not understanding the new, intimate nature of the music, and the plumpness of the prima donna who, as everybody knows, has to die of consumption in the last act, made everybody laugh. It was not till its revival a year later that *La Traviata* entered upon its career of triumph. It is difficult for us now to understand that the opera was regarded as even more erotic, even more subversive of morality, than Dumas' *La Dame aux Camélias* on which it is founded. The English critics in particular were much shocked by it. In a sense this is the best possible tribute to its merits, for, beyond question, Verdi's music gave to the merely theatrical effectiveness of Dumas' play a quality altogether more sincere and more fundamental. From the technical point of view *La Traviata* is principally interesting perhaps as rising once again to the orchestral distinction of *Rigoletto*. As a work of art it may claim to be classed as genuine music drama, in that the music is throughout linked with and conditioned by the movement of the drama.

'Viva Verdi'

Between 1853 and 1858 Verdi divided his time in the main between his country estate at Sant'Agata, just outside Busseto, and Paris. He had bought Sant'Agata some five years previously, a farm of moder-

* A complete and, I hope, a lucid account of it will be found on page 311 of my book on Verdi.

ate dimensions, with vines and arable land, on which he had since spent a good deal of money in improving the house and the property. There can be little doubt that he passed the happiest days of his life there, for, except for a short period in early manhood, he always preferred the country to the town. Thoroughly conversant with the practical details of farming, he himself managed the estate, ruling it with the same iron discipline as he demanded in the theatre. Some time during this period, much to the scandal of certain worthies in Busseto, he took Giuseppina Strepponi to reside with him in Sant'Agata, where he lived the life of a confirmed, though extremely hard-working, recluse.

One of his main artistic preoccupations was the preparation of a libretto on the theme of Shakespeare's *King Lear*, a subject that always attracted him. He never, in fact, set it to music, though on one occasion he would undoubtedly have done so but for the accident that a suitable cast was not available at the moment. Till the very end of his life, however, he never entirely abandoned the idea.

His frequent and long visits to Paris were due to the invitation to write an opera on the occasion of the Great Exhibition of 1855. Verdi disliked and despised Paris, but it was at that time the cultural capital of Europe, and to be asked, as he was, to set to music an opera by Scribe for such an event set the seal on his reputation as an international composer. The opera in question, *I Vespri Siciliani*, caused Verdi a great deal of worry. Scribe's libretto offended his patriotic susceptibilities, and there was endless trouble at rehearsal, eventually surmounted only by his inflexible determination. It was finally produced in June 1855, with considerable, though not overwhelming success. Perhaps its main interest to us nowadays is that it shows for the first time traces of Meyerbeer's influence on Verdi, though some of the music remains as individual as it is delightful.

After a battle royal with the Théâtre Italien, he returned to Sant' Agata, where he occupied himself with the music to two operas, one *Araldo*, which was in fact a revised version of a previous opera, *Stiffelio* of no particular importance, and another, *Simon Boccanegra*, produced in Venice in 1857, which is one of his most significant works. *Boccanegra* always remained one of Verdi's own favourites; twenty years later he persuaded Boito to revise the libretto, and he himself revised the score. It is true that the best parts of the music date from this joint revision, but there is much even in the original score of the opera to command respect and admiration, though it was not in fact well received in Venice at the time. Apparently the opera struck contemporary Italian taste as too gloomy and cold.

In January 1858, Verdi sailed from Genoa to Naples to produce the opera now known as *Un Ballo in Maschera.* This, a setting of a play by Scribe about Gustavus III of Sweden, for which Auber had already written music, is perhaps the most interesting of all Verdi's earlier operas. To begin with, it was the occasion of his most famous contest with the Censorship, which, frightened by the attempted assassination of Napoleon III, was even more unreasonable than usual. It would have nothing to do with a libretto that portrayed not only the assassination but the loose character of a reigning price. The disappointed Neapolitans took up the cudgels on behalf of Verdi, whom they identified with the Italian national cause, placarding the walls with '*Viva Verdi*', a seditious acrostic on '*Viva Vittorio Emmanuele, Re d'Italia*', the first letters of the last five words forming by a fortunate coincidence the name of the composer. Finally the production was moved to Rome, where the impresario of the Apollo Theatre mollified the Papal Censorship by transferring the action to Boston, of all unlikely and unsuitable places in the world.

Apart from these alarums and excursions *Un Ballo in Maschera* (1859) is of interest in that it marks yet another development in Verdi's style. The new elaboration and the original touches in the orchestration, the new sense of humour shown in the Conspirators' Chorus and Oscar's music, combine to make the opera not only charming in itself but exceptionally important as foreshadowing the attributes of Verdi's music in his later and greater compositions.

Farming and Politics

Music played but little part in Verdi's life during the next two years. He had been working continuously at high pressure for a long time and he felt the need of a rest. This, however, he found rather in change of occupation than in inactivity. Even at Sant'Agata, where he spent most of the time, he was up at sunrise every morning attending to his crops, his garden, and his horses. Occasional excursions to Genoa with Giuseppina, shooting on the banks of the Po with the conductor, Mariani, with whom he had become very friendly, a game of cards or billiards in the evening, were his sole recreations. Of social life in the ordinary sense of the words there was none. He never even went to

Busseto if he could avoid it, for he never seems to have forgiven the malicious gossip about himself and Giuseppina, whom, it may here be mentioned, he formally married in April, 1859, on the very day the Austrians invaded Italy.

Inevitably the Austrian war disturbed the tranquillity of life at Sant' Agata. All the more so since he received an anonymous warning at the very outbreak of hostilities that the Austrian authorities, who still governed the Duchy of Parma, regarded him (with reason) as highly suspect. The war, however, was short; it was the peace that affected his life the more, for, at the peace, Cavour instituted the first Italian parliament and asked Verdi to stand as a candidate for election. Nothing could have been less palatable to him, but, since Cavour insisted, Verdi felt he could not disappoint a man for whom he felt such veneration and respect. He was elected deputy in 1860 and so remained until 1865, four years after Cavour's death. It cannot be said that Verdi played any glorious part in the deliberations of the Italian legislative assembly. Far too independent to belong to any party, he disliked equally the extreme Right and the extreme Left. His policy, as he himself confessed, was blindly to follow Cavour, who, in his eyes, could do no wrong. That is why he was never a Garibaldian, for Garibaldi and Cavour by no means saw eye to eye, though he much admired and sympathized with the former's expedition to Sicily and Naples.

St Petersburg, London, Paris

It was not till 1861 that music once again replaced farming and politics as the predominant interest in Verdi's life. The Imperial Theatre at St Petersburg wanted an opera, which eventually materialized as *La Forza del Destino*, with a libretto taken by Piave from a famous Spanish play. In January of the following year Verdi went to St Petersburg to supervise the production, which was, however, postponed, so that we find him in the spring in London, where he had been commissioned, as representative of Italy, to write a cantata for the International Exhibition of 1862. Perhaps the most interesting thing about this cantata, called *Inno delle Nazioni*, was that it first brought Verdi into association with Boito, who wrote the not very distinguished words. Apparently Boito's contribution was viewed by the authorities with even less favour than Verdi's music. Boito's poem ended with an aspiration for a free and united Italy, while the *Marseillaise*, still regarded as a revolutionary tune, figured prominently in Verdi's score. On one ex-cause or another the cantata was not performed at the Exhibition at all, but by Mapleson at Her Majesty's Theatre, where it achieved a considerable success.

In the autumn Verdi returned to St Petersburg for the production of *La Forza del Destino* (1862). It was not unreservedly successful, partly owing to Nationalist opposition, partly owing to the fact that Russian audiences expected Italian Opera to be light and fluent. Since *La Forza del Destino* is one of the gloomiest operas ever written, their disappointment is scarcely a matter of surprise. Even Verdi himself felt the ultra-Shakespearean massacre of all the characters at the end to be excessive and a few years later had the last scene changed. Perhaps the outstanding quality of the opera is its wealth of melody, in fact it contains some of the most beautiful and expressive tunes every written by the composer. For this reason it has always been a greater favourite with the public than with the critics, though in recent years it has been revived with marked success in Germany and Austria and does not lack admirers even in England.

Verdi contrived to pass the summer and autumn of the year 1863 at Sant'Agata, but his parliamentary duties often took him to Turin and professional business to Paris, where his revised version of *Macbeth* was produced in 1865 with only moderate success. Verdi was not himself present at the production, though he spent the winter in Paris negotiating for a new work to be produced at the Opéra itself. This was *Don Carlos*, with a French libretto adapted from Schiller's famous play of the same name. Verdi went home to write the music, but once again war broke out with Austria; he himself has told us that the music was written in the midst of flame and fire.' Even when he left Italy for France his troubles were by no means at an end, for the news of his father's death so upset him that he could not attend rehearsals for some time. Besides which there was a lawsuit between the management and a singer, which considerably retarded the production of the opera.

Finally, however, *Don Carlos* was produced in the early spring of 1867, being received with respect rather than enthusiasm. Some of Verdi's warmest admirers, notably Bizet, thought that he had capitulated not only to Meyerbeer but to Wagner; the opera was certainly too long, and people felt the absence of those direct and incisive strokes in which Verdi particularly excelled as a writer for the theatre. Nevertheless *Don Carlos*, apart from the numbers familiar to everybody and the auto-da-fé scene that so excited Théophile Gautier's enthusiasm, contains some splendid music. Those who have heard it will not easily forget the beauty of the love scenes or the magnificent interview between the Grand Inquisitor and the King of Spain, as fine as anything in operatic literature. Besides, without that striving after deeper significance characteristic of *Don Carlos* Verdi would never have been able to achieve the masterpiece of expressiveness that is *Aïda*.

Much Unhappiness

The day after the production of *Don Carlos* Verdi left Paris for Genoa, where he kept a flat for use during the winter months. He was, we know, delighted to go home again, for Paris, though of great importance in his career, was always distasteful to him. He especially disliked the worries and intrigues connected with the Opéra, to which he always contemptuously referred as '*La Grande Boutique*'.

Whatever expectations of peace and happiness he may have entertained were, however, destined to be disappointed, for the year 1867 was, as he himself said, one of the saddest in his whole life. In the summer his father-in-law, benefactor and life-long friend, Barezzi, died – a loss that Verdi felt most keenly. Then in December, Piave, to whom he was sincerely attached, had a stroke. Piave did not, in fact, die until eight years later, but he was unable to move or speak. Verdi generously rewarded his devoted, if not always felicitous, services as a collaborator by assuring the future of the illegitimate daughter on whom, apparently, with the exception of Verdi himself, all his interest and affection were exclusively concentrated.

The death of Rossini in 1868 led to another disturbing experience, though of a different kind. Verdi's relations with Rossini had always been friendly, though never intimate; the temperaments of the two men were too diverse to admit of real intimacy. But Verdi, who felt the death of Rossini as a national loss, thought that the musicians of Italy should make some gesture in honour of his memory. With this object in view he endeavoured to secure the collaboration of a dozen other Italian composers in writing a Requiem Mass to be performed in Bologna on the first anniversary of his death. Though he was under no illusions as to the artistic value of such a patch-work composition, he thought that in this instance national should outweight aesthetic considerations. Owing to jealousy or laziness or both the project came to nothing, and the fiasco touched Verdi to the quick, for, apart from any other consideration, he dearly loved having his own way.

Moreover there was a personal side to the matter. He had reason to hink that his intimate friend, the conductor Mariani, had not supported him as wholeheartedly as he should. It is said that Mariani, who was lso a composer, felt aggrieved at not being included among those sked to collaborate in the Mass. Whatever the reason, a breach was ormed between the two men and it was never to be healed. Indeed, it gradually became wider and wider. Verdi, the very soul of probity, hought he had reason to disapprove of certain personal actions of Mariani. Some, probably without reason, say that a further cause for lisagreement was found in the singer, Teresa Stolz, who was Mariani's wife in everything but name. The two men drifted further and further apart. Mariani, who had been the great Verdian conductor par excelence, went over bag and baggage to the Wagnerian camp; he was eventually responsible for those first performances of *Lohengrin* at Bologna that so delighted Wagner. When he died, miserable and lone, in 1873, Verdi merely sent a formal telegram of condolence to he relatives. It is rather a pitiful story.

Aïda *and the* Requiem Mass

In 1869 Verdi was offered a very large sum of money 'to write an opera for a very distant country.' He refused the offer at least twice, out changed his mind after having read a précis of the libretto, sent him by one of his Paris friends, in which he sensed, quite rightly, exceptional theatrical possibilities. The scenario – it was nothing more – was the work of one Mariette Bey, a Frenchman in close touch with he Khedive of Egypt, who wanted a new opera to celebrate the opening of the Suez Canal. But there was a great deal to be done before the opera we know as *Aïda* came to birth. To begin with, Mariette's story had to be turned into a regular operatic libretto, and in this Verdi himelf played an important part. Even when this had been accomplished and the music written, unexpected difficulties arose to delay the production of the opera. The chief of these was the Franco-Prussian war, or the scenery and costumes of *Aïda* were being made in Paris, and Paris was closely besieged by the Germans.

Finally, however, on Christmas Eve, 1871, *Aïda* was produced with he utmost magnificence in Cairo. Verdi himself had refused to go to Egypt, but he took considerable trouble in the selection of the cast and of conductor. The result was a triumphant success, for critics from taly and France were unanimous in asserting that Verdi, in his latest

opera, had broken entirely new ground. This was also the opinion o
both press and public when, six weeks later, *Aïda* was produced ir
Milan. Not everybody, however, found this new orientation to hi
taste. *Aïda* was accused, strangely enough, of being too 'metaphysical'
too complicated. Above all Verdi was reproached with having abandoned the Italian tradition in favour of new-fangled Wagneriar
theories.

It is difficult for us, to whom *Aïda* appears as the very quintessenc
of Italianism – for, despite their swarthy skins, the characters in th
opera belong, psychologically, wholly to Italy – to understand such a
attitude. At the time, however, the exceptional importance attache
to the orchestra, the comparative subservience of the set numbers t
free vocal declamation, must have seemed revolutionary to the Italiar
public, even though there was in fact nothing in *Aïda* that could no
be deduced from Verdi's previous operas. For this reason the charge o
imitating Wagner particularly annoyed him. It was not only not true
it was silly. Extraneous events served to exacerbate Verdi's resentment
The disasters of France in the Franco-Prussian war revealed him, perhaps to his own surprise, as an ardent Francophile. He deplored th
triumph of 'the barbarians'; thought that Italy, at whatever cost t
herself, should have thrown in her lot with France, prophesying, wit
much acumen, that the German victory must inevitably lead in th
end to another European war. He admired, we know, much o
Wagner's music, but Wagner seems to have come to represent in hi
eyes Germanism triumphant in the sphere of music as in the sphere o
war.

The death of Manzoni in 1873 turned his thoughts in other directions. He had, in his own words, venerated the author of *I Promes-
Sposi* like a saint, so he wrote to the municipality of Milan offering t
compose a *Requiem Mass* in his memory. The offer accepted, Verd
retired to Sant'Agata to write the music. He had already at his dispos
the final number, which he had composed for the ill-starred Rossir
Mass, beside other sketches that he had written in the meantime. Th
Mass received its first performance in May 1874, at the church of S
Mark, Milan, but immediately afterwards three further performanc
were given at La Scala, and, in the following year a European tour w
arranged, which included a performance in the Albert Hall.

Readers interested in the aesthetic questions raised by this magnificent work must be referred to my book on Verdi. Here there is onl

space to state the bare fact that the Mass, though it immediately achieved a great success in every country, aroused opposition in certain quarters owing to the theatricality of its idiom. Its genius was obvious at once to no less a person than Brahms, but the famous pianist and conductor, von Bülow, though he subsequently became one of its most fervent admirers, found nothing good to say of it in the first instance. Beyond question the Mass must be regarded essentially as a dramatic work, as was indeed inevitable with a composer so intimately linked with the theatre during his entire career. But this in no way detracts from the emotional sincerity that is in fact one of its outstanding characteristics; while its general vitality, the skill of the choral writing, the vivid colours of the orchestral score, remain as striking today as ever. Indeed it seems probable that the value set by musical opinion on Verdi's Mass at the present time is greater, not less, than that claimed for it by its contemporaries.

Two Musical Miracles

There was another definite break in Verdi's life after the tour of the Mass, when he settled down again at Sant'Agata. He was sixty-two years of age, tired, very pessimistic about political affairs in Italy. In all probability he never expected to write much more music. He devoted himself with greater assiduity than ever to his agricultural interests, attending the weekly stock market at Cremona, schooling his horses, and trying to induce the peasants to cultivate their vines properly.

It was not until 1879 that any serious musical project again occupied him. In the summer of that year his friends, Ricordi and the conductor Faccio, entered into a kind of benevolent conspiracy to bring him into contact with Boito. Boito, it will be remembered, had already provided him with the words for a cantata more than twenty-five years previously, but since then he had become very hostile to Verdi, favouring Wagner. After the Requiem Mass, however, his opinions changed completely and, though he had in the meantime himself achieved a great success with the opera *Mefistofele*, his keenest desire was to provide Verdi with a worthy opera libretto.

Things did not go too well at first. Verdi was a little suspicious, but, after Boito had shown proof of his goodwill by doing his best to revise the libretto of *Simone Boccanegra*, gave him not only his complete confidence but his warmest affection. Even then, however, the music progressed slowly, so that it was not till November 1886, that their joint masterpiece, *Otello*, was finished.

When it was produced at La Scala on 5 February 1887, *Otello* provided the world with a first-class sensation. Musicians from all over Europe came to hear it and agreed with their Italian colleagues that here was something quite new in Verdi's orientation. The blending of word and music was as intimate as Wagner's, yet quite different; the declamatory recitative, without ever abandoning a melodic basis, achieved a perfect plasticity of expression; the orchestra was treated with a mastery and psychological insight never even imagined possible in Italy. In particular everybody was amazed by the vitality, hardly if at all inferior to the vitality of *Aïda* or *Il Trovatore*, that permeated this score by an old man of seventy-four. I have always felt this to be one of the major miracles of music. Thanks to this vitality, and not a little to the genius of Boito's libretto, Verdi's *Otello* equals in poetry, passion, and intensity its Shakespearean original.

Otello had made Verdi the hero of the hour, and, to escape the publicity he so much disliked, he retired almost immediately to Sant'Agata. Despite his triumph he was in a very black mood. One by one his lifelong friends were dying, and Verdi hated death. Even the death in 1883 of Wagner, whom he had never known and who was generally regarded as his great adversary, had moved him strangely. His state of mind is obvious in the attitude he adopted towards the proposal to celebrate the jubilee of his first opera. 'Among all the useless things in the world,' he wrote to Ricordi, 'this is the most useless. If some concession must be made, propose that this jubilee should be celebrated fifty days after my death. Three days suffice to wrap men and events in oblivion.' Yet he was not averse to commemorating the exploits of other men. He accepted Joachim's offer to associate his name with the Beethoven Festival, and, at the age of seventy-nine, he made his last appearance as a conductor to celebrate the centenary of Rossini's birth by directing the Prayer from *Mosé*.

To Boito, and in all probability to his own tactful and devoted wife must be ascribed the credit for arousing Verdi from his depression. He had always wanted to write a comic opera, largely, it appears, because Rossini had once said that he was unable to do so. Boito now provided him with the opportunity by fashioning a first class libretto on the subject of *Falstaff*. The writing of the music, which was probably begun in 1889, afforded Verdi great enjoyment. He worked on it at his leisure and he always seems to have regarded the opera as essentially his own private possession, to be shared with the outside world only on the strictest imaginable terms. When *Falstaff* was produced at La Scala on 9 February 1893, the public were not perhaps so enthusiastic as they had been about *Otello*, but the musicians were even more impressed. Well they might be, for *Falstaff*, from the technical point of view, is the most remarkable score of its kind in the world. For delicacy, for brilliance and subtlety of orchestration, for mellowness, for perfect blending of voice and instruments, there has never been anything quite like it. Into it Verdi had poured the ripe and accumulated experience of a lifetime. And he was eighty years old!

The Last Act

During the next few years life passed tranquilly for Verdi, in the summer at Sant'Agata, in the winter at his flat in Genoa. The feud with Busseto was finally healed, and he seems to have taken great pleasure in following the success of *Falstaff*. Indeed, he actually went to Paris in 1894 to attend the first French performance at the Opéra-Comique. In 1896 he made himself responsible for the building in Milan of a Home for Aged Musicians, the endowment being subsequently provided for in his will.

But at the end of 1897 his wife died, and the shock left him a broken man; there were still left friends like Boito, Ricordi, and Teresa Stolz, to come and see him, but, apart from his great love for Giuseppina, the last link that bound him to the various vicissitudes of his career was now broken. He still, however, had enough energy to complete the *Quattro Pezzi Sacri*, of which at least two had been written before her death. They were played for the first time in Paris in 1898 and a few weeks later, under the direction of Toscanini, at Turin. Two of them, the *Te Deum* and the *Stabat Mater*, are very beautiful, forming what may justly be called a fitting epilogue to Verdi's musical career.

He himself, becoming increasingly feeble, lingered on for another two years. He died on 27 January 1901, in Milan, where he had gone to spend Christmas with his most intimate friends. Italy observed his death as that of a national hero. Two hundred thousand people lined the streets when the body was carried to burial in the oratory of the Musicians' Home that he himself had founded. It was fitting that this should be so, for Giuseppe Verdi was one of the greatest of Italians, in his character, in his patriotism, and in his music. Unlike his predecessors, he possessed sufficient determination to rise above the conditions and circumstances of his environment. Of all composers he must be reckoned one of the sanest, strongest, and most sincere.

HENRI VIEUXTEMPS

1820–81

F. BONAVIA

The piano has attracted quite a number of musicians who were not only executants but also composers of genius. The violin has not been so fortunate in the last century. Tartini and Corelli had no direct successor. The literature of the instrument has not anything to compare with the work of Liszt, Schumann, Chopin, Brahms, or Rachmaninov – to say nothing of Mozart and Beethoven. But there are violinists who wrote music of some worth, whose resting place is not on the summit of Olympus with the gods, but on the lower slopes among the minor prophets. It would be absurd to claim for them a glorious immortality; it would be unjust to ignore them. Such men were Paganini, Wieniawski, Spohr, and Henri Vieuxtemps. Today they get scant recognition from the public, but they left their mark on the history of musical art.

Vieuxtemps was, above all, a great virtuoso in an age of great virtuosos. He can hardly be blamed if most of his compositions were so devised as to give him every opportunity to display the peculiarities of style in which he excelled. Many another violinist has done the same. Vieuxtemps did it better than most. Nature had endowed him with special aptitude for violin playing, with good taste, and a certain *savoir faire* that enabled him to master the elements of composition with ease. It had not given him the power of concentration, the individual vision of the true-born composer. Success at an early age and the applause of his fellows did not encourage self-criticism or foster a desire for new and better things. He became a genial man of the world, generous in recognizing merit in others, not given to discriminating sharply between depth and superficiality, an interpreter of consummate genius, a composer who delighted in graceful periods and melodies of a slightly sentimental cast.

His life is that of the great virtuoso – travel, concerts, overwork; rest, more travelling, and more concerts. Born at Verviers in Belgium on 20 February 1820, he began to study the violin with his father at a very early age. He must have been a fairly proficient musician at the age when other little boys are learning the alphabet, for he made his first public appearance at six with a Rode concerto. The training of the lad had been undertaken by a local teacher who did not scruple to send him about to display his accomplishments in nearby towns.

He began to travel and was fortunate to attract the notice of Charles de Bériot, a less gifted composer than Vieuxtemps, but a great violinist and the founder of the Franco-Belgian school. De Bériot took him under his wing, brought him to Paris, and sponsored his first appearance at one of the concerts de Bériot used to give together with his wife, the famous Malibran. Master and pupil passed three useful years together, after which de Bériot left France and the boy returned to Brussels. In the Belgian capital he worked hard from 1831 to 1833, but without the help of responsible tutors. A tour through Germany, begun in 1833 in the company of his father, was more fruitful. Vieuxtemps met distinguished musicians and heard *Fidelio* for the first time. Beethoven's opera made a deep impression. Immediately after hearing it he began to give attention to the music of Beethoven, to which de Bériot had not introduced him. There is nothing in de Bériot's style to show either a knowledge of Beethoven or the temperament capable of appreciating it. The success Vieuxtemps achieved in Vienna in 1834 with Beethoven's *Violin Concerto* was due entirely to his own intelligence and perspicacity. The cadenzas he wrote for the concerto, which remained in the repertory of every violinist until displaced by the cadenzas of Joachim, are probably of later date.

Vieuxtemps has been praised also for his courage in playing a concerto that at the time was 'a novelty'. This is surely an exaggeration. The concerto was undoubtedly neglected at the time, but other violinists – Paganini and Leonard among them – shared his admiration for the genius of Beethoven. The concerto was neglected; it was not unknown. From Vienna the young violinist went on to Leipzig, where he won the heart of Robert Schumann; then to Berlin and Hamburg, making friends amongst musicians and numerous admirers among the public. He also began to study composition, but it is unlikely that his labours in this field were serious. He was young and the strain of constant travel cannot have allowed much leisure for an art that needs thought and concentration.

In 1834 he paid his first visit to London where singers, rather than instrumentalists, were the rage. But the public that acclaimed Grisi, Rubini, and Tamburini had also a warm welcome for the Belgian violinist when he played at a concert of the Philharmonic Society.

The next three years were spent mostly in Paris, where he began to study composition more methodically, with occasional visits to Holland. A journey to Russia in 1838 aroused so much interest that it was succeeded by another tour in the following year. The Russian climate and the wear and tear of long journeys brought an illness that made rest and quiet necessary. He spent the whole summer in the country, but was far from idle. The composition of the best known of his concertos, in E major, a graceful work abounding in staccato passages most congenial to him, was then begun, together with the *Fantaisie-Caprice*, destined to become the battle horse of many future generations of violinists. He now often played his own compositions in public, adding to the fame of the performer the laurels of the composer.

The extraordinary interest the twenty-year-old violinist aroused at the Rubens festival held in Antwerp in 1840 added much to his reputation. He was decorated with the order of Leopold and engagements in Paris and London followed as a matter of course.

To understand rightly the impression made by Vieuxtemps on the musicians of his time as performer and composer it is necessary to remember something of the fashion then prevalent, when even in Austria and in Germany the classical concertos were looked upon as old-fashioned, while Kreutzer and Rode were applauded. The cult of technique was universal. The skill needed for a representative performance of the concertos of Mozart and Beethoven is really much greater than the skill required by one of Rode's, but, while the one implies a consummate knowledge of every shade of phrasing and finesse, the other requires mainly sound tone-production, faultless intonation, and familiarity with every possible bowing trick.

Vieuxtemps possessed these qualities in perfection. He had learnt from Charles de Bériot how to produce a robust and pleasing tone; all records agree in describing his intonation as flawless; his choice of Beethoven's *Violin Concerto* for the Vienna recital shows him to have been also a musician of taste and an intelligent interpreter. But he was above all else a specialist; his staccato bowing was more brilliant and more resonant than that of all the other violinists of his time. Today other tastes prevail and the possession of a brilliant staccato does not alone give distinction to a performance. Like the left hand pizzicatos and the double harmonics of Paganini, it belongs to the trimmings, not to the essentials, of the art of violin playing. But it is effective; it interests the amateur and, when exhibited in perfection, it has a stimulating effect. We can well imagine how thrilled were audiences that heard it for the first time executed with incomparable dash and force. At the same time neither the *E major Concerto* nor the *Fantaisie-Caprice* are mere acrobaticism. The thought of Vieuxtemps is not profound; but it is never pompous and commonplace as the thought of de Bériot too often is. The music is touched here and there by a warmth that is not found in the work of Rode; it is often truly elegant – while others aim at elegance but do not achieve it. When it is remembered that, for all its warmth and elegance, the playing of Vieuxtemps had also the solidity of de Bériot's, it will be seen that the combination could not but thrill and delight the musicians and dilettanti of his day. The adagios of Vieuxtemps art are not those of a great composer, but they are infinitely superior to those of de Bériot; his allegros are more graceful and more polished than those of his rivals.

Later Vieuxtemps tried to win fame as a composer of chamber music, writing three quartets, which were published between 1871 and 1885, and a couple of sonatas. In this he did not succeed. Quartets and sonatas are now completely and not unjustly forgotten. On the other hand the *Ballade et Polonaise* is today still a brilliant showpiece, more essentially musical and more substantial than similar compositions of Laub or Wieniawski. A *Suite in the Old Style* shows how well he had assimilated some features of the manner of the old masters. It pleased well the public that heard it played by Eugene Ysaye during the tour which that great exponent of the Vieuxtemps school made with Ferruccio Busoni at the beginning of the century.

Like other famous virtuosos, Vieuxtemps occasionally used operatic arias as patterns on which the violinist or pianist could embroider at will dashing bravura passages. His best essays in this form were based on *La Favorita* of Donizetti and Verdi's *I Lombardi*. Nothing remains of a large number of *morceaux de salon*. A *Rêverie* endured longest; some burlesque variations of *Yankee doodle* should still raise a smile. The *Études de Concert* are not forgotten, having their use in the training of students even now that the cardinal features of the style are ignored. Vieuxtemps is best remembered for the concertos, of which he wrote five. Kreisler and Menuhin have occasionally varied their programmes with the inclusion of a Vieuxtemps concerto – usually either the F sharp minor or the D minor.

Vieuxtemps went first to America when he was twenty-four years old. He had a most friendly welcome, but the fatigue of the voyage necessitated a long rest. As before, he devoted the enforced retirement to composition, writing on his return the *Concerto in A*, while taking a cure at Stuttgart. In 1846 he became professor of the violin at the conservatoire of St Petersburg and solo violinist to the Czar. He returned to France in 1852, resuming the nomadic life of the virtuoso. He visited America again in 1857 and returned to Paris in the following year. In 1868 the loss of his father and of his wife shortly after affected him deeply. He was much attached both to the father who had watched carefully over his early years and to his wife, the Viennese pianist Josephine Eder, who had been a helpful companion. He tried to forget his grief by undertaking another extended tour, which ended in America. From there he returned in 1871 to accept an appointment Gevaert had offered to him at the Conservatoire of Brussels. Two years later an attack of paralysis put an end to his violin playing. He was advised to try the effects of a milder climate and seeking health travelled as far as Algiers, only to die there on 6 June 1881.

Today Vieuxtemps is remembered mainly as one of the founders of the great school of violin playing that flourished and still flourishes in France and Belgium. Its ideals – clean attack, purity and vigour in tone, a certain elegance and warmth of style – are better seen in his compositions than in any work written by violinists of the same school. He has been compared with Meyerbeer and it is true that his themes have at times the quasi-heroic cut characteristic of the opera composer. But while Vieuxtemps was a past master of his medium, the violin, Meyerbeer was but an imperfect master of the orchestra.

WILHELM RICHARD WAGNER

1813–83

GERALD ABRAHAM

Birth and Childhood

The lives of few great men open with a biographical problem as tantalizing as the mystery of Wagner's parentage. It is true that Debussy's origin is also 'wropt in mystery', but with him the matter is of no great interest or importance. In Wagner's it is. When a man is such a bitter anti-Semite as Wagner was, it is piquant to scent a possibility – even a strong probability – that a strain of Jewish blood, no matter how thin, defiled his Aryan veins. Was the child that Johanna Wagner bore at Leipzig, on 22 May 1813, the son of her husband, the Police Actuary Karl Friedrich Wagner, or of their *Hausfreund*, the actor Ludwig Geyer, with his ever so slight taint of non-Aryan blood? No one but Johanna herself (and the potential father) ever seems to have been in a position to answer that question definitely, though we know Wagner himself had a strong suspicion that he was the son of Geyer. Contemplating the evidence dispassionately, the impartial biographer can only shrug his shoulders and admit that the probabilities are evenly balanced. Richard's predilection for the theatre proves nothing, for, although Geyer was an actor, and also a portrait-painter, Friedrich Wagner was a passionate lover of the theatre (and of pretty actresses). And four of his undisputed children, Richard's eldest brother and three of his sisters, went on the stage – two of them on the operatic stage.

After the birth of that ninth and last child of the Wagner household events followed in quick succession. The baby was only five months old when Leipzig was ringed with fire and smoke by the patriotic armies struggling to free the Fatherland from the Napoleonic yoke. War brought typhus in its train and on 22 November, barely a month after the Battle of the Nations, Friedrich Wagner fell a victim. Within two months the poor widow also lost a four-year-old daughter. Pensionless and with seven surviving children to support, Johanna's position must have seemed desperate. But the good friend Geyer, whether or not he had been her lover before, indisputably became her lover now. He married her in August 1814, and in the following February she bore him a child, Richard's half-sister (or sister) Cäcilie.

Geyer had three strings to his bow: he was actor, painter, and dramatist. He prospered. And he seems to have been the kindest of stepfathers. Wagner speaks of him with much affectionate respect in *Mein Leben*: 'This excellent man, who moved my family to Dresden when I was two, now undertook my education with the greatest care and love. He wished to adopt me entirely as his own son and, when I went to my first school, gave me his name, so that among my Dresden schoolfellows I was known until I was in my fourteenth year as Richard Geyer.' It was only when, at fifteen, he was sent to the Nicholaischule at Leipzig that he resumed the name of Wagner.

Unhappily, in September 1821, Geyer died too. Johanna's financial position was now better, but Richard sadly missed a father's guidance and control. The tiny boy with the large head and the unforgettable blue eyes had already been attending the village school at Possendorf, a few miles from Dresden. After Geyer's death, he was taken care of by the latter's brother, a goldsmith at Eisleben. Then in December 1822, he was sent to the famous Dresden Kreuzschule.

As a child, Wagner was abnormally sensitive and imaginative. He had his full share of healthy boyish energy. But that too vivid imagination, the *embodying* imagination of the future dramatist, was a two-edged gift. It sharpened his delight in the theatre, for instance; but it was also a source of torment. 'My family still remained closely allied with the theatre, and I was enthusiastically attracted by it. *Der Freischütz* – or rather its supernatural subject – above all produced an extremely characteristic effect on my imagination. The excitements of horror and of fear of ghosts formed quite a special factor in the development of my spiritual life. From my earliest childhood certain inexplicable circumstances produced an overpowering impression on me. I remember how, when left alone in a room for some time, my imagination would fasten on inanimate objects, such as the furniture – and I would suddenly shriek with fear, for they used to seem to me to come to life.' Another important factor in his development was the predominantly feminine element that surrounded him in the home. As with so many men of genius, the erotic side of his nature developed precociously.

Schooldays

Wagner remained at the Kreuzschule from 1822 till 1827. Judging from the school reports, he was a good pupil, but it is typical of his approach to things in general that, although he was fascinated by Greek mythology, 'the actual grammar (of the Greek language) seemed to me only a tiresome hindrance'. The boy worshipped Shakespeare and was already trying his hand at writing poetry, but so far music seems to have attracted him but little. His life needed an inner focus as well as external guidance. Yet he demanded more 'emancipation', left the family with whom he was supposed to be living and set up housekeeping – at fourteen – in a tiny garret. It was at this period that he produced his first play, the horrific tragedy of *Leubald und Adelaide*, a bloody-and-thunderous variation on the *Hamlet* theme, of which he wrote in later years (with considerable humorous exaggeration) that having killed off forty-two of the characters in the course of the action, he was obliged to bring them back as ghosts to finish the play.

In January 1828, Wagner was sent to the Nicholaischule at Leipzig – and was very disgusted at being put back to the 'easier Greek prose-writers', after having translated twelve books of Homer at Dresden. (Or so he claims – quite incredibly.) But this return to Leipzig marks a definite stage in the boy's development, above all in his musical development. In the Dresden days he had had a few piano lessons, but at twelve, as at nine, the whole of his musical experience reached its apogee in a performance of the *Freischütz* overture. It was the only thing he wanted to play; when he could stumble through it he was satisfied. His sister Clara was a singer at the Dresden Opera and Weber occasionally came to the house in those days, so an element of hero-worship possibly contributed to this *Freischütz* craze. But at Leipzig the boy discovered a fresh musical idol in Beethoven, who had died only a few months before. He had made the acquaintance of Beethoven's music in Dresden, through the *Fidelio* overture. Now in Leipzig he got hold of the *Egmont* music and some of the piano sonatas and heard the *A major Symphony* at a Gewandhaus concert. 'Its effect on me was indescribable.' Even the lithographed portraits of Beethoven fascinated him. 'In ecstatic dreams I met Beethoven and Shakespeare, and talked with them; I awoke, bathed in tears.' The boy friends of real life were less satisfactory; he asked to much and they gave too little.

First Compositions

Wagner was now on fire to write incidental music for *Leubald und Adelaide* and to that end borrowed a copy of J. B. Logier's *Thoroughbass*, his first musical text-book. He also had harmony lessons in secret from an orchestral player named Müller. But it was now with music as formerly with Greek. 'Music was to me a daemon, a mystically exalted monster.' Text-book harmony had no more connexion with this mighty daemon than Greek grammar with the Greek heroes. What Wagner failed to find in the dry grammar of Logier and Müller – fuel for his fiery imagination – he found in the fantastic stories of E. T. A. Hoffmann. And if he did not learn from others he somehow contrived to teach himself a great deal. He attempted various compositions, including a *Piano Sonata in D minor* and a *String Quartet*, and studied orchestration from a full score of *Don Giovanni*. In other words he learned to compose as one learns to write one's native language – by doing it; not as one learns a foreign language, by memorizing rules.

So occupied with music, the lad was neglecting his other studies. One fine day his family were shocked to find he had not attended school for six months! But they seem to have been reasonable. At any rate they accepted the inevitable. If Richard was so eager to be a musician, a musician he must be – though to them a 'musician' was one who played an instrument. To Richard, on the other hand, a 'musician' was a composer; he never did learn to play an instrument properly. His mother now bought him a fiddle and paid for violin-lessons; for two or three months he practised – to the torment of the rest of the household; but his teacher, Robert Sipp, who died as recently as 1899, has left it on record that Wagner was his worst pupil. 'He was intelligent, but lazy, and would not practise.' In the meantime Wagner continued his true musical education – which he gave himself by transcribing Beethoven's *Fifth* and *Ninth Symphonies* for piano solo and performing similar labours of love.

It was an exacting period of *Sturm und Drang* in more directions than one. The old childish love of the theatre, 'only the interest of a fanciful curiosity', now became 'a deep-rooted, conscious passion'. Wagner heard Wilhelmine Schröder-Devrient in *Fidelio* and was completely bowled over. That night he sent her a wild note telling her that his life had only now begun to have true meaning. And he wrote many years later, in *Mein Leben*, that 'when I took back over my whole life, I find scarcely any experience comparable with this in its effect on me.'

His school-work was seriously neglected and, though he entered Leipzig University as *studiosus musicae* in February 1831, he was attracted solely by the drinking, gambling, duelling side of the student life; the academic world knew him scarcely at all.

Still, he composed industriously and on Christmas Day, 1830, had the doubtful satisfaction of hearing one of his various overtures performed in public under Heinrich Dorn, the *Kapellmeister* of the Leipzig Theatre. The performance was a fiasco. The 'new overture' (given anonymously) was written with mystic intention in three inks – black, red, and green (or blue, according to Dorn); the music itself seems to have been as bizarre as one would expect; and the audience was amused accordingly. This disaster seems to have piqued Wagner into resuming his study of the dull technique of composition, for in October 1831, we find him taking lessons in fugue and sonata form from Weinlig, Cantor of Bach's old church, the Thomaskirche. He studied for only about six months with Weinlig, but, by his own account, made marvellous progress. Weinlig not only interested him in the mysteries of counterpoint but helped him practically by inducing Breitkopf and Härtel to publish a couple of his compositions, a *Piano Sonata in B flat* and a *Polonaise*. Wagner actually received £3 down for the sonata! Moreover the lad's new overtures, one to Raupach's *King Enzio* and two others, were successfully performed in 1832 – and in the sacred Gewandhaus at that. The same summer a *Symphony in C major* was tried out at Prague, and in January 1833, it was also heard at the Gewandhaus.

In the World of the Theatre

During the visit to Prague, under the influence of an unlucky passion for one of Count Pachta's daughters, Wagner had begun his first opera, *Die Hochzeit*. (From the first he was his own librettist.) Nothing came of it. But the very next year he embarked on *Die Feen*, which he completed and of which the overture is still occasionally played. By that time he was launched once and for all on his professional career as a theatre musician, for, a few days after the Gewandhaus performance of his symphony, the twenty-year-old Wagner had been given his first professional appointment. Thanks to his brother Albert, actor, singer, and stage-manager at the Würzburg Theatre, he was engaged as chorus-master there. He was quite unqualified for the post, but as the chorus numbered only fifteen and his salary was a bare pound a month the good Würzburgers had little to grumble at. At Würzburg Wagner worked at his opera, gained much practical experience of the theatre, and enjoyed two rather disreputable love-affairs with ladies of the chorus. Then, early in 1834, he returned to Leipzig with the completed score of *Die Feen*.

His hopes of a Leipzig production of his first opera were soon dashed. (*Die Feen* was not performed at all during his lifetime.) Nevertheless he began the libretto of a new opera, *Das Liebesverbot*, based on Shakespeare's *Measure for Measure*, which he transmuted into a glorification of free love and sensual indulgence, characteristic of his views at this period. This in turn was interrupted in the summer by a suggestion that he should become musical director to the Magdeburg Theatre Company (a non-subsidized company, unlike most of those in Germany). Wagner went to Lauchstädt, where the company was performing during the summer months, and was so disgusted by the conditions there that he was on the point of declining the post. But a trivial incident turned the scale – and modified the whole course of Wagner's life for many years.

Minna Planer

He was going back to Leipzig, but he needed a night's lodging, and a young actor who had met him at Würzburg promised to find him one under the same roof as 'the prettiest and nicest girl in Lauchstädt', the juvenile lead of the company, Fräulein Minna Planer. 'By chance she actually met us at the door of the house. Very charming and fresh in appearance, the young actress was distinguished by great composure and serious assurance of movement and carriage – all of which gave a pleasantly fascinating dignity to the friendliness of her facial expression. . . . I engaged the room on the spot, agreed to direct *Don Juan* on the Sunday, much regretted that I had not brought my luggage from Leipzig and hastened back there, so as to be all the quicker in returning to Lauchstädt.'

When Wagner conducted *Don Juan* that Sunday he was actually making his début as an operatic conductor. Indeed, he had little conducting experience of any kind. But he contrived to scrape through, learning as he went on, and by the time the company returned to Magdeburg in the winter he had acquired confidence and experience. Much of the work was uncongenial; he had to conduct many light and trivial pieces. But this labour was made less irksome than it might have been by a self-confessed 'decline in classical taste' during the next few years, a period of 'aesthetic demoralization' during which he acknowledged strange gods – Bellini and Auber and Meyerbeer – to his shame in later days. And, above all, there was Minna's presence to sweeten all the unpleasant routine of life with a petty inefficient theatrical company. True, she was three or four years older than he and had a six-year-old illegitimate daughter, but in drab surroundings and beside not very pleasing colleagues she stood out in bright relief. She may have had 'no culture', but the evidence suggests that she was a more successful actress than Wagner in later years would have had people believe. Her behaviour after her first meeting with Wagner was evidently irreproachable His first sudden infatuation cooled, as his infatuations so often did; then rekindled. She, quiet, level-headed woman that she was, consistently treated him with kindness but modest reserve. (She had not forgotten the lesson of her early betrayal.) That reserve was no doubt natural, but it was also obviously first-rate strategy, probably unpremeditated strategy. One of Wagner's ruling passions from his childhood was a possessiveness that brooked no obstacle and, especially in later years, completely ignored the rights of others. Now he desired above all to possess Minna.

One evening he went to her house so drunk that, contrary to all precedent, she allowed him to spend the night there. 'When I saw where I was, on waking,' says Wagner, 'the morning light showed me more and more clearly that I had entered on a long, infinitely fateful period of my life. Without frivolous jests or anything of that kind, we soberly and decorously breakfasted together . . . and in the morning went for a long walk beyond the town gate. Then we parted, but henceforth openly gratified our tender interests as a pair of lovers, freely and without embarrassment.' But it was not till 24 November 1836, twenty months or so later, that they married.

The Art of Getting into Debt

The Magdeburg episode had by that time ended in débâcle. The company had gone bankrupt. Wagner's benefit concert only added to his already heavy debts, despite the participation of the great Schröder-Devrient herself. (From his boyhood Wagner's expenditure had always recklessly exceeded his capacity to pay. Then, and perhaps still in his twenties, this chronic insolvency was probably due to naïve

Micawber-like optimism. He *would* be able to pay somewhen. But as his fibre coarsened in the long struggle with adversity he became less and less scrupulous. 'My' need always seemed to him greater than 'thine', and he quickly developed into the perfect prototype of the Nietzschean amoral genius, to whose greatness all common mortals ought to be delighted to sacrifice themselves.) The production of *Das Liebesverbot*, in March 1836, had to be cancelled owing to quarrels among the company. Finally, Minna got an engagement at Königsberg. Wagner, madly in love and madly jealous, followed her as soon as he could and married her there. The wild, spendthrift Bohemian and apostle of free love had bound himself to a quiet, gentle bourgeoise who was in fact, despite her profession, essentially a level-headed German *Hausfrau;* the genius to a woman who had little confidence in his talents.

Wagner had left Magdeburg in debt. He ran into debt at Königsberg even before his marriage. Nor do the concerts he gave at Königsberg, where he probably produced his *Rule Britannia Overture*, appear to have brought in much money. In despair at the straits to which they had been so quickly reduced, Minna ran away from her husband in May 1837, fleeing to her parents in Dresden with her daughter Natalie (who always passed as her sister). Wagner pursued her; there were recriminations, threats of divorce, a reconciliation, and a second flight in which she was actually guilty of infidelity. But at the end of August Wagner went to Riga, where he had just been appointed musical director of the theatre, and two months later the penitent Minna rejoined him.

It was during the two years he spent at Riga, directing a wretched little theatre band of twenty-four players, that Wagner planned and partially completed the grandiose *Rienzi*, a work laid out on the most lavish scale in Meyerbeer's style. He was here in real life the familiar poverty-stricken genius of romantic fiction, confidently planning the conquest of the world in his humble lodging in the Alexanderstrasse, as he sat smoking by the open window in fez and dressing-gown. But still his debts grew steadily heavier until, as the theatre manager put it, 'the pecuniary situation of the *Kapellmeister* was such that he could no longer remain in safety in the town'. In March 1839, the unlucky *Kapellmeister* found himself dismissed and, after four months' ignominious suffering from duns, the Wagners still more ignominiously (but rather excitingly) fled.

London and Boulogne

Their ultimate objective was Paris, which seemed at that distance a kind of El Dorado. But in the meantime they were on Russian territory with little money (that little of course not rightfully theirs) and with their passports held by their creditors. They were obliged to cross the border by a smugglers' route at grave risk of being shot by the frontier-guards. Even when safe in East Prussia, their troubles were not at an end, for they dared not show their faces in Königsberg; their carriage upset and Minna sustained internal injuries; when they reached the port of Pillau they had to hide for some days till they could be smuggled on board the English vessel that was to take them to London; and finally the normal voyage of eight days was protracted by appalling storms to three or four weeks. Yet although they both appear to have been sea-sick during the greater part of the voyage, Wagner was already nursing the idea of *The Flying Dutchman* and found that 'it had gained a distinct poetic-musical colouring from these new impressions'.

In London, which they reached at last on 13 August, they stayed for a week at the long since demolished King's Arms, Old Compton Street. Wagner immediately tried to find the two distinguished Englishmen on whom he felt he had some claim: Smart, to whom he had sent his *Rule Britannia Overture* a couple of years before, and Bulwer Lytton, whose *Rienzi* he had – without permission – turned into an opera. He saw neither. But making the most of this quasi-connexion with Lytton, he did contrive to get admission to the strangers' gallery of the House of Lords and to hear a debate there. He spent the rest of his London week in sightseeing, with an expedition to Gravesend – the first train journey of his life – as the grand finale. On 20 August the Wagners left for France.

On the steamer that took them to Boulogne, Wagner was lucky enough to make the acquaintance of two Jewish ladies who knew Meyerbeer, Wagner's model at that period and the Supreme Pontiff of the world of Parisian opera. Meyerbeer was indeed staying at Boulogne, and Wagner, armed with a letter of introduction from his new acquaintances, hastened to call on him. The great man received him affably, listened while he read three acts of the *Rienzi* libretto (which he praised very highly), and promised to examine the music of the first two acts. (Ferdinand Praeger, the author of *Wagner as I Knew Him*, says that Wagner played it to Meyerbeer. But Praeger was 'a greater liar than Sir John Mandeville', the Munchausen of Wagner literature; we dare not believe his most plausible statements.) Wagner spent nearly a month in Boulogne and when he left for Paris he bore letters of introduction from Meyerbeer in his pocket – certain passports (he felt sure) to immediate success. Indeed, Wagner continued for the next year or two to pester Meyerbeer with requests for recommendations and other forms of assistance, all of which Meyerbeer appears to have given good-naturedly enough. As late as 1845 Wagner wrote to him that 'it is a great happiness to be indebted to *you*' and remained 'Your everlastingly indebted Richard Wagner'. Five years later he was blackguarding him anonymously in *Das Judenthum in der Musik*.

The Hell of Paris

The years Wagner spent in Paris, from September 1839 to April 1842, were vitally important in the development – or perhaps we should say the *warping* – of Wagner's character. He arrived full of high hopes, with letters of introduction from Meyerbeer himself, bringing with him the partly completed score of an opera that was not only by far the best thing he had done so far, but a work admirably calculated to win success in the city where Meyerbeer reigned supreme. Instead of the success that seemed so certain, he met not merely with repulse but with disaster. Within a year or so he and Minna were faced with poverty worse than any they had experienced in their fifth-rate German theatrical world. In retrospect that world must even have seemed one of security and plenty. The almost incredible bitterness of these Paris years left an indelible mark, as large as it was ugly, on Wagner's soul. If before he had been careless and far from scrupulous in money matters, an immoralist in affairs of sex, it had all been in a free-and-easy Bohemian way. He was a born cadger, but not a born cad. But now, as Ernest Newman puts it, 'he had not only suffered material miseries; his pride as an artist had been grievously wounded, his idealism had been outraged, and the luxury-loving soul and body of him were resentful of the wealth enjoyed by others but denied to him.' The world had offered him no quarter. Very well, then. Let the world look out for itself in future. And he proceeded to make war on it ruthlessly, taking from it all he could get, plundering friend with foe. If he wanted another man's money or wife – so much the worse for the other man. Wagner triumphant was the Complete Cad. And yet the magnificence of the feat – one little German *Kapellmeister* pitting his genius, his will, his personal charm, his cunning, against an indifferent or hostile world, and winning – compels the admiration even of Perfect English Gentlemen. It is curious that Wagner willy-nilly made a cad of himself through his intense pursuit of an ideal; curious that that ideal would have remained a dream if Wagner had always behaved like a Perfect English Gentleman.

From their lodging in the Rue de la Tonnellerie (now No. 31, Rue de Pont-Neuf), Molière's wrongly reputed birthplace, Wagner sallied forth with his samples of work and his letters of introduction – to the Director of the Opéra, to the Director of the Renaissance Theatre (who accepted *Das Liebesverbot* and promptly went bankrupt), to Liszt, to Scribe the Universal Librettist, to the conductor Habeneck, to singers like Lablache and Pauline Viardot. Everywhere with much the same result: compliments, polite meaningless promises, at the very best half fulfilment. Habeneck rehearsed the *Columbus Overture*, but would not play it in public. (When another conductor did play it, it was mangled and failed miserably.) The Director of the Opéra was not interested in Wagner's music, but wanted his scenario for *The Flying Dutchman* – for another composer, Pierre Dietsch, who twenty years later was to conduct the unlucky Paris première of *Tannhäuser*. And Wagner was so hard pressed that he was glad to part with it for 500 francs. He composed some French songs, but no prominent singer would take them up and (Wagner knew the hateful method, though not the hateful word) *plug* them. The publisher Schlesinger printed his setting of a French version of Heine's *Two Grenadiers*, but only at the composer's expense; and since Wagner had no money to pay him – he and Minna having not only pawned all their belongings within six months of their arrival in El Dorado, but sold the pawn-tickets – Schlesinger suggested that he should balance the account by writing articles and feuilletons for his paper, *La Gazetta musicale*.

Wagner made the most of that opening – though, being unable to write French, he had to pay a translator. Schlesinger gave him other hack-work, work of the dreariest kind most wretchedly paid – the making of piano arrangements of the operas of Halévy and Donizetti, cornet pot-pourris and the like. But by dint of all this sweated labour, by wholesale borrowing, by taking a lodger (whose boots Minna had to clean), by desperate economy, the Wagners kept their heads above water, though twice, in October-November 1840, when Richard was imprisoned for debt, and again in the same months of 1841, they were almost literally starving. Yet with all this, Wagner contrived to finish *Rienzi* by November 1840, sending the score to Dresden, and encouraged by news of its acceptance (June 1841), to compose and score the whole of *The Flying Dutchman* during August-December. The *Dutchman* was sent to Berlin. (Wagner had long given up all hope of Paris.) Meyerbeer sent a strong recommendation in its favour, and it, too, was accepted in February 1842.

The tide had turned. There were many later occasions when it flowed against Wagner again, but he had passed his low-water mark for ever. Even now there were exasperating delays in the production of *Rienzi* and Wagner had to borrow the fare to Dresden from his brother-in-law. But he knew that the worst was past. He and Minna left the city of bitter tribulation on 7 April 1842, bearing with them some record of that bitterness in the score of the *Faust Overture* (written early in 1840), an utterance far more personal than anything in the two operas of the same period.

Triumph of Rienzi

Even before leaving Paris, Wagner had been attracted by the legend of Tannhäuser and the Venusberg. Now, at Töplitz, during the summer of 1842, while the preparations for *Rienzi* still dragged on interminably, he sketched out the scenario of *Tannhäuser and the Contest of Song on the Wartburg*. But the Dresden rehearsals began at last in August; the two principal artists, his old friend Schröder-Devrient and the great Tichatschek, who was singing the name-part, were well disposed to him; and the first performance of his first produced opera (20 October) was an overwhelming triumph. (In *Mein Leben* Wagner says the success was endangered by the enormous length of the work, the performance not ending till 'after midnight'. In fact it seems to have been over by 11.15.)

The success of *Rienzi* had two sequels. For one thing, the Dresden authorities became anxious to produce the *Dutchman*, so Wagner withdrew his score from Berlin, and the work was immediately put into rehearsal. Meanwhile, Weber's old enemy Morlacchi and his assistant at the Court Opera had both died within a month of the *Rienzi* production, and the Royal *Kapellmeister*-ship was offered to the twenty-nine-year-old composer who only twelve months before had been starving in Paris. The situation had changed so radically that

Wagner was for a time undecided whether or not to accept this glittering prize! He soon succumbed to the magnetism of the 'safe job', but something of the spirit that had upheld him in the hell of Paris lingered on in that desire to accept the risks of independence by single-mindedly following his own creative path. On 2 February 1843, just a month after the not very successful première of *The Flying Dutchman*, Wagner was appointed Royal *Kapellmeister* for life, at a salary equivalent to about £225 a year.

Royal Kapellmeister

The six years that Wagner spent in Dresden are not a period of enthralling interest and importance. We find him writing a *Love Feast of the Apostles* for a male voice choir festival in Dresden, coming into passing contact – never very friendly contact – with Berlioz, Schumann, and Mendelssohn. Wagner's attitude to colleagues was almost invariably compounded in equal parts of contempt and suspicion. He gives an electrifying performance of Beethoven's *Choral Symphony*, less historic but artistically sound readings of the operas of Gluck, Mozart, Beethoven, and Weber, Spohr, Marschner, and Spontini, performs various other routine and official labours to everyone's satisfaction....

Meanwhile, *Tannhäuser* was completed in April 1845, and produced, with but moderate success, on 19 October. Wagner's nineteen-year-old niece, Johanna, who had recently joined the Dresden company, sang Elisabeth – and soon won such widespread fame that Richard, when he visited England ten years later, suffered the humiliation of being referred to in the London Press as 'the uncle of the celebrated prima donna'. But if the initial reception of *Tannhäuser* was doubtful, largely because of the ineptitude of singers unable to grasp Wagner's new type of melodic recitative, later performances turned the tide of popular success. 'You are a man of genius', complained his 'Venus', the friendly Schröder-Devrient – now perhaps a little jealous of Johanna, 'but you write such eccentric stuff that it is hardly possible to sing it.' Yet the more cultured part of the Dresden lay public seems to have begun to like the 'eccentric stuff'.

Wagner had already sketched out scenarios for operas on the subjects of Lohengrin and the Mastersingers and he finished the poem of *Lohengrin* a month or so after the production of *Tannhäuser*. He seemed to be in the full swing of march from victory to victory. Yet things were not quite what they seemed. Wagner, for reasons both spiritual and material, was unable to enjoy his success. Spiritually, he was chafed by the chain of routine, by the immense differences between the real world of the musical theatre, with all its conventions and traditions, its pettiness and intrigue, and the romantic ideal of dramatic art that he cherished in secret. And materially he was galled by the ever-increasing burden of debt: old debts that he could never hope to pay, new ones incurred by living beyond his modest salary – for Wagner was so constituted that he could not live without the luxuries of life. And he now recklessly worsened his position by publishing his opera scores at his own expense.

Wagner as Revolutionist

At this period – the period of *Lohengrin* – two fresh characters become prominent among the dramatis personae of the Wagnerian tragi-comedy. One, Anton Pusinelli, was a Dresden doctor who attended Minna till her death in 1866 and at the same time remained Richard's intimate friend till his own death in 1878. The other was Wagner's official assistant and enthusiastic admirer, August Röckel, a nephew of Hummel and the brother-in-law of Albert Lortzing, 'the German Sullivan'. Both Pusinelli and Röckel were among the numerous unfortunates from whom Wagner levied 'loans' in the spirit of a Plantagenet monarch. But his debt to Röckel was intellectual as well as financial. Notwithstanding that the authorities had helped him out of his worst financial difficulties by a loan of seven or eight hundred pounds, he was growing more and more unhappy and disgruntled, surer than ever that there was something fundamentally wrong with the existing order of things – an order of things in which he, Richard Wagner, could have neither full leisure to devote himself to his creative work nor the luxuries without which life was intolerable. Even his proposals for the reform of the Dresden orchestra were pigeon-holed for a year and then turned down. He began to neglect the weekly theatre committee meeting and to treat his official superiors first with contemptuous indifference and then with open defiance. Yet when he asked for an increase in salary, it was granted, though with a threat of dismissal if he should 'plunge into further pecuniary embarrassments'.

In this state of profound personal discontent, it was only natural that Wagner should sympathize with any movement that promised a change in the general *status quo*. In the middle of a rehearsal of *Martha* Röckel brought him the news of the proclamation of the Second Republic in Paris. Within a month – the month in which *Lohengrin* was finished (March 1848) – all Germany was in ferment, and the great majority of German intellectuals, disgruntled or not, took the Liberal side. How far Wagner would have gone if he had not been on bad terms with his superiors and had not come within Röckel's sphere of political influence, it is impossible to say. His Liberalism might have remained chastely Platonic. But Röckel was a prominent member of the socialist, republican Vaterlandsverein in Dresden, and on his invitation Wagner read an article on the republican question to a great public meeting of the Verein. In spite of the official storm that this provoked, Wagner was still allowed to retain his post. He consorted with the Russian anarchist Bakunin and under the influence of the latter's ideas began to work out the philosophical basis of a new opera, *Siegfried's Death*, the germ of the whole *Ring*, fantastically bestowing on the figure of the legendary hero a new allegorical significance – as a modern revolutionary socialist!

Wagner was now caught up in a current of political affairs altogether too strong for him. On 3 May 1849, the people of Dresden, alarmed by the King's reactionary measures, demonstrated in the streets and were fired on by the troops. Barricades were improvised and on the 6th fighting broke out. It is difficult to determine just what part Wagner took in the actual hostilities; his own accounts, eye-witness reports, and police records provide us with too much conflicting evidence. But the Vaterlandsverein was deeply implicated and when the rising collapsed Röckel and Bakunin were among those sentenced to death. (They were afterwards reprieved.) Wagner fled with the 'provisional government' to Chemnitz and then slipped quietly off to Weimar where Liszt, with whom he had lately become friendly, was preparing to produce *Tannhäuser*. But on the 19th came news of the issue of a warrant for his arrest and with Liszt's assistance he fled to Zürich, where Minna and her daughter soon joined him. In October he became a citizen of Zürich and for twelve years remained a political exile.

Theorist in Exile

Relations between Richard and Minna had been growing less and less sympathetic during the Dresden period. She had stuck to him nobly through the Parisian ordeal, and the success of *Rienzi* and his subsequent official appointment had justified her faith in him. But as he acidly wrote years later: 'As *Frau Kapellmeister* she had obviously reached the pinnacle of what she demanded of life.' She could not understand why he must needs write 'eccentric stuff' like *Tannhäuser*, instead of steadily manufacturing disguised replicas of *Rienzi*. In the present situation she saw unmitigated disaster and not unnaturally failed to sympathize with Richard's strange elation at his escape from official shackles. To make matters worse, he seemed to have abandoned composition for theorizing and pamphleteering. Minna knew there was no money to be made from books and essays on musical and theatrical aesthetics, and she was exasperated by the series of tracts, from *Art and Revolution*, *The Art-work of the Future*, and *Judaism in Music* to the colossal thesis *Opera and Drama*, that occupied Wagner from 1849 to 1852 at Zürich. (Liszt produced *Lohengrin* at Weimar in August 1850, but its composer wrote hardly a note of music in the period between its completion in March 1848 and the beginning of *Das Rheingold* in November 1853.) Minna completely failed to recognize the publicity value of these provocative dissertations, which, in conjunction with Wagner's growing reputation as a serious composer and his new reputation de scandale as a political firebrand, soon made him the most talked of composer in Germany.

The Affair of Jessie Laussot

Minna had another cause for irritation against her husband. For the first time (as far as we know) he was being seriously unfaithful to her. In Dresden, early in 1848, through Frau Julie Ritter, the mother of a youthful admirer of his, he had made the acquaintance of a charming twenty-year-old English girl, Jessie Laussot, the wife of a Bordeaux wine-merchant. Jessie had begun by falling in love with *Tannhäuser* and she seems to have fallen in love at first sight with its composer. Wagner, of course, was always the most susceptible of men. But the affair made little progress till February 1850, when Minna at Fate's ironic prompting urged her husband to go to Paris and try to get his operas produced there. While he was in Paris, Jessie invited him to stay with her and her husband in Bordeaux. The situation that developed may easily be imagined.

The infatuated Jessie even proposed (in conjunction with Frau Ritter) to settle on her hero an annual pension of 3,000 francs. However, Eugène Laussot began not only to suffer pangs of jealousy but to feel that his well-to-do young wife was being exploited by an unscrupulous adventurer. His mother-in-law, a Mrs Taylor, backed him up and they finally succeeded in poisoning Jessie's mind against Wagner, who characteristically consoled himself by deploring Jessie's 'weakness of character'. 'The woman who was to have brought me salvation has proved herself a child.' he lamented to Frau Ritter. 'Forgive me if I can only regard her as pitiable. . . .' And at the same time he himself was writing distinctly 'pitiable' letters of excuse and explanation to Minna. In July, however, there was a reconciliation and Wagner rejoined his wife at Zürich.

Planning the Ring

Opera and Drama being finished, Wagner returned to his old *Siegfried's Death* project, only to find the original plan swelling to unheard-of proportions. 'When I tried to dramatize the most important moment of the Nibelungen legend in *Siegfried's Death* (which was to become *Götterdämmerung*), I found it necessary to indicate a vast number of antecedent facts so as to put the main incidents in the proper light. But I could only *narrate* these subordinate matters – whereas I felt it imperative that they should be embodied in the action. Thus I came to write *Siegfried*. But here again the same difficulty troubled me. Finally I wrote *The Valkyrie* and *The Rhinegold* and thus contrived to incorporate all that was needful to make the action tell its own tale.' However, the whole colossal poem of the *Ring* was finished by Christmas, 1852, and privately printed.

Wagner had recently made the acquaintance in Zürich of 'Herr Otto Wesendonck, several years younger than I, who had amassed a not inconsiderable fortune through his connexion with a big New York silk business and who appeared to be guided in all the affairs of life by the inclinations of his young wife. Both came from the Lower Rhineland, and bore the pleasant blonde stamp of that province. . . .' To be rich and to know Wagner was a fatal conjunction. The Prince of Cadgers wanted an Italian holiday before embarking on the composition of the *Ring*, and Wesendonck was granted the privilege of paying for it. In September 1853, Wagner crossed the Alps for the first time, visiting Turin and Genoa. Ill with dysentery, he moved on to Spezia and there one afternoon, returning to his inn in complete exhaustion, 'I stretched myself on a hard couch to await the longed-for hour of sleep. It did not come, but I sank into a sort of somnambulistic state in which I suddenly had the feeling that I was sinking in strongly flowing water. Its murmur presented itself to me as the chord of E flat, broken up in wavy figuration. . . .' The opening of the *Rhinegold* prelude had been conceived.

The composition was not itself begun until November. In the interval Wagner made an expedition to Paris with Liszt, and for the first time met the latter's two daughters by the Countess d'Agoult – Cosima, aged sixteen, and Blandine. By June 1854, the full score of *Das Rheingold* was finished and *Die Walküre* begun. But just at this period Wagner made the acquaintance of Schopenhauer's pessimistic philosophy; it captivated him as completely as it later captivated Nietzsche and Tolstoy; 'now for the first time I understood my own Wotan', he confessed long afterwards. He read *The World as Will and Idea* four times in nine or ten months and 'it was probably partly the serious mood that Schopenhauer had induced in me, and now demanded ecstatic expression, that suggested the conception of *Tristan and Isolde*'.

The composition of *Die Walküre* was further hindered early in 1855 by a visit to London to conduct eight concerts for the Philharmonic Society. A great part of the scoring was actually done in London (at 22 Portland Terrace, Regent's Park), but the corrections and copying were finished only in March 1856. Wagner rested for nearly six months, worn out and irritable. Then he plunged into *Siegfried* and had sketched out the first two acts by August 1857, when the whole vast scheme was interrupted – for no less than twelve years, as it proved – by an emotional storm.

Mathilde and Tristan

Wagner's friendship with Wesendonck, and more particularly with the latter's twenty-eight-year-old wife, Mathilde, had grown more and more intimate. Wesendonck had been building a handsome new villa at Zürich. Quite close to it was a charming little house (since known as the 'Asyl') that Wagner coveted. Wesendonck bought it for the Wagners and let it to them at the nominal rental of 800 francs a year. The Wagners moved to the 'Asyl' in April 1857, and the Wesendoncks occupied their big new house four months later. 'Then began a new phase in my intercourse with this family,' Wagner innocently remarked in *Mein Leben*, 'one that had much influence on the external course of my life. Immediate neighbourhood strengthened our ties through daily intercourse. . . . Curiously enough, this neighbourly intimacy coincided with the beginning of my poem of *Tristan and Isolde.*

It is true there were other reasons beside passion for Mathilde Wesendonck clamouring for musical expression, for the laying aside of the *Ring* in favour of a new work of only normal length. Wagner doubted whether the *Ring* could ever be performed. And he had just been invited to compose an opera for the theatre at Rio de Janeiro, of all places. Still, Mathilde seems to have pressed the button that released this great outpouring of love and pessimism.

The Laussot situation now began to repeat itself, with certain variations and intensifications. Wesendonck was far more magnanimous than Eugène Laussot had been. (His jealousy had been keenly aroused even before the purchase of the 'Asyl'.) But the proximity of the four protagonists soon made the whole situation intolerable. Minna and Mathilde quarrelled openly and matters were brought to a head when Minna intercepted one of Richard's letters to her rival. The Wesendoncks made a trip to Italy and a further armistice was imposed by a visit from Liszt's daughter Cosima and her husband, Hans von Bülow. How Fate must have smiled as she looked into the future! But in August 1858, Richard fled to Venice, gloomy and alone, to work at *Tristan,* while the broken-hearted but ever-devoted Minna journeyed to Dresden to intercede for his pardon. Still, Richard did not break off relations with Mathilde or even with her husband. In fact, some sort of friendship with them subsisted all his life. When he decided to settle in Paris in September 1859, he did so with money obtained from Otto Wesendonck on the security of the *Ring* copyrights.

Tannhäuser *in Paris*

Minna rejoined her husband in Paris, after fifteen months' separation, only a find a fresh cause of dissension in Cosima von Bülow's sister Blandine, who had married the French politician Ollivier. The affair was probably not serious, but Wagner and Blandine at least flirted outrageously. Nevertheless Minna did not relax her efforts to obtain her husband's pardon – he had certainly recanted his political errors in sufficiently abject terms – and she at last succeeded in getting permission for the scapegrace to enter any German State except Saxony itself. In August 1860, therefore, Wagner once more set foot on German soil for a few weeks. But for the time being he was held in

Paris by the preparations for a production of *Tannhäuser* at the Opéra, a production secured by backstairs diplomacy involving Napoleon III himself. So profoundly had conditions changed since the needy days of 1840.

This first performance of *Tannhäuser* (13 March 1861), for which Wagner wrote the so-called *New Venusberg Music*, has become famous through the scandalous uproar engineered by hostile elements in the audience, though the celebrated Jockey Club demonstration, when the aristocrats of the Second Empire expressed their displeasure by means of dog-whistles, did not occur till the second performance five days later. Wagner had little reason indeed to love Paris, though nothing can excuse the childish and repulsive spitefulness of his rejoicings over the humiliation of France and his benefactor, Napoleon, nine years later.

He was now again heavily in debt. But in August he was able to settle once more in his own country.

Wife and Mistresses

'Settle' is perhaps the wrong word, for while Minna took up her abode permanently in Dresden, Wagner moved restlessly about, campaigning for his works. We find him at Weimar with Liszt and the Bülows, in Vienna trying to get *Tristan* produced, with the now reconciled Wesendoncks in Venice (where he decided to write his long projected *Die Meistersinger*), back in Vienna, in Paris and (early in 1862) at Biebrich near Mainz. Biebrich became his temporary headquarters and he worked there at *Die Meistersinger*.

His personal affairs were in an extraordinary state of entanglement at this period. He had not yet finally broken with Minna, who visited him at Biebrich; he and Cosima von Bülow were already in love, though they had not yet openly confessed it to each other; and he had just acquired a new mistress, the charming young actress Friederike Meyer. In November (1862), the Saxon ban having at last been raised, Wagner visited Minna in Dresden for four days. At parting, 'she accompanied me to the station where, full of the most fearful forebodings of never seeing me again, she took a very anxious farewell of me.' Poor faithful Minna's forebodings were justified. Till her death in January 1866, Wagner saw that she was well provided for, but they never met again. It had long been obvious that their life together was impossible.

For the next eighteen months Wagner led a wandering life. He lived for a time in Vienna with Friederike Meyer; gave concerts in Prague, St Petersburg, Moscow, and Berlin; settled at Penzing near Vienna with a fresh mistress, the daughter of a Viennese butcher; met the Bülows again in Berlin in November. And it was on this last occasion that he and Cosima, driving alone on the Promenade, 'gazed silently into each other's eyes . . . A violent longing to avow the truth gave us strength to confess that which needed no words for its expression – the infinite unhappiness that oppressed us. With tears and sobs we sealed our vow to belong to each other alone.'

The object of all these journeyings and concert-givings was partly financial, partly propagandist. In the latter respect they were very successful, in the former corresponding unfortunate. By the beginning of 1864 Wagner's financial position was so desperate – for the *n*th time – that in March he was obliged to fly to Switzerland to escape his creditors. Thence he crept a month later to Stuttgart, hoping to find a haven of peace where he could work at *Die Meistersinger*. And there at the beginning of May occurred the most dramatic incident of his whole dramatic life.

Rex Ex Machina

Late on the evening of 3 May, at a friend's house, he was startled by a servant handing him the card of the 'Secretary of the King of Bavaria'. His conscience being doubly guilty by reason of his political past and financial present, he sent a message that he was 'not at home' – and fled in alarm to his hotel, where he spent an unquiet night. Next morning the royal secretary called again, bringing the incredible news that his master – the eighteen-year-old Ludwig II, who had just succeeded to the throne – had decided to constitute himself the Fairy Godfather of Wagner and his art.

Wagner promptly went to Munich and at once became the intimate friend of his passionate royal admirer. Ludwig moreover obligingly accepted the Wagner entourage as well as Wagner himself. Wagner wanted Cosima, so von Bülow was made Court Pianist and by November they too were installed at Munich. The King however had no suspicion of the relations between Richard and Cosima, and Hans von Bülow himself seems to have been a complaisant, if unwillingly complaisant, husband; when, in April 1865, Cosima bore Richard a daughter (Isolde), Hans accepted the child as his own. The position was curious in the extreme, but from the beginning it was dominated by the strong-minded and ambitious young woman at its centre. Her husband, fine musician and noble-hearted man as he was, was not a strong character. Wagner, like most men of his type, could easily be managed by a determined young woman with the skill to harness his love. The sentimental young King, already half-mad, was only an occasionally troublesome cipher.

The Triebschen Idyll

Royal favourites are proverbially unpopular and public feeling in Bavaria became so hostile to Wagner that he was obliged to go abroad. In March 1866, he settled at Villa Triebschen, on Lake Lucerne. The victory of Prussia over Austria, Bavaria, and the other South German States in the Seven Weeks' War having brought about the downfall of his most influential enemy, the Minister von der Pfordten, Wagner was able to return to Munich for a year or two and to superintend the first performance of *Die Meistersinger* there on 21 June 1868. But the Bülow situation was gradually moving to a crisis. Despite the cliché, such triangles as these are never very long-lived, much less eternal. Cosima had borne Wagner a second daughter, Eva, in February 1867, and still the crazy young King remained blind. But after the production of *Die Meistersinger* conducted by the unhappy third member of the matrimonial triangle, Wagner's longing for escape from 'the hell of Munich', with its calumnies and jealousies, for a quiet family life with the woman who had made herself essential to him, obliged him to take his courage in both hands and confess the truth to his royal benefactor. Ludwig was hurt and angry, and refused to have anything more to do with Cosima. In the autumn of 1868 the guilty pair went into their self-imposed exile at Triebschen and there, in domestic quiet, idyllically happy, Wagner resumed the composition of *Siegfried* after a break of twelve years.

To Bülow's everlasting honour, he did not allow even this final blow to interfere with his service of Wagner the artist. Wagner the man had done him the cruellest wrong, yet he remained a Wagnerian. 'If it had been anyone but Wagner,' said Bülow, 'I would have shot him.'

In the following year, Cosima gave birth to a son, Siegfried, but she was not divorced till July 1870. A month later (25 August), while the rest of Germany had temporarily forgotten them in the excitement of the war with France, she and Richard were married at Lucerne. That Christmas her husband gave her the loveliest of all birthday presents – her birthday fell on Christmas Day – the surprise first performance outside her bedroom door of the *Staircase Music* or *Triebschen Idyll*, now better known to the world as the *Siegfried Idyll*.

Friendship with Nietzsche

One very important new friendship developed at Triebschen, that with the young Nietzsche, then Professor of Philology at Basel. Wagner was now working at *Götterdämmerung*, the last part of the great *Ring* tetralogy. The time had come to think of realizing his dream of a special Festspielhaus where his colossal masterpiece could be presented as he conceived it. A great campaign of propaganda had to be carried out to raise subscriptions. Wagner Societies had to be formed all over Germany to focus enthusiasm and organize financial support. And in all this Nietzsche played an important part. He also assisted Wagner in the secret printing of his autobiography up to 1864 – *Mein Leben*. Germany has always shown profound respect for her university professors, and in those days, when Wagner's aesthetics were widely regarded – not altogether without reason – as the equivalent of what we now know as 'Wardour Street' or 'Metro-Goldwyn-Mayer', it was of value to him to have the public support of a Professor of Classical Philology – even if he were professor only at a small Swiss university.

Bayreuth

As it happened, Germany – the new Imperial Germany whose advent Wagner had celebrated in his *Kaisermarsch* – was just entering on a new phase of cultural (or anti-cultural) development, a phase of blatant, patriotic self-satisfaction. And, ironically enough, it was this wave of bourgeois complacency and 'beer-mug patriotism' that carried Wagner's art to its crowning triumph. The idealist had produced a wonderful new art that perfectly expressed the spirit of *this* age. He must surely have recognised the irony of it himself, but we shall never know whether he was embittered by it or whether the intoxication of worldly success had really, as well as apparently, numbed his artistic conscience. But Nietzsche, the intellectual aristocrat, the fanatical idealist who remained an idealist till his own bitter end, recognized it and turned away in sorrow at the very hour of victory.

The four years from 1872, when on Wagner's sixtieth birthday the foundation-stone of the new Festspielhaus was laid at Bayreuth (where the Wagners now moved from Triebschen), to 1876, when the theatre was opened with a performance of the complete *Ring* (13–17 August), were full of bitter disillusionment for Nietzsche.

Those years were also full of anxiety for Wagner himself, for a vast sum of money was needed and there were times when it seemed as if the whole great project would have to be abandoned in mid-career. Even after the unprecedented triumph of the opening of the Festspielhaus, attended by the German Emperor, a dozen minor German princes, the Emperor of Brazil, a Russian Grand Duke, and a horde of celebrities, musical and other, from all over the world, there still remained an appalling deficit of £7,500. To clear off this debt, for which he was personally responsible, Wagner had recourse to his ever-present help in time of trouble – concert-giving.

Among other efforts a great Wagner Festival was organized at the Albert Hall in May 1877, by the composer's English admirers. Wagner paid his third and last visit to London and (with Richter) conducted eight concerts of excerpts from all his works. But his devoted champion, Dannreuther, whose guest he was on this occasion, admitted that as a conductor 'Wagner did not do himself justice. His strength was already on the wane. The rehearsals fatigued him, and he was frequently faint in the evening. His memory played him tricks, and his beat was nervous. Still there were moments when his great gifts appeared as of old.' But owing to the heavy expenses the profit on the eight concerts amounted to little more than £700.

Christianity and Parsifal

Notwithstanding his 'waning strength' Wagner was hard at work on a new 'Christian' music-drama. The one-time freethinker and Feuerbachian sensualist had, under the influence of Schopenhauer's teaching of resignation, gradually accepted a form of Christianity, though a form much different from the combative, very human Lutheranism so well adapted to the German spirit. Precisely in its denial of the senses, Wagner's brand of Christianity remains curiously sensual, and in *Parsifal* he wallows in humility and suffering like one of Dostoevsky's heroes, abandoning himself to the delights of spiritual abnegation as voluptuously as he had bathed in the delights of the flesh in *Tristan*. There is little reason to believe that his 'conversion' was insincere, an attempt to curry further favour with the Powers that were in the new, united Germany, as his enemies asserted. On the contrary, there were signs that Wagner was drifting towards some sort of Schopenhauerian Buddhism.

The libretto of *Parsifal* was already completed at the time of the London Festival and Wagner began to work at the music during the following winter. The composition was finished by April 1879, but the scoring occupied another two and a half years. Strength was gradually failing. There were, moreover, other reasons for the dragging out of the work, besides waning energy. The campaign of propaganda had to be continued and Wagner was not the man to leave it to his disciples. He contributed copiously to the *Bayreuther Blätter*, the new monthly organ of the Wagner Societies, conducted, studied Carlyle, meditated new flights into the empyrean of 'abstract', purely instrumental music. And then in November 1879, he had been seriously attacked by erysipelas.

The Last Phase

Erysipelas was an old trouble of his. He had suffered from it even in childhood. It had reappeared about 1855–6 and it was this, quite as much as his love of the voluptuous, that led to his indulgence in luxurious silk underclothes and obliged him to have his trousers and jackets lined with fur and wadding. His 'coloured satin trousers with jackets to match and slippers of the same shade', his 'twenty-four silk dressing-gowns of different colours', the luxurious rugs and carpets and cushions and silk hangings of his study are another matter. But it is unfair to Wagner to forget that hypersensitive skin of his. In the winter of 1879–80 his erysipelas was particularly trying and, hoping for relief in the Mediterranean climate, he went to Naples. Again in 1881–2 he wintered at Palermo and finished scoring *Parsifal* there.

The first performance of *Parsifal* was given at Bayreuth on 26 July 1882, six months after its completion. The preparations had been very exhausting and Wagner's heart was weak; how weak no one seems to have suspected. But the performances of *Parsifal* continued all through August and it was mid-September before the Wagner household could leave Bayreuth.

This year they went to Venice, occupying part of the Duke of Grazia's beautiful fifteenth-century Palazzo Vendramin-Calergi. Wagner's health remained indifferent, but he enjoyed his surroundings and delighted in exploring the city. Then his father-in-law, Liszt, stayed with them for a month or two, himself weary almost to death, and Wagner pressed him to make his home with them once and for all. But Cosima's father and Cosima's husband, genuine as their mutual affection seems to have been, were too different ever to live comfortably together. Liszt recognized that and declined the offer. 'This time we've both got in each other's way,' said Wagner laughingly when Liszt departed on 13 January. It was not far from the unpleasant truth.

The Mysterious Cause of Wagner's Death

From the beginning of January 1883, Wagner had been busy drawing up the cast for the next performances of *Parsifal*, and it appears from a letter written the day after Liszt's departure that some incident connected with this matter had caused him a great deal of anger and annoyance. There is nothing unusual about a composer losing his temper over difficulties of casting, but a man with a weak heart – and Wagner was now suffering from angina pectoris – cannot lose his temper with impunity. Moreover a responsible French writer, Lacassagne (a doctor and jurist of the highest repute), has printed a story – otherwise uncorroborated – that accounts for the outbreak of temper and for other incidents reported by 'official' eye-witnesses. Briefly, Lacassagne's version is that Wagner had been particularly anxious to include a certain lady in the cast and that 'the family' had violently opposed the choice. The obvious inference is that Cosima was jealous. The official biographer, Glasenapp, says nothing of this, but he does give us the accounts of Wagner's doctor, Keppler, and of his young Russian admirer, Paul Zhukovsky, son of Glinka's friend, the well-known poet and critic. And they agree in describing the household as being in a curiously disturbed state early in February.

On 10 February, Keppler found Wagner excited and out of humour as a result of a conversation with one of the Bayreuth conductors; he declared that he wanted to get away from Venice for a while and to take his son, Siegfried, with him. Next day he had another fit of ill-humour and, on the 13th, Zhukovsky, on coming back to lunch, found Cosima in tears and Wagner not very well. Before sitting down to the table, Cosima went to her husband's room – he had been writing an article on 'The Feminine Element in Human Affairs'. She soon re-appeared, saying, 'My husband has had a rather bad attack, but it's better to leave him alone,' and they began their meal, but as they were chattering at the table, Wagner's bell rang violently twice and a frightened maid called Cosima to his room. Keppler, hastily summoned by gondolier, arrived at about three o'clock, but by that time the master was already dead.

CARL MARIA VON WEBER

1786–1826

EDWIN EVANS

Origins

Like most occupational names, that of Weber (weaver) is common enough all over Germany and Austria, but the particular family of Webers from whom the composer was descended were Catholic landowners of Lower Austria. In 1622 the Emperor Ferdinand II bestowed the title of Freiherr upon Johann Baptist Weber. Little else is known of him, but more concerning his younger brother, Joseph Franz Xaver Weber, who had a small theatre and concert-room erected on his estate and thus qualified to become the direct ancestor of the musical Webers. But this splendour was short-lived. The family estates were lost in the confusion of the Thirty Years' War, and, although in 1738 the title passed from the elder to the younger branch, its bearers were then reduced to accept service with more fortunate members of the landed aristocracy, such as Freiherr von Schönau-Zella, the management of whose property near Freiburg-im-Breisgau (Baden) was entrusted to Fridolin von Weber, who died in 1754. Of his two sons, the elder, another Fridolin, dropped the title, whilst the younger, Franz Anton, retained it. Both brothers entered the service of Karl Theodor, Elector of the Palatinate, at Mannheim, then one of the most important musical centres of Germany. Fridolin had four daughters, all of whom became noted singers, the most famous being Aloysia, the second. Mozart, who visited Mannheim at that time, first courted Aloysia. However, he eventually married Constanze, the third sister, but he wrote one great part and many arias for his sister-in-law, who had meanwhile married an actor named Lange. Fired by the example of Mozart, Franz Anton, the other brother, cherished dreams of becoming the father of a musical prodigy and placed his two sons by his first marriage with Haydn as pupils, but his ambition was not fulfilled in them, although they displayed some talent. When over fifty he married again, his bride being Genovefa von Brenner, a Viennese girl in her teens; on 18 December 1786, she gave birth to Carl Maria von Weber, in whom the father's ambitious dreams were destined at last to be realized.

This Franz Anton appears to have been an aristocratic scallywag, or so we would judge him to-day, though some allowance must be made for the times in which he lived. In the service of Karl Theodor he had fought against Frederick the Great in the Seven Years' War and was slightly wounded at Rossbach on the Saale in November 1757, after which he was fortunate enough to step into the shoes of his recently deceased father-in-law as steward to the Elector Clement Augustus of Cologne. His luck however did not hold out under the Elector's successor, and, having meanwhile squandered his first wife's fortune, he led a drifting life. For a time he found employment with Friedrich August, Bishop of Lübeck and Eutin, and was conductor of the town band at the latter place when Carl Maria was born there. But the following year he was again adrift as director of a strolling company. His second wife died at Salzburg in 1789 and on 19 January 1799, he wrote to a friend that he had given up theatrical life and resumed his military rank, without pay. As he was then sixty-four the prospects of Major Franz Anton von Weber were not rosy.

Boyhood and Youth

Meanwhile he had taken in hand his son's musical training. Carl Maria was a sickly lad. He suffered from a disease of the hip-bone, was unable to walk until he was four years old, and was fated to limp for the rest of his life. Delicate as he was, he was taught to play the piano and to sing almost before he could speak. He was not at first a very promising pupil, and his elder brother Fritz is said to have declared that, whatever else he might become, he would never be a musician. But at the age of nine, during a stay at Hildburghausen, he had lessons from Johann Peter Heuschkel, oboist and organist in the Court Chapel, to whom in later life he acknowledged his deep indebtedness. His earliest known composition, an organ-piece on the chorale 'Vom Himmel Hoch', dates from then. In the first half of 1798, when he was eleven, he had six months' tuition under Michael Haydn, the composer's younger and less famous brother. The autumn found the family at Munich, where he had lessons in piano-playing and composition from Johann Nepomuk Kalcher, the Court organist, and in singing from Wallishauser, who had Italianized his name into Valesi.

Four years later he became a pupil of the Abbé Vogler, in Vienna, who launched him upon his official career by securing for him the appointment of conductor of the Opera at Breslau. This was in 1804, when he was seventeen. But if, officially, his career begins at this point, he was far from being a novice. Haphazard as his musical training had been, he had profited diligently by every opportunity of improving it. But most of all the precarious existence of his father, harmful as it had been in most respects, had provided him with an admirable environment for the acquisition of empirical knowledge. He was already an experienced composer, and there was little he had not learnt about the stage and its musical requirements. Colloquially speaking, he knew every trick of the trade. From his earliest years he had constantly contributed to the family exchequer by writing to order all kinds of music. Most of these early compositions were burnt, including his first opera, *The Power of Love and Wine*, written at Munich in 1799. Of another opera, *The Dumb Girl of the Forest*, produced on 24 November 1800, at Freiburg in Saxony, only three unpublished fragments remain, though it was performed on several other stages. His third opera, *Peter Schmoll and His Neighbours*, composed at Salzburg in 1802, has remained unpublished, but the overture, revised in 1807, appeared as Op. 8 with a dedication to King Jerome of Westphalia. A few unimportant works, variously dated from 1798 to 1804, have survived, the most characteristic being a part-song, *Leis' wandeln wir, wie Geisterhauch*, published posthumously. Among these works there is, however, one that throws light upon a curious episode. It is a set of *Variations*, Op. 2, dedicated to Kalcher and printed in 1800, by the composer. The previous year he had become acquainted with a strange erratic genius who, failing to find a publisher for his works, had sought a means of printing them himself. This was Aloys Senefelder, known to fame as the inventor of lithography. He took a fancy to young Weber and initiated him into the art he had developed only three years before. The young composer was much attracted to lithography and might even have made it his career. Happily for music, his father quarrelled with the inventor.

Breslau

Young Weber reached Breslau in June 1804, and took up his new duties after the summer recess. His position there was from the first somewhat difficult. At the outset Joseph Schnabel, the deputy conductor, left the theatre, declining to serve under a lad not yet eighteen. J. G. Rhode, the managing director of the company that financed the theatre, took kindly to him at first and wrote the libretto of *Rübezahl* for him to set. Not much has survived of this opera. It is not even known whether he completed it, but the overture was revised some years later under the title *Ruler of the Spirits*. Another composition of this period is an overture on a Chinese theme, *Lieu-Ye-Kin*, which he found in Rousseau's *Musical Dictionary*. This he remodelled in 1809 when writing incidental music to Schiller's version of Gozzi's *Turandot*, under which title the overture has come down to us. Early in 1806 he met with a serious mishap. He accidentally drank some nitric acid which his father was using for experiments in etching. His singing voice was ruined and even his speaking voice suffered permanently. A little later his difficulties became such that he resigned his appointment in May 1806. His life in Breslau had been anything but happy. His salary was insufficient, he had his father to maintain, and an ill-advised liaison ran him into heavy debts which took some years to clear. Fortunately, he found employment with Duke Eugen Friedrich of Württemberg, who maintained an orchestra at Carlsruhe in Silesia, for which the young composer wrote two symphonies. But those were troublous times. The war with France was draining the resources of Germany, and the Duke found himself compelled to give up his establishment. He recommended Weber to his two brothers, the King of Württemberg and Duke Ludwig, the latter of whom appointed him his private secretary. After a short concert tour he took up his new duties at Stuttgart on 1 August 1807.

Stuttgart and Darmstadt

The newly created King Frederick of Württemberg was married to the English Princess Royal, Charlotte Matilda Augusta, daughter of George III. He was talented, but tyrannical, mean, and unscrupulous, and fond of coarse jests at the expense of those who could not retaliate. His brother, Duke Ludwig, having failed to secure the throne of Poland, was entirely dependent upon him, and the secretary's duties were mainly concerned with obtaining funds in circumstances that were generally humiliating. The King's favourite was an adventurer named Dillen, who, from being a groom in the ducal stables, had risen by devious ways to be a minister of state. Weber found friends in Danzi, the conductor of the Royal Opera, and Lehr, the royal librarian, but, surrounded as he was with temptations, it is not altogether surprising that he gave way to dissipation under the influence of Franz Carl Hiemer, a fascinating man of letters, who belonged to a club called 'Faust's Ride to Hell'. It was, however, Weber's father, the Major, then in his seventy-fifth year, who precipitated the catastrophe. At the end of 1809 the composer discovered to his dismay that the old reprobate had pocketed certain sums of money that the Duke had entrusted to his son for the purpose of paying off a mortgage on the Carlsruhe estate in Silesia. The son decided to shield his father and take the blame on himself. On 9 February 1810, a body of police invaded the theatre during the rehearsal of Weber's new opera *Silvana* and marched the composer off to prison, his father being ordered not to leave their apartment. In due course the two Webers were escorted to the frontier in the most ignominious fashion and expelled from the kingdom. The exiles did not have to travel far. First at Mannheim and then at Darmstadt they found a hospitable refuge and Weber soon settled down again to serious work. At Darmstadt he met his former master, the Abbé Vogler, renewed acquaintance with his fellow pupil from Vienna, Johann Gänsbacher, and formed a friendship with another of Vogler's pupils, Jakob Meyer Beer, who was destined to win fame in later years as Giacomo Meyerbeer. To him is dedicated the well-known *Momento Capriccioso* for piano, which Weber had brought with him from Stuttgart. Otherwise the most important of the many compositions that originated there is the opera *Silvana* already mentioned. He rewrote a considerable portion of it and it was eventually produced at Frankfurt on 10 September 1810, the day of a sensational balloon ascent by the celebrated Mme Blanchard, which considerably reduced the numbers of the audience. The principal part in it was taken by a young singer, then in her eighteenth year, Caroline Brandt, who little knew that she was destined to become the composer's wife.

Munich, Berlin, Some Tours, and Marriage

Early in 1811 Weber set out from Darmstadt, and in March he reached Munich, where he found favour with the Court. Here was produced, on 4 June, the one-act opera *Abu Hassan*, dealing with the 'Arabian Nights' story of Fatima and Hassan who, to escape from their creditors, pretend to be dead. The libretto was by Hiemer, and the opera was in reality a humorous satire on its impecunious author's difficulties at Stuttgart. It brought better luck, for the Grand Duke of

Hesse, Ludwig I, to whom it is dedicated, sent Weber 440 florins, which was then a handsome sum. The merry little overture *Alla Turca* composed at Darmstadt on 12 January 1811, is still popular. The success of the opera, however, was a chorus of creditors: 'Geld! Geld! Geld! Ich will nicht länger warten!' It was during the composition of this opera that Weber, whilst on a tour with a friend, came across Apel's volume of Ghost Stories, one of which, *Der Freischütz*, attracted his attention as a subject for an opera, though seven years were to elapse before he took it up again.

At Munich the composer formed a close friendship with Heinrich Joseph Bärmann, the greatest clarinet-player of his day, for whom he wrote several works, and with whom he continued his tour. During their progress, Weber inadvertently entered Württemberg, and was placed under arrest, but, as the frontier to which he was conducted lay in the direction of his journey, he suffered nothing worse than a 'lift' on his way. After they had visited Prague, Dresden, and Leipzig, they accepted an invitation from that eccentric prince, Duke Emil Leopold August of Saxe-Gotha, whose hobby was to appear in female attire and who wore every day a differently coloured wig. Spohr was then his *Kapellmeister* and was not overjoyed at meeting again with Weber, of whose way of living he had disapproved at Stuttgart. But the Duke kept the composer busy during his short stay, after which they proceeded to Weimar where the Grand Duke and his daughter-in-law, Maria Pavlovna, sister of the Tsar, gave them a cordial welcome. It was here that Weber met Goethe, but without deriving much pleasure from the privilege, for the poet had no ears for anyone but Zelter and talked through the music, barely acknowledging the introduction.

Another visit to Dresden, and then the wandering pair turned to Berlin, where they arrived on 20 February 1812. This first visit to the Prussian capital lasted until 31 August and resulted in several new friendships that were to prove valuable on Weber's return. But his wanderings were not yet over. He again visited Gotha, Weimar, and Leipzig and reached Prague in January 1813, just as the directorship of the theatre had become vacant. He was appointed to the post with a mission to reorganize the opera, which had sadly deteriorated since the days when Mozart, a generation earlier, had produced there his immortal *Don Giovanni*. The new duties involved a journey to Vienna in search of artists. On his return he plunged into work. There was no department of the theatre that did not receive his attention, and when he found that his unwelcome diligence was discussed by his subordinates in a language he did not understand, Czech, he promptly learned it. He opened his first season on 10 September 1813, and retained his post until 30 September 1816. During those years much history was made and the map of Europe considerably altered. Commemorative compositions appear in the list of his works, but no operas. He was too much occupied in staging those of other composers.

In his private life, however, there occurred serious developments. Attached to the theatre was a dancer named Brunetti, whose wife, though the mother of several children, still possessed youthful charm. Thinking thereby to gain influence with the director, Brunetti appears to have connived at a liaison which caused the composer much suffering in the end. He was infatuated, but Thérèse Brunetti merely preyed upon him. This, however, did not prevent her from indulging in terrible scenes of jealousy. His diary is evidence of what he went through at this period. Meanwhile he had not forgotten the favourable impression made upon him by Caroline Brandt at the first performance of *Silvana*. Since then she had made considerable progress on the various opera stages of Germany, and Weber engaged her for Prague. She made her début there on New Year's Day, 1814, in Isouard's *Cinderella* and reaped an immediate success. His interest in her was at first purely professional but gradually he came to admire her sterling qualities, her modest charm, her discretion, and her filial devotion until, whilst still believing himself in love with Thérèse Brunetti, he unconsciously developed a tender regard for Caroline. Needless to say this did not escape the jealous alertness of Mme Brunetti, and there were renewed scenes, but his eyes were opened by her conduct, and he became betrothed to Caroline. The course of true love did not, however, run any smoother than usual, and many misunderstandings intervened before their marriage took place on 4 November 1817.

Meanwhile he had revisited Berlin during his summer vacation in 1814, produced *Silvana* there and composed some patriotic songs that stirred the nation. The following year, after the battle of Waterloo, he wrote a cantata, *Kampf und Sieg*, which was performed at Prague in December, and in Berlin on the first anniversary of the battle, 1816, with great popular success. The post of *Kapellmeister* in Berlin was then vacant, and he hoped to obtain the appointment, yet even the active intervention of his friend Count Brühl, the Intendant, failed at that time to secure it for him. But he was not to remain unattached.

On his way to Berlin he had been summoned to Pillnitz, the country palace of King Friedrich August of Saxony, to receive an acknowledgement, in valuable form, of a copy of *Kampf und Sieg*. It was handed to him on his sovereign's behalf by Count Vitzthum, the King's equerry, whose brother, the Court marshal, was director of the Royal Theatre at Dresden. The latter was then staying at Carlsbad, where his brother persuaded Weber to visit him on his way back. As a result of this meeting he was given in December 1816, the appointment as conductor of the German Opera at Dresden. He took up his duties there on 13 January 1817. Less than six months later the Berlin appointment again fell vacant, and this time Count Brühl was in a position to offer it to him. It had some advantages over Dresden, but while Weber was hesitating the decision was placed beyond his power by the burning down of the Berlin theatre. At Dresden, therefore, he remained. On 13 September his appointment was confirmed for life, and in December he brought home his bride.

Dresden and the New Opera

His years of wandering were thus ended. This did not stand in the way of frequent professional visits to Berlin, where efforts continued to be made to induce him to stay, to Prague and Vienna and subsequently to London, but Dresden became his permanent domicile. His works at that date included, apart from those already named, his two piano concertos and several concert works for other instruments; three of his four piano sonatas and several shorter works for piano; his piano quartet, six violin sonatas, many songs, and a large number of occasional pieces.

The position at Dresden was at first somewhat difficult. Whereas in all other musical centres of Central Europe German opera had firmly established itself, in Dresden the Italian tradition so long fostered under the eighteenth-century Electors still remained firmly entrenched. Court Marshal von Vitzthum had succeeded, with difficulty, in inducing the King to sanction the establishment of German opera, but Count Einsiedel, the Prime Minister, was bitterly opposed to it, and to Weber as his protagonist. It had been understood when Weber was appointed that he should rank equally with his Italian colleagure, Francesco Morlacchi, but when the appointment came to be gazetted a lower title was given him. The tussle that ensued was symbolical of much that was to follow, but it ended in his favour. Another complication was that the King of Saxony had sided with Napoleon and been punished in the settlement by losing some provinces to Prussia. He was compelled to acquiesce in the new situation, but resented any reference to the past struggle, in which he had been on the wrong side. Weber's patriotic songs thus became counters in the intrigues against him and his popularity in Berlin was reckoned almost a crime. At first Morlacchi and he got on fairly well together, but in these conditions mischief-making was easy and soon became rife. In fact, for a time the Italo-German musical struggle was as acute as the similar conflict in Paris in the eighteenth century. That Weber in the end 'won through' is evidence not only of his great gifts, but perhaps even more of his tenacity of purpose. Having set his hand to the plough he did not turn back. He did far more than establish German opera in Dresden. He became the founder of romantic German opera and the precursor of modern music-drama. From the date of his appointment to that of his death was little more than nine years, but the effect of what Weber accomplished in that short time is with us yet.

Der Freischütz *at last*

Soon after he had settled in Dresden, Weber had formed a friendship with Friedrich Kind, who, like many a barrister before and since, had deserted the law for literature. The suggestion having naturally arisen that Karl should provide the composer with a libretto, the latter recalled the vivid impression made on him seven years earlier by Apel's story *Der Freischütz*. They discussed the scenario together on 21 February 1817, and a week later, on 1 March, the book was ready. Composition, however, proceeded at first slowly, Weber's time being so much occupied with his duties connected with the opera and with other tasks, notably several compositions for the Court, such as the cantata *L'Accoglienza* for the marriage of the Princess Maria Anna Carolina of Saxony to the Grand Duke Leopold of Tuscany, a *Mass in E flat* for the King's name-day, a *Jubilee Cantata* and the well-known *Jubilee Overture* for the 50th anniversary of his accession, and a *Mass in G* for his golden wedding. He also wrote the incidental music to several plays produced at the Court Theatre. Three of his best-known piano works, the *Rondo brillante*, the *Invitation to the Dance*, and the *Polacca brillante*, also date from this period, as well as the *Trio for piano, flute, and cello*, Op. 63, and numerous smaller works. Thus it happened that, although isolated numbers of *Der Freischütz* were composed in 1817,

1818, and 1819, it was not until the autumn of that year that he was able to work continuously at it, and the overture, which was the last portion to be written, was completed on 13 May 1820. Meanwhile Count Brühl, who had been unremitting in his efforts on Weber's behalf in Berlin, had pledged himself to produce the opera at the new theatre which Schinkel was constructing to replace the one that had been burned down. But before this took place another dramatic work made its appearance. Count Brühl, being dissatisfied with the incidental music that Traugott Maximilian Eberwein had composed for Wolff's melodrama, *Preciosa*, commissioned Weber to write the music for its production, in Berlin, which, the new theatre not being ready, took place at the Court Theatre, 14 March 1821.

More Operas

On 2 May 1821, Weber left for Berlin and found himself confronted by a situation resembling in one respect that which he had left behind at Dresden. Spontini had recently been appointed to the Opera. He was favoured by the Court, whose opinions were only too readily adopted by society. His operas *The Vestal*, *Cortez*, and *Olympia* had been produced in a spectacular manner, with great success, and the adherents of national opera, though the music of *Preciosa* had aroused their interest in the coming production, were a little despondent about its prospects. Weber alone remained unaffected by any such misgivings. On the very morning of the first performance, 18 June, he surprised his wife and his pupil, Julius Benedict, by playing to them a composition he had just completed for piano, and detailed to them its poetic basis. This was the *Concertstück* for piano and orchestra, of which the first idea had occurred to him in Dresden the previous February, but which he had worked at during the last fortnight and finished that very morning. It was to become one of his most popular compositions. The success of *Der Freischütz* was never in doubt. At the outset the overture was greeted with such a storm of approval that it had to be repeated before the opera could proceed. The evening ended in triumph. The partisans of national opera were jubilant. The only dissentients were Spohr, who was never responsive to Weber's music, and Zelter, who wrote disparagingly to Goethe, as he so often did on new composers.

In October the opera was produced at Vienna, amid similar scenes, and Barbaja, the astute impresario of the Kärnthnerthor Theatre, promptly commissioned another opera from the same pen. Weber had one in hand, begun before the completion of *Der Freischütz*, but it was a comic opera, *The Three Pintos*, on Seidel's novel *Der Brautkampf*, and it would not have been suitable. This work was destined to remain unfinished. A libretto was suggested by Helmina von Chezy, whom Benedict describes as 'a stout elderly lady, with all the qualities of a real blue-stocking, careless and slovenly in her appearance, not blessed with any earthly goods, but with a great deal of self-sufficiency.' She had discovered an old legend: '*Histoire de Gérard de Nevers et de la belle et vertueuse Euryanthe, sa mie.*' She submitted two acts which Weber accepted, subject to alteration, and thus was born Weber's penultimate opera *Euryanthe*. It was completed in August 1823, and produced at the Kärnthnerthor Theatre on 25 October. The music won him a good reception on the first night, but it was too severely handicapped by its libretto to be an enduring success. Frau von Chezy was no genius, as Schubert was to learn afterwards, when he wrote the incidental music, which is all that survives of another of her dramatic works, *Rosamunde*.

England and the End

Meanwhile the success of *Der Freischütz* had been making operatic history, and it continued to create a furore wherever it was performed. In London it had been presented at three theatres simultaneously, Covent Garden, Drury Lane, and the Lyceum, and its popularity induced Charles Kemble to invite the composer to write an opera in English for the first-named theatre. Weber by then was in such a state of health that before accepting he consulted his physician, who declared that unless he went to a warmer climate and rested he would have no more than a few months to live. But Weber, who had known many years of poverty, thought that the profits from the London engagement would enable him to make better provision for his family, and accepted, after Kemble's terms had been raised to £1,000. He set himself to learn English, in which he had 153 lessons from a certain Mr Carey between 20 October 1824 and 11 February 1826, the last being five days before his departure for London. Meanwhile the subject of *Oberon* had been chosen and J. R. Planché entrusted with the task of writing the libretto, which was sent to the composer early in 1825. He set to work upon it at once, but laid it aside for a time during the summer. He resumed work in the autumn, and in

January 1826, little was needed to complete the opera except the overture, which he added in London, where he arrived on 5 March. He stayed in Great Portland Street at the house of Sir George Smart, whose acquaintance he had made the previous summer at Ems. The first performance of the opera took place on 12 April under the direction of the composer, whose contract stipulated that he should conduct the first twelve. Apart from that he gave several concerts and was kept busy with engagements of all kinds, including many that, in his precarious state of health, might have been spared him. The result was what his Dresden physician had foreseen. The disease from which he suffered was aggravated and he died on 6 June 1826, not yet forty years old. He was buried at Moorfields Chapel, but in 1844 the coffin was removed to Dresden and reinterred with a ceremonial of which the musical portion was under the direction of Richard Wagner, who spoke an eloquent farewell over the grave.

Not Without Honour

There are some aspects of those last years that call for comment. How came it that, he being a State official at the Saxon capital, his last four dramatic works were produced elsewhere, in Berlin, Vienna, and London? The answer is that, as happens often in the case of genius, his immediate environment was the last to learn of his greatness. At Dresden he lived in a world of intrigue and of acrimonious controversy, which belittled him to his fellow townsmen. Some, of course, knew him for what he was, but to many it may never have occurred that a man of whom this and that was said – for slander was rife – could be a genius. Hence he was regarded as a man who performed competently the duties entrusted to him and little more. This is vividly shown by the remark of the Dresden Intendant, von Lüttichau, who happened to be in Berlin when *Euryanthe* was performed there for the first time. After a rehearsal he saw a large crowd waiting outside the theatre to catch a glimpse of the composer and said to him in surprise: 'Weber, are you then really a celebrity?' This was less than six months before Weber's death, at a time when all operatic Europe was acclaiming him. The attitude explains how Dresden, which could have demanded the privilege of producing his works, allowed them to go elsewhere and followed in the wake of other opera houses.

Limitations of space preclude our dwelling upon the anecdotal side of those later years, on his many friendships in the world of art and letters, no less than in that of music, or on his meeting with Beethoven. Life then was less adventurous than it had been in his youth, but just as full of vital interest. As with many consumptives, Weber's intellectual activities were in inverse ratio to his constitutional weakness. Like Mozart, Schubert, and Mendelssohn he was doomed to die young, but he made history.

Some other Pelican books are described on the following pages

CHAMBER MUSIC

Edited by Alec Robertson

A372

Chamber music has frequently and rightly been described as the music of friends, in allusion to the intimate team work the playing of it involves and its special character. The term itself covers a huge field of beautiful, and still far too little known, music, the exact limits of which no one has been able to define precisely. For the purpose of this book it is taken to range from duet works to octets, and to cover the time from the early eighteenth century to the present day.

Haydn is given pride of place as having developed the string quartet, the central medium of chamber music, to a wonderful peak of perfection. Chapters follow on the various kinds of chamber music by Mozart, Beethoven, Schubert, and many others, up to Bartók, whose six string quartets are considered to be in the great classical line. The remaining composers are grouped together according to their countries of origin.

THE CONCERTO

Edited by Ralph Hill

A249

This is the companion volume to *The Symphony*. It follows the same plan, was completed before the editor's death in the autumn of 1950, and, though he did not live to see it through the press, it is in conception and arrangement as much his work as its companion volume.

It deals with the well-known piano, violin, and ello concertos of the present-day repertoire, and its analyses are illustrated by a wealth of musical examples. The composers whose work is considered begin with Bach, and end with William Walton; special chapters are devoted to English compositions, to the general lines of development of the concerto, and to variation forms.

THE SYMPHONY

Edited by Ralph Hill

A204

This volume devoted to the symphonies of the great composers is addressed to serious students of music, students who *think* about music as well as *listen* to it, and do not merely approach music sensuously, like a hot bath or a pipe of tobacco. We grant that the sensuous appeal of music is a vital and important part of appreciation, but it is only a part and not the whole. Our first reaction to music is an emotional one, after which, if we are intelligent listeners, we want to know something about its construction, how the composer obtains this or that effect, and the process of his thought. The purpose of this book is, therefore, to guide the intelligent and serious listener towards a deeper understanding of the masterpieces of symphony, which he is likely to hear frequently in the concert hall, over the air, or on the gramophone.

JAZZ

Rex Harris

A 247

After the long and wearisome years of 'swing' which overlaid the traditions of jazz, there has arisen a new generation which is anxious to learn of the roots and growth of this fascinating folk music.

So much confusion exists in the public mind regarding the word 'jazz' that it was felt necessary to trace its ancestry and present a genealogical table which would clarify the subject.

This book is not intended to serve as a discography, or jazz directory filled with minute details of obscure gramophone records, but many examples of good jazz recordings are included, and care has been taken to select in almost every case those which are available in Great Britain at the time of writing.

The book has been recently revised to make it completely up to date in all details.

PHILHARMONIC

Thomas Russell

A 264

Philharmonic was first published in 1942 and rapidly ran into several editions. Its initial success was, perhaps, due to its double vision: that of an experienced orchestral player and of an orchestral administrator. Some of the ideas put forward showed considerable originality, but were soon accepted and acted upon by the author's colleagues. The realization of these ideas has led to the re-writing of several chapters, for Thomas Russell does not believe that the social development of music can be allowed to stand still.

A faith in the capacity of the man-in-the-street to appreciate the best in music, and an abhorrence of cliques, give to this book a sane optimism which is as good a tonic to-day as when it first appeared.

THE PENGUIN SCORES

Edited by Gordon Jacob

This series has been planned to meet the needs of concert-goers who wish to follow orchestral performances with a pocket score. Those listed below belong to the period dealt with in this book.

BEETHOVEN: Coriolan and Egmont Overtures

BEETHOVEN: Symphony No. 1 in C

BEETHOVEN: Symphony No. 2 in D

BEETHOVEN: Symphony No. 3 in E flat

BEETHOVEN: Symphony No. 7 in A

BEETHOVEN: Symphony No. 9 in D minor (The Choral)

BRAHMS: Variations on a Theme of Haydn

BRAHMS: Violin Concerto in D

CÉSAR FRANCK: Symphonic Variations

MENDELSSOHN: Violin Concerto

SCHUMANN: Piano Concerto in A minor

TCHAIKOVSKY: Overture Romeo and Juliet

WAGNER: Meistersinger Overture

WAGNER: Siegfried Idyll

RECORDED JAZZ: A CRITICAL GUIDE

Rex Harris and Brian Rust

A417

This book has been devised to help those who wish to acquaint themselves with the enormous progress which has been made since 1950 in the field of LP and EP recorded jazz music. It must not be regarded as a comprehensive discography, but nevertheless the authors have presented a reasonable cross-section of real jazz, together with biographical notes of performers and a critical assessment of the records listed.

The arrangement is alphabetical with regard to instrumentalists, but when the musician is also to be found under the heading of other bands, the fact is stated. Used in conjunction with Rex Harris's Pelican A247 – *Jazz* – the book will prove extremely useful to the enthusiast and student for elucidating obscure points regarding personnel and dates of performance and for general information.

MOZART'S LETTERS

Edited by Eric Blom

Translated and Annotated by Emily Anderson

A238

As a letter-writer Mozart is excelled among composers by Mendelssohn alone, and by him only in grace of style and range of interest, not for the self-revelations of a professional artist and a human being. Eric Blom has selected these letters of the composer himself from Emily Anderson's translation of *The Letters of Mozart and His Family.*

The book was published in January 1956 to commemorate the bicentenary of Mozart's birth, and it makes a most enthralling biography which will allow lovers of Mozart's music to gain a new insight into his work and a new affection for his personality. Mozart the man is not by any means as faultless and elegantly aristocratic as his art, but in his way as lovable and perennially fresh. There are crude and occasionally rather mean things in his letters, but he is what those most deserving of one's truest love always are in the end – forgivable.